TRANSFORMED
IN CHRIST

TRANSFORMED IN CHRIST

ESSAYS ON THE RENEWAL OF MORAL THEOLOGY

John S. Grabowski

SAPIENTIA PRESS
OF AVE MARIA UNIVERSITY

Sapientia Press
of Ave Maria University
5050 Ave Maria Blvd.
Ave Maria, FL 34142
800-537-5487

Distributed by:
The Catholic University of America Press
c/o HFS
P.O. Box 50370
Baltimore, MD 21211
800-537-5487

Cover Image: Transfiguration, by Raphael, 1516–20. Pinacoteca of the Vatican Museum. Courtesy Wikipedia.com

Printed in the United States of America.

Library of Congress Control Number: 2016948441

ISBN: 978-1-932589-80-1

Contents

Preface

In his document heralding the Church's entry into the third millennium, St. John Paul II wrote: "I feel more than ever in duty bound to point to the Council as the great grace bestowed on the Church in the 20th century: there we find a sure compass by which to take our bearings in the century now beginning."[1] Pope Benedict, reflecting on these words in an audience near the end of his own pontificate, added: "I think this is an eloquent image. The Second Vatican Council Documents … are a compass in our time too that permits the Barque of the Church to put out into the deep in the midst of storms or on calm and peaceful waves, to sail safely and to reach her destination."[2]

One such course charted by the teaching of the Council was toward the renewal of theology as a whole. This renewal was to be accomplished not only by opening to the modern world and its questions (*aggiornamento*), but also through a return to the sources of the faith on which theology reflects (*ressourcement*). These impulses were not opposed to one another but closely connected in the theological renewal that preceded the Council and its own teaching—the Church engages the questions of the modern world by more deeply reflecting on the sources of Her own faith—Scripture, tradition, the liturgy, and the teaching of the Fathers of the Church.[3]

---

1. John Paul II, Apostolic Letter, *Novo millennio ineunte*, no. 57.

2. Pope Benedict, Weekly General Audience of October 10, 2012, The Holy See, accessed September 26, 2016, https://w2.vatican.va/content/benedict-xvi/en/audiences/2012/documents/hf_ben-xvi_aud_20121010.pdf.

3. On this, see Marcellino D'Ambrosio, "*Ressourcement* Theology, *aggiornamento*, and the Hermeneutics of Tradition," *Communio* 18 (1991): 530–55. This is also part of what Pope Benedict XVI described as the Council's "hermeneutic of reform and renewal." See his Christmas address to the Roman Curia of December 22, 2005, The Holy See, accessed September 26, 2016, http://w2.vatican.va/content/benedict-xvi/en/speeches/2005/december/documents/hf_ben_xvi_spe_20051222_roman-curia.html.

What was true for theology as a whole was particularly necessary for the discipline of moral theology. The self-enclosed moral teaching of the manuals that had emerged after the Council of Trent was in danger of foundering on the shoals of a sin-centered rigorism, legalism, objectivism, and the atomization of the moral life into a series of individual acts.[4] The effort to make greater room for individual freedom through a casuistic study of cases of conscience failed to guide the Church's moral teaching away from these troubled waters—indeed, some would argue that they only increased their turbulence.[5]

It is in this context that one can locate the summons of the Council fathers to a renewal in Catholic moral teaching:

Likewise let the other theological disciplines be renewed through a more living contact with the mystery of Christ and the history of salvation. Special care must be given to the perfecting of moral theology. Its scientific exposition, nourished more on the teaching of the Bible, should shed light on the loftiness of the calling of the faithful in Christ and the obligation that is theirs of bearing fruit in charity for the life of the world.[6]

It is worth noting the hallmarks of renewal toward which the "compass" provided by the Council's teaching point the Barque of the Church. Such

---

4. The preoccupation with sin had its roots in the evolving forms of the sacrament of penance in the early and medieval Church, as can be witnessed in the early medieval pentitentials. For an overview of these developments, see John Mahoney, SJ, *The Making of Moral Theology: A Study of the Roman Catholic Tradition* (Oxford, UK: Clarendon Press, 1987), 2–36. The focus on law and discreet acts was compounded by the reemergence of nominalism in the fourteenth century and its influence on subsequent Western thought, including the post-Tridentine manuals. On this, see ibid., 224–58, and especially the incisive historical analysis of Servais Pinckaers, OP, *The Sources of Christian Ethics*, trans. Mary Thomas Noble, OP (Washington, DC: Catholic University of America Press, 1995), 254–79, 327–53.

5. For an overview and critique of the various "moral systems" that grew out of modern casuistry, see Pinckaers, *Sources of Christian* Ethics, 254–79; and Romanus Cessario, OP, *An Introduction to Moral Theology*, rev. ed., Catholic Moral Thought Series (Washington, DC: Catholic University of America Press, 2013), 229–42. For a more sympathetic consideration of this impulse and some of its contributions in modern and contemporary settings, see James Keenan, SJ, and Thomas Shannon, eds., *The Context of Casuistry*, Moral Traditions Series (Washington, DC: Georgetown University Press, 1995).

6. Decree on Priestly Formation, *Optatam totius*, no. 16. The citation is from the Vatican translation, The Holy See, accessed September 26, 2016, http://www.vatican.va/archive/hist_councils/ii_vatican_council/documents/vat-ii_decree_19651028_optatam-totius_en.html.

points are found not only in the text of *Optatam totius* cited above but are also confirmed and elaborated elsewhere in the Council's teaching.

First, theological renewal, including moral theological renewal, involves "more living contact with the mystery of Christ." To look to Christ is to bring the human person and his or her vocation into focus. After all, the Council teaches in its Pastoral Constitution on the Church that "Christ, the final Adam, by the revelation of the mystery of the Father and His love, fully reveals man to man himself and makes his supreme calling clear."[7] This statement has rightly been hailed as the "short formula" of the Constitution as a whole insofar as the human person was *the* key question and subject of the document.[8] Christian anthropology is inescapably Christological. In order to answer the question that is the human person, one must look to the person of Christ.

Second, this moral teaching must be "more nourished on the teaching of the Bible" and "the history of salvation." This too conforms to the larger vision of the Council. *Dei verbum* describes the study of Scripture as "the soul of sacred theology."[9] Both the overall structure of the manuals and their case-based analysis were not deeply informed by Scripture. The manuals dealt with general moral theology under headings dealing with the human act, law, conscience, sin, and special moral theology in relation to the commandments or the virtues (though these did not have a deep impact on their largely juridical structure).[10] The overarching themes of Scripture and salvation history were generally not considered. When Scripture was em-

7. Pastoral Constitution on the Church in the Modern World, *Gaudium et spes*, no. 22. The citation is from the Vatican translation, The Holy See, accessed September 28, 2016, http://www.vatican.va/archive/hist_councils/ii_vatican_council/documents/vat-ii_cons_19651207_gaudium-et-spes_en.html.

8. See Walter Kasper, "The Theological Anthropology of *Gaudium et spes*," *Communio* 23, no. 1 (1996): 129–41.

9. Dogmatic Constitution on Divine Revelation, *Dei verbum*, no. 24. The citation is from the Vatican translation, The Holy See, accessed September 28, 2016, http://www.vatican.va/archive/hist_councils/ii_vatican_council/documents/vat-ii_const_19651118_dei-verbum_en.html.

10. See Kathleen Cahalan, *Formed in the Image of Christ: The Sacramental Moral Theology of Bernard Häring, C.Ss.R.* (Collegeville, MN: Michael Glazier, 2004), 136–37; and Thomas Petri, OP, *Aquinas and the Theology of the Body: The Thomistic Foundations of John Paul III's Anthropology*, Thomistic Ressourcement Series (Washington, DC: Catholic University of America Press, 2016), 35–36.

ployed, it was often by way of proof texts rather than through deep engagement of its teaching.

Third and finally, the Decree on Priestly Formation speaks of the responsibility of the discipline to "shed light on the loftiness of the calling of the faithful in Christ" and their responsibility to "bear ... fruit in charity for the life of the world." This language recalls the recovery of the universal call to holiness forcefully articulated in the Dogmatic Constitution *Lumen gentium* that "all the faithful of Christ of whatever rank or status, are called to the fullness of the Christian life and to the perfection of charity."[11] The primary way in which this "most characteristic of the Council's doctrines" has been instantiated is through the development of the virtues, both in their acquisition in the deepening of Christian moral living and in a resurgence of interest in the scholarly study of virtue ethics in recent decades.[12] This dimension of theological renewal—like the Council's Christological focus—entails an anthropology.[13] This is because the language of virtue as a way to describe the human capacity for moral growth and development presupposes certain capacities of the person capable of being developed through moral praxis and habituation. The language of practices, moral growth, and habits in turn raise questions about the role of experience in the moral life and therefore in the theological enterprise.

The essays in this volume, written over twenty-five years of teaching moral theology, reflect the course for renewal charted by the Council's teaching. Therefore they consider the human person in the light of Christ. Such persons are created male and female in the image of God (cf. Gn 1:27), and reflecting on the anthropological "weight" of this sexual difference can shed surprising light on disputed questions of sexual ethics that have vexed Catholic moral theology over the last fifty years, as well as on newer questions about the equality of men and women as persons (chap. 1). The Christological language of nature and person and how these are understood are

11. Dogmatic Constitution on the Church, *Lumen gentium*, no. 40. The citation is from the Vatican translation, The Holy See, accessed September 28, 2016, http://www.vatican.va/archive/hist_councils/ii_vatican_council/documents/vat-ii_const_19641121_lumen-gentium_en.html.

12. The phrase is that of Peter Bristow, *Christian Ethics and the Human Person: Truth and Relativism in Contemporary Moral Theology* (Leominster, UK: Gracewing, 2009), 28. Bristol's concern here is more focused on the actual development of the virtues in Christian praxis, though his work also engages the renewal of virtue ethics.

13. This is true of morality generally; see ibid., 19.

also at the root of key differences that have emerged in the personalist turn of Catholic moral thought in the twentieth century, as illustrated in the debate over birth control (chap. 5). Other disputed moral issues too can be illumined by a consideration of their anthropological underpinnings and presuppositions, including the oft-misunderstood nature of the Church's opposition to assisted reproductive technologies (chap. 8) or same-sex sexual relationships (chap. 11).

At the heart of the concept of "person" as it emerged in the Christology and Trinitarian theology of the early Church is relationality. While much of the Western Christian tradition has understood this concept in largely individual and substantialist terms, there are numerous threads in recent Catholic thought that have attempted to understand the human person in more relational language, thereby more closely reflecting the God in whose image we are created (chap. 2). But it is vital to understand this relationality in ontological rather than merely volitional terms, especially when considering the personhood of the unborn—to exist as human is to be in relation to God and to others and therefore to be a person (chap. 7).

As the "soul of sacred theology," many of these essays engage Scripture in varying degrees. Catholic theological reflection on the human person flows from the revealed Word of God, and thus many of the more anthropological essays engage scriptural categories as a source (e.g., chap. 2) or insofar as it illumines the person in reference to particular issues (e.g., chaps. 8 and 11). Others reflect on the methodology of reading Scripture as the basis for articulating an anthropology found within magisterial documents (chap. 9). Still others locate key biblical concepts, such as that of covenant as the basis for the Catholic understanding of marriage as a sacrament and the role of sexual intercourse within it (chap. 4).

The final group of essays considers the renewal of virtue ethics as a way to concretize the universal call to holiness. These essays examine the way in which a multidisciplinary approach to virtues such as chastity can bring both the nature of the virtue and the means to acquire it into sharper relief (chap. 3). A shift in lens to a discussion of specific moral practices productive of virtue can also shed new light on questions that have proved vexing for other lines of argument, such as the moral difference between contraception and the various forms of natural family planning (chap. 6). As mentioned above, to consider moral growth and progress is to inevitably raise the question of experience and its place in theology. Much recent moral theology has invoked the category in order to challenge traditional moral positions, often appealing to a revised version of the "Wesleyan quadrilateral," which gives experience (whether of individuals or groups assessed through social scientific data) priority over Scripture, tradition, and reason. Two final essays consider this emerging trend and argue that experience only becomes useful for theological reflection in light of the purifying encounter with Christ and subsequent growth in holiness or virtue (chaps. 10 and 11).

Many of the figures who are studied in these pages were themselves involved in the theological renewal before, during, or after the Council. This is particularly true of Karol Wojtyła / Pope John Paul II, who made significant contributions to the renewal of Catholic personalism prior to the Council, participated in the Council itself as a bishop, and oversaw its implementation in his long and prolific pontificate. Joseph Ratzinger served as a *peritus* at the Council and then as Cardinal Prefect of the Congregation for the Doctrine of the Faith and a close collaborator of Pope John Paul II. Some describe his papacy as an extension of that of his predecessor, but that fails to account for the profundity of Ratzinger / Benedict XVI as a brilliant thinker and teacher in his own right. Other significant figures considered in these essays made their impact primarily as private scholars before and after the Council, but in their own way contributed to the renewal for which the Council called (e.g., Dietrich von Hildebrand, Servais Pinckaers, Hans Urs von Balthasar, Walter Kasper, and Alasdair MacIntyre). As representatives of the tradition of Western Christian thought, all of these thinkers were deeply influenced by the teaching of SS Augustine and Thomas Aquinas. The thought of these two great Doctors suffuses this work.

For both Aristotle and St. Thomas, one of the things most formative of virtue and therefore productive of the happiness to which it leads is friendship. The essays in this book have been shaped, refined, and improved by the contributions of many friends over the years—colleagues, students, and family members. Many of these acknowledgments are made in the individual essays to which these friends contributed. I would also like to express my gratitude to those who played key roles in pulling this volume together into its final form. I am particularly indebted to Matthew Levering and

Roger Nutt for the invitation to contribute a volume to the *Faith and Reason: Studies in Catholic Philosophy and Theology Series* and for their encouragement and assistance throughout this process. I would also like to thank Ashleigh McKown for her patient, prompt, and thorough copyediting of this manuscript, and Julie Amajuoyi for her invaluable research assistance and work in compiling the index. I am also grateful to Toni Gallo, who provided invaluable technical assistance in converting PDFs of some of the older essays to a more usable form.

Ultimately, the renewal of the Church and its theological life for which the Council called, like the Council itself, is a grace, "a beautiful work of the Holy Spirit."[14] This renewal, as has been emphasized in the last four major pontificates, depends upon a renewed encounter with the Person of Christ at the heart of the Church's life and mission."[15] But the work of the New Evangelization is nourished and sustained by ongoing contact with Christ in prayer, liturgical worship, and Scripture.[16] It is to these life-giving sources of renewal that the Council charts a course and offers a "sure compass" for the work of theology.

14. See Pope Francis, Homily, April 17, 2013.

15. See, e.g., Pope Francis, Apostolic Exhortation, *Evangelii gaudium*, no. 3; Pope Benedict XVI, Encyclical Letter, *Deus caritas est*, no. 1, Pope John Paul II, Encyclical Letter, *Veritatis splendor*, no. 7, Pope Paul VI, Apostolic Exhortation, *Evangelii nuntiandi*, no. 14.

16. Pinckaers wisely observes that the renewal of the Church's life for which the Council called depends upon the fact that God still speaks to his people in prayer and prayerful reading of the scriptures. See *Sources of Christian Ethics*, 318–23.

TRANSFORMED
IN CHRIST

CHAPTER 1

The Status of the Sexual Good as a
Direction for Moral Theology

Anyone who is even remotely aware of contemporary Catholic moral theology has heard something of the ongoing debate that now rages within it.
Revisionist and traditionalist moral theologians are engaged in a seemingly
endless critique of each other's methodology and viewpoints. Nowhere is
this debate more sharp than in the area of sexual ethics. Thus revisionists
charge their opponents with a "classicist" approach to reality that seeks to
deduce moral norms from a static and unchanging human nature,[1] and a
"physicalist" understanding of natural law and human action that attempts
to deduce the moral character of actions purely from their physical structure and therefore reduces the rational individual to the status of a slave to
his or her physical processes.[2] Traditionalists counter that revisionist meth-

---

Originally published as "The Status of the Sexual Good as a Direction for Moral Theology,"
Heythrop Journal 35 (1994): 15–34.

1. A good overview of the two differing world views that undergird these moral methods
from the revisionist perspective is provided by Richard Gula, SS, *What Are They Saying about
Moral Norms?* (New York: Paulist, 1982), 18–22. For more extensive treatments of this change
in outlook, see Michael J. Himes, "The Human Person in Contemporary Theology: From Human Nature to Authentic Subjectivity," in *Technological Powers and the Person*, ed. A. Moracze-
wski (St. Louis, MO: Pope John Center, 1983), 270–312; and Charles Curran, "Natural Law," in
Directions in Moral Theology (Notre Dame, IN: University of Notre Dame Press, 1985), 137–55.
It is not self-evident that all revisionist approaches are in fact less classicist than their traditionalist counterparts, however.

2. For a good summary of the charge of physicalism advanced by revisionist theologians,
see Vincent J. Genovesi, SJ, *In Pursuit of Love: Catholic Morality and Human Sexuality* (Wilm-
ington, DE: Michael Glazier, 1987), 359–63. For a more detailed presentation of this notion

odology is impractical in its emphasis on weighing future consequences of an act in determining its morality,[3] and that it is dangerously relativistic in its refusal to allow for absolute moral norms.[4] These debates will no doubt continue.

After listening to these discussions for a time, one gets the impression that they have reached something of an impasse. Those engaged in these mutual critiques seem to be talking past one another, and there seems to be little hope of a substantive agreement on any of these matters in the near future. Is there any prospect of freeing this logjam, which constitutes much present ethical discussion?

It would seem that one possible way to advance the present discussions is by taking a more foundational and theological approach to some of the issues at stake in the present debate. That is, one must focus not merely on the morality of particular sexual acts, but on the meaning and status of sexuality in relation to the person as the necessary precondition of such analysis.

There are a number of reasons for expressing optimism that such an approach might prove fruitful. First, in current discussions, much is made of the fact that the Second Vatican Council opened the way for new reflection on sexual morality by refusing to speak of the procreative and unitive aspects of marital sexuality as the "primary" and "secondary" ends of marriage, as had previous formulations (cf. *Gaudium et spes*, nos. 49–51). Nevertheless, it is no less important to observe that the Council also gave an implicit endorsement to an anthropological focus as an agenda for these new moral reflections by urging that the objective moral criteria employed in evaluating methods of birth regulation be "based on the nature of the human person and his acts" (*Gaudium et spes*, no. 51). Second, it appears that this grounding of the sexual good within theological anthropology has

in regard to traditional natural law theory and its use in Church teaching, see Charles Curran, "Moral Theology and *Humanae Vitae*," in *Transition and Tradition in Moral Theology* (Notre Dame, IN: University of Notre Dame Press, 1979), 29–58, esp. 32–37.

3. See Bartholomew Keily, SJ, "The Impracticality of Proportionalism," *Gregorianum* 66 (1985): 655–86.

4. For a critique of proportionalist methodology and especially its account of moral norms, see Germain Grisez, *Christian Moral Principles*, vol. 1, *The Way of the Lord Jesus* (Chicago: Franciscan Herald, 1983), 141–71. For a similar critique and defense of the traditional notion of absolute moral norms, see John Finnis, *Moral Absolutes: Tradition, Revision and Truth* (Washington, DC: Catholic University of America Press, 1991); and William E. May, *An Introduction to Moral Theology* (Huntington, IN: Our Sunday Visitor, 1991), 99–138.

been neglected in current discussions of moral theology by both revisionists and traditionalist authors. Third, this sort of approach can also address the growing consensus that an adequate approach to sexual ethics must also be able to speak to the contemporary awareness of the equal dignity of men and women as persons.[5] While both revisionist and traditionalist thinkers are aware of this changed situation, it is not self-evident that the methodologies that they promote are able to effectively address issues of sexual equality (often called "gender issues") as well as to evaluate sexual activity.[6]

In light of such considerations, this essay considers the theological meaning of sexuality in relation to the person as a means to shed light on these current debates. The specific question this essay examines is the status or locus of the sexual good within a theological anthropology as a ground for moral action. By "sexual good" I mean the whole person to the degree that he or she is a sexual being.[7] The term therefore refers primarily to the interrelationship of a person's sexuality and the manner in which this sexuality is seen to be possessed. Specifically, this essay argues that a consideration of various models of the sexual good identified by feminist and other theologians in current discussions of theological anthropology can shed light upon certain disputed questions within the field of sexual ethics as well as provide a more theological foundation for future discussion.

The procedure followed in the remainder of this essay is to consider the

5. See Philip Keane, SS, *Sexual Morality: A Catholic Perspective* (New York: Paulist, 1977), 20–34; and Lisa Sowle Cahill, *Between the Sexes: Foundations for a Christian Ethics of Sexuality* (Philadelphia: Fortress, 1985).

6. An exception to this observation is Cahill's *Between the Sexes*, which attempts to construct a methodology based on the four interrelated sources of Scripture, the tradition of the faith community, philosophical anthropology, and the empirical sciences in order to be sensitive to both issues of sexual equality and sexual morality. The term "gender" is not used here because of the fact that for some feminists scholars it has become a technical term opposed to "sex." In this view, "gender" is the social or cultural valuation of the biological reality of "sex." For a good overview of the sex/gender distinction in feminist thought, see Anne Carr, BVM, *Transforming Grace: Christian Tradition and Women's Experience* (San Francisco: Harper and Row, 1988), 76–84. While both feminist and nonfeminist proponents of such a position can be found, this view is but one among several possibilities that this essay explores below. Therefore, to avoid prejudging this issue and the possible confusion caused by using a word with multiple meanings, the term "gender" will be avoided in this study.

7. I am indebted to Joseph Murphy, SJ, for this usage of the phrase "the sexual good." For some thinkers, this good encompasses the biological, social, psychological, and even spiritual dimensions of the person, while for others, it is primarily a biological and/or social reality.

status of the sexual good in recent discussions of sexual ethics. It then outlines a number of models of the sexual good identified by feminist theologians and subsequently utilizes these as a basis for organizing the insights found elsewhere in recent systematic reflection about sexuality. These more developed models provide alternate foundational stances from which to consider controverted questions of both sexual equality and sexual ethics. Each of these is then evaluated in terms of its theological strengths and weaknesses, particularly in its ability to address issues of sexual equality and sexual activity. In order to give focus to a potentially large topic with multiple issues attached to it, special attention is given to the relationship of the unitive and procreative dimensions of human sexuality mentioned by the Second Vatican Council.

Models of the Sexual Good

The Sexual Good in Recent Sexual Ethics

Both revisionist and traditionalist discussions of sexual ethics have struggled to root their discussions in a coherent theological vision of the person. Likewise, both approaches betray certain inconsistencies in the methodologies that they do propose to evaluate particular acts.

Revisionists such as Charles Curran and Richard McCormick, SJ, often speak of the need to integrate sexuality within an understanding of the person and urge that data from the natural and behavioral sciences be taken into account in this project.[8] Yet neither has fully articulated a complete theological anthropology in which to integrate such an understanding of

---

8. See Curran's own description of the place of anthropology within his methodology in "A Methodological Overview," in *Directions in Moral Theology*, 3–27. Something of Richard McCormick's views can be gleaned from the approbation with which he cites the position of Louis Janssens, that to adequately consider the person is to consider all of his or her essential aspects. Among these features, Janssens (and McCormick) includes things such as subjectivity, embodiment, materiality, other-directedness, sociality, a call to know and worship God, historicity, originality, and equality. McCormick opines that these fundamental aspects can provide a basis for integrating scientific data about the person but does not attempt this integration himself. See his *Notes on Moral Theology, 1981 through 1984* (Lanham, MD: University Press of America, 1984), 49–52; and "Moral Theology since Vatican II: Clarity or Chaos?," in *The Critical Calling: Reflections on Moral Dilemmas since Vatican II* (Washington, DC: Georgetown University Press, 1989), 3–24, esp. 14–16.

sexuality, nor is it fully clear that the anthropological reflections that they do entertain are determinative for their respective moral methodologies.[9]

Furthermore, these thinkers sometimes seem unable to provide a convincing rationale for the procreative character of sexual love. Thus it is commonly argued that this dimension is to be predicated of the duration of a sexual relationship rather than any of its particular acts.[10] There are a number of potential difficulties in this approach. First, there seems to be an unjustified dichotomy between this assertion and the fact that in order to be morally good sexual activity must necessarily be in some sense unitive even though this love will only be fully expressed over the course of the relationship—otherwise, such acts can take on the character of violence, exploitation, or manipulation.[11] If this is the case, then it is not immediately clear why the procreative dimension of sexuality must not also be present *in some fashion* in individual sexual acts even though a couple's fertility will only be fully expressed over the whole course of their relationship. It is difficult to

9. The gap between an "ethics of being" and an "ethics of doing" in McCormick's thought has been pointed out by Kenneth Himes, OFM, "The Contribution of Theology to Catholic Moral Theology," in *Moral Theology: Challenges for the Future*, ed. Charles Curran (New York: Paulist, 1990), 40–73, here 67. The same idea is made even more pointedly by James J. Walter, who notes the lack of a "developed metaphysics and moral anthropology" in the writings of McCormick and other revisionist authors that could ground the account of the human goods that they propose. See his "The Foundation and Formulation of Norms," in *Moral Theology: Challenges for the Future*, 125–54, here 146. This is less evident in the case of Curran, whose "relational-responsibility" model might seem to lend itself well to reflection on the person. Yet Curran's anthropological remarks frequently consist of observations on theories of freedom, moral development, and the virtues or dispositions that should guide one in relationships with God, self, and world. See, e.g., his "A Methodological Overview," in *Moral Theology: Challenges for the Future*, 15–18. When Curran considers such anthropological themes in relation to human sexuality, he will add an emphasis on human bodiliness and sin as checks on the freedom of an individual or couple in relation to their reproductive choices. He does not consider the more basic question of the status of sexuality in relation to the person. See, e.g., his "The Contraceptive Revolution and the Human Condition," in *Moral Theology: A Continuing Journey* (Notre Dame, IN: University of Notre Dame Press, 1982), 141–69, esp. 154–58.

10. Cf. Richard McCormick, "Catholic Moral Theology: Is Pluralism Pathogenic?," in *Critical Calling*, 147–62, esp. 151–53; Charles Curran, "Official Catholic Social and Sexual Teachings: A Methodological Comparison," in *Tensions in Moral Theology* (Notre Dame, IN: University of Notre Dame Press, 1988), 87–109, esp. 102–4. Yet both hold that a relationship characterized by a "contraceptive mentality" intending that all of its sexual acts be nonprocreative cannot be considered a valid Christian marriage.

11. Cf. Cahill's observations in *Between the Sexes*, 149.

see how such a dichotomy can be justified without some underlying pre-supposition of the sexual good—or at least its procreative aspect—as something extrinsic to the person and therefore to some degree dispensable.[12] Second, the argument that the overall relationship rather than particular acts of lovemaking is most important overlooks the fact that relationships and indeed one's character are in large part constituted by particular acts.[13] If such acts are morally questionable because of their failure to respect the value of procreation, can they not serve to undermine both the relationship and the character of those within it? Third and finally, the inability to con-cretize or enflesh the procreative component of sexuality in particular acts has led in some more extreme formulations to an inability to render moral evaluations of virtually any kind of sexual activity.[14]

12. It is true that McCormick protests the characterization that he and other revision-ists "hold that the body is a mere instrument to be manipulated dualistically for our purpos-es." *Notes on Moral Theology*, 59. Nevertheless, McCormick and others clearly do argue that at times the procreative end of sexuality can rightly be suppressed in order to achieve certain desirable ends. See, e.g., his description of contraceptive sterilization as "a *marriage*-stabilizing and *family*-stabilizing procedure." See "A Commentary on the Commentaries," in *Doing Evil to Achieve Good*, ed. Richard McCormick, SJ, and Paul Ramsey (Chicago: Loyola Universi-ty Press, 1978), 193–267, here 241 (emphasis original). Curran echoes McCormick's position when he argues that "for the good of the person or for the good of the marriage it is legitimate at times to interfere with the physical structure of the act." See his "The Development of Sexual Ethics in Contemporary Roman Catholicism," in *Tensions in Moral Theology*, 74–86, here 76. There is thus a certain tension in this approach between human reason and embodiment, since at least some of the biological aspects of the sexual good are viewed as something that can be suppressed without detriment to the person.

13. See Kiely, "Impracticality of Proportionalism," 666–68. See also the discussion of *habi-tus* provided by Romanus Cessario, OP, *The Moral Virtues and Theological Ethics* (Notre Dame, IN: University of Notre Dame Press, 1991), 34–48.

14. A good example is provided by Catholic Theological Society of America study by An-thony Kosnick et al., *Human Sexuality: New Directions in American Catholic Thought* (New York: Paulist, 1977). This work advocated a broadening of the language concerning the pur-poses of sexuality from "procreative and unitive" to "creative and integrative," with the under-standing that such sexual expression will also be self-liberating, other-enriching, honest, faith-ful, socially responsible, life-serving, and joyous (86–95). The general consensus regarding this proposal is that such criteria are so vague that it is difficult to exclude virtually any form of sexual activity. The authors seem to come closest to such a prohibition in the case of bestiality (230). Hence James Burtchaell's tongue-in-cheek description of the work's "liberating norms … whereby about the only discouraged form of sex is doing it with a Doberman." See James Burtchaell, CSC, *The Giving and Taking of Life: Essays Ethical* (Notre Dame, IN: University of Notre Dame Press, 1989), 288.

On the other hand, traditionalists such as Germain Grisez and John Finnis identify certain "basic human goods" that are the sources of human fulfillment toward which we are naturally inclined and that ought not be acted against, but they do not see the need to integrate their revision of natural law theory into an understanding of the human person.[15]

Neither Grisez nor Finnis speak of the "sexual" as a good in its own right—in their system, it is assumed or subsumed in other goods, especially that of "life."[16] Insofar as sexual sins are generally characterized as sins against the good of life, it would seem that such a view is inclined toward an understanding of intercourse as ordered primarily to procreation rather than affirming the equal importance of the unitive and procreative ends of marital sexuality envisaged by the Second Vatican Council. Therefore these thinkers seem to neglect the development of a rationale for the intrinsic value of the unitive dimension of sexual love. Furthermore, it would seem that such a view renders it impossible for these thinkers to give a convincing rationale for their position that each act of intercourse must be simultaneously both unitive and procreative.[17] How can this be, as these dimensions are logically separable and grounded in goods that are incommensurable with one another? Their condemnations of contraceptive activity seem to be belied by the logic of their own method.

There are also attempts to understand human sexuality in relation to the

15. Responding to this criticism of his position, advanced by Russell Hittinger, Germain Grisez argues that "the moral *ought* cannot be derived from the *is* of theoretical truth—for example of metaphysics and/or philosophical anthropology." See his "A Critique of Russell Hittinger's Book, *A Critique of the New Natural Law Theory*," *New Scholasticism* 62 (1988): 438–65, here 465 (emphasis original). Grisez and Finnis therefore depart from Scholastic natural law theories, grounded as they are in a specific understanding of "nature."

16. That this is in fact the case can be seen in Grisez's defense of "bodily life" as a basic human good. *Christian Moral Principles*, 137–39. After a long discussion of the good of bodily life from both philosophical and theological perspectives, Grisez notes that "sins against bodily life and sexuality lead to a distorted consciousness of one's self" (138). Here it is clear that sexuality is simply one aspect of the deeper and more basic good of life. Finnis likewise rejects treating procreation or any other aspect of sexuality as distinct goods, insisting that the values inherent in sexuality are adequately grounded in other goods such as "life," "friendship," or "truth." Cf. *Natural Law and Natural Rights* (Oxford: Clarendon, 1980), 86–87.

17. See Germain Grisez, Joseph Boyle, John Finnis, and William E. May, "'Every Marital Act Ought to Be Open to New Life': Toward a Clearer Understanding," *The Thomist* 52 (1988): 365–426. For an extensive critique of the arguments of these authors, see Gareth Moore, OP, *The Body in Context: Sex and Catholicism* (London: SCM Press, 1992), 165–81.

person as a whole, evidenced by thinkers on both sides of the debate; however, these are often either undeveloped or undercut by an inability to integrate them with the methodology for moral decision making proposed by these authors. Hence Philip Keane in his *Sexual Morality* makes the following important observation: "the gift of sexuality is a gift that touches persons on all levels of their existence ... thus becoming a basic or ontological determinant of human existence or personality."[18] Yet this viewpoint is apparently lost in the subsequent discussions of method and concrete issues that blend Curran's relational responsibility model and proportionalist reasoning. Likewise, Vincent Genovesi, SJ, in his *In Pursuit of Love* provides an excellent account of sexuality as a language of committed self-giving.[19] When examining particular questions of sexual morality such as premarital sex, however, Genovesi drops this approach and reverts to the proportionalist language of ontic evil and proportionate reason.[20] Even Lisa Sowle Cahill is not fully adequate on this point in spite of the attempt to achieve a balanced methodology in *Between the Sexes*, which incorporates the insights of philosophical anthropology. The only explicitly anthropological reflection that Cahill offers is the natural law theory of Aquinas. She critiques this heavily but does not attempt to supplement or replace it.[21] The same point can be made in regard to more traditionalist authors. Thus Ronald Lawler, Joseph Boyle, and William May assert that "sexuality is a modality affecting our entire being as persons."[22] But in their discussions of method or concrete questions of sexual activity, they revert to the language of Grisez and Finnis concerning basic human goods—language that resists such theological reflection concerning the meaning of sexuality in relation to the person.[23]

Much has been made of the recent "paradigm shift" from more physicalist to personalist approaches to questions of sexual ethics.[24] Here too,

18. Keane, *Sexual Morality*, 4.

19. Cf. Genovesi, *In Pursuit of Love*, 139–56.

20. Ibid., 177–88.

21. Cf. Cahill, *Between the Sexes*, 105–22.

22. Ronald Lawler, Joseph Boyle, and William May, *Catholic Sexual Ethics: A Summary, Explanation, and Defense* (Huntington, IN: Our Sunday Visitor, 1985), 129.

23. Ibid., 70–78, 88–97.

24. See, e.g., the important discussion and overview provided by B. V. Johnstone, CSsR, "From Physicalism to Personalism," *Studia Moralia* 30 (1992): 71–96.

however, one finds sharp disagreements about the nature and meaning of this "personalism" and its relationship to disputed questions of sexual ethics. For example, some have recently proposed that the subordination of the procreative to the unitive dimension of sexuality implicit in much revisionist methodology is in fact demanded by the logic of personalism.[25] At this point, however, such an assertion remains largely unsubstantiated in the absence of a more careful theological examination of sexuality and its status in relation to the person.

Thus both revisionist and traditionalist discussions of sexuality demonstrate varying degrees of inability to integrate basic theological reflection about the meaning and relation of sexuality to the person into the methodology that they propose in order to make moral judgments. In this sense, both sides have shown themselves to be slow to respond to repeated calls for the development of an anthropology to ground such evaluation.[26] The reason for this seems to be either an implicit or explicit acceptance of Hume's axiom, developed by Ayer and Hare, that the "ought" of moral obligation cannot be derived from the "is" of statements of fact or being.[27] This principle has served to widen the disastrous rift between moral and systematic theology that has plagued Catholic theology since the Council of Trent. This essay considers whether this gap between these two kinds of discourse can be bridged through a consideration of more explicitly theological presentations of the sexual good.

---

25. See Lisa Sowle Cahill, "'Catholic Sexual Ethics and the Dignity of the Person: A Double Message," *Theological Studies* 50 (1989): 120–50. In more recent work, however, Cahill has been far more tentative in advancing this notion. See her "Is Catholic Ethics Biblical? The Example of Sex and Gender" (Warren Lecture, University of Tulsa, Tulsa, OK, March 15, 1992), 4.

26. This call was first issued by G. E. M. Anscombe, "Modern Moral Philosophy," *Philosophy* 33 (1958): 1–19. More recently it has been echoed by Cahill, "Teleology, Utilitarianism, and Christian Ethics," *Theological Studies* 42 (1981): 601–29, esp. 617; and Walter, *Moral Theology: Challenges for the Future*, 146.

27. Both Grisez and McCormick explicitly invoke this principle, albeit in somewhat differing fashion. Grisez invokes this axiom to defend himself from charges that his account of the basic human goods is inadequate because it is not grounded in a philosophical account of human nature (see note 15 above). McCormick utilizes this principle as a tool to criticize those who mix factual and evaluative language in their formulations of absolute moral norms. See, e.g., his "Moral Argument in Christian Ethics," in *Critical Calling*, 47–69, esp. 58–59.

The Contribution of Feminist Theology

Among the first theologians to identify various "models" of the sexual good were feminists seeking to explore the impact of various ways of conceiving sexuality on the quest for sexual equality.[28] Early writings on this topic focused on various "faces" or impulses to be found within feminist thought and the visions of humanity that they generated.[29] Among these visions, three were seen to stand out: (1) a unisex ideal that attempted to suppress sexual differences and to have one sex conform to the standard of the other; (2) an androgynous view that depicted sexual differences as purely biological and encouraged the sexes to adopt qualities and roles traditionally associated with the other; and (3) the heavily criticized traditional view of polarity between the sexes, which emphasized their complementarity and difference.[30]

Subsequent feminist thought has systematized these basic impulses into a number of distinct models, each of which has feminist and nonfeminist adherents and critics. The first of these is the single-nature model, which picks up on the androgynous ideal by insisting that there is a "primordial unity in human nature" and that "there are no preordained roles or functions, beyond the biological, for either men or women since the appropriate activities of the individual are extracted from spiritual and personal characteristics."[31] Yet this view has been seen as unsatisfactory by other feminists who regard it as philosophically inadequate because of its maintenance of an outmoded static concept of human "nature" and its embeddedness in an oppressive social context.[32] These feminists often adopt a process ontology in their description of a "transformative anthropology," which sees the human person as "self-creating" within the context of his or her own historical existence.[33]

28. This is not to say that feminists were the first to discuss the theological or moral significance of sexuality. See, e.g., Mary Aquin O'Neill, RSM, "Toward a Renewed Anthropology," *Theological Studies* 36 (1975): 725–36.

29. Ibid., 734–36.

30. Ibid.

31. Sara Butler, ed., *Research Report: Women in Church and Society* (Mahwah, NJ: CTSA, 1978), 37. This work advocates such a view on the basis of its compatibility with modern science and historical consciousness.

32. See Mary J. Buckley, "The Rising of the Woman is the Rising of the Race," *Proceedings of the CTSA* 34 (1979): 48–63. Cf. Carr, *Transforming Grace*, 127–33.

33. Cf. Carr, *Transforming Grace*, 117, 131–33. Carr bases this ontology on the work of Karl

In opposition to these first two models, which tend to downplay the differences between the sexes, stands a third model that emphasizes the fundamental polarity between them. This view is often called the dual-nature view because it so emphasizes sexual distinctions that it appears to root them in two different human natures: male and female. While many feminists criticize such a view as an obstacle to the achievement of sexual equality, others approximate it through their emphasis on sexual difference or separation.[34]

Because of the critique of traditional ontology inherent in the transformative model, some feminists have abandoned discussions of the sexual good in relation to human nature, preferring to focus instead on specific social and linguistic constructions of gender and embodiment.[35] Others, however, have continued to utilize these categories in their analysis of contemporary theology and ethics concerning sexuality.[36] Especially noteworthy in this ongoing discussion are proposals that could be identified as a

---

Rahner, whose writing sees human nature as a dynamic reality that arises out of the exercise of human agency and freedom. Carr does not give a systematic presentation of such an ontology or consider its implications, however. Such deficiencies can be corrected by consulting the more developed process anthropology presented in the work of Rosemary Radford Ruether. See, e.g., her *Sexism and God-Talk: Toward a Feminist Theology* (Boston: Beacon, 1983), 244–58.

34. For critiques of the dual-nature view, see O'Neil, "Toward a Renewed Anthropology," 734–35; Butler, *Research Report*, 36–37; and Carr, *Transforming Grace*, 123–24, 128–33. Among feminists inclined toward some version of this model are many French feminists who utilize the insights of psychoanalysis and linguistic theory to emphasize the value of the difference between the sexes, certain proponents of goddess spirituality such as Carol Christ, and others of a radical separatist bent such as Mary Daly.

35. See, e.g., Elizabeth A. Clark, "Sex, Shame, and Rhetoric: En-gendering Early Christian Ethics," *Journal of the American Academy of Religion* 59 (1991): 221–45; Caroline Walker Bynum, *Holy Feast and Holy Fast* (Berkeley: University of California Press, 1987); Ulrike Wiethaus, "Sexuality, Gender, and the Body in Late Medieval Women's Spirituality," *Journal of Feminist Studies in Religion* 7 (1991): 35–52; Bonnie J. Miller-McLemore, "Epistemology or Bust: A Maternal Feminist Way of Knowing," *Journal of Religion* 72 (1992): 229–47. One might also note the awareness of particular social contexts in emerging *mujerista* and womanist theologies.

36. See, e.g., Susan A. Ross, "The Bride of Christ and the Body Politic: Body and Gender in Pre-Vatican II Marriage Theology," *Journal of Religion* 71 (1991): 344–61, esp. 359. For a more extensive feminist analysis of the sexual good in relation to human nature, see Lynne Broughton, "Find the Lady," *Modern Theology* 4 (1988): 267–81; and Susan A. Ross, "'Then Honor God in Your Body' (1 Cor. 6:20): Feminist and Sacramental Theology on the Body," *Horizons* 16, no. 1 (1989): 7–27.

fourth model that seeks to integrate an emphasis on a common human nature with an affirmation of individual diversity (including sex differences) and the impact of culture.[37]

Having briefly considered some of the primary models of the sexual good identified by feminist scholars, these can be used to organize and identify the reflections of other theologians on theological anthropology and sexuality. These basic models will have to be further nuanced in their application to particular scholars or trends within recent systematic reflection.

The Sexual Good as Accidental to Human Nature and Human Persons

The first viewpoint to be considered is one that regards sexuality as accidental to both human nature and actually existing human persons. In such a view, sexuality is basically a physical or biological dimension of the person, unrelated to other aspects of human personality or being. Descriptions of male or female psychology, while they may in a certain sense be accurate, do not reflect the order of being, but rather the conditioning of the various societies or cultures from which they emerged. Theologically, such a view would deny the presence of any divine or human exemplars for masculinity or femininity derived from nature or grace, since these realities are constituted by each individual person and cannot be defined. On a social level, such a view would urge a virtually complete interchangeability of roles and qualities traditionally associated with one or the other of the sexes.

A good example of this model of the sexual good is provided by the theology of George Tavard.[38] Tavard has also noted the lack of a substantive

---

37. Thus Katherine E. Zappone observes that "women's difference from one another is *as significant* as their difference from men." See "'Women's Special Nature': A Different Horizon for Theological Anthropology," *Concilium* 6 (1991): 87–97, here 88 (emphasis original). In the same volume, Elizabeth A. Johnson argues for "one human nature celebrated in an interdependence of multiple differences." See "The Maleness of Christ," *Concilium* 6 (1991): 108–16, here 110. Cf. Mary Frohlich, "From Mystification to Mystery: Lonergan and the Theological Significance of Sexuality," in *Lonergan and Feminism*, ed. Cynthia Crysdale (Toronto: University of Toronto Press, 1994), 175–98.

38. One can find similar views expressed in some of the later writings of Karl Rahner. See, e.g., "The Position of Women in the New Situation in Which the Church Finds Itself," in *Theological Investigations*, vol. 7, trans. David Bourke (New York: Herder and Herder, 1971), 75–93; his letter of December 19, 1975, to a member of the Pontifical Study Commission on Women

theological foundation in current discussions of sexual ethics and has endeavored to fill this lacuna by his investigations of the theology of sexuality throughout his career.[39] Taking his stand with some of the more Neoplatonic strains of the patristic tradition, such as Basilius of Ancyra, Tavard argues that sexuality is primarily a biological reality—at the level of their souls, male and female are identically human.[40] Thus it follows that "men and women are complementary in sexual activity, yet identically human in everything else."[41] What are identified as male or female traits are nothing more than stereotypes or statements of cultural prejudice inculcated in children through socialization.[42] Sexual differences are therefore without ontological foundation or real theological significance.

Given this context, it follows that there are no sex-specific exemplars for the sexes, whether these be understood along the lines of the Jungian *animus* and *anima* (except as these point to the need for integration) or, as in the case of traditional Catholicism, of Christ and Mary.[43] It is the Risen Christ, whom Tavard regards as androgynous, who serves as the model for all Christians, men and women. As androgynous, Christ also reveals both humanity's original created state and final resurrected state to be one of androgyny.[44] In light of such an exemplar, the two sexes should be free to de-

in Church and Society published in *Pro Mundi Vita Bulletin* 108 (1987): 21–24; or his conversation with German journalist Anita Röper, *Ist Gott ein Mann? Ein Gesprach mit Karl Rahner* (Düsseldorf: Patmos-Verlag, 1979).

39. Thus he observes, "one gets the impression from reading in the area of sexual ethics, that no theological tradition is considered, if not normative, at least relevant." See George Tavard, "Theology and Sexuality," in *Women in the World's Religions, Past and Present* (New York: Paragon House, 1987), 68–80, here 69.

40. Ibid., 70. Tavard is attracted to Basilius because he represents the Neoplatonic vision of human androgyny without equating sexuality and fallenness, unlike Ambrose and some of the Greek fathers whose thought he reviews favorably in his earlier *Woman in Christian Tradition* (Notre Dame, IN: University of Notre Dame Press, 1973), 72–96. For an authoritative overview of early Christian views of the body and sexuality, see Peter Brown, *The Body and Society: Men, Women and Sexual Renunciation in Early Christianity* (New York: Columbia University Press, 1988).

41. Tavard, "Theology and Sexuality," 78; cf. idem, *Woman in Christian Tradition*, 206.

42. Tavard, "Theology and Sexuality," 78; cf. idem, *Woman in Christian Tradition*, 200.

43. Tavard, *Woman in Christian Tradition*, 194, 227–28; cf. idem, "Theology and Sexuality," 74, 78.

44. Tavard, *Woman in Christian Tradition*, 31–32. Cf. idem, "The Ordination of Women," *One in Christ* 23 (1987): 200–211, esp. 202–4.

velop any of the roles or traits traditionally associated with the other, since these are related neither to human nature nor to who they are as persons.

In addition, Tavard asserts that there is no distinction between the sexes in their imaging of God or in their relation to other human persons.[45] This is because the seat of the *imago dei* is not the isolated individual, but the human being as a person understood as being in relation to others and to God. This relationality is not sex-specific, however, since there is no human or divine exemplars for the sexes. Thus for Tavard the image of God is understood as dynamic and Trinitarian in character—it is that which is "grown into" through participation in the divine life, just as personal sexual identity is something grown into in unique fashion by the individual.[46] On the grounds of such considerations, Tavard rejects any suggestion of "complementarity" between the sexes and in its place advocates what he calls an anthropology of "supplementarity." In this view, members of both sexes are seen to possess the fullness of humanity in themselves, while "relation with persons of the other sex brings a supplement of humanity which could be compared to a gratuitous gift."[47]

Even though Tavard argues that the image of God does not reside in the sexual duality of the man-woman relationship, he is willing to allow that this relationship can be regarded as significant insofar as it is an image of other types of human interrelatedness or friendship.[48] Seen in this light, sexual relations are understood as "the means to make most concrete and particular the oneness of the children of God and their sharing in his life, by bringing the whole body into play as an expression of this oneness."[49] Given the insights of modern psychoanalysis concerning the role of sexuality in personality development, this unitive dimension may be regarded as the objective component of human sexuality rooted in the exigencies of human nature. And because procreation is often naturally unrelated to this dimension, "the principle of Paul VI, that 'each and every marriage act must remain open to the transmission of life' does not seem too absolute."[50]

---

45. Tavard, *Woman in Christian Tradition*, 188–91.
46. Ibid., 191–92.
47. Tavard, "Ordination of Women," 208; cf. idem, "Theology and Sexuality," 79.
48. Tavard, *Woman in Christian Tradition*, 191; cf. idem, "Theology and Sexuality," 79.
49. Tavard, *Woman in Christian Tradition*, 205.
50. Tavard, "Theology and Sexuality," 75.

Tavard's understanding of the sexual good with its emphasis on androgyny shows a good deal of convergence with what feminist theologians describe as a single-nature anthropology. There are also some echoes of what feminists describe as a transformative model of anthropology in his dynamic conception of personhood, as well as in the fact that for Tavard there are no models for the sexes to be found either in nature (which cannot be separated from its cultural manifestations) or in the realm of grace. This approach has a number of important theological and ethical implications, among which can be found both strengths and weaknesses.

On the positive side, it is clear that Tavard's view attempts to uphold the full humanity and equal dignity of both sexes and therefore can demonstrate the evil of sexual discrimination. Furthermore, Tavard's description of the human person as the seat of the *imago dei* with an analogous referent to the "persons" of the Trinity is a suggestion that is rich in theological possibilities.

Yet there are difficulties with Tavard's presentation as well. Presupposed by the reduction of sexuality to a merely biological reality seems to be a certain tension between the bodily and the rational or spiritual dimension of a person, with a rather dualistic equation of the person with the latter. Furthermore, Tavard's presentation of an androgynous Christ as an exemplar and goal for humanity seems to suggest that sexuality and its manifestations is primarily something to be ultimately overcome rather than a positive good. This impression is deepened by his insistence on an original and eschatological androgyny for humankind. Such a view bespeaks a Platonist mistrust of sexuality and tends (more explicitly in his early work) toward an identification of sexuality and sin or fallenness. Finally, while Tavard's argument does provide a certain (albeit weak) rationale for the unitive purpose of sexual love in that it concretizes and symbolizes human or Christian unity, he can find little to say about its procreative dimension, viewing it as something dispensable. Coupled with the rather dualistic anthropology, it seems that such a view could find little morally significant difference between cosmetic surgery and a surgical sterilization insofar as both are merely expressions of the person asserting rational control over his or her biological makeup.

The Sexual Good as Essential to Human Nature

The second model to be considered here stands as a logical counterpoint to the first. It views the sexual good as primarily an ontological reality rooted in the very order of being. Sexual differences in this view are not merely biological, but rather such physical differences between the sexes are signs of a more fundamental polarity on the level of their natures. As a result, men and women are seen to have markedly different psychological and even spiritual qualities. Theologically, much is made of Christ as an exemplar for masculinity and Mary or the Church as symbols of "the eternal feminine," to the degree that the value that these persons or entities have for both sexes is not always clear. On a social level, this model tends to insist on the maintenance of rather rigidly defined sex-specific qualities and roles.

A good example of the tendency to locate the sexual good on the level of nature is provided by the thought of Louis Bouyer.[51] Bouyer's thought is characterized by an Augustinian rather than a Thomist or Neo-Thomist approach to theology, and therefore he tends to speak somewhat less about "nature" and natural law, or when he does, to locate their meaning within revelation. Because of this, he makes much of the sexual or marital imagery found within the scriptures as illuminating the distinctions between the sexes. Woman in this typology is identified with feminine but still creaturely figures such as Mary or the Church. Whereas man, while himself still a creature, is depicted as mediating between creation and the divine figures of the Father and Christ, whom he is called to represent. Therefore woman for Bouyer "represents the very type of creatureliness," while in a certain fragmentary sense, man images God, whose divine fatherhood is the source of all life.[52] The sexual differences found within nature are thus taken up into the order of revelation and grace, where they are confirmed rather than transcended.

This leads Bouyer to an affirmation of an anthropology of "complemen-

51. One can find similar views expressed by Hans Urs von Balthasar. See, e.g., Benziger Verlag, trans., *A Theological Anthropology* (New York: Sheed and Ward, 1967), 306–14; "Epilogue," in Louis Bouyer, *Woman in the Church*, trans. Marilyn Teichart (San Francisco: Ignatius, 1979), 113–21; "Ephesians 5:21–33 and *Humanae Vitae*: A Meditation," in *Christian Married Love*, ed. Raymond Dennehy (San Francisco: Ignatius, 1981), 55–73; Mary Theresilde Skerry, trans., *A Short Primer for Unsettled Laymen* (San Francisco: Ignatius, 1985), 90–91.

52. Bouyer, *Woman in the Church*, 29–39.

tarity." Men and women are seen to have rather rigidly defined (although equally important) roles in sex, marriage, Church, and society.[53] These complementary roles are based on what are understood to be the complementary qualities inherent within the sexes. For example, women are said to be more receptive, intuitive, nonobjective, and prone to empathy, while men are understood as more aggressive, rational, and detached.[54]

Differing traits or qualities between the sexes point to their polarity on the level of nature. This grounding of sexuality on the level of nature can be seen in the convergence of a number of factors within Bouyer's analysis. For example, he will assert that the theological utilization of sexual symbolism within Scripture, tradition, and the Church's liturgy "rests on what is fundamentally symbolic in that creation itself, and particularly in human nature."[55] Within this basic symbolic approach, each of the sexes represents and to that degree *is* something fundamentally different than the other. This ontological characterization of sexual difference is further underscored by Bouyer's insistence on the close correspondence between the body and the soul that informs it. Thus an individual's "physical being will reveal and define his metaphysical being itself."[56] Therefore the physiological differences between the sexes bespeak the same sort of differentiation on the level of their souls.

Bouyer is careful to stress that these complementary differences do not suggest any sort of inferiority, especially in regard to women, and that there are in fact numerous ways in which woman may be said to be superior to man. At times, Bouyer goes out of his way to denigrate the ephemeral character of human fatherhood (vis-à-vis that of God, who is the true paternal source of life) and the "fundamentally unstable" character of the masculine being as opposed to its female counterpart.[57]

---

53. E.g., Bouyer calls for a revival of "traditional feminine ministries" such as orders of virgins and widows that existed within the early Church and enumerates as possible jobs for such women living in society "typist, seamstress, salesgirl in a department store, nurse, or laboratory worker, etc." Ibid., 103.

54. Ibid., 53–70.

55. Bouyer, *Woman in the Church*, 53.

56. Ibid., 89. For a more extended consideration of the role of symbolism within Bouyer's theological method, see his *Cosmos: The World and the Glory of God*, trans. Pierre de Font-nouvelle (Petersham, MA: St. Bede's, 1988), 3–36.

57. Bouyer, *Cosmos*, 34–35, 56–58.

This view shows a close correspondence to what feminist authors de-scribe as a dual-nature model of theological anthropology. As in the case of the preceding model, this particular view of sexuality raises important ques-tions for theology and ethics.

On the positive side, the views of Bouyer, like the Neo-Scholastic natu-ral law theory of many of the manuals, provide a clear basis for making cer-tain moral judgments. Unlike the previous model, a rationale is provided for the intrinsic value of the procreative character of sexual love, since the natural union of man and woman has as its norm and exemplar the image of the always fruitful relationships of God and creation, or Christ and the Church. Furthermore, unlike the previous model, the sexual good is clear-ly not subject to human control or manipulation because it is rooted in the order of being. Hence sterilization cannot be equated with cosmetic surgery because in it one tries to alter or control not only one's body, but also one's very nature.

Yet this model is also attended by numerous problems. The rather rigid link made between sexuality and nature raises the question of biologism, often leveled against traditional natural law theories. One might also note in passing that the particular biology invoked, which extrapolates from the supposed passivity of the female and activity of the male in intercourse, can hardly be regarded as tenable.[58] A further difficulty with this model is that it (also like the Neo-Scholastic natural law theory) has difficulty providing a rationale and positive estimation of the unitive end of sexual love. Thus Bouyer will argue that the two ends of intercourse are not only "inseparable but indistinguishable." Merely mutual love that is not also fruitful can only be destructive.[59] It seems that even while maintaining the inseparability of the two ends of intercourse there is a subtle tendency to subordinate the unitive to the procreative dimension. Thus sex only has meaning insofar as it images the spiritual fruitfulness of the archetypal relationships between

58. In a more theological vein, Margaret Farley, RSM, has observed that receptivity ought not be equated with passivity—one can receive in active fashion. Nor should such receptivity be identified exclusively with females or even with humans (insofar as there is receptivity in God's intra-Trinitarian life). See *Personal Commitments: Beginning, Keeping, Changing* (San Francisco: Harper and Row, 1986), 131–32.

59. Bouyer, "The Ethics of Marriage: Beyond Casuistry," in *Christian Married Love*, 33–53, here 39. Cf. ibid., 44–45.

God and Creation or Christ and the Church. Sexual love has no value in itself, but only in its orientation toward procreation. It is not clear how such a view would find value in postmenopausal sex or intercourse between an infertile couple, both of which cases have no possibility of natural fertility. Bouyer's suspicion concerning sexuality seems to recall the ambivalence found in parts of the Augustinian tradition.

Furthermore, it is not clear that this view can do justice to the contemporary appreciation of the equal personal dignity of the sexes. In spite of the acknowledgment of the equality of the sexes, there is the danger that this metaphysical polarity between them will be used to subtly portray the "otherness" of women as inferiority.[60] As feminist theologians have observed, behind the rather Romantic glorification of "the eternal woman" can lie a denigration of actual women.[61] In addition, because the roles and traits of the sexes are bound so closely to their male or female natures, it would seem to leave little room for individual choices and history in realizing one's life vocation.[62] Finally, the division of humanity into two separate natures seems to raise insoluble theological questions concerning human solidarity in salvation and in the moral life.[63]

In fairness to Bouyer, it seems that he is aware of the problem of the unity of the sexes, but his solution—to insist that all created reality and even the persons of the Son and the Spirit are ultimately feminine in relation to God the Father—is hardly adequate.[64] On the human level, such a view again reveals the problematic identification of femininity and receptivity, while at the same time voiding the sexual identity of men of any lasting significance. On the divine level, such a view tends to introduce a kind of subordinationism into the Trinitarian relationships, while simultaneously

60. Cf. Karl Lehmann, "The Place of Woman as a Problem of Theological Anthropology," trans. Robert E. Wood, in *The Church and Women: A Compendium*, ed. Helmut Moll (San Francisco: Ignatius, 1988), 11–33, here 18.

61. See, e.g., Rosemary Radford Ruether, ed., "Misogynism and Virginal Feminism in the Fathers of the Church," in *Religion and Sexism: Images of Woman in the Jewish and Christian Traditions* (New York: Simon and Schuster, 1974), 150–83.

62. Lehmann, "Place of Woman," 18.

63. On these soteriological issues, see Ruether, "Can a Male Savior Save Women?," in *To Change the World: Christology and Cultural Criticism* (London: SCM, 1981), 45–56; Carr, *Transforming Grace*, 52, 112; and Johnson, "Maleness of Christ," 109.

64. Bouyer, *Woman in the Church*, 36–39, 44–46.

identifying masculinity and divinity (only the Father is genuinely masculine and paternal and therefore fully divine). Finally, such a view calls into
question the whole of Bouyer's sexual typology and ontology, and ultimately appears to render his thought hopelessly contradictory.

Sexuality as Accidental to Human Nature but Essential to Existing Human Persons

The third model to be considered stands between the extremes delimited by
the first two. In this view, sexuality is regarded as accidental on the level of
human nature but essential to actually existing human persons. Hence there
is a single human nature, shared equally by both sexes, that is always embodied in two irreducible ways by existing male and female persons. The physical
differences between the sexes do illuminate deeper differences that touch the
whole of who they are as persons, but these differences do not divide them
on the level of human nature. Descriptions of male or female psychology or
spirituality are generally regarded as mixing traits that are genuinely rooted
in the person along with social or cultural interpretations. Theologically, this
model might be willing to consider Christ or Mary as sexually specific exemplars, provided that this does not undermine the importance of each for
both sexes. Yet it will argue that the highest model of personal diversity existing within a unity of nature can be found in the Trinity. On the social level,
this model will urge a greater flexibility in predicating qualities and especially roles of the sexes, without advocating their wholesale abolition.

An example of this model can be found in the proposal made in this
regard by Walter Kasper.[65] Kasper's point of departure is the basic equality
of women and men as persons. Noting the challenge presented by contemporary feminism, Kasper asserts, "the Christian view of woman as a person
can incorporate the legitimate demands of the philosophy of emancipation.
However, it also can and must reflect critically on it and deepen it, thus pre-
venting the emancipation of woman becoming her emancipation from being a woman."[66] While admitting the androcentric character of some bib-

---

65. Karl Lehmann has echoed Kasper's proposal (see note 62 above). One can also find a
certain correspondence in the insistence on sexuality as personal in the "theology of the body"
developed in the teaching of Pope John Paul II.

66. Ibid, 55. Cf. his remarks on the positive aspects of the feminist critique of God as Father in Matthew O'Connell, trans., The God of Jesus Christ (New York: Crossroad, 1986), 135.

lical and patristic writings, Kasper argues that the thrust of the biblical tradition supports the equal personhood of women and men. For Kasper, one reason why woman may be understood as fully in the divine image is that within the scriptures God can have feminine and maternal attributes as well as masculine ones.[67] The value or dignity of the sexes as persons cannot come from any particular role, or from one another, but can only come from God. Hence Kasper offers the following formal definition of the notion of person:

"Person," in the sense which the Christian tradition understands it, means the unique being who exists "in himself" and "for himself," a value and an end in himself, never a means to an end, an inviolable dignity with an absolute right to respect. The foundation of this dignity, from the Christian point of view, is that every human being has a direct relationship to God as his image, so that man is ultimately beyond the ken of man. On the face of every human being shines something of the glory of God.[68]

This personal autonomy and equality of men and women must be concretized in the educational, economic, legal, and political spheres.[69]

In spite of this insistence on their equal dignity as persons, Kasper is just as determined to uphold the differentiation of the sexes as significant. Thus he will argue that there are no "persons in the abstract," only male or female persons who are the "two equally valuable but different expressions of the one nature of humanity."[70] For Kasper, one cannot view human beings in either a materialistic or an idealistic fashion—they are inseparable composites of body and spirit, the body being the "real symbol" or "excarnation" of the spirit.[71] Kasper likewise rejects both the Gnostic contempt for the body (and its many reincarnations throughout history) as well as the romantic polarization of the sexes echoed in the preceding model.[72]

While there are certain qualities that are generally seen to be specific to one of the sexes, these are understood as being fewer in number and more

67. Kasper, "The Position of Woman as a Problem of Theological Anthropology," trans. John Saward in *Church and Women*, 51–64, here 53.

68. Ibid., 57.   69. Ibid., 58.

70. Ibid., 58–59.

71. Ibid., 58. It is interesting to note Kasper's novel use of a Rahnerian term because Rahner never extended his reflections on the symbolic character of the body to sexual differences.

72. Ibid., 59.

fluid in their application than those envisaged by the previous model. In a fashion reminiscent of some of Rahner's reflections on freedom, Kasper recognizes that humanity has a responsibility to cultivate the nature given to it by God within its two distinct personal roles. Thus the sexes must creatively realize the possibilities of their being male or female. Kasper believes that the basic vocation of women is "service to life"; however, this basic maternal orientation can be fulfilled through a variety of ways in marriage, family, the single life, or through religious celibacy.[73] He calls for the deeper assimilation of this "feminine value" through respect for life, protection of the environment, and a movement on the part of the Church away from a rigidly masculine appearance in its liturgy, prayer, and ministry.[74] In addition to this there must be a "redistribution of roles" in marriage, family, and society—so that women are not squeezed in a "murderous, dual role" of assuming primary responsibility for their families while trying to pursue a career.[75]

In this vein, Kasper will speak of the need to recognize men and women as partners rather than competitors or opponents. This is especially true in the partnership of marriage. Thus Kasper writes, "men and women find themselves by finding each other and by becoming one flesh, that is to say a 'We person.' Thus being a person—being in and for oneself—becomes a reality in being in and for the other: self-fulfillment is not achieved by means of egotistical self-assertion and self-aggrandizement, but only in self-giving, self-surrendering love. A person is fulfilled in relationship and communication."[76] Furthermore, because the human being exists within time, the unconditional character of the person as a norm is only fully recognized when this self-giving love takes the form of an exclusive and irrevocable commitment that endures through time, that is, within a monogamous and indissoluble marriage.

In its attempt to affirm both unity and difference, this model shows some correspondence to the emerging fourth model in feminist thought mentioned above. In this approach, too, there is an attempt to account for both unity and diversity while neither suppressing difference in the name of

---

73. Ibid., 61.   74. Ibid.

75. Ibid., 63.

76. Ibid., 62. Cf. his more extended treatment of the personalist characteristics of marital love and partnership in his *Theology of Christian Marriage*, trans. David Smith (New York: Crossroad, 1986), 15–24.

equality nor reifying difference at the expense of unity and equality. While not denying other aspects of individual difference, however, this approach does view the sexual good as primary among other forms of personal distinctiveness. Hence the focus is not purely on the individual, but on the person whose being is constituted relationally and whose sexuality bespeaks a call to realize that being in communion and community with others. It is no accident that the terminology employed here—two kinds of persons (understood relationally) who share a single nature—echoes that used in describing the Trinity as three Persons, each of whom possesses the one divine nature. Because men and women are created in the image of this triune God, their diversity in unity images the divine communion. Thus the final ground or exemplar for understanding men and women as persons is the mystery of the Trinity.[77]

Like the preceding models, this approach has a number of positive features to commend it. First, it clearly affirms the equal dignity of men and women and can identify the evil of discrimination. Second, this view is able to affirm the importance of both unitive and the procreative dimensions of sexuality without thereby subordinating one to the other. The self-giving love of the spouses is ordered toward mutual communion and community ("the one flesh" union spoken of by Kasper). Yet the personal love spoken of by Kasper is not self-enclosed but has an inherent fruitfulness that is ordered to and completed by the wider community of children, family, and, by analogy, the human community of society.[78] Yet as this progression suggests, this love can retain its fruitfulness even when the possibility of biological procreation is absent. Hence both the unitive and procreative ends have an inherent value that is not derived from devaluing one at the expense of the other. There is therefore a morally significant difference between cosmetic surgery and surgical sterilization insofar as the latter affects something integral to the person and his or her relationships (but not necessarily human nature itself as in the preceding model).[79] Third, unlike the previous

77. Cf. "'One of the Trinity'... Re-establishing a Spiritual Christology in the Perspective of Trinitarian Theology," in *Theology and Church*, trans. Margaret Kohl (New York: Crossroad, 1989), 94–108, esp. 103–8.

78. Cf. Kasper, *Theology of Christian Marriage*, 17–21.

79. Kasper does not deny the connection between human nature and personhood (nor between nature and procreation), but seeks to integrate them within his discussion of personal love. See *Theology of Christian Marriage*, 20.

models, which demonstrate a stasis suggestive of a classicist approach, this model is consciously historical in character, identifying sexuality as essential to actually existing historical persons.

The primary weaknesses of this model lie in its novelty and relative lack of development. While Kasper's proposal is devoted to the status of women, it would seem that his presentation is fundamentally incomplete without some indication of what basic qualities or vocations are appropriate for male persons. Furthermore, the notion of person as a relational entity distinct from human nature needs further elaboration.[80] Finally, critics have argued that it is not completely clear that the personalist notion of human dignity can necessarily serve as an adequate ground for moral evaluation or generate norms that would apply to concrete actions.[81]

Conclusion

This essay began by surveying the current stalemate in discussions of sexual ethics and observing inadequacies in the arguments of both sides. Such difficulties suggest the need for a more theological form of reflection on the meaning and status of human sexuality in relation to the person. Using models developed by feminist theologians, three differing positions have been outlined. Each of these provides a different vision of the sexual good and hence a different foundation from which to address issues of sexual equality and sexual ethics. None is necessarily the last word in this debate, since all have strengths and weaknesses particular to them.

---

80. Kasper recognizes this, and in recent essays asserts the importance of developing a relational ontology. See his "Revelation and Mystery: The Christian Understanding of God," in *Theology and Church*, 19–31; and in the same volume "Christology and Anthropology," 71–93.

81. Bruno Schüller, "Die Personwürde des Menschen als Beweisgrund in der normativen Ethik," *Theologie und Glaube* 53 (1978): 538–55. While these remarks are aimed primarily at the personalism of John Paul II, they are also applicable to an approach such as Kasper's. Kasper, however, believes that Schüller's failure to see the normative significance of this method results from his separation of human dignity from its foundation in a grasp of truth generated by the apprehension of natural law. See *Human Rights and the Church: Historical and Theological Reflections* (Vatican City: Pontifical Council on Justice and Peace, 1990), 47–71, esp. 56. Kasper's approach is criticized more directly by John Milbank, who labels it "an uneasy amalgam of personalist and Kantian perspectives." See his "The Second Difference: For a Trinitarianism without Reserve," *Modern Theology* 2 (1986): 213–34, here 217.

It may seem that the preceding analysis has done nothing more than replicate in more theological terms the impasse described in the opening section. In response to this objection, a number of observations are in order. First, unlike some of the methodologies utilized by moralists, each of these models has shown itself to possess an immediate relevance to questions of sexual equality (albeit in differing fashion depending on the model). Second, this analysis has at least reframed the debate in more theological terms so that it can perhaps move beyond some of the wrangling over questions of method that have come to dominate it. Third, it has revealed some interesting connections between the way in which the sexual good is viewed and one's approach to particular questions of sexual morality. A view that regards the sexual good as merely a biological reality tends to downplay the procreative dimension of human sexuality. Conversely, a model that regards the sexual good as essential to human nature will emphasize procreation even at the expense of the unitive end. Fourth, in spite of its limitations, the third model described above shows some promise of being capable of mediation within the current climate of polarization by attempting to account for the values of love and procreation without devaluing either. It thus attempts to integrate both the biological givenness of nature and the demands of freedom and individuality in its insistence upon sexuality as essential to the person. Hence, in spite of the need for further exploration of the models developed above and their implications, this presentation has demonstrated that reflection on the status of the sexual good within a theological understanding of the human person can provide a fruitful direction for future moral reflection.

CHAPTER *2*

Person

Substance and Relation

The roots of the notion of "person" are closely interwoven with those of Christian theology. Historical study has demonstrated that the ancient world, whether in biblical or classical sources, did not have an equivalent concept, even though both provide important linguistic and conceptual antecedents to its development.[1] It is only as the Church sought to articulate

Originally published as "Person: Substance and Relation," *Communio* 22 (Spring 1995): 139–63.

1. The scriptures, while not using the term, do provide conceptual and linguistic antecedents such as the understanding of God as personal, the presentation of divine or human agency in biblical narrative, the notion of a "name" as integral to one's identity, the concept of "face" (*panim* in Old Testament (OT) usage, usually translated as *prosopon* in the Septuagint (LXX) and New Testament, or the various "personifications" of the divine wisdom, word, or glory in the OT. See Walter Kasper, *Theology and Church*, trans. Margaret Kohl (New York: Crossroad, 1989), 26; and Lawrence B. Porter, "On Keeping 'Persons' in the Trinity: A Linguistic Approach to Trinitarian Thought," *Theological Studies* 41 (1980): 541. The early biblical usage of *panim* shows a certain correspondence to the original Greek meaning of *prosópon*, which designated the mask worn by an actor, and then an actor's role, and finally the "role" played by anyone in life. The Latin term used to translate *prosópon* is *persona*, whose derivation is debated but whose meaning eventually became linked with that of its Greek counterpart. Early scholarship on the topic usually held that the word *persona* was derived from the verb *personare* "to sound through," which implied the projection of a voice through the mask worn in a theatrical production. Aloys Grillmeier thinks it likely that the word derives from the Etruscan *phersu*, which was the term used to describe the masks worn in the worship of the goddess Persephone. Regardless of how it acquired its connotation of "mask," by the time of Cicero, *persona* had evolved to include the meanings of a dramatic character, grammatical person, and individuality. On these developments, see *Christ in Christian Tradition*, vol. 1, *From the Apostolic Age to Chalcedon (451)*, trans. John Bowden (London: Mowbrays, 1965), 125–26; *New Catholic*

its faith concerning the unity of humanity and divinity in Christ or as to express the idea of plurality within the unity of the divine essence did this concept emerge and begin to take shape. In this sense, it is correct to assert that the notion of person is a uniquely Christian theological insight and contribution to the broader intellectual history of humanity.[2]

But a closer look at the theological tradition reveals that the concept of person is not a univocal one, but rather one that had been understood in different ways by different theological schools or thinkers. In part, this is the result of its application to seemingly diverse mysteries within the Christian faith: the Trinity, the Incarnation, or humanity made in God's image and likeness. Yet there have also been basic differences of emphasis or different conceptual starting points behind such disagreements as well. This study traces one such fundamental difference—that between person understood as substance and that which sees person as constituted by relation. In particular, it argues that these two strands are not necessarily mutually exclusive, but rather converge in the understanding of subsistent relation and in the present movement to view the human person as a being whose subsistence is relational.

This essay first examines the origin of a relational understanding of person in patristic teaching, especially in the theology of the Cappadocians. It then looks at the more substantialist definition offered by Boethius and the partial synthesis of this approach with the more relational view found within parts of the Augustinian tradition effected by Aquinas. A final section analyzes the impulses within contemporary thought that have added impetus to this convergence by making possible an understanding of the human person as constituted by relation, focusing in particular upon new developments in the understanding of human subjectivity, the contribution of the dialogical philosophers, the theology of human sexuality, and the emergence of a Trinitarian metaphysic.

Encyclopedia, 1967 ed., s.v. "Person (in Philosophy)"; and John D. Zizioulas, *Being as Communion: Studies in Personhood and the Church* (Crestwood, NY: St. Vladimir's Seminary Press, 1985), 25–36.

2. A number of authors forcefully argue this point: Joseph Ratzinger, "Concerning the Notion of Person in Theology," trans. Michael Waldstein, *Communio* 17 (1990): 439–54; Hans Urs von Balthasar, "On the Concept of Person," *Communio* 13 (1986): 18–26; and Zizioulas, *Being as Communion*, 27–49.

Patristic Beginnings: The Emergence of Person and Relation

Study of the Christian concept of person seems to have progressed from an earlier focus on Jewish and Christian angelology to a consideration of a method of biblical interpretation known as "prosopological exegesis."[3] The roots of this approach to the scriptures can be found in Philo's practice of distinguishing revelation through the "person" of Moses from other modes. Though it was in its origins a literary and grammatical tool, in Christian usage it developed into a means of discerning the presence of the *Logos* speaking in and through the sacred text, thus identifying the role with the reality. As Ratzinger observes, "the word [*prósopa*] no longer really means 'roles,' because it takes on a completely new reality in terms of faith in the Word of God. The roles introduced by the sacred writer are realities, they are dialogical realities.... The literary artistic device of letting roles appear to enliven the narrative with their dialogue reveals to the theologians *the one who plays the true role here*, the *Logos*, the *prosópon*, the person of the Word which is no longer merely role, but person."[4] Such a process can be observed in the work of Justin, Irenaeus, Tertullian, Athanasius, and Origen.[5] Prosopological exegesis proved to be the fertile soil from which the Christological and Trinitarian use of person grew in subsequent centuries.

Given this development, it is unsurprising that when Tertullian sought to express the idea of plurality in God in his arguments against the modalist position of Praxeas, he employed the term *persona*. The unity of the three

---

3. For a representative account of an approach centered on angelology, see Jean Daniélou, *The Theology of Jewish Christianity: The Development of Christian Doctrine before the Council of Nicea*, vol. 1, trans. John Baker (Chicago: Regnery, 1964), 117–46. Important studies that mark the development of research on prosopological exegesis include: Carl Andresen, "Zur Entstehung und Geschichte des trinitarischen Personbegriffs," *Zeitschrift für die neutestamentliche Wissenschaft* 52 (1961): 1–39; Marie-Josèph Rondeau, *Les commentateurs patristiques de Psautier (IIIe-Ve siècles)*, vol. 1, *Les Travaux des Pères grecs et latins sur le Psautier. Recherches et bilan* (Rome: Oriental Institute, 1982); idem, vol. 2, *Exégèse prosopologique et théologie* (Rome: Oriental Institute, 1985); and Michael Slussler, "The Exegetical Roots of Trinitarian Theology," *Theological Studies* 49 (1988): 461–76.

4. The statement is made in regard to Justin's remarks in his *Apologia Prima*, 36, 1–2, *PG* 6:385. See Ratzinger, "Concerning the Notion of Person," 441–42. Emphasis original.

5. Cf. Slussler, "Exegetical Roots of Trinitarian Theology," 463–66; and Rondeau, *Exégèse prosopologique*, 39–40.

divine persons Tertullian located in their possession of the divine *natura* or *substantia*.[6] It is clear that the term "person" was used in a Trinitarian context prior to Tertullian by Hippolytus and after him by Novatian.[7] It seems safe to assume that the term *persona* enjoyed a growing currency in third-century Western theology, probably as a result of the prosopological method of exegesis described above.

The theology of the East had to contend with a unique set of difficulties. In spite of the speculative possibilities afforded by the philosophical background of many Eastern theologians, consensus was clouded by an overabundance of terms. Thus *prosópon*, *phusis*, *hupostasis*, and *ousia* could equally designate the idea of person, and the latter three could also mean nature.[8]

It was the contribution of the Trinitarian theology of the Cappadocian Fathers to chart a course that led out of this linguistic morass.[9] In their understanding, the one Godhead (*ousia*) exists concurrently in three modes of being or hypostases (*prosópon* or *hupostasis*). Thus, according to Basil, "*Ousia* and *hupostasis* are differentiated exactly as universal and particular are, e.g. animal and particular man."[10] The difference in origin coupled with

6. The closest Tertullian comes to a classical formulation is in the phrase *teneo unam substantiam in tribus cohaerentibus* in *Adversus Praxean*, 12, *PL* 2:168. See Porter, "On Keeping 'Persons' in the Trinity," 545. Cf. Zizioulas, *Being as Communion*, 36–37.

7. Hippolytus actually used the Greek term *prosópon*. Cf. Grillmeier, *From the Apostolic Age to Chalcedon*, 127; J. N. D. Kelly, *Early Christian Doctrines* (New York: Harper and Brothers, 1959), 125. Kelly notes that the term was regarded with some suspicion by the Popes Zephyrinus (198–217 AD) and Callistus (217–22 AD), who seem to have been influenced by a modalist bent within Roman theology (see 123–25).

8. On the various uses of these terms and the conflicts that they generated in Eastern thought, see Marcel Richard, "L'introduction du mot 'hypostase' dans la théologie de l'incarnation," *Mélanges de Science Religeuse* 2 (1945): 243–70; and A. de Halleux, "Hypostase et Personne dans la formation de dogma trinitaire (ca. 375–381)," *Revue d'Histoire Ecclesiastique* 79 (1984): 313–69, 625–70.

9. Zizioulas traces the precursors of the Cappadocian's achievement from the Eucharistic soteriology of Ignatius and Irenaeus, where being is understood as life (as opposed to the rationalism of much classical Greek philosophy, which viewed life as a quality appended to being). This particular emphasis, which arose from the experience of Eucharistic community, shattered the monism of Greek metaphysics still reflected in the more "academic" approaches of Justin, Clement, and Origen, and made possible the more relational notion of substance pioneered by Athanasius and perfected by the Cappadocians. See *Being as Communion*, 72–87.

10. Basil, *Epistulae*, 236, 6, *PG* 32:884. The citation is from Kelly, *Early Christian Doctrines*, 265. Some scholars attribute this work to Gregory of Nyssa.

their mutual relation distinguishes the divine Persons from one another.[11] Hence while each of the divine hypostases is the very essence of the Godhead, they are discernable as Persons according to their unique characteristics, such as paternity or being ungenerate on the part of the Father, sonship or being generate on the part of the Son, and mission and power for sanctification on the part of the Holy Spirit.[12] The notion of person, and indeed the very notion of being, is here understood in communitarian or relational terms. This understanding would be echoed in the teaching of the Second Council of Constantinople, which affirmed that the Father, Son, and Holy Spirit are a Trinity of one *ousia* in three *hupostases* or *prosópa*.[13]

But there is an even more radically relational stance within the thought of the Cappadocians—the very being (*ousia*) of God is understood as personal through its identification with the person of the Father. The oneness of God is not attributed to the divine substance as a whole, but is located within the Person of the Father as source of the processions of the Son and Spirit. Substance never exists alone in a "naked" state, but only within a particular "mode of existence" (*hupostasis*).[14] The attempt to ground the unity of the Godhead in the *monarchia* of the Father is characteristic not only of the Cappadocians, but also of Greek patristic theology as a whole.[15] But when joined to their relational understanding of the divine substance, the very being of God is understood as personal and relational: God is "a sort of continuous and indivisible community."[16] As Zizioulas states, "the substance of God, 'God,' has no ontological content, no true being apart from

11. Kelly, *Early Christian Doctrines*, 265. Cf. John D. Zizioulas, "On Being a Person," in *Persons Divine and Human*, ed. Christoph Schwöbel and Colin Gunton (Edinburgh: T&T Clark, 1991), 39–40.

12. Cf. Basil, *Epistulae*, 214, 4, *PG* 32:789; 236, 6, *PG* 32:884; Gregory of Nyssa, *Contra Eunomium*, II, 29, *PG* 29:636–40; Gregory Nazianzen, *Orationes*, 25, 16, *PG* 35:1220ff.; 26, 19, *PG* 35:1252; 29, 2, *PG* 36:76.

13. See Centro di Documentazione, Istituto per le Scienze Religiose, ed., *Conciliorum oecumenicorum decreta* (Bologna, 1962), 90–92.

14. Basil, *Epistulae*, 38, 2, *PG* 32:325ff. Cf. Gregory of Nyssa, *Contra Eunomium*, I, *PG* 45:337.

15. See Karl Rahner, *The Trinity*, trans J. Donceel (New York: Crossroad, 1970), 58ff. The problem with this approach, of course, is the attendant danger of subordinationism.

16. Basil, *Epistulae*, 38, 4, *PG* 32:332. The translation is from Maurice Wiles and Mark Santer, eds., *Documents in Early Christian Thought* (New York: Cambridge University Press, 1970), 34.

communion."[17] Such a view introduces a Copernican revolution of sorts into Greek metaphysical categories, which had tended to accord primacy to notions of being that were abstract and impersonal.[18] It is precisely the failure to take seriously the consequences of this novel ontological view that many today regard as the unfinished business of this "revolution."

Medieval Synthesis: Substance and Subsistent Relation

Patristic theology clearly yields an understanding of person distinct from nature. This made possible the classical Christological confession of Chalcedon that Christ is "one Person" (*prosópon* or *hupostasis*) in two natures, each of which retain their characteristic properties.[19] It also made possible the growing precision in Trinitarian theology described above. In the minds of many, however, it still did not seem to offer a sufficiently precise definition of personhood.

Boethius was one who took up this challenge and sought to provide a more precise definition of the term "person" with the aid of Aristotelian categories. His now-famous definition is "persona est definitio: naturae rationabilis individua substantia," or "definition of person, viz: 'an individual substance of a rational nature.'"[20] The two key terms in this definition are "substance," by which Boethius meant to exclude the notion of accidents as

17. Zizioulas, *Being as Communion*, 17. This is most accurate in regard to the thought of Gregory of Nyssa.

18. On this point and its implications, see Zizioulas, *Being as Communion*, 39–49, 88–89; idem, "Human Capacity and Incapacity: A Theological Exploration of Personhood," *Scottish Journal of Theology* 28 (1975): 409–10; and Colin Gunton, *The Promise of Trinitarian Theology* (Edinburgh: T&T Clark, 1991), 8–11.

19. Cf. E. Schwartz, *Acta conciliorum oecumenicorum* II, 1, 2 (Berlin, 1927–28), 129–130.

20. See *Liber contra Eutychen et Nestorian*, also known as *De persona et daubis naturis*, 3. The citation is from the Loeb text *Boethius: Theological Tractates and the Consolation of Philosophy*, ed. H. F. Stewart and E. K. Rand (Cambridge, MA: Harvard University Press, 1918), 84–85. For a good exposition of this definition in the context of Boethius's thought, see Horst Seidl, "The Concept of Person in St. Thomas Aquinas: A Contribution to Recent Discussion," *The Thomist* 51 (1987): 435–38. For a more extensive treatment of Boethius's understanding of person and nature, see M. Lutz-Bachmann, "'Natur' und 'Person' in den Opuscula Sacra des A.M.S. Boethius," *Theologie und Philosophie* 58 (1983): 48–70. After an extensive examination of its Neoplatonic and Aristotelian roots and its meaning, Bachmann concludes that Boethius's definition is insufficiently theological.

constitutive of the person, and "of a rational nature," by which he specified that the term "person" can only be predicated of intellectual beings. In spite of its greater precision, this definition is not wholly satisfactory in that if applied literally, it would also identify the souls of men and women as well as the human nature of Christ as persons.[21]

This definition is picked up and employed by Aquinas, but not without further modification.[22] When wedded to Aquinas's ontology of being, this definition takes on a new form. Like Boethius, Thomas sees the person as a *hypostasis* or first substance distinguished by its rational or intellectual nature, which implies dominion over its own actions.[23] The "individual substance" of Boethius now indicates a substance that is complete, subsists by itself, and is separated from others.[24] Because of the fact that personhood involves self-subsistence and the possession of a complete rather than a partial human nature, the soul cannot be considered a person, even when existing separately. Because the human nature of Christ subsists not on its own but in the Person of the Word of God, it too cannot be called a person.[25] In addition, because of this complete and self-subsisting character, there is a definite incommunicability or uniqueness to the person. This then raises the question of how something that is properly regarded as incommunicable can be defined. To this, Thomas replies while it is true that a being that is singular or unique cannot be defined, nevertheless one can define the category of singularity, and this is analogous to both Aristotle's definition of first substance and Boethius's definition of person.[26]

---

21. Ratzinger criticizes it on a more radical basis. According to him, personhood ought not to be conceived in substantialist but rather existentialist terms. As it stands, the definition "cannot clarify anything about the Trinity or Christology; it is an affirmation that remains on the level of the Greek mind which thinks in substantialist terms." See "Concerning the Notion of Person," 448. Gunton is likewise less than sanguine: "Not only is there a stress on individuality—*un*relatedness—but the tendency that was to play so important a part in modern individualism, of defining our humanity in terms of reason (Descartes again!) is given strong prominence." *Promise of Trinitarian Theology*, 94 (emphasis original).

22. For a good exposition of Aquinas's understanding of Boethius's definition and his application of it in the *Summa theologiae* (*ST*) I, q. 29, see Seidl, "Concept of Person in St. Thomas Aquinas," 438–60. Seidl's study is a good one, except for the fact that he tends to overemphasize the continuity between Boethius and Thomas and does not always recognize Aquinas's innovation.

23. Cf. *ST* I, q. 29, a. 1.

24. Cf. *ST* III, q. 16, a. 12, ad 2; cf. III, q. 2, a. 2, ad 3.

25. See *ST* III, q. 16, a. 12, ad 3.   26. See *ST* I, q. 29, a. 1, ad 1.

The term "person" adds to the notion of *supposit* the idea of rationality and a corresponding dignity that surpasses that of all other beings.[27] But this distinction does not hold in the case of the Trinity on account of Aquinas's understanding of divine simplicity.[28] Here each of the Persons is identical with the divine nature and distinct from one another only by virtue of their origin and mutual relation.[29] The divine nature therefore subsists in the relations that constitute the Persons of the Trinity.[30] Thus in regard to the Trinity, the distinction between person and nature is notional, rather than real, even though the divine Persons are really distinct from one another.[31]

While some tend to treat all other reflection on the notion of person as a mere footnote to the reflection of Boethius and Thomas, there is in fact another, seemingly opposed, tradition concerning personhood that views it in more relational and existential terms and draws its inspiration from Augustine.[32]

In his Trinitarian theology, Augustine described God as a being in three Persons.[33] Like much Western Patristic theology before him, Augustine begins with the unity of the Trinity.[34] As opposed to the characteristically

27. Cf. *ST* III, q. 2, a. 2, ad 2; I, q. 29, a. 3.   28. Cf. *ST* I, q. 3, aa. 1–8.
29. Cf. *ST* I, q. 28, aa. 1–4.   30. See *ST* I, q. 29, a. 4.
31. See *ST* I, q. 39, a. 1; cf. III, q. 2, a. 2, ad 1.
32. So, e.g., L. W. Geddes and W. A. Wallace in their article on "Person (in Philosophy)," after treating Boethius and Aquinas, remark that "further scholastic discussions of the notions of person have been largely disputes over the ultimate foundation of personality, i.e. to ascertain the precise determination of a nature that, if present, will make it subsistent and a person, and if absent, will not." They go on to give the opinions of Scotus and certain later Thomists such as Cajetan and Suárez on this matter. Yet to present the history of the term in this way is to relegate all other ideas to the status of footnotes or appendices to those of Boethius and Aquinas. A similar tendency can be observed in Seidl, "Concept of Person in Aquinas."
33. Of course, Augustine is a patristic theologian, but because of his significance for Western medieval theology, he is treated here.
34. Colin Gunton throughout his *Promise of Trinitarian Theology* (esp. chap. 3) harshly criticizes Augustine for this emphasis. Gunton argues that Augustine's Neoplatonism produces this emphasis on divine unity at the expense of Trinitarian plurality, and it is ultimately he who is responsible for the separation of the treatises concerning *De Deo Uno* and *De Deo Trino* in later medieval thought, and the subsequent collapse of Trinitarian faith into mere monotheism and ultimately into the individualism and atheism of modern Western thought. While not all of Gunton's criticisms are unfounded, he produces little evidence for such sweeping historical claims, he fails to note that the emphasis on the divine unity was characteristic of all

Eastern tradition, which made the Father the ground or origin of the God-head, Augustine begins with the divine essence and affirms that whatever is affirmed concerning God must be confirmed equally of all three Persons.[35] Hence each of the three Persons is identical with the others or with the divine essence.[36]

The question then arises as to how the divine Persons may be said to be distinct from one another. Arian critics of the doctrine of the Trinity attempted to demonstrate its incoherence by casting it in Aristotelian categories.[37] To say that the distinction was accidental was rejected because God's essence does not admit of accidents. Yet to say that the distinction was one of substance is to imply that the three are separate substances or individuals who are described as God (a reason for which Augustine was also unhappy with the term "person").[38] In response to this dilemma, Augustine argued that the Three are constituted by their relations with one another, that is, begetting, being begotten, and proceeding. Such relations are real or subsistent in that they are that in which the divine essence subsists.[39] When transferring this notion to the anthropological level in his famous Trinitarian analogies, however, Augustine fails to follow through on this insight and locates the image of the essence in the human person as a whole and the vari-

---

Western patristic theology and not merely Augustine, his analysis treats only *De trinitate* (*De trin.*) and not the whole of Augustine's thought, and his reading of Augustine is highly selective and unsparingly unsympathetic.

35. See *De trin.*, 5, 9, *PL* 42:917ff.

36. See *De trin.*, 6, 9, *PL* 42:930ff.; 8, 1, *PL* 42:947. This fact is not sufficiently grasped by Gunton, who implies that for Augustine "the true being of God *underlies* the threeness of the persons." See *Promise of Trinitarian Theology*, 45. Emphasis original.

37. Cf. Kelly, *Early Christian Doctrines*, 11, 274.

38. Cf. *De trin.*, 5, 10, *PL* 42:918; *De civita dei*, 11, 10, *PL* 41:325ff. On the patristic development of the notion of person and Augustine's unease with it, see B. Studer, "Der Person-Begriff in der frühen kirchenamtlichen Trinitätslehre," *Theologie und Philosophie* 57 (1982): 161–77.

39. See *De trin.*, 5–7, *PL* 42:911–46; *De civ. dei*, 11, 10, *PL* 41:325ff. Ratzinger cites the notion of relation as a new category created under the impetus of Christian faith. See "Concerning the Notion of Person," 444–45. Yet Kelly notes that there are historical antecedents to the idea of a real or subsistent relation in the thought of Plotinus and Porphyry, with whom Augustine was familiar. See *Early Christian Doctrines*, 275. Gunton is suspicious of the very notion of relation, complaining that it marks a step backward from the innovative ontological distinction of *hypostasis* and *ousia* worked out by the Cappadocians in that it remains on the level of Aristotelian logic rather than that of being. See *Promise of Trinitarian Theology*, 39–42. Such a criticism, however, misses the point that the relations of which Augustine speaks are real ones that constitute the divine essence and exist from all eternity.

ous persons of the Trinity in the psychological processes of the individual.[40]

A more thoroughly relational and existential notion of personhood was developed in the Middle Ages by Richard of St. Victor, who defined the person as *spiritualis naturae incommunicabilis existentia* "the incommunicably proper existence of spiritual nature."[41] Unlike Augustine, who allowed for a disjunction between his relational view of divine personhood and its psychological reflection within the human individual, the Victorine approach holds for a fundamental analogy between divine and human personhood, both of which are constituted by relations among existing persons. Both divine and human persons in this view may be defined as *ex-sistentia*—spiritual subjects that become personal by going out from themselves (though in God only in a relative sense).[42] Richard even appealed to natural reason to demonstrate that the very notion of person and of love demands the existence of another person with whom to be in relation.[43] Thus one is or becomes a person precisely in relation to others or, in more modern terms, in community.

40. Cf. *De trin.*, 14, 11ff., *PL* 42:1047ff. For this he is criticized by Ratzinger, who argues that Augustine failed to grasp the significance of the Trinitarian notion of person in the anthropological sphere. The result of this, he believes, is that the person was increasingly conceived in isolated and individualistic terms, and that the divine Persons were increasingly enclosed within God's interior life and seen as irrelevant to the economy of creation and salvation. See "Concerning the Notion of Person," 447, 453–54. In this he approximates something of Gunton's thesis described above. In a later note appended to this article (originally published as "Zum Personverständis in der Theologie," in *Dogma und Verkündigung* [Munich: Wewel, 1973], 205–23), however, Ratzinger places more of the blame for these events on Aquinas's separation of the treatment of *De Deo Uno* and *De Deo Trino*, ignoring the fact that (as Gunton observes) this approach is Augustinian in its roots and inspiration. A similar criticism of Augustine is made by Christopher Kaiser, who argues that Augustine's "complete dissociation of eternal intra-trinitarian relations from ordinary human relations forced him into a rather static concept of the deity, on the one hand, and an individualistic concept of humanity, on the other." See *The Doctrine of God: An Historical Survey* (London: Marshall, Morgan and Scott, 1982), 81.

41. *De trin.*, 4 xxii, in G. Salet, ed., *Sources Chrétiennes, 63* (Paris: Les Editions du Cerf, 1959), 280ff. Ratzinger notes (in apparent contrast to Boethius and perhaps Thomas) that "in its theological meaning 'person' does not lie on the level of essence but existence." See "Concerning the Notion of Person," 449.

42. See *De trin.*, 4, xii, *SC* 63:252ff. Cf. the remarks made by von Balthasar, "On the Concept of Person," 22. For a more complete exposition of Richard's Trinitarian theology, see P. Hoffman, "Analogie und Person: Zur Trinitätspekulation Richards von St. Victor," *Theologie und Philosophie* 59 (1984): 191–234.

43. See *De trin.*, 3, xix, *SC* 63:208ff. On this point, see Ewert Cousins, "A Theology of Interpersonal Relations," *Thought* 45 (1970): 56–82; and Walter Kasper, *The God of Jesus Christ*, trans. Matthew J. O'Connell (New York: Crossroad, 1986), 268.

A similar approach is continued in Bonaventure, who combines the ter-minology of Boethius and Richard, viewing the latter as a correction of and commentary on the former.[44] Furthermore, he sharply distinguishes the idea of person from the philosophical concept of *individuum* on the basis of the person's "exalted dignity."[45]

While at first glance these two traditions concerning personhood—the Thomist and the Augustinian—might seem to stand in simple opposition to one another, a closer examination reveals this to be a false conclusion. While Thomas closely follows Boethius (and with him Aristotle), he nevertheless incorporates much of the Augustinian tradition. He vigorously defends the identification of person with relation, especially on the divine level, although in God the term denotes a subsistent, or nonaccidental, relation, while in reference to humanity it does not.[46] His understanding of the subsistent re-lations among the members of the Trinity noted above draws heavily on Au-gustine. He also cites Richard of St. Victor's understanding of person as a valid corrective of Boethius's definition in regard to God inasmuch as God's individuality does not come from matter but from the incommunicability of the divine Persons, and because substance when applied to God can de-note self-subsistence.[47] Furthermore, the distinction made in Thomist on-tology between essence and existence (which are identical in God but not in creatures) allows for an existential understanding of human personhood not completely dissimilar to that found in parts of the Augustinian tradi-tion.[48] In fact, substance itself has a relational character for Aquinas because the need for active self-expression (*agere*) is inscribed in the very being (*esse*) of things.[49] One can assume that what is true for things in general is also

44. See Bonaventure, *Commentaria in Sententiarum*, lib. 1, d. 25, a. 1, qq. 1–2.

45. *In Sent.*, lib. 3, d. 5, a. 2, q. 2; d. 10, a. 1, q. 3.

46. See *ST* I, q. 29, a. 4. The idea of subsistent relation represents a fundamental revision of Aristotelian categories. See William Hill, *The Three-Personed God* (Washington, DC: Catholic University of America Press, 1982), 234–35, 266–68.

47. See *ST* I, q. 29, a. 3, ad 4.

48. Cf. the remarks made by Walter Principe on the existential notion of person developed by Aquinas in *The Theology of the Hypostatic Union in the Early Thirteenth Century*, vol. 2, *Alex-ander of Hales' Theology of the Hypostatic Union*, Studies and Texts 12 (Toronto: Pontifical Insti-tute of Medieval Studies, 1967), 34; and vol. 6, *Philip the Chancellor's Theology of the Hypostatic Union*, Studies and Texts 32 (Toronto: Pontifical Institute of Medieval Studies, 1975), 208–9.

49. Cf. *Summa contra Gentiles* II, ch. 7; III, ch. 64; III, ch. 113; *ST* I, q. 16, a. 2; I, q. 105, a. 5. For a fuller treatment of this notion in Aquinas, see W. Norris, Clarke, "Action as the

true of persons in particular.[50] Finally, Aquinas too emphasizes the incommunicability and dignity of the person. As von Balthasar points out, Aquinas demonstrates a remarkable grasp of the theological meaning of the term "person" and of its origin in the following passage:

Although we cannot use "person" of God in its original sense we can extend this perfectly well for our present purpose. Since in comedies and tragedies famous men were represented, the word "person" came to be used in reference to men of high rank. It then became customary in the ecclesiastical world to refer to personages of rank. This is why some theologians define person by saying that a person is "a hypostasis distinguished by dignity." To subsist in a rational nature is a characteristic implying dignity and hence, as already mentioned, every individual with rational nature is called "person." Of course the dignity of the divine nature surpasses all others, and so it is completely fitting to use "person" of God.[51]

That Thomas is thus able to incorporate many of the features of the Augustinian tradition concerning personhood is not mere eclecticism on his part, but testimony to his remarkable synthetic ability and evidence for the dependence of Thomist theology on the Augustinian tradition.

Having said all of this, it must be admitted that differences still remain between the two approaches. The heart of these seems to lie in the somewhat greater consistency of representatives of the Augustinian tradition, such as Richard in attempting to understand all personhood in relational and existential terms, while Thomas makes a distinction between the divine Persons, who are defined solely by their relations, and human persons, who are described in substantial terms and for whom relationality is accidental.[52]

Self-Revelation of Being: A Central Theme in the Thought of St. Thomas," in *History of Philosophy in the Making*, ed. Lines Thro (Lanham, MD: University Press of America, 1982), 63–80; idem, "Fifty Years of Metaphysical Reflection: The Universe as Journey," in *The Universe as Journey: Conversations with W. Norris Clarke*, ed. Gerald McCool (New York: Fordham University, 1988), 68–75.

50. Clarke attempts to achieve a "creative completion" of Aquinas's thought in this regard by synthesizing his dynamic notion of being or substance with his philosophical notion of personhood. See "Person, Being, and St. Thomas," *Communio* 19 (1992): 601–18. For a critique of Clarke's presentation as still insufficiently relational, see David L. Schindler, "Norris Clarke on Person, Being and St. Thomas," *Communio* 20 (1993): 580–92.

51. *ST* I, q. 29, a. 3, ad 2. The citation is from the Blackfriars edition, vol. 6 (New York: McGraw-Hill, 1965), 55. For von Balthasar's comments on this text, see "On the Concept of Person," 23.

52. See *ST* I, q. 39, a. 1, ad 1. This seems to be the heart of Ratzinger's criticism of Thomas

Here Ratzinger may be correct when he notes that there is an unfortunate disjunction between Aquinas's more philosophical approach to human personhood and his theological application of the same idea. The fact that relationality is accidental on the human level, especially when coupled with Thomas's insistence on the self-subsisting and individual character of human nature, can lead to an ontologically isolated and individualistic conception of the human person.

Yet even these differences may not be finally insurmountable, as will be demonstrated by modern attempts to bring together the more substantialist views of Boethius and Aquinas with the more existential and relational approach of the Augustinian tradition. Some of these attempts are considered briefly in the following section.

Modern Thought: Deeper Convergence

Turning to the modern notion of person, one is immediately confronted with a new set of problems in addition to the controversies of the patristic era and the differing approaches between and within the Augustinian and Thomist traditions. These difficulties are those presented by the modern notion of person as a distinct center of consciousness, often described in highly individualistic terms.[53] Attention has been drawn to this problem by Karl Barth

---

when he remarks that his theological treatment of the Trinity and Christology was not extended to the whole of spiritual reality (i.e., human persons) and that he did not integrate this understanding with his philosophy. See "Person in Theology," 449. Cf. von Balthasar, "On the Concept of Person," 22. It can be argued, however, that Thomas does not always relegate relationality to a secondary metaphysical status but holds it in tension with his understanding of the person as an individual nature. This is especially evident when one realizes that "accidents" (especially proper accidents) are a necessary part of the perfection of substance. See C. Lefèvre, "La relation personelle chez Saint Thomas d'Aquin," *Mélanges de Science Religieuse* 31, no. 3–4 (1974): 121–44; and Clarke, "Person, Being, and St. Thomas"; idem, "Response to David Schindler's Comments," *Communio* 20 (1993): 593–95.

53. For a good exposition of the evolution of the concept of person from its ancient roots to its modern usage, see Kenneth L. Schmitz, "The Geography of the Human Person," *Communio* 13 (1986): 27–48. Schmitz points out that a certain self-consciousness has always attended Western religious thought, as evidenced in Augustine's *Confessions* or his *Soliloquies*. But this consciousness became infected with a kind of pessimism toward the end of the Middle Ages (perhaps on account of the Great Plague and the long-standing conflict between the Church and the Holy Roman Empire), and this deepened to an even more profound awareness of human sin and depravity following the Reformation and the religious wars that followed it. This

and Karl Rahner, both of whom have criticized the notion of person as inadequate for Trinitarian theology.[54] The response to such criticism has varied from virtual agreement,[55] to evasion,[56] to attempts at understanding the Trinity in more dialogical or communitarian terms.[57] It seems that the most incisive responses have argued that the notion of subjectivity need not deform the Christological or Trinitarian concepts of person, especially when this idea is freed from its individualism and placed within a more relational framework.[58]

There are four ways in which this movement toward a more relational

religious introversion gave rise to a secular one in attempts of Locke and Descartes to ground knowledge within human consciousness. This turn to the self was broadened in the rationalistic individualism of the Enlightenment, the Kantian ethical autonomy of the moral agent, and in the political and social liberalism of the eighteenth century. All of this has given rise to the uniquely modern notion of privacy with its implication of psychological isolation (see 36–40). A parallel account of these developments that is more extensive (but not always as incisive) is provided by Charles Taylor, *Sources of the Self: The Making of the Modern Identity* (Cambridge, MA: Harvard University Press, 1989).

54. See Karl Barth, *Church Dogmatics*, vol. 1/1, *The Doctrine of the Word of God*, trans. G. W. Bromiley (Edinburgh: T&T Clark, 1975), 355–59; Rahner, *Trinity*, 42–43, 100; and idem, "Divine Trinity," *Sacramentum Mundi*, vol. 6 (New York: Crossroad, 1970), 301–2.

55. Some have sought to affirm the divergence between the modern notion and the traditional usage, arguing that the term "person" ought to be retained even while maintaining a clear distinction between its theological and dogmatic usage on the one hand and the modern understanding on the other. See, e.g., Rowan Williams in his study "'Person' and 'Personality' in Christology," *Downside Review* 94 (1976): 253–60; and F. X. Bantle, "Person und Personbegriff in der Trinitätslehre Karl Rahners," *Münchener Theologische Zeitschrift* 30, no. 2 (1979): 11–24.

56. Others admit of a multiplicity of meanings of the word throughout its history and would use this very ambiguity to hold the modern notion in tension with other meanings of the term. This is the argument of Porter, "On Keeping 'Persons' in the Trinity," 530–33, 541–48. Such an approach is more promising; however, it attempts to dodge the legitimate theological question of the meaning of the term, opting instead for a system of linguistic checks and balances. Furthermore, it too neglects the historical character of language, which allows it to grow and develop even while maintaining a certain organic continuity with its origin. Ratzinger notes in the case of the concept of person that "Although this thought has distanced itself far from its origin and developed beyond it, it nevertheless lives, in a hidden way, from this origin." See "Concerning the Notion of Person," 439. Cf. the excellent discussion in Schmitz, "Geography of the Human Person," 27–48.

57. A good overview of developments in this regard is provided by John O'Donnell, "The Trinity as Divine Community: A Critical Reflection upon Recent Theological Developments," *Gregorianum* 19 (1988): 5–34.

58. See, e.g., Czeslaw Bartnik, "'The Person' in the Holy Trinity," trans. Norbert Karava, *Collectanea Theologica* 53 (1983): 17–30; Jean Galot, *Who Is Christ? A Theology of the Incarnation*, trans M. Angeline Bouchard (Chicago: Franciscan Herald Press, 1981); and idem, "La définition de la personne, relation et sujet," *Gregorianum* 75 (1994): 281–99.

notion of person can be seen in contemporary thought: in certain reflections on the philosophy of consciousness, in considerations of the dialogical constitution of the person, in human sexuality understood as a means of community and relation, and in the movement toward a more relational metaphysic in general.

The Person as Subject

Given that it is the notion of individual subjectivity that has proved so vexing, it is rather surprising that this very "turn to the subject" could be the point of departure for recovering a more adequate and relational concept of the person. But this is indeed the case with accounts of consciousness that utilize phenomenological reflection in order to uncover the dynamism of the person revealed through action.

A good example of this kind of approach can be found within Lublin Thomism, whose best-known proponent is Karol Wojtyła, or Pope John Paul II.[59] According to Wojtyła, the older philosophy of being considered consciousness as an attribute of human beings (e.g., rational animals). But this overlooks conscious being and acting from within the experience of the subject who acts.[60] When viewed from this perspective, consciousness is seen to have two fundamental aspects: (1) a "reflecting" function that mirrors the content of what is experienced in action and (2) a "reflexive" function that encompasses the experience of self as the subject of the act.[61] This latter function serves to "form or shape" the personal subject in the experience of authoring his or her own acts. Actions thus reveal and express the person who authors them. "Person" here is not merely an "individual substance of rational nature," but a dynamic subject who authors acts and determines himself or herself in so doing.[62]

59. Good overviews of Wojtyła's philosophical account of personal consciousness are provided by Josef Seifert, "Karol Cardinal Wojtyla (Pope John Paul II) as Philosopher and the Cracow/Lublin School of Philosophy," *Alethia* 2 (1981): 133–45; Jerzy W. Galkowski, "The Place of Thomism in the Anthropology of K. Wojtyla," *Angelicum* 65 (1988): 181–94; and Kenneth Schmitz, *At the Center of the Human Drama: The Anthropology of Karol Wojtyla / Pope John Paul II* (Washington, DC: Catholic University of America Press, 1994).

60. Cf. Karol Wojtyła, *The Acting Person*, trans. Andrez Potocki, *Analecta Husserliana*, vol. 10 (Boston: D. Reidel, 1979), 47–48.

61. See the helpful treatment of this distinction in Schmitz, *At the Center of the Human Drama*, 70–76. Cf. Wojtyla, *Acting Person*, 31–33, 42–43, 46.

62. See ibid., 42–42, 47, 69–71. In a moral sense, this "personal becoming" accomplished

But neither human action nor personhood occurs in a vacuum. Because he or she is made in the image of the Triune God, the human person is fulfilled only in community, only in solidarity with others. The individual is called to form a "communion of persons" with other human beings.[63] This occurs through what Wojtyła describes as "participation." Participation is fundamentally an intersubjective form of "acting together with others" that constitutes the very basis of the personalistic value of the action of the individual.[64] Therefore human action, and the person it discloses, finds its value precisely in this social and communal dimension. There is, then, a close relation between the individual subject and human community.[65] In his papal teaching, John Paul finds the highest exemplar and analogy for his dynamic and communitarian conception of personhood in the Trinity. Amplifying a text from the Second Vatican Council, John Paul II explains:

Man—whether man or woman—*is the only being among the creatures* of the visible world *that God the Creator "has willed for its own sake"*; that creature is thus a person. Being a person means striving towards self-realization (the Council text speaks of self-discovery), which can only be achieved *"through a sincere gift of self."* The model for this interpretation is God himself as Trinity, as a communion of Persons. To say that man is created in the image and likeness of God means that man is called to exist for others, to become a gift.[66]

The term "person," when applied to God, denotes the subsistent relations that differentiate the Persons of the Trinity in their possession of the one

---

through human choices is what Wojtyła terms "self-determination." Cf. ibid., 150–52; and "The Degrees of Being from the Point of View of the Phenomenology of Action, in *Analecta Husserliana*, vol. 11 (Boston: D. Reidel, 1981), 127. Robert A. Conner sees Wojtyła describing a real change in the being of the person, in which the person grows through relation rather than an accidental modification of a substance. See "The Person as Resonating Existential," *American Catholic Philosophical Quarterly* 66 (1992): 39–56.

63. For an exposition of the notions of participation and community in Wojtyła's philosophy, see Elzbieta Wolicka, "Participation in Community: Wojtyła's Social Anthropology," *Communio* 8 (1981): 108–18. For a more extensive analysis of the same ideas, see Alfred Wilder, "Community of Persons in the Thought of Karol Wojtyla," *Angelicum* 56 (1979): 211–44.

64. Cf. Wojtyła, *Acting Person*, 269–70.

65. Wojtyła in fact distinguishes between the older metaphysical approach, which viewed society as constituted by a set of accidental relations among multiple human *supposita*, and his own more dynamic view. See "Person, Subject and Community," in *Person and Community: Selected Essays*, trans. Theresa Sandok (New York: Peter Lang, 1993), 239–42.

66. Apostolic Letter, *Mulieris Dignitatem*, 7. Emphasis original. The allusion is to *Gaudium et spes*, no. 24.

divine nature. As described by Wojtyła, on the human level, "person" is not purely relational. Even while denoting beings who are ordered to relationship and community with other persons, "person" still indicates individually subsisting subjects whose unity with one another can only provide an image of the oneness of nature in the Trinitarian communion of Persons. Nevertheless, a phenomenology of conscious action does provide a more dynamic view of personhood that can illuminate the analogy between divine and human persons.

The Person as Dialogical

The nature of human subjectivity illumined by phenomenological analysis already reveals an interpersonal structure to human consciousness. This structure encompasses not only human subjectivity, but also the whole of personal identity. One discovers oneself as a person, an "I," only when standing in relation to another, a "Thou."[67] Such a relation is evident in the experience of human knowing, but even more distinctly in the encounter of love because love encompasses the totality of the person. So a child discovers her own identity in the love of her parents, or a person in love finds himself anew in his beloved. It is in giving oneself to another, "making a sincere gift of self," and in receiving the love of others, that one becomes most authentically and fully personal. Individuality is not here opposed to relation, but rather flows out of interpersonal communion.

Even the "I-Thou" relation is most real and genuine when it stands in relation to a third term, one who can be addressed by the first two as a "We." This is true in the interpersonal relationships that constitute an organization or community united in the pursuit of some good.[68] The members of such an organization have a common identity forged in shared activity in relation to the wider society. It is also, and perhaps more profoundly realized, in the intimate community of family where parents stand together as a

---

67. See Martin Buber, *I and Thou*, trans. Walter Kaufman (New York: Charles Scribner's Sons, 1970), 53–85. A good introduction and overview of the thought of Buber and the other dialogical philosophers is provided by B. Casper, *Das dialogische Denken, Eine Untersuchung der religionphilosophischen Bedeutung Franz Rosenzwiegs, Ferdinand Ebners, und Martin Bubers* (Freiburg: Herder, 1967). See also Robert E. Wood, *Martin Buber's Ontology* (Evanston, IL: Northwestern University Press, 1969), esp. 38*ff*.

68. Cf. Wojtyła, "Person, Subject and Community," 242–46.

"We" in relation to their children, who are the very fruit of their self-giving love.

This understanding of the dialogical structure of human love and identity, enriched by the cross pollination of insights from the dialogical philosophers and personalism, has yielded an even deeper grasp of the profound analogy between the communitarian character of divine and human personhood. Such a line of enquiry was already anticipated in medieval theology by Richard of St. Victor but has flowered in the diverse winds of modern thought.[69] The fruitful character of human love enables one to find an analogy between the love of the Father (the "I" relation), the Son (the "Thou" relation who is born of this love), and the Holy Spirit, who is the bond of their mutual love (of the "We" relation) and that of a married couple with their child.[70] Hence personhood (both human and divine) is manifested through a dialogical relationship of opposition.[71]

The Person as Sexual

The communitarian character of the person revealed in the dialogue of fruitful love sheds light upon a further relation inscribed in the fabric of human existence—the duality of male and female. The mutual relation of male and female to one another and the fruitfulness of their union provide an image of Trinitarian life and love.[72] How is this so?

69. Von Balthasar describes the "simultaneous emergence of the 'dialogue principle'" in thinkers as diverse as Buber, Ebner, Marcel, and Rosenzweig as "one of the strangest phenomena of 'acausal contemporaneaity' in the history of the intellect." See *Theo-Drama*, vol. 1, *Theological Dramatic Theory*, trans. Graham Harrison (San Francisco: Ignatius, 1988), 626.

70. See Herbert Mühlen, *Una Mystica Persona: Eine Person in vielen Personen* (Paderborn: F. Schoningh, 1964); idem, *Der Heilige Geist als Person*, 2nd ed. (Münster: Verlag Aschendorff, 1967); Hans Urs von Balthasar, *Spiritus Creator* (Einsiedeln: Johannes Verlag, 1967), 152; idem, *Pneuma und Institution*, Skizzen zur Theologie IV (Einsiedeln: Johannes Verlag, 1974), 225; and idem, "Reflections on the Discernment of Spirits," trans. Kenneth Batnovich, *Communio* 7 (1980): 200. The problem with this analogy is that it can imply a kind of subordinationism in regard to the Person of the Holy Spirit, who is here compared to a child.

71. See Galot, *Who Is Christ?*, 296.

72. See von Balthasar, *A Theological Anthropology*, trans. Benziger Verlag (New York: Sheed and Ward, 1967), 312–13. Von Balthasar also frequently compares the male-female relationship to that between Christ and the Church. See, e.g., *Love Alone*, trans. Alexander Dru (New York: Herder and Herder, 1969), 96–111; *The Christian State of Life*, trans. Mary Frances McCarthy (San Francisco: Ignatius, 1983), 224–49; *The Glory of the Lord*, vol. 7, *Theology: The New Covenant*, trans. Brian McNeil, CRV (Edinburgh: T&T Clark, 1989), 470–84.

An inescapable feature of being a human person is having a body. Hence there are no "abstract" or disembodied persons, but only actual and embodied ones.[73] An integral component of this bodiliness is sex or gender—persons are either male or female.[74] This fundamental difference, when understood in light of the dialogical quality of human existence, suggests a further communitarian dimension of the person. The body may be described as "nuptial" insofar as one's sex is a unique way of being for another as well as a concrete means of giving oneself to another in love.[75] Sex thus incarnates or enfleshes the relational quality of human existence.

But this personal difference of male and female exists within a common humanness, a shared nature. Men and women are thus "persons in different but equal modes"[76] or the "two equally valuable but different expressions of the one nature of humanity."[77] To state the matter with greater precision, gender may be seen as accidental to human nature but essential to existing human persons.[78] The term "essential" here need not be restricted to the person understood substantially—one can also speak of the essence or being of a relation.[79] Hence there is a fundamental analogy between male

73. As noted above, for Aquinas, the soul of a person separated from the body after death cannot be considered a person. The exact status and mode of existence of such an entity is a fundamental problem for Thomistic anthropology.

74. Cases of so-called "ambiguous sexuality" usually involve confused genital sex or secondary sex characteristics; on the genetic level, one's gender is always clear. Cf. James Monteleone, "The Physiological Aspects of Sex," in *Human Sexuality and Personhood* (St. Louis, MO: Pope John XXIII Medical Moral Center, 1981), 71–85.

75. Cf. John Paul II's treatment of the nuptial meaning of the body in his general audience of January 9, 1980, in *The Original Unity of Man and Woman* (Boston: Daughters of St. Paul, 1981), 106–12.

76. Karl Lehmann, "The Place of Women as a Problem in Theological Anthropology," trans. Robert E. Wood, in *The Church and Women: A Compendium*, ed. Helmut Moll (San Francisco: Ignatius Press, 1988), 29.

77. Walter Kasper, "The Position of Women as a Problem of Theological Anthropology," in *Church and Women*, 58–59.

78. See John S. Grabowski, "The Status of the Sexual Good as a Direction for Moral Theology," *Heythrop Journal* 35 (1994): 15–34.

79. The term "essence" and its adjectival form "essential" derive from the Latin *essentia*, which is a form the verb *esse* "to be". Given this, it would seem that the essence of a thing refers properly to its being. As Galot and Ratzinger point out, being does not necessarily have to coincide with the substance of a thing. If in fact relation is a genuinely new ontological category—neither substance nor accident yet nevertheless real—it is possible to speak of the essence of a relation.

and female, whose relational difference constitutes them as irreducible to one another as persons within a common nature and the Trinity as a communion of three divine Persons, each of whom possesses the fullness of the one divine nature.[80] This analogous referent to Trinitarian communion inscribed within marriage also illuminates the possibility of the simultaneity of genuine equality with personal difference.[81]

Toward a Relational Metaphysic

The fact that within the Trinity the notion of relation is accorded primacy in the understanding of the divine Persons has led many to argue that this requires a radical rethinking of ontological categories.[82] In dramatic fashion, Ratzinger argues that within Trinitarian theology "lies concealed a revolution in man's view of the world; the undivided sway of thinking in terms of substance is ended; relation is discovered as an equally valid primordial mode of reality."[83]

In this view, substance is understood as a characteristically Greek mode of thinking whose primacy has been displaced by the revolution unleashed in metaphysics by Christian revelation. In addition to shattering the insoluble polarities of the one and the many through its insistence on unity and diversity as equally basic and coexistent, the doctrine of the Trinity challenges the priority of substance over relation. If God as Being Itself is personal, and God is the highest and all determining reality, it becomes possible to see that *"being as a whole is personally defined."*[84] And because God is not merely personal, but tri-personal, *"love is the all-determining reality*

---

80. This analogy can also explain why feminine as well as masculine qualities are sometimes attributed to God in the scriptures, even though God as a spiritual being transcends biological sexuality. Cf. *Mulieris Dignitatem*, 8.

81. The danger of a subordinationist doctrine of the Trinity has anthropological implications for anthropology as well, insofar as it eclipses the "mutual submission" of husband and wife highlighted by many feminist scholars as well as by Pope John Paul II (cf. *Mulieris Dignitatem*, 24).

82. This is argued within the studies of Zizioulas, Gunton, Ratzinger, Bartnik, and Galot cited above. One can find similar views expressed by others. See, e.g., Kasper, *The God of Jesus Christ*, 156–57; idem, *Theology and Church*, 26–31; and Catherine Mowry LaCugna, *God for Us: The Trinity and the Christian Life* (San Francisco: Harper, 1991), 243–50, 255–66, 288–305.

83. Joseph Ratzinger, *Introduction to Christianity* (New York: Herder & Herder, 1970), 132.

84. Kasper, *Theology and Church*, 29 (emphasis original). Cf. idem, *God of Jesus Christ*, 156.

and meaning of being."[85] It is for this reason that the New Testament can say that God is *agape* "love" (1 Jn 4:8). Just as the very being of the Trinity is constituted by the infinite self-giving love of the divine Persons for one another, so do human persons find the meaning of their own existence in giving and receiving this same love.

It must be admitted, however, that in spite of numerous calls for the development of a thoroughgoing ontology of relation and some initial sketches, such a project has yet to be fully explicated. In particular, it is not fully clear what happens to concepts such as "substance" or "nature" in such a view. Hence attempts to invoke such an ontology must be regarded as somewhat provisional in character and in need of further philosophical and theological analysis.

Conclusion

This study has traced two rather different understandings of person—as relation and as substance. It has argued that in spite of their apparent opposition there has been a growing convergence between them in the Trinitarian theology of subsistent relation and in certain currents of modern thought that have viewed the person in more relational terms. Yet it must finally be admitted that there has not yet been a fully developed relational ontology. How, then, ought one finally understand the concept of person? As substance? As relation? As both?

To view the person simply as substance devoid of relationality creates a highly isolated and individualistic concept of the person.[86] To understand the person as purely relational or ecstatic with no reference to substance is to opt for some form of process thought with its inherent pitfalls.[87]

Short of these extremes, there are a number of possibilities that have surfaced in the course of the above analysis. First, one can view the created per-

85. Kasper, *Theology and Church*, 29–30 (emphasis original).

86. An approach reflected in the individualism of American culture. See David Schindler, "Is America Bourgeois?," *Communio* 14 (1987): 262–90.

87. Some arguments for a relational metaphysic incline toward some form of process thought. See, e.g., the Whiteheadian approach of Joseph Bracken, *The Triune Symbol: Persons, Process, and Community* (Lanham, MD: University Press of America, 1985). One can find a more attenuated Rahnerian process approach in LaCugna, *God for Us*, 300–305.

son as a substance for which relationality is a constitutive part—a proper accident. Substance is ordered toward relational self-expression. This seems to be a traditional Thomistic understanding, but it creates the unfortunate disjunction between divine and human personhood noted above. Further, it seems that such an approach makes the ideal of personhood only fully realized in humanity and somewhat lacking in God.[88]

Second, one can attempt to locate relation within the being (*esse*) of the person rather than in his or her operations (*agere*). In such a view there is a threefold character to being: being as subsistent in itself (*esse-in*), being as receptive (*esse-ab*), and being as communicative (*esse-ad*).[89] This position brings to light the important insight that receptivity as well as creativity is a fundamental relation that defines and perfects the person. Such a view seems an important clarification of the Thomist position, but it is not fully clear if it can synthesize insights from the Cappadocian or modern notions of person.

Third, and closely related to the preceding approach, is the attempt to make substance and relation equally primordial modes of personal existence. Hence one can see the person as a "deep ground" whose outward persona conveys the "rumblings of … transcendence."[90] Or one can speak of the person as "neither substance nor relation in isolation but rather an existential core which is mysterious in itself but emergent as a resonating two-dimensional structure, a dyad, of progressive substantiality and relationality."[91] In this view, the person grows substantially by relating. This accords well with the dynamic view of the experience of consciousness described above and also seems to integrate aspects of both the Thomistic and Augustinian view of person. But there seems to be an echo of Lockean metaphysics in the view of person as an unknowable substratum underlying both substance and relation.[92] It also seems to obscure the analogy between divine and human personhood.

---

88. Cf. Galot, *Who Is Christ?*, 301.

89. See Schindler, "Norris Clarke on Person, Being and St. Thomas," 585–88; and Clarke, "Response to David Schindler's Comments," 595–96.

90. See John Caputo, "Being and the Mystery of the Person," in *Universe as Journey*, 110–11.

91. Conner, "Person as Resonating Existential," 50.

92. The formulation has similarities to Locke's description of the real essence of an entity as an unknowable substratum that is commonly supposed to underlie the outward appearance of things. See his *Essay Concerning Human Understanding*, 2.23.1; cf. 2.13.19.

Fourth, and more radically, one can make relation more basic than substance—to see substance constituted by relation or communion. Here the proper mode of existence for substances is within a *hypostasis*-understood relationally. Substances are either ordered to or exist most fully within personal communion—persons *hypostasize* being.[93] This is perhaps the most thoroughgoing relational view, and it accords well with the Cappadocian theology of the Trinity. Yet it too creates some problems, as can be witnessed in the insistence that human beings possess not merely an individual nature, but the totality of it (paralleling Trinitarian life).[94] This seems, by most accounts, an odd notion of "nature." Further, as noted above, the notion that the unity of the divine nature is grounded in the Person of the Father creates problems as well as solving them.

Fifth, and finally, one can hold the fundamental analogy between divine and human personhood by speaking of human persons as "subsisting relations" or "hypostatic relations."[95] This upholds the idea that personhood is fully realized in God and analogously in humanity—God is thus the model for all genuine community. Yet as with any analogy, there is an even greater discontinuity between Divine personhood and its human counterpart. Galot identifies three such differences: the uniqueness or originality of the human person is less radical than the originality of the divine Persons that flows from their differing relations of origin, marking the three as unique and totally original; human persons possess an individual nature, whereas each of the divine Persons wholly possesses the same totally identical divine nature without limit, enjoying an unlimited union of thought and love; and while in God the Persons are perfectly established from their origin and do not increase in perfection, human personality grows and matures through the activation of one's relational dynamism, gradually passing from potency to act during the course of one's life.[96] While this proposal seems to offer a

---

93. Cf. Zizioulas, *Being as Communion*, 39–41, 84–88; Gunton, *Promise of Trinitarian Theology*, 9–11. Writing from a more Western and existential approach, Bartnik also approximates this position. See "'The Person' in the Holy Trinity," 25–26.

94. Cf. Zizioulas, "Human Capacity and Incapacity," 408n3.

95. Galot, *Who Is Christ?*, 299; cf. idem, "La définition de la personnne," 296.

96. Cf. Galot, *Who Is Christ?*, 303–5. Perhaps another way to express this third point is to distinguish between relation (one's ontological relatedness to God and to other human persons) and relationship (one's activation of this manner of being through conscious choice and action).

potential synthesis of elements of the Augustinian, Thomist, and modern notions of personhood, it too could benefit from a more completely developed relational ontology and its grounding vis-à-vis substance and nature.

None of the positions surveyed is without ambiguities or could not but benefit from further development. What the preceding analysis does make clear is that it is not necessary to regard substance and relation as antithetical ways of describing the person. The mystery of the human person, created in the image of the Triune God, is illumined by revelation as a being who subsists in the communion of love.

CHAPTER 3

Chastity

Toward a Renewed Understanding

Certainly one of the most maligned and misunderstood virtues in contemporary culture is that of chastity. The word often evokes connotations of inhibition, prudery, dysfunction, and perhaps even neurosis. The recent resurgence of interest in the notion of virtue as the basis for the moral life in the wake of Alasdair MacIntyre's ground-breaking work has not yet removed such associations.[1] The contemporary revival of virtue theory has not yet fully turned its attention to the area of sexuality. The treatment of chastity in the *Catechism of the Catholic Church* (*CCC*, 2337–59) contains some of the strengths and ambiguities of the older classical approach as well as some indications of avenues that could be further explored in pursuing a renewed understanding of this virtue within a contemporary setting. This essay considers the classical understanding of chastity with its inherent strengths and ambiguities as these are reprised in the *CCC*. It then considers other approaches to this virtue suggested by the treatment in the *CCC* and found elsewhere in contemporary theological reflection—personalist, developmental, and culturally situated approaches. The aim of this essay is to con-

Originally published as "Chastity: Toward a Renewed Understanding," *Living Light* 32, no. 4 (Summer 1996): 44–51. Portions of this essay were reworked and published in "Sex and Chastity," in *Sex and Virtue: An Introduction to Sexual Ethics*, Catholic Moral Thought Series (Washington, DC: Catholic University of America Press, 2003), chap. 4; see esp. 71–95.

1. Alasdair MacIntyre, *After Virtue* (Notre Dame, IN: University of Notre Dame Press, 1981).

tribute toward the reformulation and rehabilitation of a virtue, which is at once badly understood and sorely needed in contemporary life and culture.

The Classical Tradition

From the perspective of the classical Aristotelian Thomist tradition of virtue, chastity is a specification of the virtue of temperance related to matters of sex, enabling reason to control and moderate sexual impulses.[2] This virtue is so named because it is that which "chastises" the concupiscence, which comes from venereal pleasure.[3] This is not to say that all pleasure is evil, since Aquinas, like Aristotle, held that pleasure is a natural accompaniment and perfection of all human action. Hence it is the goodness or badness of the act itself that determines the moral quality of the pleasure it produces.[4] This Aristotelian teleology of pleasure introduced by Aquinas would open the way for a more positive estimate of sexual pleasure in succeeding centuries.[5] Nevertheless, this tradition would insist that virtue enables reason to moderate and control such pleasure.[6] Chastity is thus reasonable self-control of one's sexual appetites, but it does not necessarily wholly exclude either sexual activity or the pleasure that accompanies it.

Earlier sources in the theological tradition had a more negative view of pleasure and hence a somewhat more stringent view of chastity and its demands. Many early Christian writers were influenced in varying degrees by Stoicism with its ideal of *apatheia*—the notion that the virtuous person was utterly unmoved by passion, which was the enemy of reason.[7] Others were affected by Neoplatonism, which added to the Stoic focus on reason an additional mistrust of the body and sexuality. Chastity in such a view was not

2. See Aquinas, *Summa theologiae* (*ST*) II-II, q. 151, a. 3. For a lucid exposition and overview of the Thomist understanding of chastity, see Josef Pieper, *The Four Cardinal Virtues* (South Bend, IN: University of Notre Dame Press, 1966), 153–75.

3. See Aristotle, *Nichomachean Ethics* III, 12; *ST* II-II, q. 151, a. 1.

4. See Aquinas, *Commentary on the Sentences*, 4.31.2.3; 4.49.3.4.3.

5. On this development, see John T. Noonan, *Contraception: A History of Its Treatment by the Catholic Theologians and Canonists* (Cambridge, MA: Harvard University Press, 1966), 292–95, 305–12, 321–30, 395, 491–504.

6. See *ST* II-II, q. 151, a. 1; cf. I-II, q. 64, a. 1.

7. For examples of Stoic influence on patristic and early monastic thought, see Noonan, *Contraception*, 75–77, 144.

always sharply distinguished from continence (refraining from sexual activity altogether). For the married, the possibilities for exercising chastity were limited—they could either content themselves with a second-class exercise of the virtue or foreswear sexual relations altogether.[8]

Such currents were given a persuasive theological rationale by Augustine's doctrine of concupiscence. According to the bishop of Hippo, *concupiscentia* is the result of original sin and disorders all human desires—the greater the desire, the greater the disorder. Because of its intensity, sexual desire is profoundly affected by concupiscence and casts down the human mind from the heights of rationality, which it ought to occupy.[9] There is thus little room here for a positive estimate of sexual desire or pleasure. Adding to these views were the Neoplatonic strains of Augustine's thought that identified sex with the fall into materiality and diversity.[10] In this context, the renunciation of sexual desire and activity become a way to return to a primordial unity: "Indeed it is through chastity that we are gathered together and led back to the unity from which we were fragmented into multiplicity."[11]

The *CCC* blends elements of these various traditions into its treatment. It too sees chastity as an aspect of temperance that "seeks to permeate the passions and appetites of the senses with reason" (*CCC*, 2341). Yet, as indicated by the quote above, it also recalls some of the more Neoplatonic motifs present within the Augustinian tradition. Like both monastic and medieval thought, it juxtaposes its treatment of virtue with considerations of opposing vices (e.g., *CCC*, 2351–56). Unlike patristic theology and some medieval theology, however, it does so within a primarily legal framework

8. This undoubtedly contributed toward the impulse toward "spiritual marriage"—the practice of couples taking vows of continence at some point in their marriages, at times immediately following their vows—within later patristic and medieval thought. On this phenomenon, see Dyan Elliott, *Spiritual Marriage: Sexual Abstinence in Medieval Wedlock* (Princeton, NJ: Princeton University Press, 1993).

9. Cf. Augustine, *Soloquies*, 1, 10; cf. *On Marriage and Concupiscence*, 1, 6; *City of God*, 14, 16. For an overview and analysis of Augustine's mistrust of pleasure, see John Mahoney, *The Making of Moral Theology: A Study of the Roman Catholic Tradition* (Oxford: Clarendon, 1987), 61–66.

10. But Augustine never went so far as some of the more Neoplatonic Eastern thinkers such as Gregory of Nyssa, John Chrysostom, Theodoret, and John Damascene, who saw sexual differences and reproduction as introduced by God only after human sin.

11. Augustine, *Confessions*, 10, 29, 40. The citation is from *CCC*, 2340.

(considering chastity under the heading of the sixth commandment).[12] This undoubtedly adds a strongly normative or deontological cast to its treatment.[13]

In the *CCC* all of these elements are united under the rubric of personal integration. This along with the *Catechism*'s use of language describing sexuality as a form of self-giving invites a consideration of chastity from a personalist perspective.

Chastity and Personalism

The treatments of chastity within the moral manuals, which were the standard textbooks of moral theology between the Council of Trent and Vatican II, were fairly standardized expositions of the classical approach and its application to various kinds of sexual sin. The rise of personalist philosophy and ethics and its application to matters of sexuality by Catholic moralists in the 1920s and 1930s made possible the development of new and more experiential perspectives on sexuality and chastity.

Personalist approaches highlighted the fact that there is more to the experience of conjugal love than its orientation to procreation. For Dietrich von Hildebrand, even if procreation is the primary purpose of marital intercourse, love is its primary meaning.[14] Herbert Doms, while echoing this formulation, went even further, arguing for the primacy of the "two-in-one-

---

12. Historical studies have demonstrated that the use of the Ten Commandments as a catechetical basis for all moral instruction emerged only through a convergence of factors in the High Middle Ages (rather than in patristic thought, as has sometimes been held). Such developments were then codified in the *Roman Catechism*, which was issued after the Council of Trent. See Joseph A. Slattery, "The Catechetical Use of the Decalogue from the End of the Catechumenate through the Later Medieval Period" (PhD diss., Catholic University of America, 1980). For a specific consideration of the sixth commandment, see John S. Grabowski, "Clerical Sexual Misconduct and Early Traditions Regarding the Sixth Commandment," *Jurist* 55, no. 2 (1995): 527–91.

13. While Aquinas suggests that all moral precepts can be located within the Decalogue (as first principles of the natural law), he does not treat chastity or lust under this heading. Cf. *ST* I-II, q. 100, a. 1. It is equally instructive to compare the relative brevity of the treatise on natural law within the *Summa* to the extensive tract on the virtues.

14. See Dietrich von Hildebrand, *Marriage: The Mystery of Faithful Love* (London: Longmans Green, 1942), 6–7, 19–27; and idem, *In Defense of Purity* (Baltimore: Helicon Press, 1962), 10–12.

ship" that intercourse effects and seeing biological ends such as procreation as secondary.[15] Both of these thinkers would describe sex as a privileged form of self-giving between spouses that both expresses and fosters their communion of love.[16] The pleasure that accompanies sexual love is unique, then, from the pleasure of other forms of activity precisely because it serves to engage the full attention of the lovers in their mutual gift of self and because it effects their unity of consciousness.[17]

In this perspective, chastity is not merely the mastery of reason over the passions, nor still less a flight from all sexual activity, but rather a form of self-possession that makes sexual and other forms of self-donation possible. Chastity serves to integrate rather than repress or sublimate both sexual desire and the range of human affectivity in the service of love.[18] The *CCC* builds on this perspective through its suggestion that "self-mastery is ordered to the gift of self" (2346).[19] A person can only truly give as a gift that which they themselves first possess. This is particularly true in the case of the gift of self. To give oneself in the absence of this possession is to be compelled by various kinds of drives or impulses rather than to genuinely offer oneself in freedom.[20]

In this perspective, chastity is needed equally by single, married, and celibate persons (cf. *CCC*, 2348–49). Because the vocation of all believers is to love, chastity enables them to give themselves in love to others in a way specific to their own vocations. Chastity makes possible the integration of one's sexuality into the commitments that structure the person's life. John Paul II, in his catechesis on the body, has observed the fundamental analogy

15. Herbert Doms, *The Meaning of Marriage*, trans. George Sayer (London: Sheed & Ward, 1939), 67–69, 85–88, 93–94, 119.

16. See, e.g., von Hildebrand, *Marriage*, 19–20; Doms, *Meaning of Marriage*, 14–15, 23, 50.

17. See Doms, *Meaning of Marriage*, 187. Cf. von Hildebrand, *In Defense of Purity*, 12.

18. This is the primary point of the long exposition of chastity offered by Karol Wojtyła in *Love and Responsibility*, trans. H. T. Willets (New York: Farrar, Straus, and Giroux, 1981), 143–73.

19. See also the extensive personalist consideration of human sexual love and chastity as forms of self-giving in the recent document of the Pontifical Council for the Family, "The Truth and Meaning of Human Sexuality: Guidelines for Education within the Family," nos. 8–25, 31. The text can be found in *Origins* 25, no. 32 (February 1996): 530*ff.*

20. Von Hildebrand contrasts the free self-surrender of self-donation with the experience of throwing oneself away in sexual excess in the absence of chastity. See *In Defense of Purity*, 21–26.

between the married and celibate vocations, as both are ways of giving one-self in which the body expresses the person and his or her commitments.[21] Thus one can refrain from sex out of unchaste forms of repression, and one can be quite chaste in the midst of a passionate sexual relationship.[22]

The *CCC* draws on some of this rich personalist tradition and language under the heading of "the integrality of the gift of self" (2346–47). But much of this treatment is occupied by the relationship between chastity and the good of friendship. While it is true that friendship occupies a central role in the ethics of both Aristotle and Aquinas and hence is an important component of the tradition of virtue, here in the *Catechism* there is more a juxtaposition than a real synthesis of this notion of friendship and modern personalism.[23] This too points to the need for further theological reflection, which can unite the current retrieval of virtue theory and personalist perspectives on sexuality. While the *CCC* draws upon personalist language and ideas in its treatment, it also makes at least passing reference to other possible avenues of development.

Developmental Perspectives

One such approach that is given passing mention by the *CCC* in its consideration of chastity is an approach informed by the insights of developmental psychology. Thus the *Catechism* states that self-mastery entails "renewed effort at all stages of life" (2342) and that it "has *laws of growth* which progress through stages marked by human imperfection and too often by sin" (2243).[24]

---

21. See the pope's weekly general audience of April 28, 1992, "Celibacy Is a Particular Response to the Love of the Divine Spouse," in *The Theology of Marriage and Celibacy*, trans. L'Osservatore Romano, English ed. (Boston: Daughters of St. Paul, 1986), 120–27.

22. See William F. Kraft, *Sexual Dimensions of the Celibate Life* (Kansas City, KS: Andrews and McNeil, 1977), 130.

23. For good expositions of the notion of friendship in the classical tradition of virtue and in contemporary accounts of the moral life, see Gilbert Meilaender, *Friendship: A Study in Theological Ethics* (Notre Dame, IN: University of Notre Dame Press, 1981); Paul Wadell, *Friendship and the Moral Life* (Notre Dame, IN: University of Notre Dame Press, 1989); and L. Gregory Jones, *Transformed Judgment: Toward a Trinitarian Account of the Moral Life* (Notre Dame, IN: University of Notre Dame Press, 1990), esp. 98–119.

24. Emphasis original. For further specification of age-appropriate education in human sexuality, see also "Truth and Meaning of Human Sexuality," nos. 64–111. While some of the

This insight can serve as a link to the growing awareness of human cognitive, affective, and moral development upon which ethicists have begun to draw.

While there has always been a certain recognition of human growth and development within the moral tradition, at times this insight was hampered by an exaggerated importance attached to the notion of the "age of reason." This term seemed to function as a watershed in the passage to moral agency and hence responsibility. In regard to virtue, one would thus move from a prerational stage where virtues functioned in somewhat inchoate fashion to a context of full-blown culpability for one's acts.[25] In the case of chastity, the matter is complicated further by the fact that puberty emerges sometime after the age of reason and by differing cultural evaluations of when an individual was sufficiently mature to commence a sexual relationship.

Modern developmental psychology has offered a helpful corrective to this apparent chasm between prerational innocence and moral responsibility. The work of Erik Erikson on human affectivity, Jean Piaget on cognition, James Fowler on faith, Robert Kegan on the self-concept, and Lawrence Kohlberg on moral reasoning have uncovered important patterns in human development over the course of the life cycle. It is true that approaches such as Kohlberg's, while particularly important from the standpoint of moral theory, are not without limitations imposed by certain philosophical presuppositions or a bias toward male experience.[26] Nevertheless, they make an important contribution toward uncovering some of the basic patterns of development within the human personality. For this reason, moralists such as Walter Conn have begun to use them to provide developmental perspectives on the moral life as a whole.[27]

---

principles that this document proposes (e.g., respect for the individuality of the child, the interconnection between biological information and moral and religious values) are genuinely helpful, its delineation of the four "principle stages of children's development" (innocence, puberty, adolescence, and the approach to adulthood) could benefit from a more intensive conversation with the developmental disciplines mentioned below.

25. Hence the Scholastic axiom that the first act of an individual after attaining the age of reason will either be an act of virtue or a mortal sin. See *ST* I-II, q. 89, a. 6.

26. For an incisive critique of some of the philosophical presuppositions underlying Kohlberg's account of moral reasoning, see Gilbert Meilaender, *The Theory and Practice of Virtue* (Notre Dame, IN: University of Notre Dame Press, 1984), 84–99. For a critique of the androcentric bias of Kohlberg's data and some proposals that are more inclusive of women's experience, see Carol Gilligan, *In a Different Voice: Psychological Theory and Women's Development* (Cambridge, MA: Harvard University Press, 1982).

27. See Walter Conn, *Conscience: Development and Self-Transcendence* (Birmingham, AL:

This developmental perspective can also aid in the renewal of virtue-centered accounts of moral agency. The primary place where this integration has begun is in the elaboration of the theology of the fundamental option, which often self-consciously draws on such developmental perspectives.[28]

In relation to sexuality, such perspectives can serve to provide a broader perspective on sexual acts. They can do so, first, by overcoming an isolated focus on individual sexual acts, abstracted from the whole of a person's growing moral character and the concreteness of the relationship in which they take place. Second, this perspective can serve to clarify and nuance the limitations placed on the moral agent's culpability by what was traditionally designated the impediment of immaturity. Hence some kinds of sexual acts at particular stages of personal development, such as masturbation by adolescents, may be more symptomatic of an immature sexuality in need of integration rather than being in themselves constitutive of one's moral character and goodness.[29]

In spite of these broader perspectives that they provide, there are further questions that developmental approaches must address. Critics of fundamental option theory have argued that it tends to neglect the reflexive character of moral action maintained by traditional virtue theory.[30] That is, particular moral acts not only express one's developing moral character but also serve to shape it. Hence even at earlier stages of development some attention ought to be paid to concrete acts (although perhaps not in the sense of determining personal culpability) because these affect further moral growth. There is thus a recognized need for further work to harmonize the classical tradition of virtue with the insights of developmental psychology.[31]

Religious Education Press, 1981); and idem, *Christian Conversion: A Developmental Interpretation of Autonomy and Surrender* (New York: Paulist, 1986). These works also contain helpful overviews of the work of the various developmental theorists listed above.

28. See, e.g., Bernard Häring, *Free and Faithful in Christ*, vol. 1, *General Moral Theology* (New York: Seabury Press, 1978), 164–222.

29. On this point, see, e.g., Charles Curran, "Sexual Ethics: A Critique," in *Issues in Sexual and Medical Ethics* (Notre Dame, IN: University of Notre Dame Press, 1978), 44–45, 49.

30. See Ronald Lawler, Joseph Boyle, and William May, *Catholic Sexual Ethics: A Summary, Explanation and Defense* (Huntington, IN: Our Sunday Visitor, 1985), 96–97.

31. On this need for synthesis, see Charles Curran, "The Historical Development of Moral Theology," in *Toward an American Catholic Moral Theology* (Notre Dame, IN: University of Notre Dame Press, 1987), 14–15.

Developmental perspectives do make clear, however, that the acquisition of chastity is closely interrelated with one's overall intellectual, affective, and moral development. One cannot expect precisely the same kinds of manifestations of the virtue from even two adults of the same age and background if they are at different developmental stages. This awareness is particularly important for those engaged in pastoral ministry in areas related to human sexuality, those who deal with the interrelationship of sexuality and spirituality, and parents and religious educators who attempt to instill values related to sexuality in the young.[32] Both the exercise and the acquisition of chastity are developmentally conditioned. If the acquisition of chastity is conditioned by one's personal development, it is equally shaped by the culture in which one lives.

Chastity and Culture

A final line of inquiry briefly suggested by the *CCC* is the consideration of the relationship of chastity to human culture. Thus the *Catechism* observes that chastity "involves a *cultural effort*, for there is 'an interdependence between personal betterment and the improvement of society'" (2344).[33]

Even the most classicist approaches recognize that not all of the particular moral excellences that produce human flourishing are rooted solely in human nature. The perception of many such values and even of human nature itself is shaped in part by the symbols and ideas of the culture in which they are viewed. Hence the effort to present or inculcate moral values must take into account this complex and far-reaching effect of cultural influence.

Modern proponents of virtue theory have recognized this cultural locus of virtue in describing the process of the passing on of a "tradition of virtue." Such a tradition is mediated by specific narratives that describe particular moral values and seek to engender specific practices that make possible their assimilation in differing cultural settings.[34]

32. For a pastoral analysis of issues related to chastity in various states in life and its integration in spirituality, see Benedict Groeschel, *The Courage to Be Chaste* (New York: Paulist, 1985). For a more thoroughgoing exposition of a spirituality of sexuality from a developmental perspective, see Joan Timmerman, *Sexuality and Spiritual Growth* (New York: Crossroad, 1993).

33. Emphasis original. The citation is from *Gaudium et spes*, no. 25.

34. See MacIntyre, *After Virtue*, 186–96. For a more thoroughgoing narrative approach to

If this is true for virtue in general, then it is also true of chastity in particular. To some degree or other, chastity is a virtue mediated by moral and religious narratives whose acquisition will be shaped by particular cultural contexts and symbols. This observation suggests a few basic implications.

It will at times be the case that the Church in its teaching, preaching, and religious education has to attempt to offer prophetic criticism to deficient understandings of sexuality in specific cultures.[35] Thus the view of sex as a commodity for nothing more than pleasure or profit widespread in popular culture, the manner in which the media often undercuts any notion of chastity or sexual restraint,[36] or rigid and stereotypical understandings of gender roles are all examples of inadequate views of sexuality that deserve to be challenged and rejected.

How does one offer such a challenge? Obviously this can be done through public critique and moral argument. Yet it can also be done through concrete efforts to build and develop cultural practices that support a better understanding of sex and chastity. This can take the form of the development of alternative media that can effectively compete in the marketplace of ideas. It can occur through the effort to forge differing perceptions of sex activity and more flexible gender roles through effective moral and religious catechesis. It can even be found in popular movements such as the efforts of many teens to offer a countercultural witness through signing a chastity pledge. All of these can contribute to what John Paul II has recently described as building a "culture of life" in which human sexuality is more adequately understood and respected.[37]

But in this engagement with culture—whether through critical evaluation or the elaboration of alternative views and practices—care must be taken that this is not heard as mere prudery or the reintroduction of a more

virtue theory, see Stanley Hauerwas, *The Peaceable Kingdom* (Notre Dame, IN: University of Notre Dame Press, 1983).

35. See the description of the sickness that can invade human culture in John Paul II, "Letter to Families," *Gratissimam sane*, nos. 13–14. The text can be found in *Origins* 23, no. 37 (March 1994): 637ff. See also the indicators of a "culture of death" described in *Evangelium vitae*, nos. 10–17. The text can be found in *Origins* 24, no. 42 (April 1995): 690ff.

36. On this effect of the media in undermining the efforts of parents and other religious educators, see "Truth and Meaning of Human Sexuality," no. 56. Unfortunately, the document's comments on the media are somewhat brief and predominantly negative.

37. See John Paul II, *Evangelium vitae*, nos. 95–100.

negative view of sex. Religious educators who focus only on the critical aspect of the engagement with culture run this very risk. The message of chastity, foreign as it may be in popular culture, will only be heard if it is linked to a compelling and positive vision of human sexuality and to the development of specific culturally attractive practices that can allow it to flourish. The Church, which in its teaching often proclaims its possession of the "truth" about the person and his or her sexuality, needs to allow this splendor to shine not merely in clarity of specific proscriptions, but in the radiance of a more compelling vision.

Finally, because human culture serves to mediate the particular values that shape moral character, there must also be a profound respect for genuine autonomy of human cultures and authentic variations in regard to understandings of sexuality. Thus various cultures might have differing estimates of the age or personal maturity necessary to enter into a stable sexual relationship or value motives for marriage other than romantic love or personal fulfillment often valorized in our own.[38] Such diversity of cultural perceptions can enrich and deepen an understanding of the mystery of human sexuality and its integration through chastity.

Conclusion

The presentation of chastity in the *CCC* restates the classical understanding of this virtue developed in the tradition as well as draws upon or briefly points to some contemporary currents of thought that could contribute to its further refinement and reformulation. Perspectives such as those afforded by modern personalism, developmental psychology, and an awareness of the reciprocity between moral values and human culture can shed new light on this much-maligned virtue and its effective presentation in contemporary religious education. The current renewal of interest in virtue theory could benefit from such perspectives when it more systematically engages issues of human sexuality under the rubric of chastity.

38. Thus the current Code of Canon Law (c. 1083) specifies a minimum of sixteen years of age for males to licitly enter marriage and a minimum of fourteen years for females, but recognizes the power of local bishops conferences to set such limits at an older age depending on local custom (cf. c. 1072).

CHAPTER 4

Covenantal Sexuality

The Second Vatican Council's Pastoral Constitution on the Church in the Modern World, *Gaudium et spes*, has been widely hailed by scholars for its utilization of the category of covenant in its description of marriage. According to the Council, marriage is "an intimate partnership of ... life and love ... rooted in the conjugal covenant of irrevocable personal consent."[1]

Previous versions of this essay appeared as: "Covenantal Sexuality," *Église et théologie* 27 (1996): 229–52; "Covenant and Sacrament," in *Sex and Virtue: An Introduction to Sexual Ethics*, Catholic Moral Thought Series (Washington, DC: Catholic University of America Press, 2003), chap. 2, 23–48; and "Covenantal Sexuality," in *Divine Providence and Human Freedom*, ed. Kevin A. McMahon (Lanham, MD: Lexington Books, 2015), 107–25. I am indebted to Francis Martin, Laura Millman, Christopher Begg, Stephen Miletic, Msgr. Kevin Irwin, William E. May, and Paul Wadell for helpful comments and suggestions on earlier drafts of this essay.

1. *Gaudium et spes*, no. 48. The citation is from *The Documents of Vatican II*, ed. Walter Abbott, SJ (Piscataway, NJ: New Century, 1966), 250. All citations of the Council's documents will be from this edition. On the significance of this language, see Wilhelm Ernst, "Marriage as an Institution and the Contemporary Challenge to It," in *Contemporary Perspectives on Christian Marriage: Propositions and Papers from the International Theological Commission*, ed. Richard Malone and John Connery (Chicago: Loyola University Press, 1984), 39–90, esp. 66–72; Denise Larder Carmody, "Marriage in Roman Catholicism," *Journal of Ecumenical Studies* 22 (1985): 28–40, esp. 34; Theodore Mackin, SJ, *The Marital Sacrament: Marriage in the Catholic Church* (New York: Paulist, 1989), 539–44; and Joseph Selling, "Magisterial Teaching on Marriage 1880–1986: Historical Constancy or Radical Development?," in *Readings in Moral Theology*, vol. 8, *Dialogue about Catholic Sexual Teaching*, ed. Charles Curran and Richard McCormick, SJ (New York: Paulist, 1993), 93–97. For a more critical view of the adequacy of covenant as the basis for a sacramental theology, see Tibor Horvath, SJ, "Marriage: Contract? Covenant? Community? Sacrament of Sacraments? Fallible Symbol of Infallible Love, Revelation of Sin and Love," in *The Sacraments: God's Love and Mercy Actualized*, ed. Francis Eigo, OSA (Villanova, PA: University of Villanova Press, 1979), 143–81, esp. 148–50.

This signaled a paradigm shift from a largely juridical understanding of marriage that had dominated modern Catholic thought to one that is biblical in its roots and personalist in its trajectory.[2] The document thus made possible the integration of the ongoing renewal of biblical studies into the Catholic theology of marriage.[3] In this way it was part of the Council's overall call for greater integration of biblical study into the theological endeavor in general and the field of moral theology in particular.[4] A case can be made that in spite of a concerted effort to integrate biblical teaching into moral theology as a whole, the idea of covenant has not received extensive consideration.[5]

An examination of the whole of moral theology is outside the scope of

2. For a development of the implications of this personalism in regard to the theology of sex and marriage in the present context, see Germán Martinez, "An Anthropological Vision of Christian Marriage, *The Thomist* 56 (1992): 451–72.

3. This development is reflected in the 1983 Code of Canon Law. Unlike the 1917 Code, which focused on the *ius od corpus* "right to one another's bodies" given in the matrimonial consent, the present revision sees the relationship as a covenant between spouses that establishes a "partnership of the whole life" *totius vitae consortium* (can. 1055), in which they "mutually hand over and accept each other" *sese mutuo tradunt et accipiunt* (can. 1057). See *Codex iuris canonici* (Vatican City: Libreria Editrice Vaticana, 1983). For a good overview of these developments, see Michael D. Place, " A Guide to the Revised Code," *Chicago Studies* 23 (1984): 5–36; and P. Brancherreau, "Le sacrament de marriage dans le Code de droit canonique," *Nouvelle revue théologique* 107 (1985): 376–93; Bernard Siegle, TOR, *Marriage According to the New Code of Canon Law* (New York: Alba House, 1986); and Comac Burke, "Marriage: A Personalist or Institutional Understanding?" *Communio* 19 (1992): 278–304.

4. Thus the Dogmatic Constitution on Divine Revelation teaches that "the study of the sacred page is, at it were, the soul of sacred theology." *Dei verbum*, no. 24. *Documents of Vatican II*, 127. *Optatum totius*, the Decree on Priestly Formation, specifically stated that moral theology needed to be "more thoroughly nourished by scriptural teaching" (no. 16). *Documents of Vatican II*, 452.

5. Thus even recent introductions to moral theology that make a concerted effort to engage Scripture do not offer extensive considerations of this concept. David Bohr makes frequent mention of covenant but does not use it to structure a chapter (unlike the biblical themes of conversion, discipleship, law, and sin). See his *Catholic Moral Tradition: In Christ a New Creation*, rev. ed. (Eugene, OR: Wipf & Stock, 2006). Others, because of a focus on natural law or virtue ethics, hardly mention it at all. See, e.g., Romanus Cessario, OP, *Introduction to Moral Theology*, Catholic Moral Thought Series (Washington, DC: Catholic University of America Press, 2000); William E. May, *Introduction to Moral Theology*, 2nd ed. (Huntington, IN: OSV, 2003); William Mattison, *Introducing Moral Theology: True Happiness and the Virtues* (Grand Rapids, MI: Brazos, 2008); and Paul Wadell, *Happiness and the Christian Moral Life: An Introduction to Christian Ethics* (Lanham, MD: Rowman & Littlefield, 2012).

this study, but one specific example of this interface suggested by the Council is the way in which the phenomenon of human sexuality within the marriage relationship is also informed by the biblical theology of covenant. This observation can provide a deeper understanding of the theology of both sex and marriage. This study argues that a consideration of key biblical traditions in the light of recent scholarship reveals sex to be an action that symbolizes or enacts the promise made in the marriage covenant, and that this view can shed light on the theology of both sex and marriage in the Christian tradition.

This essay first reviews certain features of the understanding of covenant highlighted by modern biblical scholarship. These insights are then used to examine biblical traditions that portray sex in covenantal terms, particularly the description of the creation of woman in Genesis 2. The explanatory power of such biblical usage is then utilized in an examination of aspects of the understanding of both marriage and sex in later Christian tradition.

The Nature of Covenant

The importance of the covenant in structuring Israel's relationship to Yahweh has long been evident to even casual readers of the Old Testament (OT). Yet modern scholarship has uncovered an extensive and multifaceted use of this category in biblical materials to describe many relationships. This section highlights certain features of the biblical theology of covenant (*berith*) that are necessary to understand its application to the marriage relationship and sexual intimacy within it.

From the perspective of biblical thought, there is a fundamental difference between the legal category of contract and the more personal category of covenant.[6] A contract is an economic or legal agreement between two parties made before witnesses that involves a pledge of one's property.[7] If one of the parties breaks the contract, that party forfeits the prop-

---

6. On the biblical basis of this distinction, see Gene M. Tucker, "Covenant Forms and Contract Forms," *Vetus Testamentum* 15 (1965): 487–503; Paul F. Palmer, SJ, "Christian Marriage: Contract or Covenant?," *Theological Studies* 33 (1972): 617–65, esp. 617–19, 639–40.

7. Extrabiblical examples of contract forms and biblical evidence for their use in Israel are considered by Tucker, "Covenant Forms and Contract Forms," 497–500.

erty pledged. A covenant, on the other hand, is an agreement or oath of fidelity between parties made with or before God in which one promises one's very self to another. This is illustrated in dramatic fashion in the account of Abram's covenant with Yahweh in Genesis 15. Yahweh "cuts a covenant" *karath berith* (Gn 15:18) with Abram by having him split in two a heifer, a goat, and a ram. Generally, in such covenant ceremonies, both parties would walk between the animal halves, indicating that if they ever broke the agreement, their own lives would be forfeit. The promise entailed in a covenant thus demands an unconditional and more personal form of fidelity, even though it can be violated or even broken.

It is precisely because of the total claim that it makes on a person that a covenant creates a new relationship between its parties. These agreements can take numerous forms. One can find "secular" variations such as an unequal treaty between a powerful party who promises protection to the weak in exchange for service (cf. Jgs 9:11–15; 1 Sm 11:1; 2 Sm 3:12*ff.*),[8] peace treaties (cf. Gn 14:13*ff.*, 26:28, 31:43*ff.*), or agreements between friends (cf. 1 Sm 23:18).[9] There are also the more "religious" presentations of the covenant between Yahweh and Israel.[10] The new relationship created by such agreements is often described in familial terms.[11] If one of the parties is the more

8. Walther Eichrodt holds that even in cases of covenants between those who are not equal, there is still a certain mutuality of obligation. See *Theology of the Old Testament*, vol. 1, trans. J. A. Baker (Philadelphia: Westminster, 1961), 37. More recent research has corroborated this position: "The reductionist idea that covenant means only 'obligation' and is essentially one-sided has been largely abandoned. Most scholars contributing to the field recognize that the covenant always involves mutuality and relationship; indeed, even when the terms only express obligations for one party, there seems to be the assumption of reciprocal loyalty on both sides." Scott Hahn, "Covenant in the Old and New Testaments: Some Current Research (1994–2004)," *Currents in Biblical Research* 3 (2005): 262–92, here 285.

9. For an extensive study of the declaration formulae of various "secular" covenants found in the OT, see Paul Kalluveettil, CMI, *Declaration and Covenant: A Comprehensive Review of Covenant Formulae from the Old Testament and the Ancient New East*, Analecta Biblica 88 (Rome: Pontifical Biblical Institute Press, 1982).

10. There is some overlap between these various kinds of covenant. The covenant between God and Israel at Mt. Horeb, e.g., is described by some biblical traditions in terms that are redolent of ancient Near Eastern (ANE) suzerainty treaties. See Dennis J. McCarthy, *Old Testament Covenant: A Survey of Current Opinions* (Richmond: John Knox, 1972); idem, *Treaty and Covenant*, 2nd ed., Analecta Biblica 21A (Rome: Pontifical Biblical Institute Press, 1978).

11. The seminal work in this area was Johannes Pedersen's study on the familial nature of covenant among the Semitic Bedouin tribes of the Arabian Peninsula. Because Semites tend to base all rights and duties on relationship, the covenant utilizes a juridical fiction to make the

powerful of the two, he becomes a "father" to the other (cf. Jer 35:18; Is 9:5) with obligations to protect and care for him.[12] In other cases, parties are said to be made "brothers" by such a pact (cf. 2 Sm 1:26; 1 Kgs 20:32–33). In every case, covenant declaration formulae serve to "extend the bond of blood beyond the kinship sphere, or, in other words, to make the partner one's own flesh and blood."[13]

Integral to most covenants is an oath. In fact, the two are so closely related as to be virtually interchangeable.[14] Such oaths often invoke God as a witness to the terms of the covenant (cf. Gn 21:23–24, 31:39–50). A similar notion is present in descriptions of covenants made in the sight of Yahweh (cf. 1 Sm 23:18; 2 Sm 5:3; 2 Kgs 23:3). Because God is witness to these pacts, he is understood to punish those who break them. Hence many covenant oaths take the form of a curse (*alah*), often self-imprecating in character, pronounced on those who fail to keep their word (see, e.g., Ru 1:17b; 1 Sm 3:17, 14:44, 25:22; 2 Sm 3:9–11, 3:35*ff.*; 1 Kgs 2:23, 19:2, 20:10; 2 Kgs 6:31).[15]

Also essential to covenant ceremonies is some act that seals or enacts the agreement. Thus, following Yahweh's revelation of himself and his laws to the Israelites at Sinai, the people three times express their consent to the words of the Lord (Ex 19:8, 24:3, 24:7) and then are sprinkled with the

---

parties into blood relatives. See *Der Eid bei den Semiten, in seinem Verhältnis zu verwandten Erscheinungen sowie die Stellung des Eides im Islam*, Studien zur Geschichte und Kultur des islamischen Orients 3 (Strassburg: Trübner, 1914), 31.

12. On the use of such language in covenant forms, see Dennis J. McCarthy, "Notes on the Love of God in Deuteronomy and the Father-Son Relationship between Yahweh and Israel," *Catholic Biblical Quarterly* 27 (1965): 144–47; and Frank Charles Fensham, "Father and Son as Terminology for Treaty and Covenant," in *Near Eastern Studies in Honor of William Foxwell Albright*, ed. H. Goedicke (Baltimore: Johns Hopkins University Press, 1971), 121–35.

13. Kalluveettil, *Declaration and Covenant*, 212. Cf. Gottfried Quell, in *Theological Dictionary of the New Testament*, vol. 2, 1964, s.v. "*diatheke*."

14. Numerous texts parallel the making of a covenant with the swearing of an oath (cf. Gn 21:22–24, 21:31–32, 26:28, 31; Jo 9:15–20; 2 Kgs 11:4b; Ez 17:13, 17:16, 17:18–19). On this point, see Pedersen, *Der Eid*, 21–51; Norbert Lohfink, *Die Landverheissung als Eid: Eine Studie zu Gn. 15*, Stuttgarter Bibel-Studien 28 (Stuttgart: Verlag Katholisches Bibelwerk, 1967), 101–13; Tucker, "Covenant Forms and Contract Forms," 488–90; and Gordon Paul Hugenberger, *Marriage as a Covenant: A Study of Biblical Law and Ethics Developed from the Perspective of Malachi*, Supplements to Vetus Testamentum 52 (Leiden: Brill, 1994), 182–84, 193–205.

15. On these conditional self-curses, see Pedersen, *Der Eid*, 103*ff.*; Friederich Horst, "Der Eid im Alten Testament," in *Gottes Recht: Gesammelte Studien zum Recht im Alten Testament*, ed. Hans Walter Wolff (Munich: Chr. Kaiser, 1961), 301–14. On the variety of forms of covenant oaths, see Tucker, "Covenant Forms and Contract Forms," 491–97.

blood of their peace offerings. In this case, the blood symbolizes the bond between God and his people and their sharing of a common life. It should be remembered that the Israelites held blood to be sacred precisely because it was understood to contain the very life of the creature (cf. Lev 17:11, 17:14; Dt 12:23). Given this, one can begin to discern the role of blood in covenant ritual. The blood indicates not only the community of life among the covenant parties, but also the sanctification or being set apart of the object or person whom it marks (cf. Ex 12:12–23, 29:20–21). Such being made holy through sacrificial blood also recalls the demands made on those who are party to a covenant. The life of the creature forfeited in the sacrifice or offering bespeaks the totality of the claim made upon the faithful Israelite in his covenant with Yahweh.

There are still other ways of sealing or ratifying a covenant that, though not utilizing the symbolism of blood, bespeak a similar consecration or offering of self. These gestures that signify a similar familial intimacy include the giving of a hand, a kiss, or a gift (cf. Gn 21:27; Hos 12:2), the sharing of a meal (cf. Gn 26:30; 31:46; Jos 9:14–15; 2 Sm 3:20), or the bestowal of a garment (cf. 1 Sm 18:3–4; Ez 16:8).[16] In the case of marriage, it is sexual intimacy that serves as the gesture that seals or symbolizes a couple's covenant oath.

Sex as Covenantal: Genesis 2

The fact that some of the prophets, beginning with Hosea, used marriage as a symbol for Yahweh's covenant with his people is well known. Influenced by this symbolism, later biblical writings also use the term *berith* for the relationship of marriage itself (cf. Mal 2:14; Prv 2:17). This has led some scholars to conclude that the idea of covenant and its application to marriage was a relatively late and rather inconsequential development within Israelite thought.[17] Such a conclusion overlooks the way in which the second

16. Cf. Hugenberger, who notes that many of these gestures can themselves be considered "oath-signs" and that some do suggest a self-maledictory character. *Marriage as a Covenant*, 193–96, 199–200.

17. See, e.g., Lothar Perlitt, *Bundestheologie im Alten Testament*, Wissenschaftliche Monographien zum Alten und Neuen Testament 36 (Neukirchen-Vluyn: Neukirchener Verlag, 1969); and Ernest W. Nicholson, *God and His People: Covenant and Theology in the Old Testament* (Oxford: Clarendon, 1986), 68–82.

creation account in Genesis, which is often thought to date from the tenth century BC, lays a foundation for these developments in its rich use of covenant language and imagery to describe the creation of woman and her subsequent union with man.[18]

After describing the creation of the man (*adam*) and his placement in Eden as its caretaker, the second creation account sounds a strikingly discordant note: "It is not good for the man to be alone" (Gn 2:18b).[19] The tension in the narrative builds as the search for an *ezer kenegdo* "suitable partner" remains unresolved in the creation of the animals (Gn 2:18–20).[20]

18. The dating of the opening chapters of Genesis, and indeed the whole documentary hypothesis concerning the composition of the Pentateuch, has been subjected to an enormous amount of controversy among scholars. For a recent overview and defense of the source critical approach to the study of the Pentateuch, see Joel S. Baden, *The Composition of the Pentateuch: Renewing the Documentary Hypothesis*, Anchor Yale Bible Reference Library (New Haven, CT: Yale University, 2012). For an overview of some of these recent challenges, see Jonathan Huddleston, "Recent Scholarship on the Pentateuch: Historical, Literary, and Theological Reflections," *Revue de Qumran* 55 (2013): 193–211. In spite of these challenges, some scholars still attribute Gn 2–3 to a larger Yahwist source. See, e.g., the reconstruction of the Yahwist history of Gn 2 through Nm 25 by Christopher Levin, "The Text of the Yahwist's History," in *Re-reading the Scriptures: Essays on the Literary History of the Old Testament*, Forschungen zum Alten Testament 87 (Tübingen: Mohr Siebeck, 2013), 25–49. Scholars also debate whether Gn 2–3 is a unified composition or the product of differing sources written at different times. For arguments for their basic unity, see Erhard Blum, "Von Gottesunmittelbarkeit zu Gottähnliekeit: Überlegungen zur theologischen Anthropologie der Paradieserzählung," in *Gottes Nähe im Alten Testament*, Stuttgarter Bibelstudien 202, ed. Gönke Eberhardt and Kathrin Liess (Stuttgart: Katholisches Bibelwerk, 2004), 9–29; and Jean-Louis Ska, "Genesis 2–3: Some Fundamental Questions," in *Beyond Eden: The Biblical Story of Paradise (Genesis 2–3) and Its Reception History*, Forschungen zum Alten Testament 2.34 (Tübingen: Mohr Siebeck, 2008), 1–27.

19. English citations are from the New American Bible Revised Edition (NABRE) unless otherwise noted. The discordant character of this statement is seen especially when juxtaposed against the affirmation of the goodness of all that God made in Gn 1:31. The author of the first creation account, who did the final redaction of this material, presumably allowed the dissonance created by this statement to remain precisely because of the importance of what it introduces.

20. Translation my own. On the basic equality of woman and man denoted by the use of the term *'ezer*, see Lisa Sowle Cahill, *Between the Sexes: Foundations for a Christian Ethics of Sexuality* (Philadelphia: Fortress, 1985), 54; and Erich Zenger, "Die Erschaffung des Menschen als Mann und Frau: Eine Lesehilfe für die sogenannte Paradies—und Sündenfalgeschichte Gen 2,4b–3,24," *Bibel und Kirche* 58 (2003): 12–15. On the enduring value of the creation accounts' anthropological reflections and their presentation of the relations between the sexes for contemporary questions, see André Wénn, "Humain et nature, femme et home: Differences fondatrices ou initiales? Réflexions à partir de creation en Genèse 1–3," *Recherches de Science Religieuse* 101 (2013): 401–20.

The stage is set for the climax of this part of the narrative in the account of the creation of woman (Gn 2:21*ff.*).

Of particular interest is the wealth of covenant language contained in this section of the Genesis narrative. Verse 21 describes Yahweh as casting a *tardemah* "deep sleep" on the man. As used in the OT, this term sometimes indicates God's activity in providing protection (cf. 1 Sm 26:12) or bringing judgment (cf. Is 29:10). It also denotes the slumber that precedes divine revelation, whether in word or vision (cf. Jb 4:13, 33:15).[21] But perhaps the closest use to this present one is that found in the narrative of Genesis 15. In Genesis 15:12, a *tardemah* falls upon Abram prior to his vision of Yahweh in the culmination of their covenant ceremony. Thus the term, while usually associated with divine action or communication, also has the particular connotation of the state that precedes a covenant. This connotation is suggested by the state of *adam* in Genesis 2:21 before Yahweh creates the woman.

The man's poetic cry of joy upon meeting the mate given him by God is also redolent of covenant imagery, but injects it into a distinctively nuptial context.[22] *Adam* exclaims "this one, at last, is bone of my bone and flesh of my flesh" (Gn 2:23). As used in the OT, the phrase "bone of my bone and flesh of my flesh" can indicate kinship (cf. Gn 29:14) or a covenant oath that expresses a claim or promise of allegiance. For example, when the northern tribes of Israel came to David in Hebron wanting to express a claim on him as to why he should be their king, they said: "Here we are, your bone and your flesh" (2 Sm 5:1b–c; cf. Jgs 9:2; 2 Sm 19:13–14; 1 Chr 11:1).[23] In the present case, the exclamation indicates both the close relationship of the man (*ish*) and the woman (*ishah*) created to be his suitable partner and the

21. On the range of usage of this term in the OT (both in the Hebrew text and the Septuagint [LXX]), see Manfred Görg, "Tardema—'Tiefschaf,' 'Ekstase' oder?" *Biblische Notizen* 110 (2001): 19–24. Görg finds an Egyptian background to the word, which denotes the "weariness of heart" associated with death. It also has connotations of incubation in a temple prior to being presented to a deity.

22. Gerhard von Rad describes the scene in this way: "God himself, like a father of the bride, leads the woman to the man." See *Genesis: A Commentary*, trans. John H. Marks (Philadelphia: Westminster, 1961), 82.

23. Claus Westermann, following W. Reiser, describes the phrase as "the formula of relationship." See *Genesis 1–11: A Commentary*, trans. John J. Scullion, SJ (Minneapolis: Augsburg, 1984), 232. For an analysis of these texts as covenant formulae, see Walter Brueggemann, "Of the Same Flesh and Bone," *Catholic Biblical Quarterly* 32 (1970): 535–38.

oath that unites them.[24] While the oath is not self-imprecating in its for-mulation, it nevertheless is made before God (since the woman is not ad-dressed in the exclamation) and indicates a promise of allegiance or loyalty that now binds the pair together.[25] As noted in the preceding section, such an oath is in fact constitutive of a covenant.

The covenantal motif continues in the succeeding verse (Gn 2:24) with the statement of the narrator that "that is why a man leaves his father and mother and clings to his wife, and the two of them become one body."[26] Both the verb *azab* "to leave, to forsake" and the verb *dabaq* "to cling" are often found in covenant formulations.

The first of these terms, *azab*, is common in the Hebrew of the OT. What is noteworthy is the variety of its uses in covenantal contexts. It is used in declarations of God's faithfulness (cf. Gn 24:27; Neh 9:17c, 19:19, 19:31; 1 Chr 28:20b; Pss 37:25, 37:28, 94:14; Ez 9:9), God's promises of fi-delity (cf. Gn 28:15; Jos 1:5; 1 Kgs 6:13), exhortations based on this fidelity (cf. Dt 31:6, 31:8), or promises of restoration (cf. Is 41:17, 42:16c, 54:7, 60:15, 62:12b). This verb can also be found in warnings against "forsaking" the covenant with Yahweh (cf. Dt 28:20; Jos 24:20; 2 Chr 7:19*ff.*), predictions of covenant apostasy and its consequences (cf. Dt 31:16–17), descriptions

24. Brueggemann too sees Gn 2:23 as a covenant oath and makes the further observation that both terms in the pair have a double meaning. Thus understood, "flesh-weakness" and "bone-power" describe the whole range of possibilities that might occur and test the fidelity of a couple's oath to one another (similar to the "in sickness and in health, in plenty and in want" of more recent wedding vows). "Of the Same Flesh and Bone," 533–35, 539.

25. Cf. Hugenberger, *Marriage as a Covenant*, 164–65. Hugenberger also gathers a wealth of ANE and biblical examples of oaths or gestures that are not self-maledictions but are in fact solemn declarations made before God or *verba solemnia*, many of which are used in the context of sex and marriage (see 185–279).

26. The text can also be translated "one flesh" because the Hebrew word *basar* has both meanings. In fact, "flesh" is the more typical OT usage. See John A. T. Robinson, *The Body: A Study in Pauline Theology* (Philadelphia: Westminster, 1952), 17–19. The verse as a whole is cu-rious given the etiological character of the second creation account, since the legal situation of woman in the rather patriarchal Israelite society was just the opposite—it was she who left her family to become part of the *bayith* "house" of her husband. Cf. Cahill, *Between the Sexes*, 55. For a range of possible interpretations of this verse that attempt to read it within this etiologi-cal context, see Paul Krueger, "Etiology or Obligation: Genesis 2:24 Reconsidered in the Light of Text Linguistics," *Thinking toward New Horizons: Collected Communications to the XIXth Congress of the International Organization for the Study of the Old Testament, Ljubljana 2007*, Beitr e zur Erforschung des Alten Testaments und des Antiken Judentums 55 (Frankfurt: Lang, 2008), 35–47.

of actual covenant infidelity (cf. Jgs 2:12–13, 10:6; 1 Sm 12:10; 1 Kgs 19:10, 19:14; 2 Kgs 17:16; 2 Chr 21:10), or pronouncements that reprove the infidelity of the people to the covenant (Jer 22:9; Ez 20:8).[27] The term also figures in prayers of repentance (cf. Jgs 10:10; 1 Sm 12:10) or those that beg the Lord for his continued fidelity (cf. 1 Kgs 8:57; Pss 27:9, 71:9, 71:18, 119:8). It is also used in covenant oaths where the people swear fidelity to Yahweh (cf. Jos 24:16). Or it can indicate an oath in which one person binds himself or herself to another (cf. Ru 1:16, 2:11; 2 Kgs 2:2, 2:4, 2:6, 4:30).

The common denominator in these varied uses is the idea of the covenant. God's faithfulness to his people demands that they leave or forsake all that deflects them from their covenant relationship to himself. It is particularly noteworthy that *azab* is sometimes used in conjunction with covenant marital symbolism either to reprove those who refuse to forsake evil (cf. Ez 23:8), or those who have forsaken the Lord (cf. Hos 4:10), or their spouse (Prv 2:17), or to promise restoration (cf. Is 54:6, 62:4). In this way, the reciprocal hermeneutic of covenant imagery becomes apparent as the exclusivity of Israel's relationship with Yahweh inscribed at the head of the Decalogue (i.e., "You shall not have other gods beside me" [Ex 20:3]) begins to color its later understanding of the marriage covenant with growing expectations of fidelity.[28] The marital symbol will in turn impart an undercurrent of love and intimacy to Israel's relationship with Yahweh.

27. One finds numerous uses of the term in the context of condemnations of infidelity of the people to the Lord or the law of the Lord, some of which may have covenant connotations (cf. Jgs 10:13; 1 Kgs 11:33, 18:18; 2 Kgs 22:17; 2 Chr 12:5, 24:20, 34:25; Is 1:4, 58:2b; Jer 1:16, 2:13, 2:17, 5:19, 16:11, 19:4).

28. One can discern a gradual evolution in OT traditions in this regard. While monogamy was regarded as a theological and practical ideal, the value of fecundity and desire for powerful family led, in some cases, to the practice of polygamy. Hence the Genesis narratives describe rather straightforwardly the fact that some of the patriarchs (e.g., Abraham, Jacob) had more than one wife. This reality is reflected in laws that prevent the children of the favorite wife from inheriting an unjust share (cf. Dt 21:15–17). But even here there is growing awareness of the pitfalls of such a practice. This is highlighted through a kind of genealogical editorializing in some traditions: the patriarchs of Seth's line are monogamous (e.g., Noah, Gn 7:7); however, Cain's descendants (esp. Lamech, Gn 4:19) are polygamous. The point is underscored by the descriptions of Esau's marriage to foreign women (Gn 26:34, 28:9, 36:1–5). Later OT traditions reveal monogamy to be increasingly normative in Israelite society. The books of Samuel and Kings, e.g., do not record one instance of bigamy among commoners (with the exception of Elkanah—cf. 1 Sm 1–2). Likewise, the Wisdom literature presupposes monogamy in its teaching on the joys and difficulties of faithful monogamous marriage.

The second of the two verbs, *dabaq* "to cling," also has covenantal con-notations. Specifically, it is found in admonitions to "hold fast" or "cleave" to Yahweh in faithful obedience (cf. Dt 10:20, 11:22, 13:18, 30:20; Jos 22:5, 23:8), in declarations of real or intended fidelity (cf. 2 Kgs 18:6; Pss 101:3, 119:31; Jer 13:11), or even in self-imprecating oaths (cf. Jb 31:7–8; Ps 137:6). It also designates the curses for disobedience that will "cling" to those unfaith-ful to God (cf. Dt 28:21, 28:60; Jer 42:16). In at least one instance, *dabaq* is used to indicate the bonds of friendship (cf. Prv 18:24). This term too can have specifically marital connotations indicating affection (cf. Gn 34:3; 1 Kgs 11:3a) or intermarriage with other nations (cf. Jo 23:12; 1 Kgs 11:2–3; Dan 2:43).

As used together in Genesis 2:24, the two terms build upon the cove-nant oath that precedes them by indicating, respectively, the termination of one loyalty and the espousal of a new one in the marriage relationship.[29] Hence when the narrative is read within the linguistic horizon of the OT, it becomes clear that the singular devotion and fidelity required by Yahweh is also to characterize the commitment of spouses to one another.

Thus the net effect of this wealth of covenant terminology used by the second creation account is to describe the relationship of male and female as covenantal in character.[30] Emerging from his covenant sleep, the man binds himself to the woman by an oath. This oath is then used as an explanation for the man's leaving his family and clinging to his wife so that together they form a new entity—"one flesh." This term denotes the new familial commu-nion that the oath creates between male and female—a communion that includes and is expressed by sexual intimacy.[31]

29. Cf. Brueggemann, "Of the Same Flesh and Bone," 540; Hugenberger, *Marriage as a Covenant*, 159–60.

30. The marriage prayer of Tobiah and Sarah (Tb 8:5–9) draws not on prophetic theology but on the account in Gn 2. Cf. Palmer, "Christian Marriage," 623. In the NT, Jesus will appeal to the same text to ground his teaching concerning marital indissolubility (cf. Mk 10:2–12 and par.).

31. While the particular expression "familial communion" is my own, it is basically a syn-thesis of two related positions. The first is that of Maurice Gilbert, SJ, whose excellent study of the term in Genesis and subsequent biblical traditions concludes that "one flesh" is to be under-stood in the sense of bondedness that results from and is expressed by sexual union. See "'Une seule chair' (Gn 2, 24)," *Nouvelle revue théologique* 100 (1978): 66–89. The second is that of Hugenberger, who adds the nuance of a "familial" bondedness. This, as he points out, creates a balance between the family of parents that is "left" in Gn 2:24 and the new one created by mar-

The relationship of the following verse to that which precedes it is less clear. The text says that "the man and his wife were both naked, yet they felt no shame" (Gn 2:25). The interpretation of the couple's "nakedness" is difficult for a number of reasons. First, the reference is obviously a transition verse to the next part of the narrative.[32] Second, there is a wealth of patristic interpretation, undoubtedly colored by various forms of dualistic thinking, which associates sex in some way with sin and thus refuses to consider the possibility of prelapsarian sex.[33] Third, in many cultures, including that of the OT, nudity can have multiple associations or meanings attached to it.[34] Thus the Israelite reader might well see here an allusion to the lack of deceit (symbolized by the absence of veils) or to the openness that characterized the communication and community of the pair.[35]

In spite of this ambiguity, however, the "nakedness" of the couple, for both the Israelite and the modern reader, is also a circumlocution that bespeaks sexual intimacy. This is especially evident when the text is considered in the context of the passage as a whole and of the preceding verse in particular.[36] Sex serves to both express and foster the "one flesh" unity of the cou-

---

riage. He also points out that *basar* is used in other OT texts with the connotation of family or kin (cf. Gn 29:14, 37:27; Lv 18:6, 25:49; 2 Sm 5:1; Is 58:7). *Marriage as a Covenant*, 162–63.

32. This is indicated both by the wordplay of *arumim* "naked" in Gn 2:25 with *arum* "cunning" in Gn 3:1 and by the contrast this verse offers to the association of shame with nakedness after the interposition of sin (Gn 3:7). Cf. Hugenberger, *Marriage as a Covenant*, 152n113. But this observation causes Hugenberger to regard Gn 2:25 as merely transitional and therefore to largely overlook its meaning.

33. On the prevalence of such ideas among various groups and thinkers of the early Christian era, see Peter Brown, *The Body and Society: Men, Women and Sexual Renunciation in Early Christianity* (New York: Columbia University, 1988), 86, 93–96, 175, 186, 268, 294–98.

34. For an overview of nudity and its associations in various cultures, including that of the OT, see Mario Perniola, "Between Clothing and Nudity," in *Fragments for a History of the Human Body*, Part II, ed. Michel Feher with Ramona Naddaff and Nadia Tazi (New York: Zone, 1989), 237–65.

35. Hence André-Marie Dubarle, OP, sees it as an indication of "mutual trust and esteem." See "Original Sin in Genesis," trans. John Higgens, *Downside Review* 76 (1958): 242. This sense of nakedness is obviously at work in Gn 3:10, where the inability to remain naked in God's presence follows the couple's sin, thus indicating the breakdown of open communication between humanity and God.

36. Gerhard von Rad argues that "the Jahwist's story of creation practically issues in this aetiological explanation of the power of *eros* as one of the urges implanted in man by the Creator himself (v. 24f.), and so gives the relationship between man and woman the dignity of being the greatest miracle and mystery of creation." See *Old Testament Theology*, vol. 1, trans. David M. G. Stalker (New York: Harper, 1965), 150.

ple. In terms of the depiction of the covenantal nature of the male-female relationship, sexual intimacy seals or enacts the covenant oath that binds them.[37] It is the embodied gesture that expresses the new relationship that their covenant creates between them. Sex, therefore, as a recollection and enactment of the covenant oath, takes on a liturgical function within the marriage relationship akin to other covenant-making gestures (e.g., the sprinkling with blood, table fellowship) described above. One of the primary functions of liturgy in biblical thought is to remember in a way that makes present the event commemorated.[38] Sexual union is thus understood as a kind of anamnesis that recalls precisely the totality of a couple's gift to one another expressed in their oath.

Covenantal Sexuality Fallen and Redeemed

The positive presentation of the equality of man and woman and the sexual union as a ratification of the marriage covenant found in Genesis 2 is sharply qualified by the account of the couple's sin in Genesis 3. At the instigation of the serpent, the woman and the man misuse their freedom by trying to "be like gods who know what is good and what is bad" (Gn 3:5c) by eating the fruit of tree of the knowledge of good and evil.[39] This act of rebellion produces dramatic consequences. No longer will they be able to be naked in one another's presence without shame (cf. Gn 3:7, 3:10), a condition in-

---

37. This is also the view of Hugenberger, though he bases it upon OT traditions other than Gn 2. His argument stands upon the convergence of a number of strands of evidence: the consensus in current scholarship against the notion of "marriage by purchase" (which views the marriage as primarily a transaction between a man and his father-in-law versus covenant between a man and woman); that there is both biblical and extrabiblical evidence for the idea that intercourse consummates a marriage; that a number of texts (e.g., Gn 34; Ex 22:15–16; Dt 22:28–29; 2 Sm 13) all evidence a view that a marriage should be formalized after sexual union (in some cases even after forced sex); that even marriages based on deception (e.g., that between Jacob and Leah in Gn 29) appear to have been regarded as irrevocable once ratified in intercourse; and the apparent connection between oath taking and genitalia evident in practices such as circumcision or placing one's hand under another's thigh (cf. Gn 24:2, 24:9, 47:29). *Marriage as a Covenant*, 216–79.

38. See, e.g., the injunctions concerning the celebration of the Passover in Ex 12:1–28.

39. Some scholars argue that the description of the Fall in the garden reflects the story of the archetypical sin of the people of Israel in worshipping the golden calf in Ex 32. See, e.g., Jan Joosten, "Que s'est-il passè au jardin d'Eden?," *Revue des Sciences Religieuses* 86 (2012): 493–501.

dicating both the entrance of deceit into human communication and the disordering of sexuality. Shame thus marks the boundary of the experience of postlapsarian sexuality, signaling the body's vulnerability to exploitation alongside its capacity for self-donation.[40] Instead of relationships founded on honest mutual attraction and lived in covenantal unity, relationships between men and women will be marked by the poles of domination and subservience in a continuing struggle for power (cf. Gn 3:16d–e).[41] Sexuality, while still understood in covenantal terms, will henceforth be lived within a markedly diminished existence.

Numerous OT traditions highlight this diminishment of historical sexuality yet also offer a trajectory of hope for its ultimate healing. One example of this can be found in the developing understanding of adultery. In what has usually been regarded as the older version of the Decalogue (Ex 20), the prohibition regarding adultery (Ex 20:14) is modified by that concerning coveting (Ex 20:17). This latter injunction begins with the basic precept that "you shall not covet your neighbor's house" and then goes on to specify the contents of this house—wife, slaves, property. Thus the prohibition focuses on the (property) rights of the husband. A man could presumably have sex with unmarried women or prostitutes. The later Deuteronomic formulation of the Decalogue (Dt 5) expands this one law into two by separating the woman (Dt 5:21a) from the neighbor's house and property (Dt 5:21b–e).[42] This development has the effect of suggesting that

40. On shame as a boundary between prelapsarian and historical experience of the body and sexuality, see John Paul II's weekly general audiences of April 30, May 14, and May 28, 1980, in *The Theology of the Body: Human Love in the Divine Plan*, trans. L'Osservatore Romano, English ed. (Boston: Pauline, 1997), 108–17. Cf. Karol Wojtyła, *Love and Responsibility*, trans. H. T. Willets (New York: Farrar, Straus and Giroux, 1981; reprint, San Francisco: Ignatius, 1993), 186–93. For Wojtyła / John Paul II, shame can also have a positive function, as it serves as reminder of the dignity of the person manifested in through the body in a fallen world. Biblical scholars have made a similar point, pointing out that the shame described in Gn 3 can have a positive function in the wider OT insofar as it prevents one from doing committing evil deeds. On this, see Alexandra Grund, "Und sie schämten sich nicht ... (Genesis 2,25): Zur altentestamentlichen Anthropologie der Scham im Spiegel von Genesis 2–3," *Was ist der Mensch, dass du seiner gedenkst? (Psalm 8,5): Aspekte einer theologischen Anthropologie. Festschrift für Bernd Janowski zum 65. Geburtstag* (Neukirchen-Vluyn: Neukirchener Verlag, 2008), 115–22.

41. On domination over the other, and particularly male domination of women as the effect of sin, see John Paul's weekly general audiences of June 18 and 25, 1980, in *Theology of the Body*, 120–25; and Apostolic Letter, *Mulieris dignitatem*, 10.

42. Some scholars have argued that the Deuteronomic version of the Decalogue is in fact

married Israelite women are not mere possessions within the household. Later biblical traditions will more clearly exclude extramarital sex for men (cf. 2 Sm 12; Jb 31:1, 31:9–12; Prv 5:15–23; Sir 9:5–9, 41:22ff.).[43]

Another example of the promise of a restored sexuality in the midst of its historical diminution can be found in the OT insistence on the holiness of sex. Over against the cosmologies and ritual practices of many of its neighbors, Israel steadfastly refused to deify sex by crudely projecting it onto God and equating it with worship. Yet this did not prevent sexuality from being seen as something holy—the demythologization of sex did not necessarily entail its desacralization.[44] This is evident both in the view of it as quasi-liturgical activity within marriage (described above) and the injunctions against specific kinds of sexual activity found in the legal traditions of the Pentateuch, such as those embedded in the Holiness Code (Lv 17–26) in Leviticus 18. Not only do such norms show significant development as outlined above, but they also serve as stimuli for deeper theological reflection. One can find adultery referred to as "the great sin" *chataah gedolah* in various traditions (e.g., Gn 20:9, 39:9). The same term is used elsewhere to describe idolatry (cf. the account of the Golden Calf in Ex 32:21, 32:30, 32:31, and its application to Jeroboam's calves in 2 Kgs 17:21).[45] Such texts suggest a parallel between adultery and idolatry. Historically, this association undoubtedly is in reaction to the fertility rituals and child sacrifice found in the idolatrous worship of many of Israel's neighbors.[46]

---

older than the material found in Exodus. See, e.g., Frank-Lothar Hossfeld, *Der Dekalog: Seine späten Fassungen, die originale Komposition und seine Vorstufen*, Orbis Biblicus Orientalis 45 (Freiburg: Universitätsverlag, 1982); and Reinhard Gregor Kratz, "Der Dekalog im Exodusbuch," *Vetus Testamentum* 44 (1994): 205–38. This is still not the view of most scholars, however.

43. On this development, see Ernst, "Marriage as an Institution," 42–46, 51.

44. On the difference between Israelite and Canaanite religion on this point, see von Rad, *Genesis*, 58–59; idem, *Old Testament Theology*, 1, 28, 146. Von Rad unfortunately uses the terms "demythologize" and "desacrilize" interchangeably, thereby obscuring an important nuance in OT thought.

45. The usage has other ancient Near Eastern parallels. See Jacob J. Rabinowitz, "The 'Great Sin' in Ancient Egyptian Marriage Contracts," *Journal of Near Eastern Studies* 18 (1959): 73; William L. Moran, "The Scandal of the 'Great Sin' at Ugarit," *Journal of Near Eastern Studies* 18 (1959): 280–81.

46. On the prevalence of "sacralized unchastity" and child sacrifice in the cultures surrounding ancient Israel and its parallel to our own culture's pursuit of sexual license and frequent recourse to abortion, see Patrick Riley, *Civilising Sex: On Chastity and the Common Good* (Edinburgh: T&T Clark, 2000), 100–113.

Theologically, however, it indicates a judgment that adultery and idolatry are both, at root, forms of covenant infidelity.

This points to yet another example of the OT's promise of a restoration of sexuality—the very idea of covenant. The analogy between the marriage covenant and the people's covenant with Yahweh found in the Pentateuch and historical books is reflected and developed further in prophetic theology. This teaching works on different levels. First, one can find condemnations of actual adultery (cf. Jer 7:9–10; Hos 4:1–2) where it is classified with other sins such as treachery (cf. Jer 9:2), misuse of God's name (cf. Jer 29:23), and oppression of widows (cf. Mal 3:5). Second, adultery is used as a symbol to condemn the people's infidelity to God. In its worship of false gods, Israel has played the harlot or adulterated her covenant with Yahweh (this imagery recurs throughout texts such as Jer 2–3, 30–31; Ez 16, 23; Hos 1–4). Third, the positive expression of this marital understanding of the covenant is found in promises of restoration when Yahweh promises that he will again marry his people (cf. Isa 54:1, 62:1–7; Zep 3:14–18).

In these various strands, one observes again the reciprocal hermeneutic between these covenant relationships, which were central to Israel's life. Both the covenant with Yahweh and the covenant of marriage demand a faithful and exclusive promise of self. To give oneself to a stranger in worshiping a false god or to have sex with someone other than one's spouse falsifies this covenant oath. The gesture is authentic only in relation to the oath that it recalls and enacts. Here one can begin to discern an analogy between sex and worship as activities that ratify or seal the covenant oath.[47] Both parallel other liturgical gestures that seal or ratify a covenant.

A related theology can be found in the New Testament (NT), transposed by the author of Ephesians to the relationship between Christ and the Church.[48] The text (Eph 5:21–33) appears to utilize the literary form of a *Haustafel* "household code" and builds upon Pauline new creation theology.[49] Here the human and divine spheres of relationship are even more tightly

---

47. In this same vein, one can also consider the increasing tendency toward allegorical interpretation of the postexilic love poetry found in the Song of Songs. While it seems remarkable to apply sexual imagery to divine/human love, it is perhaps understandable in light of the theology of covenant and the implicit parallel between sex and worship.

48. One can see the connection with some of the OT texts considered above (especially Gn 2) even though the author does not use the term *diathēkē* "covenant."

49. See Stephen F. Miletic, *"One Flesh": Ephesians 5:22–24, 5:31. Marriage and the New*

interwoven with the thread of marital symbolism as the passage moves back and forth between the two levels. The mutual self-giving love of husband and wife images the union of Christ and the Church. The head-body relationship of Christ and the Church illumines the "one flesh" unity of husband and wife (cf. Eph 5:23, 5:31).[50] The seal of this marital relation in the case of Christ and the Church is the sacrificial love demonstrated in Christ "handing himself over" for the Church "to sanctify her, cleansing her by the bath of water and the word" (Eph 5:25c, 5:26). The baptismal imagery here is an allusion to Jesus's self-giving love on the Cross.[51] This in turn demands an equally selfless love on the part of Christian spouses who are joined as *mia sarx* "one flesh" (Eph 5:31). The place of sex within this vision is largely left unstated, except perhaps in the allusion to the "one flesh" of Genesis 2:24 and an implied contrast between the holiness demanded by new life in Christ and pagan sexual excess (cf. Eph 4:19–20).

The preceding overview of select biblical traditions discloses a connection between God's covenant relationship to his people (in the NT identified as the relationship of Christ and the Church), the covenant between man and woman in marriage, and sexual intimacy, which serves to seal or enact the nuptial oath. The analogous character of the covenant relations allows a flexible application of marital imagery—idolatry is tantamount to adultery; adultery is reductive idolatry. The intensity and exclusivity of covenant relationships require a complete and faithful offering of self in worship and sexual self-donation, respectively. In this association of covenant, marriage, and sex, one finds the foundations for a theology of sexuality. It is to the historical and theological implications of this view that this chapter now turns.

Creation, Analecta Biblica 115 (Rome: Pontifical Biblical Institute, 1988). On the similarities and differences of these texts to Jewish, Greek, and Roman texts found in the broader Hellenistic culture, see Francis Martin, "Marriage in the New Testament Period," in *Christian Marriage: A Historical Survey*, ed. Glen W. Olsen (New York: Crossroad, 2001), 50–100, esp. 83–92.

50. The language of "headship" in the passage need not indicate an inferior standing on the part of wives. The context of the passage is explicitly one of mutual submission (Eph 5:21); the duties enjoined on spouses are reciprocal (unlike those in Hellenistic versions of the *Hastaufeln*); and the exhortation, while using language reflective of the culture of the time, calls both spouses to unselfish love, service, and respect. Cf. John Paul II, Apostolic Letter, *Mulieris dignitatem*, 24.

51. The verb *paredoken* is often used in the NT as a technical term for the Passion. Likewise, one can note the close association of baptism with the death and resurrection of Christ in Pauline theology (cf. Rm 6:1–11).

Intercourse as Anamnesis: Theological Developments

It is fairly clear that the early Church did not have a developed theology of marriage as a sacrament. While it is true that texts such as Ephesians 5:21–33 laid a foundation for the beginning of theological reflection on the meaning of this relationship "in the Lord,"[52] nevertheless marriage was basically a long-standing social institution that, in spite of typically religious associations in differing cultures, was usually administered by the family and perhaps regulated by the state.[53] Thus it is not surprising to find in Christian theology and practice differing understandings of marriage.

One ancient tradition with NT roots saw the essence of marriage in the marriage "debt" (cf. 1 Cor 7:3–5)—that is, in sexual intercourse—which husband and wife owe one another.[54] Marriage thus grants spouses partic-

---

52. This can be seen through the fact that the term *mystērion*, used by the Letter to the Ephesians to indicate the relationship of husband and wife, is translated by various ante-Nicene authors into Latin as *sacramentum*. In Roman society, this term had the meaning of a sacred oath (made by a soldier to the emperor). See Émile de Backer, "Tertullien," in *Pour l'histoire du mot "Sacramentum,"* ed. Joseph de Ghellinck et al. (Paris: É. Champion, 1924), 66–71. This, along with the fact that the Romans too tended to see marriage as sacred and indeed covenantal, provided an atmosphere in which the assimilation of biblical theology was possible in spite of some linguistic and cultural differences. See Palmer, "Christian Marriage," 618–19, 625–30. Cf. Pheme Perkins, "Marriage in the New Testament and Its World," in *Commitment to Partnership: Explorations in the Theology of Marriage*, ed. William P. Roberts (New York: Paulist, 1987), 26. More recent scholarship has highlighted the range of usage of such terms in patristic thought. See, e.g., Joseph Leinhard, SJ, "*Sacramentum* and Eucharist in Saint Augustine," *The Thomist* 77 (2013):173–92.

53. But the view of Edward Schillebeeckx that marriage was a basically secular institution later sacralized by "clerical intervention" is overstated. See his *Marriage: Human Reality and Saving Mystery*, 2 vols., trans. N. D. Smith (New York: Sheed and Ward, 1965), 245; cf. 194. This view is problematic on at least two counts. First, it overlooks a wealth of evidence from Roman, patristic, and liturgical sources that marriage was seen and celebrated as a religious—specifically covenantal—reality in the first millennium AD. Cf. Palmer, "Christian Marriage," 625–35. Second, it fails to observe that it was precisely a kind of secularization that enabled medieval theology to delimit marriage and the other six sacraments from the other rites in the Church's possession—a distinction rendered difficult in an earlier worldview that considered reality as indistinguishably sacral. See Walter Kasper, *Theology of Christian Marriage*, trans. David Smith (New York: Seabury, 1980), 31–32. Cf. John S. Grabowski, "And So He Revealed His Glory: Cana and the Sacramentality of Marriage," *The Thomist* 78 (2014): 37–63.

54. Authorities such as Jerome, the Emperor Zeno, and later Gratian defended this view. See P. Lyndon Reynolds, "Marriage, Sacramental and Indissoluble: Sources of the Catholic Doctrine," *Downside Review* 109, no. 375 (1991): 131.

ular rights to one another's bodies—a rather revolutionary assertion, given the prevailing view of women as the possession of men and the double standard regarding sexual morality common in the Hellenistic culture that surrounded the nascent Church.[55]

A somewhat different view, flowing from Roman law and introduced by Ambrose and Augustine, saw marriage rooted in the consent of the couple and existing even in the absence of intercourse.[56] Such a position served to underscore the freedom of the couple and aided the later emancipation of marriage from family control. It also coincided with the growing embrace of virginal or spiritual marriage on the part of the Church leaders and theologians inspired by the monastic ideal and somewhat wary of the body and sexuality.

The controversy between proponents of these two traditions came to a head in Western theology in the theological renewal of the High Middle Ages.[57] In the thirteenth century, for example, the canon law faculty of the University of Bologna held to the "debt-oriented" view, while the theology faculty at Paris championed the consensual position.[58] The outcome of the debate was basically a victory for the theologians in that consent came to be seen as that which effects the sacrament.[59]

55. Peter Brown notes that while Christian portrayals of the debauchery of the Roman world are sometimes overstated, it is nevertheless true that female infidelity was harshly punished by law, and male adultery earned no such stricture. Indeed, the "chastity" expected of the male was often thought to be limited to the walls of his house, leaving upper-class men free to seek sexual outlets in the bodies of their female (and male) servants. See Brown, *Body and Society*, 21–24.

56. See Ambrose, *De institutione virginis*, 6 (41), *PL* 16, 331A; Augustine, *De nuptiis et concupiscentia* I.11, *CSEL*, 42, 224; *De consensu evagelistarum*, 2.1.2, *CSEL*, 43, 82. For the Roman understanding of marriage as based on consent versus consummation, see Karl Ritzer, *Le mariage dans les églises chrétiennes du Ier au XIe siècle* (Paris: Éditions du Cerf, 1970), 218–19; and Christopher N. L. Brooke, *The Medieval Idea of Marriage* (Oxford: Clarendon, 1989), 128–29.

57. For the history of this controversy during the medieval period, see Brooke, *Medieval Idea of Marriage*, 129–33, 137–41; and Art Cosgrove, "Consent, Consummation and Indissolubility: Some Evidence from Ecclesiastical Medieval Courts," *Downside Review* 109 (1991): 94–104.

58. One can find canonists as well as theologians who defended the consensual view before and during this same period, however. See James A. Brundage, *Law, Sex, and Christian Society in Medieval Europe* (Chicago: University of Chicago Press, 1987), 348–55, 414–15, 433–39.

59. Hence, even though consummation is considered typical, intercourse is not seen to belong to the essence of marriage. See Bonaventure, *Breviloquium*, 6.13. This also solves the problem that the Pauline view creates in regard to the tradition concerning Mary's perpetual virginity. If one sees intercourse as the essence of marriage, doubt is cast upon Mary and Joseph's union. Cf. Aquinas, *In Sententiarum*, 4.30.2.1–3; Bonaventure, *In Sententiarum*, 4.27.2.1.

But this is not the end of the story. The Pauline emphasis on the sexual and bodily basis of the marriage relationship has been accommodated within past and present canon law through the insistence that it is consummation that renders a sacramental union indissoluble.[60] This seems an odd notion given that it has existed alongside a high sacramental theology that holds to the *ex opere operato* efficacy of the sacraments and the indissolubility of marriage. How can a sacrament be caused by the consent of the couple and yet remain dissoluble until consummation?

An answer emerges when one considers the biblical theology of covenant that provided the soil from which later theological reflection and legislation grew. The oath or promise that one makes in a covenant is indeed its central component, but the covenant is not completed until sealed or ratified. In the case of marriage, it is the mutual consent of the couple expressed in their promise to one another in their vows that causes the sacrament, but this consent remains incomplete until enacted sexually. In coition, a couple seals their covenant with one another by an embodied enactment of their complete self-giving. The unconditional and exclusive character of their mutual promise is enfleshed in the giving of their bodies completely and exclusively to one another. Sex is thus the embodied symbol of a couple's love and communion in a way similar to that in which liturgy symbolizes and enacts the communion between God and his people through gesture and ritual. Though in some sense a private act, as liturgical, sexual intimacy also completes and signifies the relation of the couple as "one flesh" and is an enactment and recollection of their public commitment within the community of faith.[61]

Pope John Paul II has aptly described this total self-donation and fidelity communicated by sexual intimacy within the marriage covenant as a dimension of the "language of the body."[62] Just as one can communicate

60. Thus the present code continues to maintain that for a Christian marriage to be valid and indissoluble, it must be *ratum et consummatum* "ratified and consummated" (can. 1061).

61. It is in this sense that we can understand the public and juridical standing of a marriage, which is *ratum et consummatum*. Cf. Karl Lehmann, "The Sacramentality of Christian Marriage: The Bond between Baptism, Faith and Marriage," in *Contemporary Perspectives on Christian Marriage*, 91–115, esp. 112–13; and Gustav Martelet, "Sixteen Christological Theses on the Sacrament of Marriage," in *Contemporary Perspectives on Christian Marriage*, 275–83, esp. 281–82.

62. See his weekly general audiences of January 5, 12, 19, and 26, 1983, in *Theology of the Body*, 354–65.

through bodily gestures as well as words, in sexual union a married couple "speak" a language on the basis of their masculinity and femininity. That which is communicated in this somatic dialogue is both a word of fidelity and of total self-giving. Fidelity because a couple gives themselves to one another in this way and to no other. Total self-donation because intercourse enacts in bodily form the unconditional promise and acceptance articulated by the couple in their wedding vows.

In this sense, marital sex is genuinely sacramental; that is, it is integral to the sacrament itself as the completion and recollection of the consent that causes it. This is true not only of the first time a marriage is consummated, as a narrow reading of canon law might suggest, but also of all of the conjugal acts that make up the sexual communion of a couple. These too recall and in fact make present the grace that a couple's consent conferred on them. They thus participate in the marriage bond that unites a man and woman as "one flesh" over the whole of their lives.

Such observations suggest a fundamental analogy between the offering of self to God in the act of worship and the sexual self-giving of spouses to one another. Both are liturgical actions that recall and symbolize a covenant relation through a bodily gesture of self-donation. They are embodied gestures meant to symbolize and deepen communion. Both are encounters of love that are basic to establishing the I-Thou relation that underlies community—whether this be the community between God and humanity in the covenant or that between male and female in marriage. An awareness of this parallel can be discerned within some of the prayers found in the liturgical tradition, such as the ancient formula for the blessing of the nuptial chamber, which names it as the place of the "worthy celebration" of marriage.[63] It is equally evident in the late medieval formula for the bridegroom's gift of the ring to his bride: "With this ring I thee wed and this gold and silver I thee give; and with my body I thee worship, and with all my worldly chattel I thee honor."[64]

---

63. The citation is from the Spanish, *Liber Ordinum*, in Mark Searle and Kenneth W. Stevenson, *Documents of the Marriage Liturgy* (Collegeville: Liturgical Press, 1992), 122.

64. *The Sarum Missal*, in *Documents of the Marriage Liturgy*, 167. The text here is somewhat modernized from the old English spelling. The Sarum rite originated in the diocese of Salisbury in the thirteenth century. From here it spread to other English dioceses and became the preferred rite of the English churches both before and after the Reformation, finding its way into both English versions of the Roman rite and the *Book of Common Prayer*. On the

Conclusion

The Second Vatican Council's Pastoral Constitution on the Church, *Gaudium et spes*, has been widely hailed for its recovery of the biblical language of covenant to describe marriage. According to the Council, marriage is "an intimate partnership of … life and love … rooted in the conjugal covenant of irrevocable personal consent," which comes into being through "that human act whereby spouses mutually bestow and accept one another."[65] One important result of this recovery is the opportunity it affords to once again situate not only marriage but also sexuality within a biblical framework.

This study has argued that, in light of both the biblical witness and aspects of the Church's liturgical and sacramental tradition, sex can be rightly understood as an activity that seals the covenant relationship between man and woman in marriage. As such, it has an anamnetic quality in that it is a recollection and enactment of what the couple promise in their vows to one another. There is a fruitful convergence here between the biblical insistence on the covenant as a personal oath and contemporary personalist descriptions of sex as embodied self-giving—a convergence that has begun to be developed by the teaching of Pope John Paul II. This convergence brings into view the analogy between worship and sex as parallel forms of self-donation that seal a covenant relationship.

That such analogous relations exist is unsurprising given the relational quality of the human person. To be in relation to God and to be in relation to other human beings is fundamental to human existence. The witness of the biblical tradition suggests that the primordial form of human relationality is the partnership of women and men in marriage. It is for this reason that the intimacy at the heart of this relation can symbolize and even mediate something of the love of God made available to humanity in the death and resurrection of Christ. It is this same self-giving love that husband and wife both promise and enact bodily in their sexual relationship.

---

rather tumultuous history of this particular form in the Anglican communion, see Paul Elmen, "On Worshipping the Bride," *Anglican Theological Review* 68 (1986): 241–49. For a contemporary Catholic consideration of this view, see Germán Martinez, "Marriage as Worship: A Theological Analogy," *Worship* 62 (1988): 332–53.

65. *Gaudium et spes*, no. 48. The citation is from *Documents of Vatican II*, 250. On the significance of this language, see Theodore Mackin, *The Marital Sacrament: Marriage in the Catholic Church* (New York: Paulist, 1989), 539–44.

Gaudium et spes describes marriage as not only "a reflection of the loving covenant uniting Christ and the Church" but also " a participation in that covenant."[66] To this theological vision the present study would append the idea that the sexual communion of husband and wife both symbolizes and mediates the grace of this covenant relation.

66. *Gaudium et spes*, no. 48; *Documents of Vatican II*, 252.

CHAPTER 5

Person or Nature?

Rival Personalisms in Twentieth-Century Catholic Sexual Ethics

Recent studies have called attention to a methodological "paradigm shift" underway in Catholic moral theology that has begun to move from a focus upon the category of nature to that of person.[1] But it is equally clear that the notion of person and its relevance to moral reflection is not univocal. Thus there are sharply different understandings of this new "personalist" approach to moral theology and its implications for issues of sexual ethics.[2]

This study argues that at the heart of these competing understandings of personalism are divergent understandings of the key concepts of "person," "nature," and sexuality and their interrelationships. By tracing these divergent understandings, this essay endeavors to identify different strands of contemporary personalism and gain some critical leverage on that which separates them.

Originally published as "Person or Nature? Rival Personalisms in 20th Century Catholic Sexual Ethics," *Studia Moralia* 35 (1997): 283–312.

1. See, e.g., John Mahoney, *The Making of Moral Theology: A Study of the Roman Catholic Tradition* (Oxford: Clarendon Press, 1987), 310; Charles Curran, "Official Catholic Social and Sexual Teachings: A Methodological Comparison," in *Tensions in Moral Theology* (Notre Dame, IN: University of Notre Dame Press, 1988), 93–96; Richard Gula, SS, *Reason Informed by Faith* (New York: Paulist, 1989), 63–64; and Brian V. Johnstone, CSsR, "From Physicalism to Personalism," *Studia Moralia* 30 (1992): 71–96.

2. On this point, see the examples and analysis offered by Johnstone, "From Physicalism to Personalism," 83–90. Cf. Lisa Sowle Cahill, "Catholic Sexual Ethics and the Dignity of the Person: A Double Message," *Theological Studies* 50 (1989): 120–50.

This chapter proceeds by first examining the historical emergence of the first generation of Catholic personalism in the thought of Dietrich von Hildebrand and Herbert Doms, noting some of the significant differences between them. It then considers the development of these different strands of personalism as refracted through the lens of the debate concerning birth control in the thought of Louis Janssens, Paul Quay, and Karol Wojtyła. In addition to different conclusions about concrete issues of sexual ethics, this analysis highlights strong methodological differences between these authors that are indicative of wider trends of thought. Such differences can be utilized to construct differing models of personalism based on the relationship of the notions of person, nature, and sexuality in each.

Historical Background: The Emergence of Personalism

While one could make the case that the seeds of a personalist approach to sexual morality were laid in the sacramental theology of the high Middle ages, which enabled the body and sexuality to once again be seen as a medium of spiritual love,[3] such an approach flowered only in the intellectual currents of the twentieth century, particularly in the light of the more experiential focus afforded by modern phenomenology. The work of Dietrich von Hildebrand and Herbert Doms proved to be an influential, if not entirely harmonious, exposition of this new approach to marriage and sex within it.

Dietrich von Hildebrand

Von Hildebrand, who long held the post of professor of philosophy at the University of Munich before coming to the United States, holds the distinction of being among the first married laymen to have a significant impact on Catholic teaching regarding sexuality.[4] Accepting the Augustinian position, which saw procreation as the primary end of marriage, von Hildebrand attempted to contextualize this teaching by insisting that self-giving love is the primary meaning of the conjugal act.[5] Sexual intimacy refracts the offer-

3. For such a reading, see Frank Bottomley, *Attitudes toward the Body in Western Christendom* (London: Lepus, 1979), 112–28.

4. Cf. John T. Noonan, *Contraception: A History of Its Treatment by the Catholic Theologians and Canonists*, enlarged ed. (Cambridge, MA: Belknap Press, 1986), 494–95.

5. See Dietrich von Hildebrand, *Die Ehe* (1929); English translation, *Marriage* (London:

ing of the couple to one another through the prism of communion in the flesh. As such, it both expresses and fosters the couple's communion of love. It is "the expression and flower of a specific kind of [i.e., wedded] love."[6] In this way, von Hildebrand is able to attribute to intercourse a sacramental meaning without overturning the understanding of consent as the primary cause of the sacrament developed in Scholastic theology.

Sex, for von Hildebrand, "is essentially deep" in its psychological power and its effect on the soul.[7] Sexual activity is thus a mystery that involves the whole person. This understanding has two implications. First, this involvement of the whole person is also true of one's sexual being as a male or female. Men and women are irreducibly unique and distinctive as persons.[8] These differences in turn become the means of personal communion in conjugal love. Second, the involvement of the whole person means that such activity must be fully conscious in order to be genuinely personal. Unlike Augustine, who gave intercourse a merely instrumental value as a means to achieving procreation and thus licitly channeling the powerful forces of concupiscence that raged through fallen sexuality, von Hildebrand saw it as intrinsically valuable and something that demanded conscious attention. Procreative intent alone cannot account for the full human and personal quality of intercourse.[9]

But this focus on the personal qualities of sex did not obscure for von Hildebrand its natural ordination to procreation. In his early works he described contraception as a sacrilege that divorced the organic union that God established between procreation and the sacramental significance of intercourse.[10] In later works he would treat this under the rubric of "super-

---

Longmans, Green, 1942), 6–7, 19–27; and idem, *Reinhart und Jungfräulichkeit* (Munich, 1928); English translation, *In Defense of Purity* (New York: Sheed & Ward), 1931, 10–12. On the antecedents to von Hildebrand's position, see Theodore Mackin, SJ, *What Is Marriage?* (New York: Paulist, 1982), 226.

6. See von Hildebrand, *In Defense of Purity*, 10.

7. Ibid., 4 (emphasis original).

8. Von Hildebrand describes this difference as "a metaphysical one" "representing ... two manifestations of the person." Further, he says: "These two types, man and woman, have a unique capacity for complementing each other ... They are made for each other in a special way, and they can, purely as spiritual persons, form a unity in which they reciprocally complement one another." See *Marriage*, 11–12. Cf. *In Defense of Purity*, 9.

9. See *In Defense of Purity*, 13–14.

10. Ibid., 10.

abundant finality." As an act of the whole person, sexual self-donation has an orientation that transcends the purely biological—a finality severed by contraception.[11] For von Hildebrand, to understand the notion of "nature" invoked by *Humanae vitae* as merely empirical or biological mistakenly constricts the reality of sexuality. Rather, it should be seen as ontological and as such deeply connected to the values of the person considered as a whole.[12] To separate intercourse from its meaning, which is the expression of love, is the source of impurity, but to artificially manipulate the act to preclude procreation is ultimately an act of irreverence toward God and his design of the person. Natural means of regulating births, on the other hand, involve no active separation of the superabundant finality of sexual self-donation.[13]

Von Hildebrand's project represents an effort to balance the demands of nature in the form of the primacy of the procreative end, with a new focus on the experience of personal self-giving love. But, as his later thought would indicate, he resisted any attempt to usurp or displace nature's purpose in the name of personalism. While the lyricism of his insights was not always balanced by precision in specific normative applications, von Hildebrand's work indicated an important direction for later reflection.

Herbert Doms

Herbert Doms, a Catholic priest and lecturer in theology at the University of Breslau, appropriated many of von Hildebrand's ideas, but also developed some of them in rather different directions. Doms too would speak of intercourse as a privileged expression of communion between a couple in which they give and receive each other. Conjugal union does not merely express such self-giving, but realizes it in a metaphysical fashion and thus shapes the very personalities of those who engage in it.[14] The condition of the possibility of this union are the differences between the sexes, which, as in the case of von Hildebrand, are understood to be rooted in the very be-

11. See Dietrich von Hildebrand, *The Encyclical Humanae Vitae: A Sign of Contradiction* (Chicago: Franciscan Herald Press, 1969), 29–38.

12. Ibid., 38–46.

13. Ibid., 47.

14. See Herbert Doms, *Von Sinn und Zweck der Ehe* (Breslau, 1935); English translation by George Sayer, *The Meaning of Marriage* (New York: Sheed & Ward, 1939), 15, 33–34, 48–51, 99.

ing of the person.[15] This act, for Doms, is rich in its symbolism, alternately denoting in analogous fashion the union of Christ and the soul in the Eucharist, Christ and the whole Church, or the processions of the Second and Third Persons of the Trinity.[16]

But the immediate end of this intercourse is not so much procreation as the personal fulfillment[17] and the *Zweieinigekiet* ("two-in-oneship") that it creates between the couple.[18] In places Doms suggests that this primacy is true only in the subjective sphere, leaving open the objective primacy of procreation, at least biologically.[19] But elsewhere he will argue forcefully that, even from the seemingly objective vantage point of science, procreation is at best an indirect and involuntary end of intercourse (given the time lapse involved and the relative infrequency of conception).[20] In addition, the fact that the meaning of the act precedes the realization of its biological purpose gives further grounds for its preeminence.[21] Such arguments convey the distinct impression that the hierarchy of the ends of marriage should not simply be abandoned, as *Gaudium et spes* would later appear to do, but perhaps reversed.[22] Doms thus anticipates the trajectory of much revisionist personalism over the course of the century. In terms of issues of family planning, Doms betrays some uncertainty regarding his final position and the arguments employed to defend it. While the biological end (procreation) and the personal end (union) ought to be bound together, it is only a voluntarist appeal to the rights of the Creator over the seed once deposited or the sexual organs that forbids the active thwarting of procreation.[23] Doms flirts with developing a personalist argument against contraception, trying to tie the biological giving of sex to the personal self-giving that is its meaning, but does not utilize this argument consistently nor free

15. Sayer, *Meaning of Marriage*, 18, 21, 54, 62. Cf. 46, 127. Doms suggests that such differences are more physical than spiritual, however (22).

16. Ibid., 18–19, 103–14, 123.   17. Ibid., 35.

18. Ibid., 23–24, 84–85, 94–95. Cf. 79, 130.   19. Cf. ibid., xix, 86, 166.

20. See ibid., 175–76, 183–84. Doms even argues in places that the primary biological end and meaning is union (cf. 68–71).

21. Cf. ibid., 186.

22. Doms himself suggests this reversal. See ibid., 83, 87–88. On the challenge posed by Doms's position to the traditional Catholic moral system, see Mackin, *What Is Marriage?*, 229–38. Cf. André Guindon, OMI, *The Sexual Creators: An Ethical Proposal for Concerned Christians* (Lanham, MD: University Press of America, 1986), 64.

23. See Sayer, *Meaning of Marriage*, 73–74, 88, 165–66.

it from the narrowly biological and voluntarist notion of nature that underlies it.[24] Furthermore, he rejects the idea that the intercourse of an infertile
couple can be said to be "ordained to procreation," including the temporary
infertility of the "safe period."[25] Thus while Doms attempts to uphold fairly
traditional conclusions on issues of sexual ethics ranging from homosexual
activity to birth regulation, the basis of this defense is a series of arguments
that are neither cohesive with each other nor fully cogent in themselves. In
particular, his use of a highly biological concept of nature as a ground for
the procreative end of intercourse, buttressed by voluntarist appeals to the
Divine will or prerogative in such matters, is clearly a weak defense of many
of the conclusions that he attempts to defend. Such arguments would un-
ravel quickly when subjected to the pressure of later developments.

Rival Personalisms and the Pill

The new and more experiential approach to sexuality introduced by these
early personalist perspectives coalesced with other factors in subjecting traditional positions in sexual ethics, particularly the proscription of contraception, to new scrutiny. Among the most important of these factors often
cited are: an increased awareness of global population and limited resources;
the new social and political role of women; the increased costs of raising and
educating children in an industrial society; and the repudiation of the traditional prohibition by other Christian churches, beginning with the decision
of the Anglican Church at the Lambeth Conference of 1930.[26] The Catholic
response to these developments was somewhat complex. On the one hand,
Pius XI unequivocally reaffirmed the Church's position that contraception
was gravely immoral under the rubric of natural law.[27] On the other hand,

24. See ibid., 166–68.

25. Ibid., 170. Yet Doms also views such recourse to the safe period as licit, primarily on the
basis of the teaching of Pius XI in *Casti connubii* (191). His own arguments in this regard are
notably weak (see 191–94).

26. For an overview of these developments, see Noonan, *Contraception*, 476–91; and William H. Shannon, *The Lively Debate: Response to Humanae Vitae* (New York: Sheed & Ward,
1970), 3–10, 24–25.

27. Pius XI, Encyclical Letter, *Casti connubii*, nos. 55, 57. The use of natural law language is
noteworthy, given that the manualist tradition usually treated contraception as a violation of
chastity.

both theologians and the hierarchy showed a growing openness to the principle of family limitation through the use of natural means in the so-called rhythm method.[28] The key difference between contraception and rhythm, it was argued, was that one respected the natural structure of intercourse and its procreative finality and the other did not. Such an argument proved unable to contend with the challenges presented by the progesterone pill, however.

Given the import and far-reaching nature of this developing controversy, it is not surprising to find invocations of personalist categories on both sides of the growing debate. This study considers three figures who are representative of methodologically and, to some degree, substantively different responses to this growing debate: Louis Janssens, a pivotal figure in the argument for revision of the traditional position on birth control and a pioneer in articulating an influential foundation for one stream of contemporary personalism; Paul Quay, representative of the traditional position, who utilizes personalist language even while advocating the continuing primacy of nature; and Karol Wojtyła, who has attempted to fuse modern personalism and the traditional concept of nature in his phenomenological Thomism.

Louis Janssens

Louis Janssens, a priest and longtime professor of moral theology at the Catholic University of Leuven, was at the forefront of the debates regarding birth control both before and after *Humane vitae*. These debates served as a catalyst for the development of his own thought regarding personalism. Originally trained in systematic theology, Janssens crossed over to morality to attempt a personalist synthesis between German thinkers such as Max Scheler and Dietrich von Hildebrand and French scholars such as Jacques Maritain and Emmanuel Mournier on the question of the relationship between the person and society.[29] Even in his early writings, Janssens sought to

---

28. *Casti connubii* gave cautious approval to the principle of birth regulation in the form of continence by mutual agreement or intercourse rendered infertile as a result of natural defects such as time. Cf. nos. 54, 60. Noonan observes that such remarks did not necessarily address the question of a systematic use of the "safe period" in order to avoid pregnancy, although it was certainly understood in this way by Doms. *Contraception*, 442. This acceptance would be expanded considerably by the criteria enumerated in the allocutions of Pius XII in 1951. On these statements and their effect, see ibid., 445–47; and Shannon, *Lively Debate*, 27–29.

29. The result was Louis Janssens, *Personne et société: Théories actuelles et essai doctrinal, Dissertationes ad gradum magistri in Facultate Theologica vel in Facultate Iuris Canonict con-*

articulate a holistic anthropology that could account for the many dimensions of personal existence. When confronted with competing or even conflicting claims between moral values, he argued that it is possible to "find a solution only if we measure every act with the objective ruler of morality, i.e. the person, adequately considered in regard to self and in relation with others."[30] This idea would become the guiding principle of much of Janssens's subsequent reflections on the topic of personalism as he became involved in the growing birth control debate.

As anovulant pills became available in the 1950s, moralists began to debate the morality of their use. Going beyond the consensus that formed around the position that allowed for indirect sterilization in the case of a therapeutic use,[31] and many others who argued for its use to correct an irregular menstrual cycle,[32] Janssens weighed in to the debate by arguing that the pill could licitly be used to suppress ovulation during the period of lactation because a woman's body normally did so in order to produce a natural spacing of births.[33] But in cases where this "mechanism of nature" was in default, then it was permissible to sustain it through this intervention.[34] The identification of "nature" with biological processes and finality invited just this line of argument and the wedge that it drove into the older natural law approach would prove fatal.

While methods of contraception based on withdrawal or the use of bar-

seauendum conscnptae, Series II-Tomus 32 (Gembloux, 1939). For a helpful overview and background on Janssens's career, see Jan Jans, "Some Remarks on the Work of Professor Emeritus Louis Janssens," in *Personalist Morals: Essays in Honor of Professor Louis Janssens*, ed. Joseph A. Selling and Franz Böckle, Bibliotheca Ephemeridum Theologicarum Louvaniensium LXXXIII (Leuven: University of Leuven Press, 1988), 319–28.

30. Louis Janssens, "Time and Space in Morals," in *Personalist Morals*, 13 (emphasis original). This essay was originally written in 1947. As early as his 1939 dissertation, he observed the need for "a complete and real revision of our being, of its structure, its activity, its relation with the surroundings and its dependence, perhaps, on realities which are beyond it." Jans, *Personne et société*, 235, as cited in "Some Remarks," 320.

31. Pius XII would affirm this position in an allocution in September of 1958. See Pius XII, Address to the Seventh International Congress of Hematology, September 12, 1958, *Acta Apostolicae Sedis* 50 (1958): 732–40.

32. On this, see Noonan, *Contraception*, 462–65; and Shannon, *Lively Debate*, 36–37.

33. Louis Janssens, "L'Inhibition de l'ovulation est-elle moralement licite?," *Ephemerides Theologicae Lovaniensess* 34 (1958): 357–60.

34. Ibid., 359. Janssens's suggestion was widely criticized by theologians and perhaps by Pius XII in the abovementioned allocution given in the same year. Cf. Noonan, *Contraception*, 466–67; and Jans, "Some Remarks," 319n1.

riers could be described as "unnatural" because of their subversion of the natural performance of the act of intercourse or its procreative finality, the pill seemed to elude such analysis. The pill merely used a hormone already produced within a woman's body to suppress ovulation. Thus it began to be argued that the pill employed no physical or chemical action foreign to the body's own processes and hence seemed a wholly "natural" way of placing human biology under the control of human reason.[35]

For Janssens, the pill was as "natural" as rhythm. Perhaps it was more so, since it not only respected the natural structure of the act of intercourse, but it also did not damage the mutual love of the couple through extended periods of abstinence and did not "mutilate" female fertility through wasting ova as rhythm did.[36] Furthermore, he observed that the temporal barrier introduced by periodic continence is as real as the spatial barrier to procreation in barrier methods of contraception.[37] Because intercourse is a unique incarnation of conjugal love, not simply from a subjective perception but as its "intrinsic sense (*finis operis*)," the pill allows the integration of mutual self-giving love into a relationship that as a whole is open to procreation.[38]

Janssens's argument successfully demonstrates the utter inability of the traditional natural law arguments, which attempt to locate "nature" and its demands in biological process and function, to contend with a phenomenon such as the pill. While his arguments would draw fire from many of Janssens's fellow moralists, their influence and cogency were such that even the minority report of the Pontifical Study Commission on Family Population and Birth Problems, which argued for a maintenance of the traditional position, would have to agree that the natural arguments were not compelling and had to rest their case on an appeal to authority.[39] So it was that the pill "was destined to push Rome beyond its theological supply lines."[40]

When *Humanae vitae* did appear, Janssens joined many other theo-

35. This was the argument offered by the Catholic physician and professor at Harvard John Rock, whose research had helped to develop the anovulant pill. See *The Time Has Come* (New York: Alfred A. Knopf, 1963). Janssens echoed this argument in "Morale conjugale et progestogens," *Ephemerides Theologicae Lovanienses* 39 (1963): 820–24.

36. Janssens, "Morale conjugale et progestogens," 820–24.

37. Ibid., 817.

38. See ibid., 807, 818, 821, 824.

39. On this, see Shannon, *Lively Debate*, 90–91.

40. James Burtchaell, *The Giving and Taking of Life: Essays Ethical* (Notre Dame, IN: University of Notre Dame Press, 1989), 38, cf. 89–115.

logians in criticizing the document. For Janssens, the chief failure of the encyclical was that, in focusing on a narrow concept of nature and its demands, it failed to follow through on the personalism of *Gaudium et spes*, which saw marriage as a covenantal communion of life and love and held that decisions about family planning should be based "on the nature of the human person and his acts."[41] He argues that the biological aspects of sexuality have only a limited impact on the person as a whole, whereas its relational and interpersonal aspects are far more profound.[42] In an authentically personalist approach, more attention should be paid to the autonomy of the human person[43] and to the historical conditioning and hence relativity of particular norms.[44]

In later writings, Janssens would expand on his notion of "the person adequately considered," identifying eight fundamental aspects of the person. The person is: a self-determining subject; an embodied being; a sharer in materiality; essentially other-directed; social; created in God's image and called to worship; a historical being; fundamentally equal but simultaneously unique.[45] He will use this foundation to defend not only contraception but also the licitness of artificial insemination as a valid expression of conjugal self-giving against an older argument that condemned it on the basis of a biologistic appeal to the finality of sexual organs and semen.[46] One cannot elevate

41. *Gaudium et spes*, no. 51, as cited by Louis Janssens, "Considerations on Humane Vitae," *Louvain Studies* 2 (1968–69): 234; cf. 251. See also the more extended consideration of the personalism of *Gaudium et spes* in Louis Janssens, *Mariage et Fécondité: De Casti connubii à Gaudium et spes* (Paris: Editions J. Duculot, 1967), 75–96, 106–18. Jans opines that, even though he was not officially a *peritus*, Janssens may have had some influence on the terminology employed in the Pastoral Constitution through his contacts with Cardinal Leon Suenens. See Jans, "Some Remarks," 323–24.

42. Janssens, "Considerations on Humane Vitae," 249–50.

43. See ibid., 237–40. Thus he writes, "man himself (autonomy) must endeavor to elaborate concrete moral norms according to available data of experience, that is, according to the acquired degree of knowledge of the laws and values of human sexual relationships" (240).

44. See ibid., 240–42. Cf. Janssens, *Mariage et Fécondité*, 96–106. Janssens would pursue this idea of the relative character of moral norms in later works that would help to forge a methodological foundation for proportionalism. See especially his "Ontic Evil and Moral Evil," *Louvain Studies* 4 (1972): 115–56.

45. See Louis Janssens, "Artificial Insemination: Ethical Considerations," *Louvain Studies* 8 (1980): 3–13. Cf. idem, "Personalism in Moral Theology," in *Moral Theology: Challenges for the Future. Essays in Honor of Richard McCormick*, ed. Charles Curran (New York: Paulist, 1990), 94.

46. See Janssens, "Artificial Insemination," 17–29; idem, "Personalism in Moral Theology," 95–98.

biological processes to the status of moral laws because the purpose of acts or organs can only be found in a consideration of the person as a whole.[47]

Janssens's approach champions the values of personal self-giving love over a biologistic concept of nature. While not excluding biological exigencies from his concept of the person, these are clearly subordinate to the person considered as a whole. In particular, the values of relationality, subjectivity, autonomy, and historicity are highlighted in the sphere of sexual morality and decision making. With Janssens, the implications of some of Doms's ideas, which pointed to the subordination of the biology of procreation to the union of the couple, reach their fruition. Nature is not denied but, as basically biological, it is made subject to the person as a whole.[48]

Janssens's elaboration of a foundation for personalism has proved widely influential in contemporary theology. His various aspects of the person are often cited as the best possible elaboration of the criteria of *Gaudium et spes* concerning decisions of sexual morality based "on the nature of the human person and his acts," or as an adequate foundation for an anthropology in general.[49] Others have invoked elements of a personalism like that of Janssens to engage other issues in sexual ethics, such as the morality of homosexual activity.[50] One can also find echoes of Janssens's approach in

47. Cf. Janssens, "Artificial Insemination," 21; idem, "Personalism in Moral Theology," 94–95.

48. Janssens will still use the notion of "nature" as a ground for human equality and as a ground for the development of a unique subjectivity. See Janssens, "Artificial Insemination," 12. For a complementary analysis that seeks to articulate the reality of nature from a perspective that gives priority to the personal, see Franz Böckle, "Nature as the Basis of Morality," in *Personalist Morals*, 45–60.

49. See, e.g., Richard McCormick, *Notes on Moral Theology 1981 through 1984* (Lanham, MD: University Press of America, 1984), 49–52; idem, "Moral Theology since Vatican II: Clarity or Chaos?," in *The Critical Calling: Reflections on Moral Dilemmas since Vatican II* (Washington, DC: Georgetown University Press, 1989), 14–16; and Gula, *Reason Informed by Faith*, 66–74.

50. Thus Margaret Farley highlights "autonomy and relationality" as "two essential features of personhood" in constructing an argument that evaluates sexual activity by homosexual partners in a manner akin to heterosexual sex. See "An Ethic for Same Sex Relations," in *A Challenge to Love: Gay and Lesbian Catholics in the Church*, ed. Robert Nugent (New York: Crossroad, 1983), 101. Guindon invokes many of Janssens's criticisms of the biologism of the older tradition and its subordination of the person to nature (e.g., *Sexual Creators*, 9, 46–47, 49), but believes that he has moved beyond the dualism still implicit in his approach by making "fecundity" apply to personal love as the integration of tenderness and sensuality, self-identity, personal worth, and community rather than simply to the biology of human procreation (cf. *Sexual Creators*, 63–80). Because sexuality primarily involves relationality rather than sexual difference, Guindon can offer an extended consideration of "gay fecundity" (cf. *Sexual Creators*, 40n34, 159–87).

some feminist accounts of human experience.[51] Where some contemporary theology has moved beyond Janssens, to some degree, is in taking still further his suggestion of the historicity of the human person to invoke a more strongly relational and processive account of nature.[52]

In spite of its widespread influence, there are questions that can be asked of such an approach. In regard to the argument that attributes procreation to the whole of a couple's relationship rather than individual acts, there are at least two problems. First, this approach seems to neglect the reflexive or self-determining character of human actions that serve to shape both the character of the agent and the quality of the relationship.[53] Second, it is not explained why the procreative end can be spread over the whole of a relationship, but presumably this is not equally true of the unitive end lest individual sexual acts lose their character of self-giving.[54]

But there are more fundamental questions that can be asked of Janssens's account of personalism. Is it accurate to regard human fertility and hence the demands of "nature" as merely biological? Or can it be argued that there is a deeper ontological dimension to such realities when they pertain to a person?[55] Furthermore, it has rightly been observed that Janssens is less than clear on how the various dimensions of the person that he identified are interrelated and what normative value they have.[56] The analysis above suggests that some of these dimensions (e.g., autonomy, subjectivity, relationality, and historicity) are weighted more heavily than others. Other factors such as embodiment with its concomitant sexual differentiation

51. Thus Farley cites a list of elements almost identical to those enumerated by Janssens (without specifically citing him) in her *Personal Commitments: Beginning, Keeping, Changing* (San Francisco: HarperCollins, 1986), 82.

52. See, e.g., the process language and sources utilized by Farley, *Personal Commitments*, 57, 82, 104–5, 123–24, 131–32, 138n3. A more overtly processive account of the sexual becoming of the person is utilized by Guindon, *Sexual Creators*, 15, 2–9, 71, 102.

53. See John S. Grabowski and Michael J. Naughton, "Catholic Social and Sexual Ethics: Inconsistent or Organic," *The Thomist* 57 (1993): 568–69.

54. See John S. Grabowski, "The Status of the Sexual Good as a Direction for Moral Theology," *Heythrop Journal* 35 (1994): 17.

55. Aquinas, at least, sees the inclinations of human nature as ontological realities unified by the exercise of reason. See Jean Porter, *The Recovery of Virtue: The Relevance of Aquinas for Christian Ethics* (Louisville, KY: Westminster John Knox, 1990), 89–90; Grabowski and Naughton, "Catholic Social and Sexual Ethics," 564–66.

56. See Johnstone, "From Physicalism to Personalism," 85–86.

are weighted less heavily.[57] The weight given to autonomy and historicity and the lack of a stable concept of nature appear to incline Janssens's view toward some kind of process thought—a direction made explicit by others influenced by him. Finally, it must be asked whether the apparent subordination of nature to the person is a tenable anthropological position given the Christological and Trinitarian origin of this distinction.

Paul Quay

A different approach to both sexuality and personalism can be found in the thought of Paul Quay. Quay, an American Jesuit and professor of philosophy, was also involved in the early stages of the birth control controversy and its aftermath and may be regarded as at least a representative, if not overly influential, example of the traditional position.[58]

Quay's thought appears to bear the linguistic and substantive marks of the personalist project. Citing the incommunicability and uniqueness of the person, he argues that the person transcends both the species and society.[59] He draws a sharp contrast between a love that treats the other as a mere thing and hence ignores the dignity of the person, and a love that regards the other as a person and seeks his or her good as such.[60] Intercourse is a form of interpersonal communication between spouses that expresses a privileged form of mutual self-giving.[61] Even the pleasure of the act has an interpersonal source.[62] Ultimately, it is the person of Christ who is the norm for human life and behavior.[63]

Yet this personalist language is potentially deceptive because it is ultimately not the anthropological or ethical center of Quay's thought. While the person may be said to "transcend the species even as he transcends civil

57. Cf. ibid., 86. Johnstone argues that the status of corporeity and biology remains unclear in Janssens's approach.

58. Cahill describes Quay as "vehement but not unrepresentative." See "Catholic Sexual Ethics," 128.

59. See Paul Quay, "Contraception and Conjugal Love," *Theological Studies* 22 (1961): 26.

60. Ibid., 27–28. Cf. 25. Cf. Paul Quay, *The Christian Meaning of Human Sexuality* (San Francisco: Ignatius Press, 1985), 32.

61. Quay, "Contraception and Conjugal Love," 28, 30.

62. Ibid., 28.

63. This Christological dimension of his anthropology emerges more in Quay's later work. See *Christian Meaning*, 8–9, 12–14.

society," this is only accomplished "by rationally working for the good of the species" and acting "in virtue of his nature."[64] While the whole of the person is physiologically and psychologically stamped by maleness and femaleness, this identity is directed toward and fulfilled in fatherhood and motherhood.[65] And while sexual intercourse is a language of intentional self-giving, such a gift is always incomplete and only genuine insofar as it is willed in accord with nature.[66] The person is thus, in a certain sense, ordered to the demands of nature.

For Quay, however, sexual intercourse has an even deeper meaning than that which is invested in it by the volition of spouses. It is first and foremost a natural sign or symbol, and as such it is rooted in human nature itself.[67] The very act of intercourse is utilized by Quay to construct a typology of sexual difference based on male activity and female passivity.[68] The two become "one flesh" in this act through the procreation of a child. Intercourse is thus "the natural symbol of willingness to become father or mother," which actualizes for the man "the deep responsibility, sobriety, long patience, and quiet nobility of fatherhood" and for the woman "the peculiar richness warmth and fullness of motherhood."[69] This natural symbolism is taken up and confirmed supernaturally in the revelation in the fruitful love of Christ for the Church or of the Persons of the Trinity for one another.[70]

This identification of the natural symbolism of sex is then used as the basis to condemn particular sexual acts such as contraception. The objective evil of such acts is their violation of the natural law; their subjective evil lies

---

64. Quay, "Contraception and Conjugal Love," 26.

65. Ibid., 25–26.

66. Ibid., 29–30; cf. Quay, *Christian Meaning*, 33–35.

67. Cf. Quay, *Christian Meaning*, 18, 20, 22.

68. Thus Quay writes: "In coition the woman gives and surrenders herself to the man by complete openness, receptiveness, submission, and a full unfolding of herself to this sole partner. The man, on his part, gives himself to the woman through his entrancement with her, his finding of his satisfaction in her alone, his yearning to protect this soft helplessness, his penetration and permeation of her with his very substance, his focusing all of his attention and activity, dominance and responsibility exclusively upon this one woman." "Contraception and Conjugal Love," 29. In spite of the addition of some more phenomenological and sociobiological descriptions of the sexually differentiated body in his later work (e.g., *Christian Meaning*, 25–29), Quay retains the language of headship and submission in intercourse itself (see ibid., 31–32).

69. Quay, "Contraception and Conjugal Love," 29; cf. idem, *Christian Meaning*, 34–35.

70. Quay, "Contraception and Conjugal Love," 32–33; cf. idem, *Christian Meaning*, 55–63.

in their deliberate falsification of "the natural word of love," which is sex.[71] Thus in contraception a woman rejects the power of her husband's seed "over her body" and hence his authority over her, while a man "no longer dominates his wife as a person" and takes "no responsibility for her."[72] This intercourse "becomes the symbol of feminine dominance instead of masculine, of masculine impotence instead of strength."[73] Such activity destroys the natural ordination of intercourse to procreative parenthood and refuses God's intervention in the process: "they are two alone at this moment and refuse to transcend themselves; their pleasure in each other is corrupted at its core."[74] On the level of supernatural symbolism, such an act bespeaks the malice of sacrilege.[75] On the other hand, when properly used, the abstinence required by periodic continence symbolizes sorrow over the limits of a sinful world that make its use necessary.[76]

While using some personalist language and ideas, the heart of Quay's project is the traditional Neo-Scholastic natural law approach read through natural and revealed symbols. This nature and these symbols form the parameters for personal action and fulfillment. So strongly is the person ordered to fulfillment through his or her nature that the notion of "person" appears to become subordinate to the broader category of nature. In matters of sex, the goodness of personal fulfillment is wholly dependent upon the ordination to procreation. As such, this position represents the logical opposite of the account of personalism developed by Janssens.

This viewing of the person through the lens of nature is fraught with problems. Quay's use of natural symbols appears somewhat arbitrary. It is not fully clear why the symbols Quay employs might not be read differently.[77] The only thing that guarantees the reading Quay develops is a presup-

---

71. Quay, "Contraception and Conjugal Love," 34. Quay will use his reading of natural and supernatural symbols to condemn other "sexual counterfeits," including masturbation, homosexual activity, and extramarital sex. See ibid., 34–35; and idem, *Christian Meaning*, 65–70.

72. Quay, "Contraception and Conjugal Love," 35; cf. idem, *Christian Meaning*, 70–71.

73. Quay, *Christian Meaning*, 71; cf. idem, "Contraception and Conjugal Love," 35.

74. Quay, "Contraception and Conjugal Love," 37.

75. Ibid., 38.

76. Ibid., 39.

77. A different reading might argue that contraceptive sex symbolizes the celebration of the unitive power of love even in the midst of tragic circumstances that require the suppression of fertility.

posed biological ordination to procreation in all sexual activity. Further, it is not clear that the act of intercourse can or should bear all of the symbolic weight attributed to it.[78] Especially problematic is the extrapolation of male and female traits based on the supposition of male activity and female passivity in sex. Such a schema seems to presuppose an Aristotelian account of procreation rather than the insights of modern biology or a phenomenological approach to the experience of sexuality. It also threatens, on the basis of its construction of symbols read from acts, to polarize the sexes on the level of nature.[79] Ultimately, it must be asked whether such an approach can be called personalist in any real sense, and whether it genuinely serves to advance beyond the physicalism of the older tradition.[80]

Karol Wojtyła

While similar in many of its conclusions, a different methodological approach to personalism is developed by Karol Wojtyła. Even before the crisis that the pill precipitated, Wojtyła, as a priest and bishop and professor of philosophy at the University of Lublin, sought to find a new philosophical basis for the traditional prescriptions of Catholic sexual ethics. Like Doms, he attempted to carry out this project in dialogue with the sciences. Like von Hildebrand, he utilized a phenomenological approach to human experience, sharpened by his own attempts to appropriate the thought of Max Scheler in his doctoral studies and later philosophical works.[81] But wedded to this phenomenological exploration of experience was a determined retrieval of Thomistic categories of natural law. Wojtyła's personalism thus

78. Quay admits that he attempts to read the meaning of symbols off of the structure of individual acts. Thus he writes: "Now we wish to consider the natural symbolism of sexual intercourse itself…to know meanings that God built into these physical acts through internal likeness and parallelism of structure." *Christian Meaning*, 24; cf. 65, 72.

79. It is precisely here that Quay's account shows affinity with other "dual nature" approaches to sexual differences and sexual activity. For an analysis of this trend and its implications, see Grabowski, "Status of the Sexual Good," 23–25.

80. On the physicalism of the Neo-Scholastic natural law tradition, see Johnstone, "From Physicalism to Personalism," 72–79.

81. Wojtyła's habilitation thesis was "The Ethical System of Max Scheler as a Basis for a New Interpretation of Christian Ethics" (1954). His efforts to appropriate Scheler continued in his later opus on personal action. The Polish original, *Osaba i czyn*, was published in 1969. The English translation by Andrzej Potocki appeared a decade later as *The Acting Person*, Analecta Husserliana X (Boston: D. Reidel, 1979).

had widely differing philosophical pedigrees and constituted an attempt to effect their fusion.[82]

The basic axiology of Wojtyła's ethics is the contrast that he draws between personalistic and utilitarian views of the person and sexuality. In the latter perspective, characteristic of much modern culture, the person is treated as a mere object for use and enjoyment.[83] In the former, the person appears as a kind of good that cannot be used as a means to an end, or, stated positively, as a good to which the only proper response is love.[84] This "personalist norm," a curious blend of Kantian personalism and New Testament ethics, provides Wojtyła with his basic analytical tool to evaluate sexual self-donation. Such activity is good to the degree that the person is given and received in his or totality and utilitarian to the extent that the person is treated as an object for use.

Like both von Hildebrand and Doms, Wojtyła argues that the phenomena of sexuality and sexual differences pertain to the person as whole. The "sexual urge" embraces the physical and psychological differences between the sexes but ultimately is deeper than them, reaching to the order of existence and thus rooted in the being of the person as a whole.[85] It is a mistake engendered by modern empiricism to reduce the order of nature from which the sexual urge proceeds to a merely biological phenomenon.[86] Self-consciously invoking the Thomistic understanding of the inclinations of human nature, Wojtyła argues that the most fundamental of these inclinations is that of existence itself, which is fostered by respect for the sexual urge and its orientation to procreation.[87] But this drive must be integrated into the demands of personal love. To use another merely for procreation

82. This bears upon the protracted debates among commentators as to whether Wojtyła's anthropology is better understood primarily as a form of phenomenology or Thomism. For different readings of this issue, see Anna-Teresa Tymieniecka, "The Origins of the Philosophy of Pope John Paul the Second," in *The Human Person*, ed. George McLean (Washington, DC: Catholic University of America Press, 1979), 16–27; Jerzy Galkowski, "The Place of Thomism in the Anthropology of K. Wojtyla," *Angelicum* 65 (1988): 181–94; and Kenneth L. Schmitz, *At the Center of the Human Drama: The Philosophical Anthropology of Karol Wojtyla/Pope John Paul II* (Washington, DC: Catholic University of America Press, 1993, 60–67.

83. *Milosc I Odpowiedzialnosc* (Krakow, 1960). English translation by H. T. Willets, *Love and Responsibility* (New York: Farrar, Straus, and Giroux, 1981), 25–39.

84. Wojtyła, *Love and Responsibility*, 41.

85. Cf. ibid., 52–53, 230. Cf. Wojtyła, *Acting Person*, 215–18.

86. Cf. Wojtyła, *Love and Responsibility*, 56–57. Cf. 230.

87. Ibid., 51–52.

is as utilitarian as to use him or her for pleasure. [88] The two-edged sword of the "personalist norm" thus cuts both ways.

In terms of the pressing question of birth regulation, Wojtyła uses this foundation to attempt to formulate a consistent personalist argument capable of supporting the traditional position. He accepts the notion established by von Hildebrand and Doms that the meaning of intercourse is one of complete self-giving love. [89] The moral quality of this action is judged by the standard of the personalist norm. If, however, human fertility is not merely biological but an aspect of the person as a whole, then to withhold it through a utilization of contraception by whatever means is to overlay the language of mutual self-giving with a contradictory language of withholding and refusal. [90] In order to be genuine, personal love must respect and integrate the order of nature and its demands. [91] Recourse to periodic continence, however, involves no such withholding of self and diversion of intentionality from the person within conjugal communion; rather, it relies on the virtue of chastity to help the couple integrate their sexual relationship within the bonds of authentic personal love. [92] Because Wojtyła's argument is not tied as closely to the interruption of biological process, it is therefore not as easily stymied by the pill.

Wojtyła's project represents an effort to achieve an integration of the experiential perspective of modern personalism and the classical natural law approach. [93] The notion of nature utilized here, however, is not merely biological but ontological. It thus attempts to integrate the realities and moral demands of human nature into its understanding of the person and personal love rather than polarizing the two or subordinating one to the other. Thus Wojtyła himself states that "Sexual morality and therefore conjugal morality consists of a stable and mature *synthesis of nature's purpose with the personalistic norm*." [94]

88. Cf. ibid., 58–59, 61–63, 233.

89. He in fact argues that there are three objective ends of marriage: *procreatio, mutuum adiutorium*, and *remedium concupiscentiae*. Of these, procreation is the primary end, but all depend upon love for their proper realization. See ibid., 66–68. The full expression of betrothed love is self-giving, which shapes the very being of those who engage in it. See ibid., 96–99.

90. Ibid., 52–53.   91. Ibid., 226–30.

92. Ibid., 234–35, 237–44.

93. This is also the interpretation of Böckle, "Nature as the Basis of Morality," 55.

94. Ibid., 61 (emphasis original). Elsewhere he states, "Some people might say that this ruling [regarding birth regulation] subordinates man, who is a person, to 'nature,' whereas in so many fields he triumphs over nature, and dominates it. This however is a specious argument,

Wojtyła's position has not been without influence, especially in his native Poland.[95] One can also find independent accounts of personalism that attempt a similar integration of nature and person.[96] Wojtyła's influence has undoubtedly been magnified internationally by his elevation to the papacy. His use of personalist language and categories to understand sexuality also has surfaced at numerous points in his papal teaching and has continued to influence discussions of sexual ethics.[97]

But this approach also has been the subject of questions. For all of his effort to articulate the precise nature of the moral difference between recourse to natural and artificial means of birth regulation, it is still not fully clear why only contraceptive means divert the intentionality of spouses from one another, as persons and natural means do not.[98] Such a question becomes even more pressing in light of Janssens's query observed above

---

for wherever man dominates 'nature' it is by adapting himself to its immanent dynamic. Nature cannot be conquered by violating its laws." Ibid., 229. This effort to integrate person and nature in human activity concerns Wojtyła in other philosophical works. See *Acting Person*, 70–84, 181–86; and idem, "The Transcendence of the Person in Action and Man's Self-Teleology," *Analecta Husserliana* 9 (1979): 203–12.

95. For an analysis of Wojtyła's place within the circle that comprised "Lublin Thomism," see Stefan Swiezawski, "Karol Wojtyla at the Catholic University of Lublin," in *Person and Community*, trans. Theresa Sandok, Catholic Thought from Lublin 4 (New York: Peter Lang, 1993), ix–xvi. For a consideration of the school as a whole and its impact, see R. Duncan, "Lublin Thomism," *The Thomist* 51 (1987): 307–24.

96. See, e.g., Walter Kasper, *Zur Theologie der christlichen Ehe* (Mainz: Matthias-Grunewald-Verlag, 1977); English translation David Smith, *Theology of Christian Marriage* (New York: Seabury Press, 1980), esp. 17–21. For an overview of Kasper's project as whole and its implications for moral theology, see Grabowski, "Status of the Sexual Good," 25–28.

97. See, e.g., John Paul II, Apostolic Exhortation, *Familiaris consortio* (1981), nos. 11, 18–19, 24–26, 32; idem, *Reflections on Humanae Vitae: Conjugal Morality and Spirituality* (Boston: Daughters of St. Paul, 1984), esp. i–34, 77–96; idem, Letter to Families, *Gratissimam sane* (1994), nos. 9, 11–12. For sympathetic expositions of this teaching and its impact on moral theology, see Daryl Glick, "Recovering Morality: Personalism and Theology of the Body of Pope John Paul II," *Faith and Reason* 12 (1986): 7–25; Richard Hogan and John Levoir, *Covenant of Love: Pope John Paul II on Sexuality, Marriage, and Family in the Modern World* (New York: Doubleday, 1986); Andrew N. Woznicki, *The Dignity of Man as a Person: Essays on the Christian Humanism of His Holiness John Paul II* (San Francisco: Ignatius Press, 1987), 1–46. He has also added a stronger biblical basis to supplement the philosophical basis of his personalism. See Alain Mattheeuws, SJ, "De la Bible à *Humanae Vitae*: Les catecheses de Jean-Paul II," *Nouvelle Revue Théologique*. 111 (1989): 228–48; and Michael Seguin, "The Biblical Foundations of the Thought of John Paul II on Human Sexuality," *Communio* 20 (1993): 266–89.

98. Cf. Wojtyła, *Love and Responsibility*, 234–35.

concerning the "temporal barrier" to fertility created by methods of natural family planning.[99] Others have made the point that the idea that sexual acts have an intrinsic meaning such that certain acts (e.g., contraception, extramarital sex) are inherently contradictory or dishonest is unconvincing because it is only the immediate context or relationship that provides the meaning for sexual gestures.[100] Still others have asked whether mutuality in self-giving is experienced equally by women and men, given that the former still bear most of the weight of procreation.[101]

In terms of broader methodological questions, others have asked whether the notion of "the dignity of the person" underlying the personalist norm can actually serve as the basis of concrete norms that can evaluate the moral quality of specific acts.[102] This deficiency in the area of ethics is sometimes seen as the result of a broader anthropological flaw in the project that flows from its use of phenomenology in the service of a preconceived ontology of the person rather than achieving a genuine synthesis of differing methods.[103] Such questions are not easily answered, given that they flow from deeply divergent accounts of the place of anthropology in the enterprise of moral evaluation.[104]

Rival Models and Prospects for Personalism

There is widespread agreement among current scholars that the self-enclosed world of the moral manuals had, in the centuries preceding the present one, become tainted by physicalism.[105] That is, the language of human nature

99. But much of the force of this position depends upon Janssens's insistence that temporality is as basic to the person as embodiment.

100. Thus Gareth Moore, OP, *The Body in Context: Sex and Catholicism* (London: SCM Press, 1992), esp. 64–113. The philosophical presuppositions of the analytic tradition from which he operates make it difficult for Moore to ascribe a natural meaning or symbolism to virtually any act.

101. Cahill, "Catholic Sexual Ethics," 145–46. Cahill's query is directed primarily to the public teaching of Pope John Paul II.

102. See Bruno Schüller SJ, "Die Personwürde als Menschen als Beweisgrund in der normativen Ethik," *Theologie und Philosophie* 53 (1978): 538–55.

103. Böckle, "Nature as the Basis of Morality," 53–55.

104. One of the most basic issues of disagreement is whether one can derive normative judgments from a philosophical or theological account of the person or whether it is impossible to so derive "ought" from "is."

105. There is less agreement as to the origins of this physicalism. Some find in it in the

and natural law in some cases had become so closely tied to biological processes that these processes were seen as morally determinative. Physical laws
were thus wrapped in a mantle of divine authority.

The impulse toward personalism in moral theology in the present century can be understood in part as a response to this phenomenon and especially to the truncated account of sexuality that it produced. As the preceding analysis has demonstrated, however, the new focus on the person has
hardly been uniform in its method or in its conclusions. Rather, from its
inception, there have been important differences that separated proponents
of this approach.

Von Hildebrand's ground-breaking work strove to balance the primacy
of procreation as the end of marriage by delineating a new category—that
of meaning—in which love could be accorded primacy. Each value was seen
as having primary importance in its own sphere. Hence the natural value of
procreation was balanced by the new focus on personal self-giving love.[106]

Doms was dissatisfied with this juxtaposition of values in separate
spheres and sought to resolve some of the tension. He did this in two ways.
First, he abandoned the hierarchical language that ranked the various ends
of marriage and necessitated the creation of a new category in which to assert a different kind of primacy for love. In this he anticipated the teaching of
Gaudium et spes. Second, he made the personal communion of the couple—
their two-in-oneship—the chief end of marriage and all other ends subordinate to it. In this he indicated a trajectory for later revisionist personalism
that has tended to subordinate the exigencies of nature, understood in largely biological terms, to personal values that are seen as more weighty.

---

thought of Aquinas insofar as he was influenced by Ulpian. See Charles Curran, "Absolute Norms
and Moral Theology," in *A New Look at Christian Morality* (Notre Dame, IN: University of Notre Dame Press, 1968), 77–84; idem, "Natural Law," in *Directions in Fundamental Moral Theology*
(Notre Dame, IN: University of Notre Dame Press, 1985), 127–31; and Timothy O'Connell, *Principles for a Catholic Morality,* 2nd ed. (San Francisco: HarperOne, 1990), 153–55. Others locate it
in later Neo-Scholastic thought under the impact of nominalism. See Johnstone, "From Physicalism to Personalism," 76–78. Cf. Servais Pinckaers, OP, *Les sources de la morale chrétienne* (Fri-
bourg, 1985). English translation (from the 3rd ed.) by Mary Thomas Noble, *The Sources of Christian Ethics* (Washington, DC: Catholic University of America Press, 1995), 244–45.

106. A similar juxtaposition is attempted by Ramón García de Haro, *Marriage and the
Family in the Documents of the Magisterium: A Course in the Theology of Marriage,* 2nd ed. (San
Francisco: Ignatius Press, 1993), 195–98, 241–45. De Haro distinguishes between procreation as
the primary end of marriage and conjugal love as the way or path of marriage.

Under the pressure of later developments, such as the development of the progesterone pill, the heavily biological conception of nature that Doms still employed to defend fairly traditional conclusions regarding birth regulation unraveled altogether. Some possibilities open to subsequent moralists were: (1) to accept the limitations of this concept of nature conceived along biological lines as they became apparent in the debate and move on to a focus on more important personal values; (2) to attempt to resuscitate this concept of nature with the aid of personalist language; or (3) to argue that "nature" represented more than mere biology and hence had to be integrated with the new focus on personal values. These are the avenues taken by Louis Janssens, Paul Quay, and Karol Wojtyła, respectively.

Janssens's approach cannot be read as a complete rejection of the notion of "nature." Rather, he rightly critiques the physicalist concept found in many of the manuals as incapable of supporting many of the conclusions of traditional sexual ethics and inadequate to the rich reality of human sexuality. Having critiqued the older concept of nature, Janssens does go on to incorporate it into his anthropology, but as one element among others and certainly not as the most important. Things such as rationality, autonomy, freedom, and historicity emerge as central to his concept of the person. The new weight accorded to history and temporality in the ontology of the person opens the way to conceive nature in more processive terms, although Janssens does not fully embrace or articulate such a process ontology.

Quay's thought, on the other hand, represents a kind of retrenchment in the face of new questions in moral theology. Rather than facing the inadequacies of a physicalist concept of nature exposed by the development of the pill, Quay attempts to reconfigure this concept through the lens of natural and revealed symbols. Personalist language is added to this reading for rhetorical effect, but little else. The primacy of nature seen in the symbolism of natural acts and physical processes is basically unchallenged. Hence the mutual self-giving of conjugal love is clearly secondary and subordinate to procreation—even following the apparent abandonment of this hierarchal language by *Gaudium et spes*.[107] The result in Quay's case appears to be an updated version of physicalism.

107. Some authors argue that *Gaudium et spes* did not repudiate the hierarchy of the ends of marriage utilized in the 1917 Code of Canon Law. See Janet Smith, *Humanae Vitae: A Generation Later* (Washington, DC: Catholic University of America Press, 1991), 47–48; De Haro, *Marriage and the Family*, 195–98, 241–45; and William E. May, *Marriage: The Rock on Which*

Wojtyła's approach to the concept of nature in his elaboration of personalism is different. Here nature is understood not so much as biological law or physical process, but as inclinations toward fulfillment rooted in the being of humanity. These inclinations are then refracted through the person as bearer of an inestimable dignity and moral value. On the one hand, the person must act in accordance with his or her nature inasmuch as it is ground of personhood and the guide to fulfillment. On the other hand, the natural inclinations must be fully personalized through self-giving in which the beloved is also respected as a person. Both union and procreation as ends of sexuality emerge as equally important and interconnected, even if different, moral values. While these values affect and modify one another, theoretically one cannot be pursued at the expense of the other.[108]

Given such methodological and substantive diversity, what are the prospects for the future development of personalist approaches to issues of sexuality? This question can be considered both on the level of foundational issues and that of more specific questions.

In terms of foundational issues, first the analysis of Quay's thought above makes it clear that not all approaches that use the rhetoric of personal self-giving are genuinely personalist in their substance. Such an observation suggests that a baseline consideration for a method to lay claim to the personalist mantle is that there must be some way in which personal values can modify the demands of nature—either univocally or reciprocally. Otherwise the approach is simply a variation on the Neo-Scholastic natural law theory, however repackaged.

the Family Is Built (San Francisco: Ignatius Press, 1995), 110–12. There are a number of problems with such a view. First, it is not the reading of most scholars. Second, it ignores the theology of covenant present within the Pastoral Constitution, which serves as the vehicle for its embrace of personalist ideas. Third, it overlooks the fact that subsequent magisterial documents, including Humanae vitae (esp. no. 12), effectively settle the question by treating the two ends as not only equally important but also inseparable.

108. The widely echoed argument that the experience of periodic continence by those who use it is precisely that it is "unnatural" in forcing a couple to abstain from intercourse on the basis of biological patterns, for all its rhetorical force is undercut by its equivocation on the term "natural" as the basis for evaluating experience. For some examples of this argument, see Rosemary Radford Ruether, "Birth Control and the Ideals of Marital Sexuality," in Contraception and Holiness: The Catholic Predicament (New York: Herder & Herder, 1964), 72–91; and Burtchaell, Giving and Taking of Life, 40–41, 104–5. But these sources do make the point that there are some conflict situations in conjugal relationships where the love and procreation seem to be at odds with each other.

A second set of larger issues clusters around the precise manner of conceiving the key concept of nature and its relation to the person. The above analysis suggested at least three different possibilities: nature understood in largely physical terms, often identified with biological process; nature understood through the lens of process ontology as a continual unfolding in time; and nature viewed from a classical ontology as a stable set of inclinations rooted in the very being of a thing. Such differing conceptions of nature yield varying accounts of what it means to be a person and which moral values receive the greatest anthropological weight. Given that all of these accounts of nature have been subjected to criticism and that the second is still rather undeveloped, further work is needed on the foundational level of theological anthropology before the debate on specific questions can be approached fruitfully.[109]

A third large-scale issue that the above analysis highlights is the vexing separation between the language of being and obligation, is and ought. While the issue has been raised most forcefully in regard to Wojtyła's attempt to derive normative conclusions from his understanding of the person, any anthropological approach to moral questions must face this question, lest its reflections be reduced to the status of mere window dressing. If a particular understanding of the person has relevance for moral questions as most personalist approaches claim, then there must be a way to overcome the dichotomy between is and ought at some level. Elaboration of the precise manner in which differing accounts of personalism move from is to ought might reveal some unexpected common ground between approaches that appear to be intractably opposed as well as provide more clarity regarding the differences that do exist.

In terms of more concrete questions of sexual ethics, the above analysis reveals some interesting connections. Janssens's account of personalism, which privileges certain aspects of personhood over a biological understanding of nature, also seems to point toward the primacy of interpersonal love over procreation as the end of sexuality.[110] The result is, in regard to specific questions of sexual morality, that procreation is treated as a negotiable good, while interpersonal love is not. Conversely, Quay's approach,

109. A helpful preliminary philosophical overview of these concepts is provided by Ambrose McNicholl, OP, "Person, Sex, Marriage and Actual Trends of Thought," in *Human Sexuality and Personhood* (St. Louis, MO: Pope John XXIII Center, 1981), 138–65.

110. Cahill also suggests this reversal of the hierarchy of ends as a trajectory that flows from her overview of twentieth-century personalism. See "Catholic Sexual Ethics," 120, 122.

which grants priority to this same notion of nature, seems to retain the older hierarchy, which saw procreation as the primary end of sexuality. Hence procreation is the dominant moral value, and the love of the couple is dependent upon it for its realization. Wojtyła's method attempts to balance and integrate the ends of sexuality as it also strives to integrate nature and personhood. This approach seems best able to capture the equal importance of conjugal union and procreation implicit in *Gaudium et spes* and explicit in *Humanae vitae*. But this attempted integration also brings unique questions concerning how these ends can be balanced in specific cases.[111]

The purpose of the preceding analysis is not necessarily to reduce all of the debates within contemporary moral theology to this one. There are certainly other methodological approaches that make no claim to be personalist in any sense and that betray equally sharp disagreements with opposing views. There are also undoubtedly other thinkers who use personalist approaches akin to those identified here but provide them with different emphases and nuances.

What this analysis has aimed to accomplish is to distill from the discussion particular models of personalism by focusing on differing accounts of "nature," "person," and sexuality in order to better understand one part of the ongoing debate in sexual ethics. Focusing on these concepts has revealed both continuity of origin and rhetoric and often unrecognized areas of methodological disagreement between these rival approaches. But it is only in recognizing these approaches as distinct and irreducible to one another and identifying the precise areas in which they disagree that genuine and constructive dialogue can continue to develop.[112] Hence, in many respects, the discussion of the real significance of the shift to the personalist paradigm has only begun.

111. Such cases are of two kinds. First, this account must seek to clarify the exact status of the moral difference between natural and artificial means of birth regulation from the vantage point of its phenomenological personalism. This issue is the fulcrum upon which the debate has turned both historically and methodologically, and hence its adjudication will have a bearing across the whole range of issues concerning sexuality. Second, this account must also address how these two ends can be balanced in situations where there is real or apparent conflict between them.

112. Alasdair MacIntyre makes a similar claim regarding the conflict produced by real dialogue between rival moral traditions within the university in *Three Rival Versions of Moral Enquiry: Encyclopedia, Genealogy, and Tradition* (Notre Dame, IN: University of Notre Dame, 1990), 228–32.

6

Public Moral Discourse on Abortion

The Contribution of Theology

One of the most vexing and contentious issues for contemporary public moral discussion is that of abortion. Claims of justice, which require even treatment for all, collide with those of care, which prioritize certain relationships over others.[1] Even when a common linguistic framework is used, this can often mask deeply differing presuppositions and viewpoints (e.g., "the right to life" versus "the right to choose"). Such rival and incommensurable claims are a hallmark of the debate over this issue.[2] This clash has

Originally published as "Public Moral Discourse on Abortion: The Contribution of Theology," *Irish Theological Quarterly* 64 (1999): 361–77. I am indebted to Lawrence J. Welch, John Berkman, and the members of the Missouri Valley Association of Catholic Professors in Theology for helpful comments on earlier drafts of this essay. I would also like to express my gratitude to the Homeland Foundation for financial support in the form of a grant, which made this research possible.

1. Cf. Carol Gilligan's work on women's moral development focuses on the abortion question: *In a Different Voice* (Cambridge, MA: Harvard University Press, 1982).

2. It is little wonder that MacIntyre uses this issue as an example of intractable moral disagreement. See *After Virtue*, 2nd ed. (Notre Dame, IN: University of Notre Dame Press, 1984), 6–7. MacIntyre, however, highlights other kinds of divergent arguments about abortion: the right to choose what happens to one's body (which yields the conclusion that abortion should be legal); the difficulty of universalizing the choice to abort given that one would not will it in one's own case (which inclines toward seeing abortion as problematic, but not necessarily something to be prohibited by law); and the view that abortion is the killing of innocent human life and therefore a form of murder (which grounds an understanding that abortion should be seen as immoral and should be prohibited by law).

spilled over into the fields of law, social science, and even the hard sciences. Far from being disinterested providers of objective information, practitioners of such disciplines often show themselves committed to specific viewpoints that color their presentation of "the facts." While philosophers of science have questioned the myth of total objectivity for decades, this debate has fully exposed its fallacious character.[3] The supposed wall of separation between is and ought statements is breached daily in activist legal decisions and partisan science. Given this situation, is public moral discussion of abortion possible? Or should the idea be abandoned? Would it be better, as MacIntyre seems to intimate at the end of *After Virtue,* to focus on the building of new communities of moral praxis and leave the public domain to the powers that be?[4]

This essay argues against such a suggestion. Public moral discourse is a crucial component of any healthy society, particularly those that organize themselves along democratic lines. And integral to this discussion is the voice of religious faith—not simply for the perspective it affords on moral issues, but as a condition of the possibility for genuine democracy.[5] Such is also the case with the vexing debate over abortion. At the heart of this discussion is the question of when human personhood begins. This chapter argues that the beginning of human personhood cannot be discerned solely through scientific or philosophical considerations but only, as John Paul II has indicated, by also attending to the theological roots and meaning of the term "person" and its implications for the public moral discussion of this issue.

This study begins by surveying the apparent impasse between various scientific and philosophical positions on the beginning of human personhood. Building on the theological vision of personhood contained in *Evangelium vitae,* it returns to the theological roots of the term "person" in the Christological and Trinitarian theology of the early Church and draws out relevant implications for the current abortion debate. Finally, this study considers the implications of this more theological approach for public moral discussion in general.

---

3. See Anthony Fisher, OP, "'When Did I Begin?' Revisited," *Linacre Quarterly* 58 (1991): 67.

4. Cf. ibid., 263. MacIntyre's more recent works do attempt to generate tradition-based forms of public moral discussion and debate.

5. Cf. Richard John Neuhaus, *The Naked Public Square: Religion and Democracy in America,* 2nd ed. (Grand Rapids, MI: William B. Eerdmans, 1984).

Inquiry at an Impasse

Premodern philosophical treatments of the issue of abortion often centered around the idea of ensoulment. For Aquinas, as for Aristotle, the developing child was "informed" by a rational soul that entered it from without at a certain point of its development—some forty days for a male fetus, eighty for a female.[6] But such a view is closely tied to an inadequate and seemingly androcentric biology.[7] After the discovery of the female ovum (1823) and its union with sperm (1875), the idea of immediate ensoulment became popular. Yet there are still many Catholic defenders of "delayed hominization" who attempt to locate ensoulment or the beginning of personhood later in the spectrum of fetal development in the new context created by modern biology.[8]

---

6. Cf. Aristotle, *De generatione animalium* II, 3; Aquinas, *Summa contra Gentiles* II, ch. 89; *Summa theologiae* (*ST*) I, q. 118, a. 2. For an overview of Aquinas's thought on this point, which also provides arguments for "delayed hominization," see Joseph F. Donceel, "Immediate Animation and Delayed Hominisation," *Theological Studies* 31 (1970): 76, 105; and Philip Smith, "The Beginning of Personhood: A Thomistic Perspective," *Laval theologique et philosophique* 39 (1983): 195, 214. For a differing reading of Aquinas, which argues that he would have defended ensoulment from conception in the light of modem biological findings, see Stephen J. Heaney, "The Human Soul and the Early Embryo," *The Thomist* 56 (1992): 19–48. Cf. Augustine Regan, CSsR, "The Human Conceptus and Personhood," *Studia Moralia* 30 (1992): 97–125.

7. For a critique of the now-standard modern reading of Aristotelian and Thomistic biology as androcentric, see Michael Nolan, "The Defective Male: What Aquinas Really Said," *New Blackfriars* 75 (1994): 156–66; and idem, "Passive and Deformed? Did Aristotle Really Say This?," *New Blackfriars* 76 (1995): 237–57.

8. For other recent defenses of delayed hominization, see Norman M. Ford, *When Did I Begin? Conception of the Human Individual in History, Philosophy and Science* (New York: Cambridge University, 1988); Carlos A. Bedate and Robert C. Cefalo, "The Zygote: To Be or Not to Be a Person," *Journal of Medicine and Philosophy* 14 (1989): 641–45; Thomas A. Shannon and Allan B. Wolter, "Reflections on the Moral Status of the Pre-Embryo," *Theological Studies* 51 (1990): 603–26; Richard McCormick, SJ, "Who or What Is the PreEmbryo?," *Kennedy Institute of Ethics Journal* 1 (1991): 1–15; Vincent Genovesi, SJ, *In Pursuit of Love: Catholic Morality and Human Sexuality*, 2nd ed. (Collegeville, MN: Michael Glazier, 1996), 341–53. For an overview of the literature and the debate, see Lisa Sowle Cahill, "The Embryo and the Fetus: New Moral Contexts," *Theological Studies* 54 (1993): 124–43. For a critique of this position, see Benedict M. Ashley, OP, "Delayed Hominization: A Catholic Theological Perspective," in *The Interaction of Catholic Bioethics and Secular Society* (Braintree, MA: Pope John XXIII Center for the Study of Ethics in Health Care, 1992), 163–79; Diane Nutwell Irwin, "Scientific and Philosophical Expertise: An Evaluation of the Arguments of Personhood," *Linacre Quarterly* 60 (1993): 18–46; and Mark Johnson, "Reflections on Some Recent Catholic Claims for Delayed Hominization," *Theological Studies* 56 (1995): 743–63.

Contemporary biology, genetics, and law have located a number of watershed moments in the development of the fetus, each of which has been championed as the beginning of human personhood: the process of fertilization resulting in conception, which forms a unique and unrepeatable genetic pattern that will govern the development of this organism until its death; segmentation or "twinning" and in some cases recombination of preembryos, which can occur up to the fourteenth day; implantation of the blastocyst in the endometrium—a point not reached by perhaps 50 percent of fertilized ova;[9] development of the cerebral cortex to a point where brain-wave activity is measurable by an electroencephalogram, or EEG (approximately eight weeks), indicating a foundation for consciousness;[10] and viability, the point at which a fetus can survive independently from its mother. While this last criterion was used by the US Supreme Court in *Roe v. Wade*, it is obviously artificial, as its rollback by advancing medical technology has demonstrated. There are still other markers that are sometimes cited.[11]

Underlying such competing scientific or legal positions, each with its own set of data and defenders, are divergent philosophical presuppositions concerning personhood—highlighting things such as individuality, rationality, or autonomy. There is no one agreed upon philosophical definition or model, however. The Boethian definition of "an individual substance of a rational nature"[12] stands over against the disembodied subjectivity high-

9. Johnson, "Reflections on Some Recent Catholic Claims," 745n8, notes that Allen J. Wilcox et al. reduce this number to 20 percent before implantation and 31 percent after this point. Cf. "Incidence of Early Loss Pregnancy," *New England Journal of Medicine* 319, no. 4 (1988): 189–94.

10. See, e.g., Hans-Martin Sass in *Health Care Systems: Moral Conflicts in European and American Public Policy*, ed. Hans-Martin Sass and Robert U. Massey (Dordrecht: Kluwer Academic, 1988). Others hold open the possibility of an earlier beginning of life but still argue that a soul can only exist in a body that has achieved sufficient neural development. See Thomas Bole, "Metaphysical Accounts of the Zygote as a Person and the Veto Power of Facts," *Journal of Medicine and Philosophy* 14 (1989): 647–53.

11. E.g., some point to blood formation, which occurs at around twenty-one days as signaling the beginning of individual life. See Shirley L. Barron, "Searching for Life's Beginning," *Christianity Today* 35, no. 13 (1991): 41. The more recent debate over partial-birth abortion suggests that birth itself is another such marker for some legal views.

12. *Naturae rationalis individua substantia*. See *De persona et duabis naturis*, 3. The citation is from the Loeb text *Boethius: Theological Tractates and the Consolation of Philosophy*, ed. H. F. Stewart and E. K. Rand (Cambridge, MA: Harvard University Press, 1918). The Boethian definition is invoked by Johnson, "Reflections on Some Recent Catholic Claims," 762–63.

lighted by Descartes,[13] the Kantian emphasis on autonomous individuality, the Marxist analysis of power relations and economic conditions, and
the postmodern socially constructed self.[14] How does one choose among
such rival positions with their widely differing estimates of what counts for
human personhood? And it is precisely the beginning of personhood that
underlies much of the debate over abortion. Such difficulties suggest that a
solution may not be fully possible on scientific grounds alone.[15]

The Theological Roots of Person

In light of this apparent impasse, it is instructive to consider the different
perspective afforded by Pope John Paul II's encyclical letter *Evangelium vitae*. Before its solemn condemnation of direct abortion, it offers a contrast
between two visions of personhood, each of which is embedded within a
differing cultural matrix. The first is a functional understanding of the person that is enmeshed in the "culture of death." The other offers a theological
and Trinitarian understanding of the person that is at the heart of a "culture
of life."

A functional understanding of the person sees personhood as constituted by performance—the ability to sustain certain kinds of activity such as
communication or work. Freedom, in this view, is understood in monadic

13. A number of authors in the debate identify personhood as a kind of "subjective
self-awareness." See, e.g., Clifford Grobstein, "A Biological Perspective on the Origin of Human Life and Personhood," in *Defining Human Life*, ed. M. W. Shaw and A. E. Doudera
(Washington, DC: Association of University in Health Administration, 1983), 1–11; Thomas J. Bole III, "Zygotes, Souls, Substances, and Persons," *Journal of Medicine and Philosophy* 15
(1990): 637–52.

14. H. Tristam Engelhardt Jr. argues that the epistemological presuppositions of postmo-
dernity make it impossible to frame a meaningful public moral argument against abortion.
See his "Personhood, Moral Strangers, and the Evil of Abortion: The Painful Experience of
Post-Modernity," *Journal of Medicine and Philosophy* 18 (1993): 419–21.

15. Thus Lisa Sowle Cahill, reviewing recent debates on the issue among Catholic thinkers
utilizing scientific data, judiciously remarks: "what is all too clear from this (ongoing) exchange
of scientific trumps is that moral theologians should be wary of finalizing their analysis on the
basis of research likely to be indefinitely in progress" (136). In this I disagree with Mark Johnson's self-described "antipathy to the project of letting theological concerns dictate the direction that what is first of all a biological investigation should take." "Reflections on Some Recent
Catholic Claims," 745n8; cf. 749, 761–62. I am not sure that the question of personhood can be
resolved apart from theological concerns.

fashion as individual autonomy, producing a society understood as a collection of individuals.[16] Human rights are simply extensions of one's personal autonomy and capacity to function, and therefore can be denied to those who lack these abilities.[17] Nature is seen simply as matter to be dominated and exploited, and the human body as a tool to be used according to the criteria of efficiency and pleasure.[18] Even fundamental values such as life come to be seen as commodities subject to human control and manipulation. This utter lack of objective moral values serves to create moralities of pleasure (hedonism) and efficacy (utilitarianism), which in turn yield the many manifestations of what the encyclical calls the "culture of death."[19]

Over against this view of personhood stands a distinctly theological one. Here it is relation that is constitutive of personhood. Human freedom is understood as "entrustment"—the actualization of such relations in relationships of self-giving love. Rights are grounded in the dignity of the person created by God and redeemed by Christ, and cannot be removed by the fiat of a group or a government.[20] Nature is understood not as mere matter but mater to be treated with reverence and appropriate stewardship. The human body is the locus of the person's relationality and the self-giving that enacts it. Morality and human freedom are therefore founded on truth, particularly the truth of the human person. Such an understanding of the person is at the heart of an authentic "culture of life."[21]

This theological view of personhood, with the concept of relation at its

16. This individualism may be founded upon a Lockeian understanding of the social contract or upon a more radical atomic individualism (such as that of Hobbes) in which "everyone else is considered an enemy from whom one has to defend himself" (*Evangelium vitae*, no. 20).

17. This denial can take place through a kind of social will to power in which stronger groups impose themselves on weaker ones. Or it can take place through a totalitarian imposition on the part of government. See *Evangelium vitae*, no. 20.

18. Conversely, some in opposing a purely instrumental view of nature go to the opposite extreme, deifying it. See *Evangelium vitae*, no. 22.

19. Among such symptoms, John Paul points to widespread abortion; the growing impetus for legalized euthanasia; hostility toward the weakest members of society; materialism and greed; war; the trivialization of sex; and the perversion of professions such as law, medicine, or politics in the service of such ends. See *Evangelium vitae*, nos. 10–17.

20. This is most clear in the case of the value of human life, in regard to which the encyclical offers a profound mediation on the value of human life revealed most fully in the blood of Jesus and the offer of eternal life. See *Evangelium vitae*, nos. 2, 25, 36–38, 51.

21. The encyclical notes many signs of the culture of life in today's world: the generosity of married couples in caring for the elderly, the handicapped, or the unborn; improved medical

heart, recalls the origin of the term "person" in the Trinitarian theology of the early Church.[22] Historical study has demonstrated the lack of a fully equivalent concept in the ancient world.[23] The earliest human cultures were basically mimetic in character, and the notion of individuality emerged slowly. Biblically, one can locate conceptual antecedents of person in the ideas of a "face" or a "name."[24] In classical thought, one finds a growing concept of individuality so that by the time of Cicero, *persona* could indicate grammatical person, a corporation, or the mask or role of an actor in a stage production.[25] But such individuality is not yet equivalent to the concept of person.

The notion of person proper grew out of the method of prosopological exegesis developed by Stoic commentators on Homer and employed by Philo in reading the Old Testament (OT). Early Christian fathers (e.g., Irenaeus, Justin, Origen) employed the method to discern the Persons of the Father, the Word, or the Holy Spirit speaking in the text of the OT.[26] But such designations named not merely literary figures, but, from the perspective of Christian faith, realities—the three Persons of the Godhead who shared a common nature (*substantia, natura*).[27]

In Greek theology the Cappadocian Fathers made, with greater preci-

---

technology in the service of life; nonviolent forms of pro-life action; the sacrifice of those who answer the call to religious life; new public opposition to war and capital punishment; and concern for the environment. See *Evangelium vitae*, nos. 26–27.

22. Other authors note but do not develop this Christological and Trinitarian origin of the term. See Regan, "Human Conceptus and Personhood," 98; and Livio Melina, "Epistemological Questions with Regard to the Status of the Human Embryo," in *Identity and Statute of Human Embryo: Proceedings of the Third Assembly of the Pontifical Academy for Life*, ed. Juan de Dios, Vial Correa, and Elio Sgreccia (Rome: Libreria Editrice Vaticana, 1998), 96–127; see esp. 125.

23. On the historical emergence and evolution of person, see Kenneth L. Schmitz, "The Geography of the Human Person," *Communio* 13 (1986): 27–43; and John S. Grabowski, "Person: Substance and Relation," *Communio* 22 (1995): 139–63.

24. See Walter Kasper, *Theology and Church*, trans. Margaret Kohl (New York: Crossroad, 1989), 26; and John L. McKenzie, "Face," in *The Dictionary of the Bible* (New York: Macmillan, 1965), 266–67.

25. See Aloys Grillmeier, SJ, *From the Apostolic Age to Chalcedon (451)*, vol. 1, *Christ in Christian Tradition*, trans. John Bowden (London: Mowbrays, 1965), 125–26.

26. See Michael Slussler, "The Exegetical Roots of Trinitarian Theology," *Theological Studies* 49 (1988): 461–76.

27. See Joseph Cardinal Ratzinger, "Concerning the Notion of Person in Theology," trans. Michael Waldstein, *Communio* 17 (1990): 442.

sion, a similar distinction between person and nature.[28] The one Godhead (*ousia*) exists concurrently in three persons or hypostases (*prosópon* or *hupostasis*). In fact, in this view, "person" precedes nature because the being of God exists in the communion of life, which has its origin in the Father and then is shared with the Son and Spirit.[29] If God is this one event of communion or life, how are the Persons of the Godhead known? The answer is through individuating characteristics that mark them as relationally distinct from one another—ungenerateness (Father); generateness (Son); and mission, procession, or sanctifying power (the Holy Spirit).[30]

In the West, Augustine worked out a similar understanding with different language. Responding to the Arian attempt to render plurality within the Trinity incoherent by casting it into Aristotelian categories of substance or accident,[31] Augustine offered the notion of relation as an alternative. The Three Divine Persons are known through their mutual relations (begetting, being begotten, proceeding). For Augustine, these relations are real because God's essence subsists in them.[32]

This brief sketch of early Christian Trinitarian theology highlights a number of important points. First, the concept of person was born within the early Church's attempt to articulate its faith in the mystery of the Trinity (as well as the mystery of Christ). From this theological origin it has passed into Western vocabulary both philosophically and in common speech, where it has undergone various mutations throughout history. But etymologically and historically, the origin of the term was theological. Second, at the heart of this theological origin in both East and West is the notion of relation. Third, it is precisely this theological view that highlights relationality, which *Evangelium vitae* uses as a backdrop for its condemnation

---

28. See John Zizioulas, *Being as Communion: Studies in Personhood and the Church*, Contemporary Greek Theologians 4 (Crestwood, NY: St. Vladimir's Seminary Press, 1993), 87–89.

29. This is because substance never exists by itself in a "naked" state, but only within a particular "mode of existence" *hypostasis*, namely, the person of the Father. See Basil, *Epistulae*, 38, 2, *PG* 32:325*ff*. Cf. Gregory of Nyssa, *Contra Eunomium*, 1, *PG* 45:337.

30. Basil speaks of "sanctifying power" or "sanctification" in regard to the Holy Spirit. The other Cappadocians hold that the Holy Spirit is known through "mission" or "procession.'" See Basil, *Epistulae*, 214, 4, *PG* 32:789; 236, 6, *PG* 32:884; Gregory Nazianzen, *Orations*, 25, 16, *PG* 35:122; cf. 26, 19, *PG* 35:1252; 29, 2, *PG* 36:76. Cf. J. N. D. Kelly, *Early Christian Doctrines* (New York: Harper and Brothers, 1959), 265.

31. See Kelly, *Early Christian Doctrines*, 11, 274.

32. See *De Trin.*, 5.7, *PL* 42:911–46; *De civitate dei*, 11, 10, *PL* 41:325*ff*.

of direct abortion. Therefore, even though the concept of person sketched above was forged within Trinitarian theology, it has implications for human persons created in the image of God, and for when this created personhood begins.

Ethical Implications

What are the implications of this more theological vision of personhood for the vexing debate over abortion? At the very least it provides an alternative to other accounts of personhood that have had an impact on this discussion.

The first of these other accounts might be called "volitional personhood." This view holds that if relation constitutes personhood, then we become persons when others (e.g., mothers, doctors) choose to relate to us. Thus George Tavard, in locating his dynamic and Trinitarian account of the image of God in the human person understood as being in relation, has argued against the full personhood of a newly born child. Rather, insofar as a child is born an individual, "he is not in the image of God; yet as soon as he interrelates with others (which means, in practice, as soon as a midwife or doctor or his mother picks him up) he then begins to become a person."[33] In a similar vein, Majorie Reiley Maguire has used a relational understanding of personhood to argue that a fetus only becomes a person when its mother makes a "personing covenant" with her unborn child (i.e., chooses to regard it as a person).[34]

This understanding of both "person" and "relation" fails to recognize that relation is ontologically prior to its volitional enactment in specific relationships. It is undoubtedly true that, in the case of the Trinitarian Persons described above, the two are inseparably united. The Father cannot repudiate his relation to the Son or Spirit because in God, who is the very fullness of love, relation and relationship are one and the same. In the case

33. George Tavard, *Woman in Christian Tradition* (Notre Dame, IN: University of Notre Dame Press, 1973), 191; cf. 192, 196.

34. Majorie Reiley Maguire, "Personhood, Covenant, and Abortion," *American Journal of Philosophy and Theology* 6, no. 1 (1985): 28–46. In more recent public statements, this author has repudiated many of these views. See Charlotte Hayes, "The Choices of Majorie Maguire," *Our Sunday Visitor*, July 23, 1995, 6–7.

of human creatures who exist in space and time, however, the two can and must be distinguished. And this is so for at least two reasons.

First, because human beings are creatures, human and divine person-hood must be understood as analogous rather than identical to one anoth-er. This means that, while there is continuity, there is even greater discon-tinuity between them.[35] Only the divine Persons are persons in the fullest and most real sense. As Jean Galot notes, the originality of the divine Per-sons inscribed by their differing relations of origin is far more radical than that of individual human persons created by God. Furthermore, while each of the divine Persons possesses the fullness of the divine nature, human per-sons possess only their own individual nature and therefore do not enjoy the same unity of thought and love. Finally, while the divine Persons are utterly perfect from their origin, human personality grows through the ac-tivation of one's relational dynamism in actual relationships, passing from potency to act over the course of a lifetime.[36]

Second, human beings are not only finite, but also fallen. As such one can have a good or bad relationship with God or with one's parents—or no relationship at all—and yet these fundamental relations still exist and will still shape the identity of this person. One will still be a creature of God and the son or daughter of this particular man and this particular woman for the whole of one's existence in spite of any estrangement or attempts to repudiate this reality.[37] And such relations affect us on a host of levels—spiritual, ontological, genetic, intellectual, affective, physical, and social.[38] Hence for human beings, relation cannot be reduced to the choice to be in a relationship—volition cannot confer personhood, only acknowledge it.

Closely related to the reduction of person to a status conferred by the choice of another is a second view, which might be called "performative

---

35. This is the classic understanding of the Fourth Lateran Council (cf. *DS* 806) and Thomas Aquinas (cf. *ST* I, q. 13, a. 5).

36. See Jean Galot, SJ, *Who Is Christ? A Theology of the Incarnation*, trans. M. Angeline Bouchard (Chicago: Franciscan Herald Press, 1981), 303–5.

37. Such consciousness of being shaped by one's family or tribe was much stronger in pre-modern societies, which were less characterized by individualism.

38. It is worth considering that analogous graced relations are established by the sacra-ments: becoming a son or daughter of God (baptism); being anointed by the Spirit and com-missioned for Christian service (confirmation); becoming "one flesh" as husband or wife (mar-riage); being conformed to Christ in his office of Priest (orders).

personhood." In this understanding we become persons to the degree that we can function at a given level.[39] Such a view is reinforced in our culture, which ties identity to performance and productivity.[40] This, at root, is the basis for identifying the personhood of the unborn in terms of rationality or viability (as in *Roe v. Wade*). It is also the basis for the view that, once we can no longer function at a required level or perform various roles, or our lives lack requisite "quality," we cease to be persons and therefore can be eliminated (i.e., involuntary euthanasia).

This view is likewise flawed by problematic presuppositions and implications. To predicate personhood on having a certain level of function is to deny the very heart of the concept. It collapses the Christian insight into the person as a being who exists in relation back into the pagan *persona*—a role, a mask, a function. Further, it subjects the whole notion of personhood and rights that inhere in it to the whim of government or other powerful interest groups in a given society. That is, it makes personhood something that can be arbitrarily given or taken away depending on where the bar of function is set.

In opposition to these problematic views, an understanding of personhood that attends to its origin in the theology of the Trinity sees the relations that constitute human beings as persons given in our very existence. Simply to be is to be in relation—to God, to parents, to one's family, to all humanity—from the first moments of our existence. Therefore the first moments of human existence are personal because they are relational. Personhood is not a status conferred by the arbitrary fiat of another or earned through achievement of a specific level of function; it is a gift inscribed in the very fabric of human existence.

39. Thus Michael Tooley argues that because fetuses (and even infants) are incapable of desire and self-awareness, they do not enjoy a right to life. See "In Defense of Abortion and Infanticide," in *The Problem of Abortion*, ed. Joel Feinberg (Belmont, CA: Wadsworth, 1984), 120–34. Joseph Fletcher ties personhood even more closely to specific quantitative levels, insisting not simply on neocortical function, but on measurable thinking by the cerebral cortex, such as a score of 20 on the Binet scale measuring intelligence, or IQ. See "Abortion," in *Humanhood: Essays in Biomedical Ethics* (Buffalo, NY: Prometheus, 1979), 134–35. Cf. "Four Indicators of Humanhood—The Enquiry Matures," in *On Moral Medicine: Theological Perspectives in Medical Ethics*, ed. Stephen Lammers and Allan Verhey (Grand Rapids, MI: William B. Eerdmans, 1987), 276.

40. This understanding is basically akin to the functional understanding of person critiqued by *Evangelium vitae* summarized above.

Having recalled the theological origins of the term person, it is possible once again to consider empirical evidence concerning the origin of personhood. As the Second Vatican Council taught: "Only in the mystery of the incarnate Word does the mystery of man take on light… Christ, the final Adam, by the revelation of the mystery of the Father and His love, fully reveals man to himself and makes his supreme calling clear."[41] The revelation of Christ, which is at the same time the revelation of the mystery of the Trinity as well as the human person,[42] offers a hermeneutical key for understanding human personhood and its origins. Having begun "from above" in understanding personhood, it is possible search for confirmation "from below."

This chapter considers but a few examples. In this vein it is surely worthy of note that when the process of fertilization is complete, the newly conceived zygote possesses an utterly unique genetic code that is different from both that of the mother and the father and sets in motion a intensive process of growth and development.[43] The zygote, while formed by the union of maternal and paternal gametes, is not reducible to either. The sum is more than either of its parts. Further, this genetic code will shape the development and function of this organism for the whole of its existence.[44] Yet this code is formed and directed precisely through the mutual relation of maternal and paternal genes. Such a biological marker is indicative, though certainly not exhaustive, of the relationality at the heart of human personhood. A person for the whole of his or her existence is the son or daughter of this particular man or woman (i.e., parents) as well as a creature of God.[45]

---

41. *Gaudium et spes*, no. 22. The citation is from *The Documents of Vatican II*, ed. Walter M. Abbott, SJ (Piscataway, NJ: New Century, 1966), 220.

42. On the inseparable connection between Christology, Trinitarian theology, and anthropology, see Walter Kasper, "One of the Trinity: Re-establishing a Spiritual Christology in the Perspective of Trinitarian Theology," in *Theology and Church*, 94–108; and idem, "Christology and Anthropology," in *Theology and Church*, 73–93.

43. For a fascinating defense of human personhood from conception, see the remarks of the renowned French geneticist Jérôme Lejeune in his interview with Robert Sasson in *The Tiniest Humans*, 2nd ed. (Stafford, VA: American Life League, 1977), 56–76. On the purposeful self-development of the pre- and postimplantation embryo, see the excellent summary in Johnson, "Reflections on Some Recent Catholic Claims," 744–54.

44. Johnson, "Reflections on Some Recent Catholic Claims," 753n18, observes that the term "blueprint" often used to describe this genetic code is potentially misleading insofar as the term implies a form utilized by another in the construction of a thing, whereas the zygote is very much an agent in its own development.

45. Obviously, such relationality is more than genetic or even biological. It is also social,

This observation can also shed some light on some of the most common objections to attributing personhood to the embryo prior to implantation in the uterus.[46] One such objection involves hydatidiform moles—uterine tumors that contain an unusually large amount of placental tissue, but no fetus. Some have argued that because such nonpersonal entities can arise from a zygote, it follows that zygotes cannot be persons.[47] However, modern genetics has found that hydatidiform moles are formed from defective or "pseudo-zygotes," resulting from a sperm fertilizing an ovum in which the female pronucleus is absent, or an ovum fertilized by multiple sperm in which the maternal pronucleus has died.[48] While one can question the assertion that hydatidiform moles disprove the personhood of the embryo on biological grounds,[49] the above analysis of the theological origins of the term "person" can raise still other questions. Namely, occasional phenomena such as hydatidiform moles lack the relation of maternal and paternal genes, which is a necessary but not sufficient condition for personhood.[50]

A second problem often cited by critics of the attribution of personhood to the embryo prior to implantation is the fact that the developing embryo at this stage seems to be dependent on extranucleic genetic information for its development, such as genetic material from maternal mitochondria or information supplied by messenger ribonucleic acid (RNA) or

---

interpersonal, and historical. All of these facets analogously bear witness to the underlying ontology of the person. On the endurance of personhood over the whole of one's existence, see Stanley Hauerwas, "Must a Patient Be a Person to Be a Patient? Or, My Uncle Charlie Is Not Much of a Person But He Is Still My Uncle Charlie," in *On Moral Medicine*, 278–81.

46. While some ethicists continue to use the term "pre-embryo," most current works of embryology have abandoned it as scientifically inaccurate. See, e.g., Ronan O'Rahilly and Fabiola Müller, *Human Embryology and Teratology*, 2nd ed. (New York: Wiley-Liss, 1996), 8, 12; and Lee M. Silver, *Remaking Eden: Cloning and Beyond in a Brave New World* (New York: Avon, 1997), 39.

47. See Bedate and Cefalo, "The Zygote," 644.

48. See Jérôme Lejeune's testimony in the custody case of the frozen embryos in Maryville, Tennessee, reprinted in *Child and Family* 21, no. 1 (August 1989): 7–52.

49. See Johnson, "Reflections on Some Recent Catholic Claims," 755–56. See also Antonie Suarez, "Hydatidiform Moles and Teratomes Confirm Human Identity of the Preimplantation Embryo," *Journal of Medicine and Philosophy* 15 (1990): 627–35; and Diane Nutwell Irving, "Philosophical and Scientific Analysis of the Nature of the Early Human Embryo" (PhD diss., Georgetown University, 1991), 72.

50. The same might be said for "dermoid cysts" in women formed by the division of a non-fertilized ova.

proteins.[51] This dependency undercuts the assertion that the early embryo has all the necessary genetic information to order its own development. Further, it calls into question the individuality and hence the personhood of the embryo prior to implantation.[52]

This suggestion too has been challenged on biological grounds.[53] In addition to this evidence, the preceding analysis suggests other issues. To assert that individuality must be marked by utter genetic autonomy on the part of the zygote is to ignore the relationality constitutive of personhood. To find further evidence of the zygote's dependence on paternal and maternal genetic influence is simply a further indication of this relationality and indeed of the dependence that characterizes the whole of unborn life.[54]

A third issue, and one that appears to pose the greatest problems for the theological approach being developed here, is that of the totipotentiality of the early embryo's cells—the fact that, in a small number of cases, cells of the preimplantation embryo can give rise to its genetic double.[55] It has also been speculated that separate embryos can combine, or divided embryos recombine, to form a single organism.[56] For a number of authors the apparent fluidity and lack of individual identity on the part of the early embryo rules out it being considered an individual and hence a person.[57] Further, in

---

51. Cf. Bedate and Cefalo, "The Zygote," 641–45.

52. Ibid.

53. Ronald K. Tacelli, SJ, observes that the claim that the postimplantation embryo requires genetic information to develop into a human being is simply false: "The mother does not give any genetic information to the conceptus, in the sense of giving something that changes this being from one kind of thing to another. It is certainly true that at and after implantation, the embryo needs certain molecules from the mother to develop properly. But note: the search for just these molecules is directed *by the embryo itself*, and this activity is determined by *what the embryo is and what it is striving to become*." See "Were You a Zygote?," *Josephinum Journal of Theology* 4, no. 1 (1997): 30 (emphasis original). Cf. Johnson, "Reflections on Some Recent Catholic Claims," 756–57.

54. It is worth recalling *Evangelium vitae*'s identification of authentic human freedom with entrustment, as opposed to autonomy noted above.

55. Johnson, "Reflections on Some Recent Catholic Claims," 759, notes that the observable number of monozygotic or identical twins is about one-quarter of 1 percent of births.

56. Regan, "Human Conceptus and Personhood," 103, observes that there have been no documented cases of combination or recombination of human embryos either through natural or artificial means.

57. See Ford, *When Did I Begin?*; Shannon and Wolter, "Reflections on the Moral Status of the Pre-Embryo," 614; and McCormick, "Who or What Is the PreEmbryo?," 2.

the light of the analysis above, it might be urged that a monozygotic twin shares the same genetic makeup as its twin, and hence one should not make too much of genetic uniqueness as a marker for personhood.

But such conclusions are perhaps premature. Biologically this seems to overlook the unity and coordination of function among the cells of the early embryo.[58] It also does not adequately deal with some emerging research that suggests that the phenomenon of twinning may not be an indicator of the complete indeterminacy of embryonic cells, but of the presence of genetic defects or mutations that are its cause.[59] Further, it fails to note that, in the rare event of twinning, an existing individual does not cease to exist and instead is replaced by two new daughter cells. Rather, the embryo continues to exist while giving rise to its genetic double.[60]

In terms of the relationality of which the genetic marker bespeaks, it is true that monozygotic twins share a common genetic makeup that is inherited from their parents (and for this reason are often profoundly similar in ways that go beyond appearance). But this in no way undermines their personal irreducibility and uniqueness. This can be seen for two reasons. First, this common makeup itself points to a unique relation that exists between them and shapes them as persons—a relation like other fraternal bonds yet unique in its nearness and intensity. Second, as noted above, the unique genetic code of each person is but one sign or marker of the relations constitutive of personhood—but the person exists in ways other than genetically or biologically. Persons are historical beings who live in specific environments and are affected by interpersonal relationships in their families, communities, and in their lives of faith.[61]

This observation suggests a qualification of the distinction drawn be-

58. See Tacelli, "Were You a Zygote?," 31–32; and Johnson, "Reflections on Some Recent Catholic Claims," 760.

59. Johnson, "Reflections on Some Recent Catholic Claims," 759, cites Judith Hall, "A New Theory on the Origin of Twins (Mutations within the Embryo)," *Science News* 146, no. 6 (1992): 84; and John Horgan, "Double Trouble: When Identical Twins Are Not Identical," *Scientific American* 262, no. 6 (1990): 25–26.

60. See Regan, "Human Conceptus and Personhood," 124. Others have likened this to a kind of asexual reproduction that in no way threatens individuality. See Nicholas Tonti-Filippini, "A Critical Note," *Linacre Quarterly* 56 (1989): 36–50; and Tacelli, Were You a Zygote?, 32.

61. Thus because of such environmental differences even genetically identical twins can differ in intelligence, temperament, interpersonal skills, and character.

tween relation and relationship above. If theologically one would insist that relation is ontologically prior to its historical enactment in specific relationships, it nevertheless remains true that one of the tasks of all human beings is to actualize the relations constitutive of personhood in relationships characterized by the communion of love.[62] Especially as such relationships are healed by grace, then one's irreducibility and spontaneity as a person can increasingly shine through the relations that constitute him or her. In this sense, it is possible to speak of such graced communion as a "way toward personality."[63]

The preceding theological argument makes it possible to move beyond probability based on disputed biological facts, or a position that gives the "benefit of the doubt" to unborn life by holding that because a human soul might be present, it is morally wrong to abort it even at early stages of fetal development.[64] This is because personhood is not dependent upon the achievement of a certain level of biological function, individual autonomy, or upon the fiat of others. It is a gift inscribed in the fabric of human existence. Human life cannot exist apart from a profound relation to God and other human beings, particularly one's parents.[65] Such relations make the person not only irreducibly unique, but also "irreplaceable." Hence direct abortion is wrong precisely because it destroys the life of an innocent hu-

62. In this sense, the observation above concerning the simultaneity of human existence, relation, and personhood also requires qualification. All created things stand in relation to God as creatures. Even such categories as substance and being may be correctly understood in relational terms. On this, see Grabowski, "Person," 159–60; and Thomas Kopfensteiner, SJ, "The Role of the Sciences in Moral Reasoning," *Science et Esprit* 1 (1998): 79–97. Not all substances or created realities are persons, however, because person-making relations are characterized by understanding, freedom, and love, which make communion possible. These qualities need not be fully actualized (as in the case of the embryo or a comatose patient), but must be present at least potentially.

63. Romano Guardini, *La realtà della Chiesa* (Brescia: 1973), 63. Cf. Livio Melina, "Moral Conscience and 'Communio': The Challenge of Ethical Pluralism," *Communio* 20 (1993): 673–86; and Kenneth L. Schmitz, "Selves and Persons: A Difference in Loves?," *Communio* 18 (1991): 183–206.

64. This "benefit of the doubt" approach was utilized by even some recent Church teaching, such as the 1974 Congregation for the Doctrine of the Faith *Declaration on Procured Abortion* (*Origins* 4 [1974]: 385–90) or its 1987 Instruction, *Donum vitae* (*Origins* 16 [1987]: 697–711).

65. Thus *Evangelium vitae*, quoting *Donum vitae*, observes: "How could a human individual not be a human person" (no. 60).

man person, regardless of his or her stage of fetal development.[66] And human persons are not merely irreducibly unique, but also "irreplaceable."[67] Having considered a theological understanding of personhood and the light it can shed on certain biological data, it remains to consider what contribution this approach can make to a polarized debate in a pluralistic society.

Implications for Public Moral Argument

In the light of the preceding theological argument against abortion, one might conclude that in a religiously diverse society it has little to contribute to the public moral debate over this issue. As theological and specifically Trinitarian, it might be found convincing by some Christians, but it has little to offer to those from other religious traditions or those with no religious faith. It might be argued that this approach is a retreat from the natural law language used by the Church to appeal to "all persons of good will" in discussing moral issues in a public context. It therefore runs the risk of lapsing into a kind of sectarianism foreign to the Catholic tradition. Such objections, however, are unfounded. This is evident for a number of reasons.

First, the above argument has a bearing on the public debate simply insofar as it offers an accurate account of the origin and history of the term "person." It can therefore question the adequacy of usage that describes personhood in purely functional or volitional terms even apart from a theological context. While it is true that the meaning of terms can change over time, and that this has happened to some degree in the case of the term

---

66. Cf. John Paul II, *Evangelium vitae*, no. 62. It seems to me that if one reads this solemn condemnation together with the previous proscription of direct killing of the innocent (no. 57) and the whole theological vision of personhood that the encyclical offers, there is some movement beyond the "benefit of the doubt" approach taken by previous teaching concerning the beginning of personhood.

67. Cf. John Paul II, Encyclical Letter, *Redemptor hominis*, no. 13. It is true that some, while acknowledging the humanity of the fetus, have argued that abortion can still be morally justified. See Judith Jarvis Thomson, "A Defense of Abortion," *Philosophy and Public Affairs* 1 (Fall 1971): 47–66; and the development of her work by F. M. Kamm, *Creation and Abortion: A Study in Moral and Legal Philosophy* (New York: Oxford University Press, 1992). But it seems that such an argument fails to account for the uniqueness and irreplaceable quality of the person. For a more specific critique of Thomson's argument and its presuppositions, see Gilbert Meilaender, *The Limits of Love: Some Theological Explorations* (University Park: Pennsylvania State University Press, 1987), 48–59.

"person," because of the historical and tradition-based character of language, there must be a certain organic continuity with this origin.[68] Hence this usage can and should have a corrective function within the debate, even simply on historical and philological levels.

Second, the assumption that natural law arguments must exclude any theological concerns is a distinctively modern, and badly deformed, account of the natural light of human reason. Historically, the first to hold for the possibility of developing an account of natural law without reference to God was the Dutch theologian and lawyer Hugo Grotius (1583–1645).[69] In this he was merely a sign of his times, indicative of the social and intellectual dislocations that gave birth to the desacralized worldview of modernity.[70] But such a view could only be unintelligible for the previous tradition, which saw creation itself as a word from God. Aquinas, to be sure, offered an account of moral precepts grounded within the inclinations of human nature (i.e., the natural law), but only as one small part of an overarching theological vision of the whole of reality coming from God and returning to him through Christ.[71] Hence within the tradition the theological character of the natural law was always understood. To invoke natural law in order to remove theological concerns from public moral discussion is to misconstrue Aquinas and the whole premodern understanding of the concept and the category.

Third, and related to the previous point, it is precisely this theological character of natural law that John Paul II attempted to retrieve in grounding Catholic moral theology in a vision of the person revealed in Christ. This is true not only in the sphere of bioethics in *Evangelium vitae*, but also

68. Thus Joseph Ratzinger remarks in the case of the concept of person: "Although this thought has distanced itself far from it origin and developed beyond it, it nevertheless lives, in a hidden way, from this origin." "Concerning the Notion of Person in Theology," 439. Cf. Schmitz, "Geography of the Human Person," 27–48.

69. Cf. Hugo Grotius, *De jure belli ac pacis*, Prologue 11.

70. Such dislocations would include the outbreak of the Black Plague in Europe beginning in the fourteenth century, the rise of nominalism, the Reformation, and the ensuing wars of religion. On the impact of these developments on modern moral thinking, particularly that of nominalism, see Servais Pinckaers, OP, *The Sources of Christian Ethics*, trans. Mary Thomas Noble (Washington, DC: Catholic University of America Press, 1995), 240–73. Cf. Gordon Leff, *The Dissolution of the Medieval Outlook* (New York: Harper and Row, 1976).

71. It must be remembered that *ST* I-II, q. 94, stands within the overall structure of the *Summa theologiae*.

in his teaching on sexuality in his catechesis on the body, in his social teaching in *Laborem exercens*, and in fundamental moral theology in *Veritatis splendor*.[72] The pope is attempting to reconnect natural law as a category for moral discourse with its revealed theological roots. In classical terms, he is arguing that natural law and revealed law share a common Christological basis.[73]

In this he is merely exegeting the teaching of *Gaudium et spes* noted above: it is Christ who reveals us to ourselves and shows us what it means to be fully human. The plan of the Father from all eternity has been to bring together all things in the Person of His Son and thereby into the communion of the Trinity. Hence this plan, also called the eternal law, finds its realization in the Person of the Son, who became incarnate. It is also in him that the natural law finds its perfect expression, since Christ is the answer to questions about human morality, and human freedom is set free in following him.[74]

It is noteworthy that *Evangelium vitae* locates specific views of the person within cultural matrices. For in many ways the two concepts are interconnected. A culture that values pleasure and efficiency will view personhood differently than one that sees human beings as created in the image of the God, who exists in the communion of love and therefore valuable in themselves. The very term "culture" is derived from the Latin *cultus* "to worship." Hence a culture is formed in large part by what it worships, and this in turn shapes its perception of human personhood. To forget or ignore the Creator is hopelessly to obscure an adequate understanding of the creatures made in his image.[75]

It is in this context that one can begin to understand just how much

---

72. For a brilliant analysis of this in regard to the pope's teaching in *Veritatis splendor* and *Evangelium vitae*, see Russell Hittenger, "Natural Law and Catholic Moral Theology," in *A Preserving Grace: Protestants, Catholics and Natural Law*, ed. Michael Cromartie (Grand Rapids, MI: Center for Public Policy / Eerdmans, 1997), 1–30. In regard to other areas of his teaching, see Alain Mattheeuws, SJ, "De la Bible à *Humanae Vitae*: Le catéchèses de Jean Paul II," *Nouvelle Revue Théologique* 111 (1989): 228–48.

73. On this point, see Lawrence J. Welch, "Christ, the Moral Law, and the Teaching Authority of the Magisterium," *Irish Theological Quarterly* 64 (1999): 16–28.

74. Cf. *Veritatis splendor*, 6–11, 20.

75. See *Gaudium et spes*, nos. 19, 21. For a masterful analysis of this understanding in the light of the intellectual currents of modernity, see Henri De Lubac, *The Drama of Atheist Humanism*, trans. Edith Riley (New York: Sheed and Ward, 1950).

religious, and particularly Christian, perspectives are needed within current public debates over the morality of abortion. The early Church, which forged the concept of person in reflecting on the mysteries of Christ and the Trinity, found itself in a society in many ways brutally hostile to the value of human life. Yet it resolutely opposed abortion, the abandonment and exposure of infants, and euthanasia, and sought to articulate this witness in both its preaching and its praxis.[76] *Evangelium vitae*, in its call to preach "the gospel of life" and build a new "culture of life," recalls the Church to these roots.[77]

Conclusion

This essay began by noting the intractable public moral debate over abortion and its reflection in the scientific and philosophical impasse over what counts for personhood and its beginning. It has argued that this question cannot be resolved on purely empirical or even philosophical grounds. Rather, following the direction that *Evangelium vitae* indicates, one must attend to the theological origin of the term in order to fully understand the concept and adjudicate the arguments that surround it. In this way one can see that personhood cannot be reduced to a level of function (whether cognitive, interpersonal, or biological), or to the arbitrary fiat of another person or group. Rather, as constituted by basic relations given in the fabric of human existence, personhood is woven into the very fabric of that existence—an existence expressed in this world in the gift of life.

This is not merely a set of esoteric theological assertions, intelligible only in the context of Christian faith. Rather, it can speak to a pluralistic society. Christian voices are crucial to the current public debate as a cultural memory and conscience. They serve as a memory insofar as they recall the theological roots of the concept of "person" that is at the heart of the de-

76. On the teaching of the New Testament, see H. C. van Zyl, "The Sanctity of Human Life: A Perspective from the New Testament," *Srif en Kerk* 14 (1993): 292–304. For a survey of Christian teaching on these points in the first three centuries, see W. M. Gessel, "Frühchristliche Voten für das ungeborene Leben," *Forum Katholische Theologie* 8 (1992): 187–95. For a comparison of Christian and Greco-Roman practice, see Michael Gorman, *Abortion and the Early Church: Christian, Jewish & Pagan Attitudes in the Greco-Roman World* (Mahwah, NJ: Paulist, 1982).

77. Cf. John Paul II, *Evangelium vitae*, nos. 78–101.

bate. They serve as a conscience because they allow the full truth about the person, created in the image of God, redeemed by the blood of Christ, and called to eternal communion with the Trinity, to shine forth and so illuminate societal and individual moral questions. Thus the defense of the life of unborn human persons, when illumined and motivated by the central mysteries of Christian faith, can offer a profound contribution to the public moral debate on the issue of abortion.

CHAPTER 7

Natural Family Planning
and Moral Education
within the Family

Practices Make Perfect

One of the still-smoldering sources of contention in the aftermath of the explosion of disagreement ignited by the encyclical *Humanae vitae* has been the exact nature of the difference between natural and artificial means of birth regulation. Are methods such as natural family planning (NFP) simply other methods of birth control that happen not to use barriers or chemicals? This is the view of many people who regard it as simply an alternative means to the same end achieved by contraception. Others argue for real moral differences between natural and artificial means of birth regulation and locate these in the intent of the couple, the intentionality of the action, or the view of the person that they presuppose. While not discounting these efforts to articulate a moral difference between the two approaches along these lines, this presentation offers a different approach. I argue that NFP is in fact a form of moral praxis that enables married couples to express and develop their bodily gift of self in accord with the virtue of chastity. As such, it has implications not just for the moral and spiritual growth

Originally presented at the Restoring Life Connections through Natural Family Planning Conference, Marquette University, Milwaukee, WI, March 25, 2000. Portions of this essay were later published as "Covenant Fidelity, Fertility, and the Gift of Self," in *Sex and Virtue: An Introduction Sexual Ethics* (Washington, DC: Catholic University of America Press, 2003), chapter 6, 142–54.

of the couple, but also for the entire family as a school of love. NFP can help parents more effectively educate their children in the authentic values of human sexuality, respect, love, and communion.

This chapter begins by reviewing some of the arguments against and for a moral difference between NFP and contraception. The second part of the essay draws on diverse sources to describe NFP as a practice related to the acquisition and expression of conjugal chastity. The third section considers the moral and spiritual effects of NFP as practice on the life of the couple. The fourth and final part of the chapter examines the impact of NFP as a practice on the family as a whole.

The Problem: Specifying the Moral Difference between Natural Family Planning and Contraception

Since Catholic moralists and official Catholic teaching began to give cautious approval to natural means in the form of the rhythm method in the 1930s and 1940s, it has often been presumed that this difference exists.[1] Thus Pope Pius XII in his allocution of November 26, 1951, "affirmed the legitimacy and, at the same time, the limits ... of a regulation of offspring [i.e., rhythm] which, unlike so-called birth control, is compatible with the law of God."[2] Likewise, Paul VI in *Humanae vitae* justified recourse infertile periods for serious motives as licit because in so doing, a couple "make legitimate use of a natural disposition while in contracepting they impede the development of natural processes."[3] The difficulty of these statements is that they were largely read through the lens of the then-dominant physicalist account of natural law, which reduced it to the operation of biological process.[4] The controversy over the pill exposed the weakness of this physicalist

1. On this gradual acceptance, see William Shannon, *The Lively Debate: Response to Humanae Vitae* (New York: Sheed and Ward, 1970), 26–31; and John T. Noonan, *Contraception: A History of Its Treatment by the Catholic Theologians and Canonists*, enlarged ed. (Cambridge, MA: Harvard University Press, 1986), 438–47.

2. Cited in Shannon, *Lively Debate*, 28.

3. Pope Paul VI, Encyclical Letter, *Humanae vitae* (1968), no. 16. The citation is from NC News Service Translation (Boston: Daughters of St. Paul, 1968), 13.

4. On the sources and impact of this physicalism, see Brian V. Johnstone, CSsR, "From Physicalism to Personalism," *Studia Moralia* 30 (1992): 71–96; and Servais Pinckaers, OP, *The Sources of Christian Ethics*, trans. Mary Thomas Noble (Washington, DC: Catholic University of America Press, 1995), 244–45.

understanding and placed a new burden upon those who would argue for a qualitative moral difference to natural means of birth regulation.[5] To many people it seemed that there was no difference at all between natural and artificial means. They were simply different avenues to the same end—avoiding pregnancy. Interestingly, this view has been put forward with equal fervor by self-described progressive Catholics who challenge the Church's ban on contraception and traditional providentialists who see NFP as a concession to a modern anti-child mentality. This view, especially as articulated by the former group, has been echoed by theologians.[6]

Some theologians have gone further than arguing for a certain moral equivalence between the two methods. According to them it is NFP that can be described as "unnatural." This argument can take a number of forms. Some have argued that the method is unnatural on biological grounds because it "mutilates" female fertility by wasting ova, whereas the pill does not.[7] Others have held that NFP does violence to the values of freedom and spontaneity in a couple's sexual relationship, reducing it to a mechanistic set of calculations based on charts and graphs. In this case, NFP is dismissed as unnatural because it is perceived as such in the couple's perceptions and experience.[8] Still other arguments combine biological and experiential con-

<hr/>

5. James Burtchaell aptly remarks that the pill "was destined to push Rome beyond its theological supply lines." *The Giving and Taking of Life: Essays Ethical* (Notre Dame, IN: University of Notre Dame Press, 1989), 38; cf. 89–115; Bernard Häring, "The Inseparability of the Unitive-Procreative Functions of the Marriage Act," in *Contraception, Authority and Dissent,* ed. Charles Curran (New York: Herder, 1969), 176–92.

6. The mainstream of Catholic revisionist theology contends that contraception has inherent disvalues (i.e., "ontic evil") but that its use may not be morally evil in every case. See, e.g., Philip Keane, SS, *Sexual Morality: A Catholic Perspective* (New York: Paulist, 1977), 121–28. Cf. Lisa Sowle Cahill, who, without the proportionalist language of ontic versus moral evil, also arrives at the conclusion that contraception is a sometimes justifiable exception. See *Between the Sexes: Foundations for a Christian Ethics of Sexuality* (Philadelphia: Fortress, 1985), 148–49.

7. This was an argument put forward by Louis Janssens at the beginning of the debate over the pill. See his "Morale conjugale et progestogènes," *Ephemerides Theologicae Lovanienses* 39 (1963): 820–24.

8. Thus Rosemary Radford Ruether argued in her essay "Birth Control and the Ideals of Marital Sexuality," in *Contraception and Holiness: The Catholic Predicament* (New York: Herder and Herder, 1964), 72–92; reprint in *Readings in Moral Theology,* vol. 8, *Dialogue about Catholic Sexual Teaching,* ed. Charles Curran and Richard McCormick (Mahwah, NJ: Paulist, 1993), 138–52, esp. 144–52. Cf. The findings of John Marshall, *Love One Another: Psychological Aspects of Natural Family Planning* (London: Sheed & Ward, 1995), 23, 31.

siderations and urge that NFP damages a couple's relationship by requiring abstinence precisely when a women's sexual desire's are strongest—at the time of ovulation.[9]

While not lacking in rhetorical force, these arguments have substantive problems. The biological appeals made share the same rather physicalist horizon as the Neo-Scholastic natural law arguments demolished by the pill—they equate human "nature" with the functioning of biological process. The more experiential appeals reduce the moral meaning of nature to that which feels "natural" to the couple. Both kinds of arguments therefore draw their rhetorical force from a basic equivocation. Neither successfully grapples with an understanding of human nature in an existential or ontological sense.

On the other hand, there are also a variety of arguments that attempt to demonstrate a real moral difference between these approaches to birth regulation. Some focus on the practical differences and consequences of the two approaches. Some of these considerations, while significant, are not necessarily moral in themselves. These would include considerations such as the fact that NFP is as effective as any other means of birth regulation short of complete sterilization,[10] that it is relatively inexpensive to use,[11] and that it has been successfully learned and effectively used by people from a whole host of economic and cultural backgrounds. Other of these kind of considerations certainly have moral dimensions but do not provide a full-blown articulation of the difference: NFP requires communication and shared decision making by the couple (and hence promotes mutuality);[12] NFP is the only reversible method of family planning and can aid couples with limited fertility in achieving pregnancy;[13] NFP, unlike contraception, has no med-

9. Cf. The testimonies cited by Marshall, *Love One Another*, 52–53.

10. For comparisons of the effectiveness of NFP versus artificial methods and related studies, see Mercedes Arzú Wilson, *Love and Family: Raising a Traditional Family in a Secular World* (San Francisco: Ignatius Press, 1996), 246–55.

11. On the costs of NFP in comparison to artificial methods, see Wilson, *Love and Family*, 256–57.

12. On this point, see the studies cited by Mary Shivanandan, *Crossing the Threshold of Love: A New Vision of Marriage in Light of John Paul II's Anthropology* (Washington, DC: Catholic University of America Press, 1999), 234–51. Cf. Marshall, *Love One Another*, 78–79.

13. See Wilson, *Love and Family*, 264; and Thomas W. Hilgers, *The Creighton Model NaProEducation System*, 3rd ed. (Omaha, NE: Pope Paul VI Institute Press, 1996), 3. Cf. Marshall, *Love One Another*, 39.

ical side effects for the woman;[14] and some forms of contraception, including forms of the progesterone pill, can actually have an abortifacient rather than contraceptive action.[15] These factors are certainly important and some will be treated further below, but in themselves none of them provide a larger framework to specify the difference between artificial and natural means of birth regulation.

One influential attempt to articulate such a larger theoretical framework has been put forward by Germain Grisez, Joseph Boyle, John Finnis, and William May, also known as GBFM.[16] In their view, every act of contraceptive intercourse involves a twofold decision on the part of a couple—a decision to have intercourse and a decision (prior to, during, or after intercourse) to negate its procreative potential. It is this second choice in which they locate the malice of contraception because it involves a choice to attack a basic human good—that of life. The will of the couple in this case involves a malice directed against the possible human persons who might result from their union. This explains, in their view, the connection between contraception and abortion in method and in use because the latter merely carries the anti-life decision of the former to its fullest expression. The use of NFP, on the other hand, while it can be used with contraceptive intent, ordinarily involves no such second anti-life choice on the part of the couple.[17]

This view, though not without merit, has been rightly criticized on a number of points. First, in loading all of the evil of contraception into the will of the couple, it seems to neglect the embodied character of human sex-

14. For an overview of the various health risks associated with different forms of chemical or mechanical contraception as well as surgical sterilization, see Wilson, *Love and Family*, 267–97. Cf. Elizabeta Wójcik, "Natural Regulation of Conception and Contraception," in *Why Humanae Vitae Was Right: A Reader*, ed. Janet Smith (San Francisco: Ignatius, 1993), 421–43, esp. 440–43.

15. See William F. Colliton, "The Birth Control Pill: Abortifacient and Contraceptive," *Linacre Quarterly* (November 1999): 26–47.

16. See Germain Grisez, Joseph Boyle, John Finnis, and William May, "Every Marital Act Ought to Be Open to Life: Toward a Clearer Understanding," *The Thomist* 52 (1988): 365–426; and idem, "NFP: Not Contralife," in *The Teaching of Humanae Vitae: A Defense* (San Francisco: Ignatius, 1988), 81–92. Cf. Joseph M. Boyle, "Contraception and Natural Family Planning," *International Journal of Natural Family Planning* 44 (1980): 309–13.

17. An important qualification of the GBFM position is offered by William Marshner, who holds that while couples can use NFP with a bad will, this misuse should not be classified as contraception. See "Can a Couple Practicing NFP Be Practicing Contraception?," *Gregorianum* 77 (1996): 677–704.

uality and of contraceptive choice as a rejection of fertility.[18] Second, there seem to be logical and ontological difficulties in determining the status of "possible persons" and hence of moral acts directed against them.[19] Third, this view does not seem to account for *Humanae vitae*'s understanding of an inseparable connection between the unitive and procreative meanings of the conjugal act, given that it grounds its teaching on sexuality in goods that are not only discreet but also necessarily incommensurable (viz. life and friendship).[20]

A more promising personalist line of argument has been advanced by Karol Wojtyła / Pope John Paul II. In this view, sexual intercourse has an inherent meaning of bodily self-donation. Spouses both give themselves to each other and receive one another in their totality in their sexual communion. Contraception undercuts and falsifies this language of self-gift with a contradictory language of withholding of self and refusal of the other in his or her totality.[21] And the fertility withheld or refused is not a superficial or merely biological dimension of the person that can be subordinated to human reason and freedom, but rather an aspect of the person as a whole.[22] Contraception thus falsifies the total personal self-gift spoken by the couple in the language of the body.[23] Recourse to periodic continence in the form

18. For a careful analysis and thoughtful critique of the GBFM position, see Janet Smith, *Humanae Vitae: A Generation Later* (Washington, DC: Catholic University of America Press, 1991), 340–70.

19. See on this point Gareth Moore, OP, *The Body in Context*: *Sex and Catholicism* (London: SCM Press, 1992), 166–76.

20. On the failure of this revised natural law theory to account for this inseparability, see John S. Grabowski, "The Status of the Sexual Good as a Direction for Moral Theology," *Heythrop Journal* 35 (1994): 18. For the articulation of the "inseparability principle," see *Humanae vitae*, no. 12.

21. See Karol Wojtyła, *Love and Responsibility*, trans. H. T. Willets (New York: Farrar, Straus and Giroux, 1981; reprint, San Francisco: Ignatius, 1993), 234. For instances of this personalist argument in the papal teaching of John Paul II, see Apostolic Exhortation, *Familiaris Consortio* (1981), no. 32; Letter to Families, *Gratissimam Sane* (1994), no. 12. Cf. The weekly general audiences of July 11, 1984, August 8, 1984, and August 22, 1984, in *The Theology of the Body: Human Love in the Divine Plan* (Boston: Daughters of St. Paul, 1997) 386–88, 395–96, 396–99.

22. Cf. Wojtyła, *Love and Responsibility*, 57, 230.

23. It follows for John Paul II that the Church's teaching in this matter is grounded not simply in the natural law, but that it has basis in divine revelation. See the weekly general audiences of July 18, 1984, in *Theology of the Body*, 380–90. For an overview of this understanding of John Paul II and its implications, see John S. Grabowski, "*Evangelium Vitae* and *Humanae Vitae*: A Tale of Two Encyclicals," *Homiletic and Pastoral Review* 97, no. 2 (1996): 7–15.

of NFP, on the other hand, involves no such withholding of self from the other and diversion of intentionality from the whole person within conjugal communion. The language of embodied self-gift is thus spoken without negation.

In places in his papal teaching, John Paul II has indicated that natural means of birth regulation are not only morally different from artificial methods, but also rest on a completely different view of the person.[24] By this he seems to have in view the contrast between understandings of fertility that see it as a merely biological component of the person to be medicated when inconvenient and those that see it in existential terms as a dimension of the whole person. But his call for further reflection on this point certainly indicates his own understanding that further research and elaboration is necessary.[25]

This appeal has not been lost on critics of the pope's position. Individual scholars have found the notion that sexual acts have intrinsic meanings to be unconvincing, holding instead that only the immediate context or relationship provides the meaning for specific sexual gestures.[26] Some feminist thinkers have wondered whether the ideal of mutual self-giving is experienced unequally by women and men on account of women bearing most of the weight of procreation.[27] Others have wondered if the dignity of the person that underlies Wojtyła / John Paul II's personalism can ground moral norms that bear upon concrete acts.[28] Thus the debate sparked by Humanae vitae finds new expression in the effort to answer the question of a moral difference between NFP and contraception.

24. Cf. Familiaris Consortio, no. 32; September 1983 ad limina address to American bishops, cited in James T. McHugh, "The Bishops and Natural Family Planning: Theological and Pastoral Implications," in Moral Theology Today: Certitudes and Doubts (St. Louis, MO: Pope John Center, 1984), 287–99, esp. 298.

25. Cf. Familiaris Consortio, no. 31.

26. This is the view of Moore, Body in Context, esp. 64–113. It should be noted, however, that the presuppositions of the analytic tradition of philosophy from which he operates make it difficult for Moore to ascribe an inherent meaning or symbolic value to virtually any act.

27. See, e.g., Lisa Sowle Cahill, "Catholic Sexual Ethics and the Dignity of the Person: A Double Message," Theological Studies 50 (1989): 120–50, esp. 145–46.

28. See Bruno Schüller, "Die Personwürde als Menschen als Beweisgrund in der normativen Ethik," Theologie und Philosophie 53 (1978): 538–55.

Natural Family Planning as a Practice

Because of the ongoing nature of the disagreement, it may be helpful to approach the problem from a different perspective. One reason it may be difficult to fully discern the difference between natural and artificial means of regulating birth is that the dominance of instrumental reasoning in a scientific and technological culture, such as that found in much of the first world, tends to reduce them to competing methods.[29] In this view the chief difference between these rival methods is to be found in quantitative measures such as effectiveness, impact on couple communication, health, and so on.[30] But this is to reduce natural methods of regulating birth to mere *techné*, while there is reason to think otherwise.

Even before the revival of interest in virtue theory in the last few decades, Karol Wojtyła in *Love and Responsibility* offered a number of important but still relatively unexplored observations. First, Wojtyła faces squarely the question posed in the last section: "Why should the natural method be morally superior to artificial methods, since the purpose is the same in each case—to eliminate the possibility of procreation in sexual intercourse?"[31] The answer comes in the form of a qualification: "To answer we must rid ourselves of some of the associations of the word 'method.' We tend to approach the natural method and artificial methods from the same utilitarian premises."[32] Understood in this way, the natural method is simply another means to ensure sexual pleasure without the risk of pregnancy. Wojtyła, however, proposes a different understanding:

the utilitarian interpretation distorts the true character of what we call the natural method, which is that it is based on continence as a virtue and this … is very closely connected with love of the person. Inherent in the essential character of continence as a virtue is the conviction that *the love of man and woman loses nothing as a result of temporary abstention from erotic experiences, but on the contrary gains*: the personal union takes deeper root, grounded as it is above all in the affirmation of the value

29. On the primacy of instrumental reason in modern Western culture, see Charles Taylor, *The Ethics of Authenticity* (Cambridge, MA: Harvard University Press, 1991), 93–108.

30. For a critique of the anthropological presuppositions underlying social scientific research on family planning studies, see Shivanandan, *Crossing the Threshold of Love*, 209–33.

31. Wojtyła, *Love and Responsibility*, 240.

32. Ibid.

of the persons and not just in sexual attachment. *Continence as a virtue cannot be regarded as a contraceptive measure.*[33]

Wojtyła contrasts calculating and self-interested expressions of continence with its disinterested expression, which is closely bound up with justice—both to the Creator and to one's spouse.[34] The same view is expressed by Pope John Paul II in his papal teaching. Thus, commenting on the teaching of *Humanae vitae*, he writes,

Even though the periodicity of continence in this case is applied to the so-called natural rhythms (*HV* 16), the continence itself is a definite and permanent attitude. It is a virtue, and therefore the whole line of conduct acquires a virtuous character. The encyclical emphasizes clearly enough that here it is not merely a matter of a definite technique, but of ethics in the strict sense as a morality of conduct.[35]

In the same audience the pope notes that "In the case of a morally upright regulation of fertility effected by means of periodic continence, one is clearly dealing with the practice of conjugal chastity, that is, of a definite ethical attitude."[36] In Wojtyła's analysis, continence is one of the components of the moral virtue of chastity.[37] While he does not disagree with St. Thomas's view of chastity as a form of reasonable control of one's sexual appetites expressive of the cardinal virtue of temperance,[38] Wojtyła's personalism understands it more as a form of self-possession that makes possible the expression of love within sexual self-giving.[39] Given this, it is difficult to reduce the whole positive reality of chastity to continence—that is, refraining from intercourse—and to understand this abstinence as virtue in itself. Wojtyła is certainly aware that continence can be practiced from bad motives, in which case it is hardly virtuous. He is also quite clear that chastity does not preclude the embodied gift of self in sexual union—only that it ensures the fully personal quality of this gift.[40] For these reasons it seems more pre-

---

33. Ibid., 241. Emphasis original.
34. Ibid.
35. General audience of August 28, 1984, in Wojtyła, *Theology of the Body*, 399–401, at 400.
36. Ibid., 401.
37. Ibid., 166–73. The other, negative, component is shame, understood as a reaction that protects the sexual values of the person from exploitation and use. Cf. ibid., 174–93.
38. Cf. *Summa theologiae* II-II, q. 151, a. 3.
39. Wojtyła, *Love and Responsibility*, 169–71.
40. "True chastity does not lead to disdain for the body or to disparagement of matrimony

cise to regard the periodic continence required by NFP not as a virtue in it-self, but as a practice integrally related to acquisition of chastity.

Alasdair MacIntyre in his ground-breaking work *After Virtue* provides a helpful analysis of practices and their relationship to moral virtue. Mac-Intyre identifies three successive logical stages in his concept of virtue: specific practices, a narrative account of human life, and an account of a moral tradition.[41] It is primarily the first of these that is of interest to my argument. MacIntyre's definition is rather complex: "By a practice I am going to mean any coherent and complex form of socially established cooperative human activity through which goods internal to that form of activity are realized in the course of trying to achieve those standards of excellence which are appropriate to, and partially definitive of, that form of activity, with the result that human powers to achieve excellence, and human conceptions of the ends and goods involved are systematically extended."[42] His use of this concept, however, is not so complex. It would exclude rudimentary activities such as tic-tac-toe or activities simply based on natural ability such as throwing a football, but would include more complex games such as chess or the game of football. It would also embrace forms of academic inquiry such as architecture, physics, or history, as well as arts such as painting and music. More to the subject of this essay, it would include the creation and sustaining of various forms of human community such as nations, cities, and the family.[43]

The goods of which MacIntyre speaks can be internal to the practice, such as a recognizable skill or excellence displayed within the practice, or external to it, such as fame or fortune. Virtue in this view can be understood as *"an acquired human quality, the possession and exercise of which tends to enable us to achieve those goods which are internal to practices and the lack of which effectively prevents us from achieving any such goods."*[44] The ability to recognize internal goods depends upon training in perception and truthfulness in regard to the facts of the actual excellence displayed. Hence

---

and the sexual life. That is the result of false chastity, chastity with a tinge of hypocrisy, or still more frequently, of unchastity." Wojtyła, *Love and Responsibility*, 171.

41. See Alasdair MacIntyre, *After Virtue*, 2nd ed. (Notre Dame, IN: University of Notre Dame Press, 1984), 186–87.

42. Ibid., 187.   43. Cf. ibid., 187–89.

44. Ibid., 191. Emphasis original.

"we have to accept as necessary components of any practice with internal goods and standards of excellence the virtues of justice, courage, and honesty."[45] Thus moral practices shape the character of both those who participate in them and those who, through their own experience, evaluate them.

What I am suggesting is that NFP is a "practice" in MacIntyre's sense of the term. It is a complex activity not based on natural ability. It requires training by those who have acquired a level of proficiency, it calls for careful observation cultivated by experience, it necessitates new levels of cooperation and communication on the part of the couple, and in the process it shapes the character of both couples who use the method and practitioners who teach it in definite ways. As in the case of other practices, this moral impact necessarily involves justice, courage, and honesty. But NFP understood as a moral practice is most directly related to the acquisition and practice of chastity.

Marital Chastity and Natural Family Planning

Within the Christian theological tradition, chastity has been understood to take differing forms dependent upon one's state in life. For single persons, religious celibates, and (in the Western tradition) those who have received holy orders, chastity has been understood to demand complete continence (refraining from genital sex). For the married, conjugal chastity requires sexual fidelity to one's spouse, respect for the dignity of the spouse as a person, and respect for the nature and purposes of sexuality.[46] It may well also require periodic continence for reasons other than issues of family planning (e.g., for reasons of health, during times of emotional crisis, etc.). In spite of the different forms that chastity can take, it is necessary for all Christians insofar as all have the vocation to give themselves in love and self-possession is the necessary precondition to this.[47]

45. Ibid.
46. Thus St. Ambrose writes: "There are three forms of the virtue of chastity: the first is that of spouses, the second that of widows, and the third that of virgins. We do not praise any of them to the exclusion of the others.... This is what makes for the richness of the discipline of the Church." *De viduis* 4, 23: *PL* 16, 255A. The citation is from the *Catechism of the Catholic Church* (*CCC*), Libreria Editrice Vaticana, trans. US Catholic Church (USCC) (Washington, DC: USCC, 1994), 2349. Cf. *CCC*, 2360–81.
47. See *CCC*, 2348, 2392, 2394. Cf. John S. Grabowski, "Chastity: Toward a Renewed Understanding," *Living Light* 32, no. 4 (1996): 44–51, esp. 46.

How does the use of NFP as a moral practice serve to shape the character of the couple? As MacIntyre's analysis suggests, NFP, like other moral practices, requires the specific virtues of justice, courage, and honesty. MacIntyre means this in the rather restricted sense that these virtues are the necessary precondition for judging accurately and honestly genuine excellence in a specific practice.[48] And certainly this is true for couples who use NFP. They must be honest and accurate in using the method, clear in applying it, willing to seek further information and training when confronting new problems, disciplined in making observations and charting, and committed to avoiding behaviors that compromise the agreed-upon purpose of the method (e.g., genital contact during fertile periods when the method is being used to avoid pregnancy). These same standards are necessary for practitioners to teach the method and evaluate its successful use by couples.

Yet there is a broader sense in which these virtues are required of those who use and teach NFP. Wojtyła makes clear that choices to use the natural methods are based upon justice and honesty on the part of the couple to one another and toward their Creator.[49] If intercourse is a language that bespeaks the gift of the whole person to the other, then the deliberate exclusion of fertility is, in fact, a dishonest expression of this gift.[50] Such an act commits an injustice toward the other insofar as it fails to treat them as a whole person. The same act is an injustice to the Creator insofar as it disregards the existential values of sexuality that have God as their author.[51] To stand firm for these personal and existential values in sexuality by using or teaching NFP in the face of personal or societal pressure to do otherwise requires the virtue of fortitude or courage. Obviously, these observations serve to revisit some of the personalist and anthropological arguments for the qualitative moral difference of NFP treated in the first section, but now set in the horizon of moral growth and virtue.

The classical tradition of virtue represented by St. Thomas understands the moral virtues (or in the person of a Christian the moral and theological virtues) to form a unity.[52] Hence justice, honesty, and fortitude require pru-

48. Cf. MacIntyre, *After Virtue*, 191.
49. Chapter 4 of Wojtyła, *Love and Responsibility*, is titled "Justice towards the Creator." See especially pp. 222–49 within that chapter.
50. Cf. ibid., 234.
51. Cf. ibid., 54–57, 230.
52. Interestingly, in *After Virtue*, MacIntyre rejects Aquinas's understanding of the unity

dence and temperance and their specific forms. Thus a certain level of chastity is required of the truly just or courageous person—even though it may not be fully developed or expressed in their character.

How does NFP understood as a practice enable a couple to acquire the moral virtue of chastity? As noted above, it is misleading to reduce the whole of conjugal chastity to the periodic continence that successful use of NFP requires. At the same time, however, it is true that this abstinence is one of the keys to a couple's growth in their freedom to love one another and hence their growth in chastity. Continence enables the couple to experience sexual union as a gift given freely to one another rather than a biological urge that must be obeyed or satisfied.[53] It thus serves as a part of that "apprenticeship in self-mastery," where chastity works within the person in effecting the self-possession necessary for genuine love.[54]

It is here that many of the narratives of couples who use NFP or practitioners who work with couples and witness the impact of NFP on them becomes important.[55] Couples often speak of a deepened respect for one another as a result of the method.[56] Men often report that the method engenders in them a new respect for their wives because of their wonder at the intricate pattern of women's fertility and its impact on the whole of their personality. Women often point to a heightened awareness of respect for them on the part of their husbands, who are willing to abstain from sex and therefore show them love in nongenital forms.[57] Ethically this is important because it speaks to a deeper perception of the value of one's spouse as a person on the part of the couple and thus to a respect that is a precondition of authentic love.

---

of the virtues (see 179–80). In more recent works he accepts this Thomistic position. See, e.g., *Whose Justice? Which Rationality?* (Notre Dame, IN: University of Notre Dame Press, 1988), x, 198.

53. See John Paul II's weekly general audiences of October 24, 1984, October 31, 1984, and November 7, 1984, in *Theology of the Body*, 408–15.

54. See *CCC*, 2339. Cf. *Familiaris Consortio*, 32; and John Paul II's weekly general audience of October 10, 1984, in *Theology of the Body*, 406–8.

55. For an individual example of such testimony, see Ruth Lasseter, "Sensible Sex," in *Why Humanae Vitae Was Right*, 475–95. For a collection of such narratives addressed to various topics, see Mary Shivanandan, *Natural Sex* (New York: Rawson, Wade, 1979).

56. For an inverse description of the effects of contraception in eroding marital trust and respect, see Lasseter, "Sensible Sex," 483–90.

57. See, e.g., Shivanandan, *Natural Sex*, 73.

There is significant evidence, both anecdotal and statistical, that NFP improves open, honest communication on the part of the couple.[58] Especially if there is shared responsibility for charting, NFP builds a "rhythm" of regular—even daily—communication regarding sexuality into a couple's relationship. The practice of NFP forces a couple to communicate regularly about their fertility, their desire for children, and their sexual relationship. This habituates such couples to talk more openly about these vital issues and may facilitate more open and honest communication throughout their relationship as a whole.

Closely related to deepened communication is deeper intimacy. Communication is merely the verbal form of intimacy. From a psychological perspective, intimacy can be understood as the closeness or sense of connectedness between a couple. Theologically, intimacy can be understood as the quality of a couple's communion with one another. NFP builds intimacy in a marriage because most forms in which the method is taught encourage couples to develop physical (but not genital), verbal/psychological, and spiritual forms of intimacy.[59] This instruction is given opportunity and impetus during periods of abstinence, when couples are forced to find ways other than genital sex to communicate affection. It is this that creates according to the experience of many couples the "courtship and honeymoon" effect of NFP—the romantic pursuit of the other during times of abstinence, which creates a greater appreciation for intercourse during times when a couple can come together sexually.[60] This awareness of other forms of intimacy also creates a heightened perception of the value of the other as a whole person and as a friend, which is integral to marital chastity.

Finally, NFP as a moral practice entails shared decision-making on the part of the couple and thus promotes a basic mutuality in the couple's relationship. Unlike the various artificial methods in which the responsibility inevitably devolves upon either the man or the woman, NFP requires not just communication but genuine collaboration on the part of the couple. Ideally, couples together take responsibility for monitoring their shared fer-

58. For more anecdotal testimony, see ibid., 77.

59. See, e.g., Hilgers, *Creighton Model NaProEducation System*, 39–45, Marshall, *Love One Another*, 84–85.

60. Cf. Wilson, *Love and Family*, 263; Shivanandan, *Natural Sex*, 77, 89–104; Marshall, *Love One Another*, 40–41.

tility (women through observation of their signs and men through record-ing them). But they must decide together whether to have intercourse and whether they are using the method to help achieve or avoid pregnancy. This practice of shared decision making regarding their sexual relationship and family planning habituates the couple to communicate and reach decisions together in other areas of their married life. Such decision making better reflects the mutual exercise of authority that current Church teaching high-lights in regard to marriage and more closely corresponds to the demands of justice in regard to the equal dignity of the spouses.[61]

The fact that NFP serves to foster greater respect, improved commu-nication, deeper intimacy, and mutuality within marriage concretizes the claim that as a moral practice it serves to shape the character of the couple. The method provides a form of moral activity that sensitizes the couple to the demands of justice, honesty, courage, and chastity required by their mu-tual love. All of these factors together may provide some explanation of the strikingly low divorce rate found in some studies among couples who use the method (2% to 5% for NFP couples vs. the national average of over 40% for US couples).[62] This observation in turn suggests that the impact of NFP as a moral practice is experienced by more than the couple, but within the whole of the family and even the whole of society.[63]

Natural Family Planning within the Family

In the Church's understanding, a married couple as *communio personarum* is already a family.[64] Hence what has already been said regarding NFP's im-

61. For John Paul II's teaching regarding the "mutual submission" of husband and wife to one another in marriage, see his Apostolic Letter, *Mulieris Dignitatem*, no. 24. For an analysis of this teaching as effecting a development in the Catholic doctrine of marriage and its ex-emplification in the use of NFP, see John S. Grabowski, "Mutual Submission and Trinitarian Self-Giving," *Angelicum* 74 (1997): 489–512.

62. See Smith, *Humanae Vitae*, 127; Jeff Brand, *Marital Duration and Natural Family Planning* (Cincinnati, OH: Couple to Couple League, 1995).

63. In this regard it becomes apparent that the Church's teaching on responsible parent-hood is more than a matter of sexual ethics; rather, it is an integral part of its social teaching. See David McCarthy, "Procreation, the Development of Peoples, and the Final Destiny of Hu-manity," *Communio* 26 (1999): 698–721.

64. Cf. John Paul II, Letter to Families, *Gratissimam Sane*, no. 7.

pact in shaping the character of the couple is a description of its effect on the family. Insofar as children add to and broaden the communion of love within the family, however, it is worthwhile to consider more closely the effect of the practice on parents and children.

In the Church's understanding, parents are the primary educators of their children in the faith.[65] This means that they have the primary right and responsibility to evangelize their children, to catechize them in the truths of the faith, and to shape their character by instruction and example. When parents share this role with religious educators, this relationship is governed by the principle of subsidiarity.[66] In regard to education in sexuality, this means that parents have the primary right and responsibility to instruct their children in an authentic human and Christian understanding of sexuality in a manner appropriate to their age and to instill in them the virtue of chastity.[67]

The difficulty in this regard is that virtue cannot simply be taught. As an acquired modification of the person's being or character, which grants a power to act excellently (i.e., a *habitus*), a virtue is not merely speculative or abstract knowledge. Virtue is rather an evaluative form of knowledge, based on an experiential grasp of the truth of particular moral values to which one has become habituated by repeated actions.[68] It is therefore something "caught" rather than "taught." It is something imparted through specific forms of human activity such as friendship, love, worship, storytelling (narrative), or liturgy. Knowledge that shapes one's character must appeal to more than the intellect—it must engage the imagination, affectivity, and activity of the person.

These observations about education in virtue shed light on the role of NFP in chastity education within the setting of the family. One cannot ac-

---

65. See *Familiaris Consortio*, nos. 36–39; *CCC*, 2221.

66. Cf. *Familiaris Consortio*, no. 40; *CCC*, 2229.

67. See the overviews of the issues here provided by the Sacred Congregation for Catholic Education in *Educational Guidance in Human Love* (Boston: Daughters of St. Paul, 1983) and the Pontifical Council for the Family in *The Truth and Meaning of Human Sexuality* (Boston: Daughters of Saint Paul, 1996). Especially note the developmental overview of chastity education in the latter document (nos. 77–111).

68. On the differences between speculative and evaluative forms of knowledge and their acquisition, see David Bohr, *Catholic Moral Tradition: In Christ a New Creation*, rev. ed. (Huntington, IN: Our Sunday Visitor, 1999),

quire specific virtues without first perceiving them, and they are most often seen in the person of others. Admiration of another's excellence inspires emulation. What basketball player who grew up in the 1980s or 1990s does not want to "be like Mike"? Yet excellence is not just perceived in heroes but is often found closer to home in the character friends or other persons we admire. For both Aristotle and Aquinas, friendship is the primary school for virtue.[69] Because of the natural admiration that young children have for their parents and because the love between parents and children is a specific form of friendship, the family provides an ideal setting to impart virtue.[70] As Pope John Paul II notes, the communion of love between spouses ought to pervade the broader community of the family and the education that occurs within it.[71] The family is thus not only a school of love, but also a laboratory for virtue.

But parents cannot model or instruct their children in qualities of character that they themselves do not possess. Thus for parents to effectively instruct their children in chastity, they must have begun to acquire and practice this virtue themselves. Insofar as NFP contributes to this acquisition in the ways described above, its use equips parents to be more effective models and teachers in this regard. At the very least, the fact that couples communicate regularly about their sexual relationship and family planning decisions and have a heightened understanding of the values that ground them can help to overcome the embarrassment or ignorance regarding the subject that is often a primary obstacle to parents in communicating an authentic understanding of human sexuality to their children. Furthermore, the parents' own witness of mutual respect, effective communication, chaste expressions of intimacy, and collaborative leadership powerfully reinforces the words that they address to their children, whether these be eloquent or ordinary.

Within the relationships between parents and children or between children and others who assist their parents in their educational responsibility, it is important to develop concrete forms of moral action that enable moral values such as chastity to be assimilated at a deeper level than that of mere information. For adolescent children and young adults, especially

---

69. See the helpful overview provided by Paul Wadell, CP, *Friendship and the Moral Life* (South Bend, IN: University of Notre Dame Press, 1990).

70. "The home is well-suited for *education in the virtues.*" CCC, 2223. Emphasis original.

71. See John Paul II, Letter to Families, *Gratissimam Sane,* nos. 7–8.

young women, this may be instruction in some form of NFP as a method for fertility awareness and record of gynecological health. Prudence might suggest reserving aspects of the method necessary for avoiding pregnancy until young adults are engaged to be married. But for children of all ages, it is necessary to develop other practices to make possible a later appreciation of the values imparted by NFP as a moral practice as well as to support growth in chastity throughout one's life. Thus forms of moral action—such as service to the poor, which inculcates justice and an awareness of the dignity of others; care for one's body and the environment, which promotes reverence for God's creation; public witness to the value and sanctity of human life, which fosters courage; friendship with others of high character, which requires prudence in selecting and maintaining these relationships; and continence as the appropriate means of expressing love and friendship outside of marriage—are all crucial to the development of chastity and for appreciating the role of NFP in fostering it within a marriage.

Conclusion

Natural family planning should not be regarded simply as one method of birth control among others. Rather, it should be seen as a moral practice integral to the development and living of conjugal chastity. Because of NFP's role in shaping the character of spouses who practice it and because these spouses are also called as parents to be the primary educators of their children, this practice can benefit the moral and spiritual development of the family as a whole. It equips parents on a number of levels to better impart the values of an authentic understanding of human sexuality to their children in both their words and the witness of their lives.

It might be objected that this argument simply reprises some of the arguments for a moral difference between natural and artificial means of birth regulation in slightly different language and therefore contributes nothing new to the debate. It is undoubtedly true that this argument converges in many ways with the personalist argument of Wojtyła / John Paul II outlined above.[72]

72. This should not be surprising because Wojtyla suggests this other line of argument in *Love and Responsibility*. What he does not do is show fully how the personalist argument against contraception and the designation of the natural means as reliant on virtue cohere with one another.

But there are a number of reasons to think otherwise. First, this presentation sets that personalist argument in a broader context of moral growth and virtue that encompasses the whole of the moral life—not simply the specific issue of birth regulation. Second, this argument in some ways provides further indication of the anthropological differences between the two approaches to which the pope alludes but does not fully describe. NFP refuses to treat fertility as a biological problem to be medicated or otherwise suppressed. Rather, it sees it as an integral part of the *person* as a whole to be given and received in love. Furthermore, to set the question in the context of virtue is to refuse to envision the moral life of the person as a set of rules in search of exceptions, but rather to see it as a quest for happiness realized through a slow (and sometimes uneven) process of growth in the capacity for love.

Third and finally, the analysis above makes clear that NFP is not simply a concession to the anti-life mentality of the modern world or a capitulation to the culture of death. Nor is it simply something merely "licit" to be tolerated as less worse than its alternatives. Rather, the method is a positive good. Not because it is identical to virtue or incapable of misuse, but because when used rightly, it is a practice integrally related to the acquisition and expression of conjugal chastity. Thus understood, it can contribute much to the healing of marriages, families, and the society that they comprise.

CHAPTER 8

The New Reproductive Technologies

An Overview and Theological Assessment

"Behold, children are a gift from the Lord; the fruit of the womb is a reward," declared the psalmist (Ps 127:3).[1] Surely among those in our society with whom this affirmation would resonate most strongly are women and men affected by infertility.[2] Fueled by new research and procedures, the treatment of infertility has become a billion-dollar industry.[3]

The Church is in a rather paradoxical situation in regard to this reality. On the one hand, the Church in its teaching and pastoral care acknowledges the reality of the anguish experienced by infertile couples.[4] Yet on the other hand, it opposes many of the new medical treatments aimed at helping such couples conceive and bear children, seeing them as morally dangerous. Thus Pope John Paul II in *Evangelium vitae* warns that such treatments

Originally published as "The New Reproductive Technologies: An Overview and Theological Assessment," *Linacre Quarterly* 69 (2002): 100–119. I am indebted to Amy Vineyard Ekeh for helpful comments on an early draft of this essay.

1. The translation is adapted from the New American Bible. Subsequent references will be to this version unless otherwise noted.

2. Studies indicate that some 8.4 percent of women between the ages of 15 and 44 have impaired ability to have children. See Howard Jones, MD, "The Infertile Couple," *New England Journal of Medicine* 329, no. 23 (1993): 1710.

3. On infertility treatments as a billion-dollar-per-year industry, see *Health Facts* 19, no. 176 (January 1994).

4. See Congregation for the Doctrine of the Faith, Instruction on Bioethics, *Donum vitae* (February 22, 1987) II, B, 8.

may in fact be covert manifestations of the culture of death: "The various techniques of artificial reproduction, which would seem to be at the service of life and which are frequently used with this intention, actually open the door to new threats against life."[5] To some, this opposition renders the Church's professed compassion as empty rhetoric.

Compounding the difficulty of the situation is the confusion of many people both inside and outside of the post–*Humanae vitae* Church regarding its teaching on human sexuality. Much of the population is quite willing to believe that the Church simultaneously holds the mutually exclusive positions of being *against* sex and *for* procreation. Yet most of the very procedures that could apparently reconcile such a contradiction by achieving procreation without the perils of sex—modern reproductive technologies—are rejected by the Church. The resulting tangle of public perceptions is a Gordian knot that could daunt the most zealous public relations team or stymie the most accomplished spinmeister.

This essay examines the reasons for the Church's teaching on reproductive technologies from the standpoint of moral theology. Against widespread popular perceptions, I argue that this opposition is neither arbitrary nor inconsistent, but rather flows from a profound insight into the nature of life, the human person, and the gift of sexuality. In the first part of this essay, I examine some of the foundational theological perspectives that underlie the Church's teaching. In the second part, I describe some existing and potential reproductive technologies and apply these perspectives to them in the form of moral evaluation.

Foundational Perspectives

Life as God's Gift

The psalmist's affirmation of children as a gift from God noted above reflects a basic tenet of biblical thought. All life, particularly human life, is a gift and blessing from God. Biblical traditions reflect this conviction in a variety of ways.

From the horizon of biblical thought, all creation comes from God

---

5. John Paul II, Encyclical Letter, *Evangelium vitae*, no. 14. The citation is from *Origins* 24, no. 42 (1995): 695.

(Gn 1:1)[6] and reveals his glory (cf. Ps 8) because created things bear luminous witness to their source and maker. Creation itself is a word from God. This conviction forms the biblical basis for the doctrine of natural law—that it is possible to know existence of God (cf. Ws 13:1–9; Rm 1:18ff.) and certain basic moral truths from that which he has made (cf. Rm. 2:14–15).

Living things share in this witness more intensely than inanimate objects. In their diversity and complexity they reflect God's wisdom and majesty, and in their lives they reflect God's own character as living and the source of all life. Thus we can understand the biblical perception of the sacredness of blood, both animal and human, because it contains the life of the creature and hence belongs directly to God (cf. Lv 17:11). While animal blood could be spilled for sacrifice or food, it could never be consumed (cf. Gn 9:4).

Human life represents the fullest expression of God's gift. The second creation account depicts God as fashioning human beings directly (from mud in the case of *adam*, from the man's rib in the case of woman) and then breathing into them the "breath of life" (Gn 2), a term that indicates more than biological life, as "breath" *neshama* recalls that God himself is "spirit" *ruach*.[7] While other creatures are alive, humanity is distinct because of receiving this life-breath directly from God. Hence there is something of God within the human person.[8] Human life is unique because it is more than biological existence.

Therefore to beget human life is a profound form of cooperation with God's own creative activity. "I have begotten a man with the help of the Lord," declares a triumphant Eve in Genesis 4:1c. Human procreation is thus a unique form of co-creation with God—a renewal of the original mystery of creation, as Pope John Paul II has noted.[9] It is this theological conviction, together with the concrete socioeconomic realities of ancient

6. The affirmation that "God created the heavens and the earth" (Gn 1:1b) in Hebrew idiom is an indication that God created everything—one names the two extremes (i.e., heaven, earth) so as to encompass everything between them.

7. For other Old Testament (OT) texts that refer to humanity being formed from the earth and yet possessing the breath/spirit of God, see Jb 33:4, 33:6, 34:14–15; and Ws 15:10–11.

8. See Francis Martin, "Old Testament Anthropology" (unpublished manuscript, 1998), 4.

9. See John Paul II, General Audiences of March 26, 1980, and October 6, 1982, in *Theology of the Body: Human Love in the Divine Plan* (Boston: Pauline Books and Media, 1997), 83–86, 333–36.

Israel (in which children and family were necessary for sustenance and security), that underlies the uniform biblical witness that regarded children as a blessing and sterility as a hardship and a curse.

The preciousness of human life receives added impetus from the message of redemption offered in the New Testament (NT). If the spilled blood of Cain cries to God from the ground for vengeance, the blood of Christ shed on the Cross pleads "more eloquently" for mercy for the whole of sinful humanity (cf. Heb 12:24). Human life is so precious that God sent his own Son to redeem it. As John Paul II notes in *Evangelium vitae*:

The blood of Christ, while it reveals the grandeur of the Father's love, shows how precious man is to God's eyes and how priceless the value of his life … Precisely by contemplating the precious blood of Christ, the sign of his self-giving love (cf. Jn 13:1), the believer learns to recognize and appreciate the almost divine dignity of every human being and can exclaim with ever renewed and grateful wonder: 'How precious must man be in the eyes of the Creator, if he gained so great a Redeemer' (Exsultet of the Easter Vigil).[10]

Yet the biblical tradition is equally aware that life is not an absolute value to be preserved or sought at any cost. The seven sons and the mother in 2 Maccabees 7, Daniel and other prophets who faced or endured death, and the young men cast into the fiery furnace (cf. Dn 3) all bear witness to the hope of resurrection of the just, for which life might be freely surrendered in order to not compromise higher values. This willingness to resist sin "to the point of shedding blood" (Heb 12:4) prefigures the faithfulness and love displayed by Jesus in offering himself on our behalf. This witness is continually renewed in the martyrs who are conformed to Christ in choosing to freely lay down their lives rather than compromise their faith.[11]

The NT also offers an important qualification to the value of begetting life by setting it in an eschatological perspective through its teaching on celibacy. Differing NT traditions make it clear that this practice, modeled on the witness of John the Baptist and Jesus, was highly regarded in early Christian communities (cf. Mt 19:12; 1 Cor 7:7–9, 7:32–35). In a world dominated by concern to reproduce offspring for one's city or nation, the practice of sexual renunciation was itself a dramatic proclamation of the

---

10. *Evangelium vitae*, no. 25, 698–99.

11. On the idea of martyrdom as witness to the highest values of the moral order, see Pope John Paul II, Encyclical Letter, *Veritatis splendor*, August 6, 1993, 90–93.

Gospel message. To deliberately step outside the seemingly endless cycle of reproduction, birth, growth, sickness, decay, and death was an announcement writ in bodies and behavior that in Christ time as it had been previously known had come to an end, and a new era of immortality had broken into human existence.[12]

The esteem given by the Church to martyrdom and celibacy is not a denigration of human life or sexual reproduction, but rather an appreciation of them in light of their relationship to the eternal destiny of the human person. In this perspective it is clear that life, while both fundamental to other human values and itself profoundly precious, is a penultimate rather than an ultimate value. This awareness underlies the Church's teaching that life need not be preserved at all costs and that one can rightly refuse extraordinary means of medical care. It also informs its teaching that the begetting of human life is neither an inalienable right nor an absolute value to be pursued at any cost.

Technology and Human Dominion

The first creation account (Gn 1:1–2:4a), near the climax of its description of the days of creation, describes the creation of human persons, male and female, in the image of God (cf. Gn 1:26–27).[13] This idea of the *imago dei* has generated countless volumes of biblical commentary and theological analysis. Without pretending to exhaust the meaning or import of the text, it is possible to find in the text important clues to its meaning.

One important meaning of the term "image" *tselem* is found in the fact that humanity is created in the dual form of male and female. Thus part of the image of God in us is relational—we are created to be in relation or communion with others. On the human level, the most basic form of this relationality is that between male and female.[14] The union of male and fe-

12. On the early Christian practice of sexual renunciation as a form of proclamation, see Peter Brown, *The Body and Society: Men, Women, and Sexual Renunciation in Early Christianity* (New York: Columbia University Press, 1988).

13. Parts of this section are adapted from my article "Made Not Begotten: A Theological Analysis of Human Cloning," *Homiletic and Pastoral Review* 98, no. 9 (June 1998): 16–21; reprint, *Ethics and Medicine* (1998): 69–72.

14. See Claus Westerman, *Genesis 1–11: A Commentary*, trans. John J. Scullion, SJ (Minneapolis: Augsburg, 1984), 142–61; cf. Karl Barth, *Church Dogmatics*, vol. 3.4, trans. A. T. Mackay et al., ed. G. W. Bromiley and T. F. Torrance (Edinburgh: T&T Clark, 1961), 116–41.

male in marriage is both the basis of human society and paradigmatic for other forms of human friendship and community. Yet this fundamental relation is dependent on a far more encompassing one—the relationship between humanity and its Creator anchored in the Sabbath worship of the seventh day. It is only on the seventh day that creation is complete, because on this day it returns through the praise of its human priests to the One who made it.[15] That which makes us most fully human is not merely our ability to reason, but to worship. Human dignity is ultimately priestly.

Another equally basic meaning of the term "image" is indicated by the twice-repeated command given to humanity to "have dominion" over the rest of creation (Gn 1:26, 1:28). Within the ascending order of the first creation account, humanity is in a sense at its pinnacle, exercising dominion over the material, vegetation, fish, birds, and animals that comprise the rest of the natural world. The problem is that in the scientific and technological culture spawned by the Enlightenment, *dominion* is often misunderstood as *domination*—untrammeled power to conquer, shape, and exploit the natural world. This results in part from the primacy of instrumental reason within our intellectual culture.[16] This distinctively modern misreading is utterly foreign to the biblical text, however.

In the biblical view, human dominion has clear limits. It is modeled on and subject to God's dominion over creation. "Image" does not necessarily indicate resemblance, but representation. Humanity must therefore image God's dominion over the earth as that which is not exercised as untrammeled power, but life-giving care and sustenance. Human dominion is thus better understood as stewardship than license. In the words of the second creation account, humanity's role is to "cultivate and care for" the earth (cf. Gn 2:15).[17] Furthermore, it is precisely the effort to acquire godlike knowledge and power that constitutes the original and perennial temptation that humanity faces—to attempt, in the words of the serpent, "to be like gods who know what is good and evil" (Gn 3:5).[18] When we succumb

---

15. On seven as the number of perfection and completion in biblical thought, see John L. McKenzie, SJ, "Seven," *Dictionary of the Bible* (New York: MacMillan, 1965), 794.

16. On the dominance of instrumental reason in Western culture, see Charles Taylor, *The Ethics of Authenticity* (Cambridge, MA: Harvard University Press, 1991), 93–108.

17. The phrase is originally used in reference to *adam*'s role in the garden.

18. My translation.

to the deceit of these whispered words, we succeed only in creating disaster, sundering our relationship to God (cf. Gn 3:8–10, 3:23) and one another (cf. Gn 3:7, 3:16), and disordering the world in which we were placed as stewards (cf. Gn 3:17–19).

One important exercise of human dominion is connected to the mutual relation of male and female in marriage in their shared fertility (Gn 1:28). God's blessing (*barak*) attends the sexual union of husband and wife so that they can exercise dominion by heeding God's directive to "be fertile and multiply; fill the earth and subdue it" (Gn 1:28b–c). In spite of the disastrous results of human sin, this original blessing, which attends human procreation, is never removed.[19]

At first glance, this "commandment" to procreate given in the context of human dominion over creation would seem to lend powerful support to the effort to employ any available medical technology in the effort to achieve conception. But this conclusion too quickly forgets the limits of human dominion over nature and its technological expressions.

Technology is basically an expression and extension of human dominion. As such, it potentially reflects humanity's creation in the image of God and yet it also has real limits. In itself, technology is morally ambiguous. On the one hand, it can be morally good when used according to God plan and purpose. Thus the story of the preservation of life on earth during the flood in the ark (Gn 6–9) may be read as a kind of parable on the use of technology in the preservation of life. On the other hand, technology can be evil when used in the service of prideful human assertion as an attempt to achieve security apart from God, as in the story of the tower of Babel, which caused further fragmentation of human communication and relationships (cf. Gn 11:1–9).

One consequence of the moral ambiguity of technology, especially in a culture such as ours, is that its creation and implementation often race ahead of moral evaluation. There is a profound gap between technical prog-

---

19. The canonical shape of the text, which juxtaposes the two creation stories, does not revoke this blessing (Gn 1:28) in the curses pronounced on the primordial couple after sin (Gn 3:14–19)—the serpent and the ground are cursed, but the man and woman are not. In the quasi-historical narratives that follow the creation stories, this blessing is primarily understood as procreation. See Peter J. Elliott, *What God Has Joined: The Sacramentality of Marriage* (New York: Alba House, 1990), 11.

ress and moral progress.[20] And many are seduced by the "technological imperative" (the idea that because we *can* do something, we *should* or *must* do it). Yet a moment's reflection indicates just how false and dangerous such thinking is. The fact that we can unleash havoc on the earth through widespread use of nuclear, chemical, or biological weapons does not mean that we should. The fact that we have refrained from using nuclear technology available for some decades to engage in all-out war belies the idea that we must. Technology, like any other human artifact, is subject to the control of human reason and freedom and therefore should be carefully scrutinized before being used.

Thus medical technology, which aims at enhancing human fertility, must be evaluated according to the same criteria—does it reflect an understanding of human dominion that is subject to God's plan and purpose, or does it reflect a human attempt to "play God"? To fully answer this question requires a brief examination of the nature of human sexuality and the place of procreation within it.

Sex as a Language of the Body

While the creation accounts of Genesis depict a surprising equality between women and men, they do not portray the sexes as interchangeable. Both together are created in the image of God and therefore possess the dignity of being able to relate directly to God in worship and exercise stewardship over creation. Both share a common humanity or nature.[21] Yet the biblical text is also aware of the profound difference necessary for the covenantal union of a man and a woman in marriage (cf. Gn 2:21–25) and the exercise of their joint fertility in the begetting of children.[22]

20. On the gap between technological progress and moral reflection in the modern world, see Pope John Paul II, Encyclical Letter, *Redemptor Hominis*, March 4, 1979, no. 15.

21. This unity of nature is especially clear in the language of the second creation account where woman is described as a "helper matching him" *ezer kenegdo*. Lisa Sowle Cahill, following Phylis Trible, observes that the term *ezer* has no connotation of inferiority in the Hebrew of the OT. See Cahill, *Between the Sexes: Foundations for a Christian Ethics of Sexuality* (Philadelphia: Fortress, 1985), 54; Phylis Trible, *God and the Rhetoric of Sexuality*, Overtures to Biblical Theology 2 (Philadelphia: Fortress, 1978), 90. This observation is also borne out in the play on words between man (*ish*) and woman (*ishah*) in *adam*'s poetic exclamation in Gn 2:23.

22. On the description of the creation of woman in the second creation account as simultaneously a description of the marriage covenant, see John S. Grabowski, "Covenantal Sexual-

Among the most keen analyses of this difference and the light that it sheds on human sexuality is that provided by Pope John Paul II in his catechesis on the body.[23] Following the example of Jesus, who when questioned by the Pharisees about divorce appealed to God's original creative intention for sexuality disclosed in the Genesis creation accounts, the pope returns to "the beginning" to frame an understanding of human sexuality.[24] He does so by pointing to three "original experiences" that the second creation account in particular narrates: original solitude, original unity, and original nakedness.

Solitude   As *adam* was alone with God, so every human person has an awareness of himself or herself as a self, a subject. It is to this experience that we make reference whenever we use the pronoun "I." Yet our experience of being a subject is mediated through our bodies—it is through our bodies that we encounter, learn from, and act in the visible world. Unlike other creatures of the visible world—the animals with whom *adam* was alone—only the human body is capable of expressing this subjectivity. Only the human body reveals personhood. Within this perception of our own uniqueness among other creatures, we become aware again of the giftedness of human existence and of the gratitude we owe to the One who made us. We also become aware of our profound need to be in communion with other human persons—an insight captured in the words of the text: "It is not good for the man to be alone" (Gn 2:18b).

Unity   God's remedy for this unquenchable need is to create an "other," a partner who is both like ourselves yet wonderfully different. Awakening from his covenant sleep, *adam* cries out with joy upon seeing the woman made from a part of himself: "This one, at last, is bone of my bones and

---

ity," *Église et Theologie* 27 (1996): 229–52. For a broader overview of marriage as a covenant in OT thought, see Gordon Paul Hugenberger, *Marriage as a Covenant: A Study of Biblical Law and Ethics Developed from the Perspective of Malachi*, Supplements to Vetus Testamentum 52 (Leiden: Brill, 1994).

23. This teaching is composed by the pope's weekly general audiences given between September 1979 and November 1984, which have been collected, together with other papal teaching, in *Theology of the Body* (see note 9 above). What follows is a summary of some of the main lines of this catechesis.

24. Cf. the General Audience of September 5, 1979, in *Theology of the Body*, 25–27.

flesh of my flesh; This one shall be called 'woman' for out of 'her man' this one has been taken" (Gn 2:23). Because the body expresses and reveals the person, the differing embodiment of men and women points to their irreducible difference ("originality") as persons.[25] Sex is more than skin deep—it touches the whole of who we are as persons (encompassing both body and soul). To the "I" of our own subjectivity corresponds the "Thou" of another form of human embodiment.

Yet the duality of maleness and femaleness is intended to summon us to communion and community with others. It is a reminder written in our bodies that we image God by being in relation and that our vocation is communion. In the words of the Second Vatican Council, "Man, who is the only creature on earth which God willed for itself, cannot fully find himself except through a sincere gift of self."[26] Every human person—of whatever state in life—is called to and fulfilled in the gift of self, which creates communion in friendship and love. The most basic and intense expression of this reality is in the unity of the marriage covenant. When lived in authentic self-giving love, marriage provides an image of the Trinity as a communion of persons. Insofar as this summons to communion is written in our very embodiment as male and female, it may be said that the body has a "nuptial meaning."[27]

Nakedness   The culmination of the unity of man and woman in marriage is their offering themselves to one another in and through their naked bodies: "The man and his wife were both naked yet they felt no shame" (Gn 2:25). The bodily gift of self—intercourse—is a ratification of a couple's covenant promise to one another in marriage. Sex is a bodily enactment and remembrance of a couple's wedding vows that continually communicate their love in new ways. This is why the biblical expression for the sexual union of husband and wife—"to know" (cf. Gn 4:1)—is especially apt, because it expresses the knowledge gained about oneself and one's spouse

25. On the "originality" of men and women as persons, see the General Audience of November 7, 1979, in *Theology of the Body*, 42–45.

26. Pastoral Constitution on the Church in the Modern World, *Gaudium et spes*, no. 24. The citation is from Walter M. Abbott, SJ, ed., *The Documents of Vatican II* (Piscataway, NJ: New Century, 1966), 223.

27. On the nuptial meaning of the body, see the General Audience of January 9, 1980, in *Theology of the Body*, 60–63.

in sexual self-donation.[28] In this way, conjugal love can be understood as a "language of the body" that expresses both unreserved self-giving and unconditional commitment.[29] Yet it is also a language of potential fatherhood/motherhood because in it one comes to know one's spouse not only as spouse, but also as potential parent. Genesis links the "knowledge" yielded by intercourse—"the man *knew* his wife Eve" (Gn 4:1a)—with parenthood—"and she conceived and bore" (Gn 4:1b). The communion of love between spouses leads to the broader community of children and family.

Here, then, is the ground for the "inseparable connection" between the unitive and procreative meanings of sexuality asserted by Paul VI in *Humanae vitae*. Many criticized the encyclical's teaching because it offered little argument for this connection. John Paul II's theology of the body addresses this lacuna by providing an analysis of marital sex as intrinsically unitive (i.e., bodily self-donation that expresses and recalls a couple's covenant vows) and procreative (i.e., open to parenthood). To deliberately negate either meaning is to falsify both.[30] And it does so not merely on the basis of an appeal to human reason (i.e., the natural law), but on the more authoritative basis of biblical revelation.[31]

In this way it becomes apparent that the Church's opposition to many reproductive technologies is the flip side of its constant opposition to artificial contraception. The totality of the gift of self includes the fertility that makes parenthood possible. And parenthood is, by God's design, a gift, received within the context of a bodily gift of self in spousal love. Far from the incoherence and inconsistency attributed to the Catholic view of sex and reproduction in some popular (mis)conceptions, there is a remarkable coherence to the Church's understanding of these matters.

28. See the General Audience of March 5, 1980, in *Theology of the Body*, 77–83.

29. On the idea of sex as a language of the body, see the General Audiences of January 5, 12, 19, and 26, 1983, in *Theology of the Body*, 354–65.

30. On the relationship of Paul VI's inseparability principle to John Paul II's analysis of the language of the body, see William E. May, *Marriage: The Rock on Which the Family Is Built* (San Francisco: Ignatius, 1995), 90–92.

31. For a consideration of this trajectory of the pope's thought, see John S. Grabowski, "*Evangelium Vitae* and *Humanae Vitae*: A Tale of Two Encyclicals," *Homiletic and Pastoral Review* 97, no. 2 (November 1996): 7–15.

Application to Reproductive Technologies

Having looked at some of the foundational perspectives that underlie the Church's opposition to many forms of assisted reproduction, they can now be brought to bear on existing and potential reproductive technologies. Rather than describing and analyzing each procedure piecemeal, I briefly summarize individual techniques and then offer a series of moral observations about them as a group, making distinctions among them where relevant.

Description

Artificial Insemination   Artificial insemination (AI) is the procedure in which previously collected semen or a sperm preparation is introduced into a woman's vagina, cervix, or uterus.[32] If the sperm is from the woman's husband, the procedure is known as homologous artificial insemination or artificial insemination by husband (AIH). If the sperm is from a male donor who is not married to the woman (either known or unknown), it is referred to as heterologous artificial insemination or artificial insemination by donor (AID).

In Vitro Fertilization   In vitro fertilization (IVF) is the oldest and best-known form of a group of procedures in which conception occurs outside of a woman's body, in a test tube or petri dish (i.e., *in vitro*). These procedures are often organized under kinder and gentler headings such as assisted reproduction therapy (ART). I describe both the original procedure and some of its more recent variants.

IVF is the retrieval of a preovulatory ovum from a woman's ovary; its placement in a laboratory culture dish, where it is fertilized by collected sperm; and the development of the conceptus to the eight- to sixteen-cell stage.[33] Once it reaches this point of development, the embryo is then transferred to a woman's uterine cavity in the hope that implantation will

---

32. See Gerald Coleman, SS, *Human Sexuality: An All-Embracing Gift* (New York: Alba House, 1992), 365.

33. Ibid., 357. Coleman says the two- to eight-cell stage. The actual steps of IVF-ET involve: hyperstimulation of multiple ovarian follicles through medication; oocyte retrieval through a needle or laparoscopy; fertilization of the oocyte through the introduction of washed sperm in a controlled environment and subsequent incubation and monitoring of the embryos; and transfer of the developing embryo(s) to a woman's uterine cavity. See ibid., 357–60.

occur. IVF then necessarily involves the related technology of embryo transfer (ET) and is often referred to as IVF-ET. Initially developed in the mid 1940s as a way to bypass blocked or diseased fallopian tubes, IVF-ET is now used to treat virtually any form of infertility (except azoospermia, or total lack of sperm). Since the successful IVF-ET birth of Louise Brown in 1978, such programs have expanded exponentially (with some one hundred IVF centers in the United States reporting over 3,000 births by the early 1990s).[34] This procedure also has homologous and heterologous forms depending on whether the man from whom the sperm is obtained is the woman's husband or an unmarried (and perhaps anonymous) donor.

Some recent variations of IVF use the fallopian tubes as a more natural setting for fertilization or for the development of the conceptus. Gamete intrafallopian transfer (GIFT) takes already-collected and washed sperm and preovulatory oocytes and transfers them into the fallopian tubes in an attempt to mimic the physiologic processes that lead to human gestation.[35] Zygote intrafallopian transfer (ZIFT) is similar to IVF except that the fertilized eggs (zygotes) are transferred to the fallopian tubes one day after fertilization in the laboratory. Tubal embryo transfer (TET) follows the same procedure as ZIFT except that the embryos are transferred to the fallopian tubes two days after laboratory fertilization.

There are also procedures aimed specifically at male infertility, such as intracytoplasmic sperm injection (ICSI), in which a single sperm is injected directly into the center of an egg through a microneedle. This can result in the fertilization of an egg by a sperm with little or no motility. In cases where a man has no sperm in his ejaculate, sperm can be obtained directly from the testes. These efforts to produce conception through micromanipulation are generally performed in the laboratory and therefore part of the IVF-ET "family" of procedures.

A common feature of IVF-ET and the cluster of related procedures that it spawned is that they usually produce multiple fertilizations. Scientists found early on that the odds of successful conception and implantation increased dramatically with multiple fertilizations and the transfer of more than one embryo. This raises the issue of the treatment of these embryos.

34. Ibid.
35. Ibid., 362. Because GIFT aims to produce conception in vivo, it can be distinguished from IVF procedures. The moral relevance of this distinction is considered below.

Embryo Treatment and Experimentation   Even though laboratory person-
nel transfer multiple fertilized eggs to a woman's uterus or fallopian tubes in
IVF or related procedures, usually not all embryos will be selected because
of number or apparent viability. The "spare" embryos are either discarded as
excess lab material, used for research or experimentation (e.g., use in stem
cell research or other prospective therapies), or frozen for later implantation or experimentation.

Surrogate Motherhood   A phenomenon that has grown up along with
these fertility technologies is that of surrogate motherhood, in which a
woman carries a child to term having agreed or pledged to surrender it to
another party on its birth. In many cases, women receive payment for this
service. In some cases the child that she carries may be genetically unrelated to her, as when it is another couple's child conceived through IVF and
then implanted in her womb through ET. In other cases the child may be
genetically her own, resulting from the union of one of her own ova and the
sperm of another man, as in the infamous Baby M case, where the surrogate
(Mary Beth Whitehead) refused to surrender the child after her birth.[36]

"Reproductive cloning" is a term employed to describe the effort to create a genetic double of a human being in the form of an embryo and to carry
that embryo to full term pregnancy. While the procedure has been successfully used on sheep and pigs, it has not, to the best of my knowledge, been
attempted on human beings, and many experts have offered ethical arguments that it should not be. Reproductive cloning is distinguished from the
effort to clone individual cells or tissues for therapeutic purposes. But some
who use this language see the effort to clone human embryos for research in
which they will ultimately be destroyed as "therapeutic" as opposed to "reproductive" cloning.[37]

Moral Evaluation

The Church opposes all of the abovementioned procedures—though not,
as is sometimes popularly held, because they are artificial or technological.

36. For an extensive analysis of the Baby M case as an argument against surrogacy, see Donald
DeMarco, *Biotechnology and the Assault on Parenthood* (San Francisco: Ignatius, 1991), 148–55.
37. This is the current usage in the United Kingdom. See Michael D. West, *Testimony before the Senate Appropriations Subcommittee on Labor, Health and Human Services, Education
and Related Agencies*, 105th Cong., 2nd Sess., December 2, 1998, pp. 2–3.

This is yet another misperception generated by the controversy surrounding *Humanae vitae*. It was precisely this line of reasoning that sent journalists scurrying to the Vatican for comment after the public introduction of Viagra. Surely, many thought, this had all the elements to reignite the fires of controversy that burned so brightly in the Church in the late 1960s and early 1970s—sex, a pill, and the pope. Imagine the chagrin of those in the media holding such assumptions when told by Vatican spokesmen that the Church applauded the development insofar as it gave couples an opportunity to restore an important part of their conjugal communion. What these journalists failed to grasp is that the issue is not technology, but the dignity of the human person and the meaning of human sexuality. The same is true with reproductive technologies. The Church opposes them not because of their technological nature, but rather because of the impact of this technology on the purposes of human sexuality, the dignity of the human person, and the value of human life.

The primary problem that runs through almost all of these procedures is that they tear apart the integral connection of the unitive and procreative meanings of sexuality.[38] As contraception aims at having sex without children, reproductive technologies aim at producing children without sex. Yet, as noted above, it is precisely within the total and unreserved gift of oneself to one's spouse in sexual union that the Church sees as the vehicle chosen by God to enable human parents to cooperate with him in the transmission of new human life.

It might be objected that such procedures merely enable us to control and modify nature when it fails to work properly.[39] Surely, medical treatment for defects in human fertility is no more objectionable than wearing contact lenses or glasses (or having laser correction) for impaired vision. Yet this objection fails because it assumes that fertility is simply another biological aspect of the person that can be manipulated by human reason in the form of technology. In fact, fertility—like sexuality, of which it is an integral part—is a reality that touches the whole of the person. It is existential (i.e., rooted in the order of existence), not merely biological. As Karol

38. Cf. *Donum vitae* II, B, 4–5.

39. Doctors and theologians advanced the same argument to justify the use of the progesterone pill in the 1960s. See, e.g., John Rock, *The Time Has Come* (New York: Knopf, 1963); and Louis Janssens, "Morale conjugale et progestogènes," *Ephemerides Theologicae Lovanienses* 39 (1963): 787–826, esp. 820–24.

Wojtyła observes, it is a mistake engendered by modern empiricism to reduce sexuality and fertility to merely biological realities.[40]

Heterologous forms of AI or IVF are additionally objectionable because they strike at the exclusivity and fidelity of the marriage covenant that intercourse recalls and signifies.[41] They also undermine the right of the child to know and be raised by his or her parents.[42] Life is difficult enough without having to go through it as the child of a withdrawal from the local sperm bank.

This observation points to a second major line of objection to these procedures—they are an affront to the dignity of the child as a person. By God's design, the mystery of human personhood emerges from the bodily enactment of the self-giving love of parents. A laboratory procedure is an unworthy beginning for a human person created in the image of God.

Such procedures are morally objectionable because they depersonalize the children conceived by them. It substitutes the personal relations constitutive of our identity as persons (mother and father to child) with the impersonal ones of producer or consumer and product.[43] This is true in existing reproductive technologies and most particularly in the specter of future attempts at reproductive cloning of human beings. And as Gilbert Meilaender notes: "What we beget is like ourselves. What we make is not; it is the product of our free decision and its destiny is ours to determine."[44] Such procedures are a denial of the dignity and equality of persons. Furthermore, cloning attacks the personhood of those it produces in yet another way—

40. See Karol Wojtyła, *Love and Responsibility*, trans. H. T. Willets (New York: Farrar, Straus, and Giroux, 1981), 57, 230.

41. See *Donum vitae* II, A, 2. Some Catholic authors attempt to distinguish the more objectionable heterologous forms of these procedures and their homologous counterparts, arguing that the "simple" cases of AIH or IVF-ET that avoid the destruction of embryos could, in some cases, be morally licit. See, e.g., John Mahoney, SJ, "Human Fertility Control," in *Readings in Moral Theology*, vol. 8, *Dialogue about Catholic Sexual Teaching*, ed. Charles E. Curran and Richard A. McCormick, SJ (Mahwah, NJ: Paulist, 1993), 251–66; and Lisa Sowle Cahill, *Sex, Gender and Christian Ethics*, New Studies in Christian Ethics (Cambridge: Cambridge University Press, 1996), 217–54. But this argument does not fully address the argument based on the inseparability principle above nor the others considered below.

42. It is true that this right is not an absolute one and might be waived in some circumstances in the interest of the child (i.e., adoption).

43. See May, *Marriage*, 95–99.

44. Gilbert Meilaender, "Begetting and Cloning," Address to the National Bioethics Advisory Commission, March 13, 1997. Reprinted in *First Things* (June/July 1997): 42.

by mocking the uniqueness and irreducibility of the person through the attempt to make a kind of genetic photocopy of the individual.[45]

Surrogate motherhood is another sign of the depersonalization effected by these technologies. The surrogate is reduced to the status of a womb for rent, and the child she carries to a bargaining chip in a business transaction. Surrogacy also attacks the natural bond between mother and child created by pregnancy, particularly if it is the mother's own child that she carries and must surrender for a price.

The social effects of these present and prospective technologies are not difficult to discern. The prospect of being able to screen donors of sperm and ova for sex selection, desirable characteristics (witness the $50,000 reward recently offered in national newspapers for a single egg from a tall, athletic woman with an Ivy League education), to genetically program them, or simply to clone them creates the chilling prospect of "designer children" made to order. Children become chattel to be bought and sold, parents become consumers, and laboratory technicians become the priests of a new eugenic religion that worships genes and generation rather than the God who made them. James Burtchaell, summarizing the Church's opposition to such procedures in the Congregation for the Doctrine of the Faith Instruction, *Donum vitae*, puts the matter well:

The Vatican is too technical, or perhaps too dainty to state graphically enough that we have been turning procreation into science fiction, and that we become monsters as a result. A society which venerates Drs. Masters and Johnson and their lab-coat lore of orgasm, or that harkens to Dr. Ruth as a *sage femme* of how men and women give themselves to one another, or that orders up children the same way it uses the Lands' End catalogue: this is a creature feature that ought not appear even on late Saturday television. Or so I take the Vatican to be telling us.[46]

To use the language of *Evangelium vitae*, this horror story is the face of the culture of death.

While the suffering of infertile couples is real, and the Church has particular pastoral responsibilities toward them, this does not justify engaging

45. See Grabowski, "Made Not Begotten," 19–20. It is true that, owing to environmental and personality factors, no clone would ever be exactly like the person from whom he or she was copied, as is also the case with genetic or "identical" twins.

46. James Burtchaell, CSC, *The Giving and Taking of Life: Essays Ethical* (Notre Dame, IN: University of Notre Dame Press, 1989), 134.

in evil for a good purpose. Children are a gift, not a right to be seized at any cost.[47] To cooperate with God in transmitting new human life is a privilege that should express the responsible stewardship of dominion, not the untrammeled self-assertion of domination. Human life is precious, but not an end in itself to be sought to the exclusion of other moral goods.

While it opposes the use of these procedures to generate human life, *Donum vitae* hastens to add that such life, once conceived, is owed respect and protection.[48] This is true whether one is speaking of the embryo in the lab dish, the child in the womb of the surrogate, or, should it occur, the human embryo produced by reproductive cloning.

This observation points to a third set of objections to many of these procedures, particularly IVF and the attempt to clone human embryos: the moral evil of destroying innocent human life. Whether excess embryos are treated as laboratory waste to be flushed down the drain of an ART clinic or used for "spare parts" that can be disassembled to perform research on stem cell therapies or created solely to be destroyed in other experimental use, the destruction of human embryos entails the same evil as direct abortion.

There are still other arguments that can be made against these procedures. They tend to be expensive, for example, and like the burgeoning field of cosmetic surgery cater to a predominantly wealthy clientele. This diversion of medical resources away from those with less means raises important questions of social justice.[49] Furthermore, there is some evidence that, in spite of their cost, for those with limited fertility these procedures are not all that more effective than continued effort to achieve pregnancy by ordinary means.[50]

---

47. See *Donum vitae* II, B, 8.

48. See *Donum vitae* I, 1.

49. On this point, see DeMarco, *Biotechnology and the Assault on Parenthood*, 115–40.

50. In a study of 1,145 couples, John A. Collins, MD, found that expensive fertility treatments offered only a 6 percent improvement in the rate of pregnancy over those couples who simply "kept trying." See *New England Journal of Medicine* 309, no. 20 (November 17, 1983): 1201. In a later study, published in *Sterility Fertility Journal* (Fall 1993), of 2,000 couples the same physician found the results of the two approaches "roughly the same." The 1997 Society for Assisted Reproductive Technology (SART) Summary, however, found that the best IVF clinics have an approximately 20 percent rate of pregnancy per cycle of IVF.

Alternatives

What recourse do couples with limited fertility have within the framework of the Church's teaching? On this point, *Donum vitae* echoes Pope Pius XII: "medical intervention respects the dignity of persons when it seek to assist the conjugal act either in order to facilitate its performance or in order to enable it to achieve its objective once it has been normally performed."[51] While gametes can be repositioned to enhance the possibility of conception, in the case of the egg prior to—or, in the case of egg and sperm after—intercourse, the criterion is respect for the integrity of the conjugal act. Unfortunately, research on some methods designed to achieve fertilization by providing medical assistance to normal intercourse, such as low tubal ovum transfer, or LTOT (which uses ovarian hyperstimulation, oocyte retrieval, and transfer of oocyte to the proximal portion of the fallopian tubes), has been discontinued owing to the low rate of pregnancies that they produced.[52] Other methods such as GIFT have created confusion among Catholic authors because they do in fact aim to produce conception *in vivo*. But it is difficult to reconcile the typical GIFT procedure with the framework of *Donum vitae* insofar as it relies on masturbation—not intercourse—to obtain sperm.[53] There are also modified versions of GIFT that collect sperm through various means from an act of intercourse prior to washing and repositioning in the fallopian tubes. As one moralist prudently concludes regarding such procedures, "As long as the husband's sperm are collected by a morally acceptable method and the repositioning of the gametes are within the context of the conjugal union of husband and wife, the process is not morally objectionable."[54]

51. *Donum vitae* II, B, 7. The citation is from *Respect for Human Life*, Vatican trans. (Boston: Daughters of St. Paul, 1987), 32–33. The document is quoting Pius XII, "Discourse to Those Taking Part in the 4th International Congress of Catholic Doctors," September 29, 1949.

52. See Coleman, *Human Sexuality*, 364.

53. Ibid., 362.

54. This is the judgment of David Bohr, *Catholic Moral Tradition: In Christ a New Creation* (Huntington, IN: Our Sunday Visitor, 1990), 289; cf. Coleman, *Human Sexuality*, 363–64. Other Catholic authors are critical even of modified versions of GIFT. See, e.g., DeMarco, *Biotechnology and the Assault on Parenthood*, 219–35.

For other potentially acceptable procedures, see: E. Cofino et al., "Transcervical Balloon Tuboplasty: A Multicenter Study," *Journal of the American Medical Association* 264, no. 16 (1990): 2079–82; J. M. Kasia et al., "Laparoscopic Fimbrioplasty and Neosalpingostomy: Experience of the Yaounde General Hospital, Cameroon," *European Journal of Obstetrical*

Conclusion

The psalmist was undoubtedly right: children are a gift from God. Yet a gift is something that cannot be demanded, only received. Human life is a precious gift, yet it is not one to be sought regardless of the cost. Just as Christians believe there are things worth dying for, so too there are things worth living without if in seizing them we disfigure our very selves.

Reproductive technologies purport to offer oases of life in the desert of sterility, yet at what price? At the price of wrenching procreation from the context of sexual self-giving, which gives it meaning and transcendent dignity; at the price of objectifying children and the women who bear them; at the price of countless human lives cast away as leftovers or sacrificed at the altar of further scientific progress. And when our limited creaturely dominion is recast as power for domination, sexual self-giving becomes procreative self-assertion. Stretching out our hands to seize the fruit of the tree of life, we find that we have eaten again from a far more bitter tree—the one that held out to us the promise of our "being like gods who know what is good and evil" (cf. Gn 3:5). The promise of reproductive technologies turns out to be an illusion, a mirage. Seeking our way back into the garden, we find ourselves deeper in the desert of our exile.

The Church's teaching on reproductive technologies is neither arbitrary nor unfeeling—it offers a compassion based in the truth of the human person and the gift of sexuality. As such, it can help dispel the mirage created by the culture of death. Yet ultimately changing this culture can only be accomplished by changing its gods. The gods of technological efficiency, progress, and personal fulfillment must be replaced by the God of life, who created us in his image and calls us into his own eternal communion as a Trinity of Persons. Only the appropriation of this Mystery through worship can ground an authentic understanding of human life, dominion, and the gift of human sexuality. To build a culture of life requires much more than scientific or moral analysis—above all, it requires the sincere gift of self, lived out in evangelization and doxology.

Gynecological Reproductive Biology 73, no. 1 (May 1997): 71–77; and K. Sueoka et al., "Fallopo-scopic Tuboplasty for Bilateral Tubal Occlusion: A Novel Infertility Treatment as an Alternative to In-Vitro Fertilization?," *Human Reproduction* 18, no. 1 (January 1998): 71–74. I am indebted to Dr. Hanna Klaus for these references.

CHAPTER 9

The Luminous Excess of the Acting Person

Assessing the Impact of Pope John Paul II on American Catholic Moral Theology

"There is nothing deader than a dead pope," or so say the cynics of Rome who have watched the parade of pontiffs passing through the walls of the Vatican over the course of years. Only time will tell just how lasting will be the imprint left by Pope John Paul II on the Church, but early indications some years after his death are that the influence from his exceptionally long and prodigious pontificate continues to be felt by the Church's members and in its institutional life. His global travels in 104 Apostolic journeys that took him to 129 different countries, his charismatic personality, and his multilingual eloquence affected millions and redefined the image of the papacy for the modern world. The international interest in his recent beatification testifies not only to the witness provided by his own personal holiness but also to the ongoing global impact of the Polish pontiff.[1] Biographers tout the geopolitical impact of his papacy through his defense of human freedom and rights and personal interventions around the globe,

Originally published as "The Luminous Excess of the Acting Person: Assessing the Impact of Pope John Paul II on American Catholic Moral Theology," *Journal of Moral Theology* 1, no. 1 (2012): 116–47. I am indebted to Joseph Capizzi, Lawrence Welch, Rae Grabowski, William Mattison, and David Cloutier for helpful comments and criticisms on earlier drafts of this paper.

1. Pope Benedict XVI beatified his predecessor on May 1, 2011. See Jesús Colina, "1M Pilgrims Make for Most Crowded Beatification Ever," *Zenit*, accessed June 28, 2011, https://zenit .org/articles/1m-pilgrims-make-for-most-crowded-beatification-ever/.

which helped encourage democracy in much of Latin America as well as played an important role in the peaceful fall of communism in Europe and the former Soviet Union.[2] His pontificate did much to heal the wounds of Christian anti-Semitism and to foster closer relationships with Jews, members of other non-Christian religions, and members of other Christian churches.[3] His teaching on the struggle between a "culture of life" and a "culture of death" has not only shaped ethical teaching and discussion, but also has become part of political discourse on life issues.[4] His call for a "new evangelization" remains programmatic for the Church as it moves into the new millennium.[5] His teaching in the area of marriage and family is the

2. This is a frequent theme in the laudatory works on the late pope by George Weigel. See his *Witness to Hope: The Biography of Pope John Paul II* (New York: Cliff Street Books, 1999); and *The End and the Beginning: Pope John Paul II—The Victory of Freedom, the Last Years, the Legacy* (New York: Doubleday, 2010). But others support this idea as well. See Jo Renee Formicola, "The Political Legacy of Pope John Paul II," *Journal of Church and State* 47 (Spring 2005): 235–42; and *The Political Papacy: John Paul II, Benedict XVI and Their Influence*, ed. Chester Gillis (Boulder, CO: Paradigm, 2006). Others highlight the late pope's efforts to build a "culture of peace" through his diplomatic activism and interventions. See Bernard J. O'Connor, *Papal Diplomacy: John Paul II and the Culture of Peace* (South Bend, IN: St. Augustine's, 2005).

3. On the late pope's effort to promote Jewish Christian dialogue, see the collection of essays in David Dalin and Matthew Levering, eds., *John Paul II and the Jewish People: A Jewish Christian Dialogue* (Lanham, MD: Sheed and Ward, 2008). On his efforts to create dialogue with Judaism and other non-Christian religions, see Byron Sherwin and Harold Kasimow, eds., *John Paul II and Interreligious Dialogue* (Eugene, OR: Wipf & Stock, 2005). On the pope's impact on relations between the Catholic Church and Evangelicals, see Tim Perry, ed., *The Legacy of John Paul II: An Evangelical Assessment* (Downers Grove, IL: Intervarsity Press, 2007). For assessment of John Paul II's ecumenical teaching from both Catholic and Protestant perspectives, see Carl Braaten and Robert Jensen, eds., *Church Unity and the Papal Office: An Ecumenical Dialogue on John Paul II's Encyclical Ut Unum Sint* (Grand Rapids, MI: Eerdmans, 2001).

4. The term was an important theme in Pope John Paul II's 1995 encyclical *Evangelium vitae*. It was subsequently adopted as a name by the Culture of Life Foundation, a Washington, DC, pro-life think tank. It entered more directly into American political discourse when used by George W. Bush in the 2000 presidential election (in a debate with Vice President Al Gore on October 3, 2000) and then subsequently in his presidency to articulate his pro-life views. For differing assessments of the language of these opposing cultures of life and death, see Marc Oullet, "The Mystery of Easter and the Culture of Death," in *John Paul II and Moral Theology*, Readings in Moral Theology 10, ed. Charles Curran and Richard McCormick (New York: Paulist, 1998), 109–19; and Charles E. Curran, "*Evangelium Vitae* and Its Broader Context," in *John Paul II and Moral Theology*, 120–33.

5. The idea has not only been frequently addressed by his successor, but also in June 2010, Benedict XVI announced the creation of a Pontifical Council on the New Evangelization. On John Paul's own understanding and implementation of the term in his outreach to

subject of ongoing study by a worldwide institute that bears his name.[6] His catecheses, known as the Theology of the Body, continue to generate wide popular interest as well as increasing scholarly scrutiny.[7]

Yet not unlike the retreat that Karol Wojtyła preached for the household of Paul VI, John Paul II's pontificate could be described in the biblical language of a "sign of contradiction."[8] The relationship of his papal teaching to the renewal called for by the Second Vatican Council has been the subject of intense debate. Some commentators see the late pope's work as a retreat from the reforms of the Council and retrenchment of older preconciliar ideas.[9] Advocates of the late pope's teaching counter that his pontificate represents instead a critical discernment and purification of the Council's vision, which had been clouded in the years immediate following it.[10] In some ways these competing readings map onto larger fault lines of theological disagreement that existed both during the Council and in its aftermath. These lines were set ablaze by the explosive debate that ensued after Pope Paul VI's encyclical *Humanae vitae* over the issue of contraception.[11] This fierce disagreement quickly and simultaneously spread to other ques-

---

youth, see Mario D'Souza, "Action and the New Evangelization: The Youthful Humanism of Pope John II," *Toronto Journal of Theology* 21, no. 2 (2005): 199–215.

6. The John Paul II Institute for Studies on Marriage and Family has sessions (or locations) in Italy (at the Lateran University in Rome), the United States (in Washington, DC), Benin, Brazil, India, Mexico, Spain, and Australia.

7. This will be considered at greater length below.

8. In this work, Wojtyła asks the suggestive question of whether the term "sign of contradiction" might be "a distinctive definition of Christ and the Church." See Karol Wojtyła, *Sign of Contradiction*, trans. St. Paul Publications (New York: Seabury Press, 1979), 7–8.

9. For a case in point in regard to John Paul II's teaching in *Veritatis splendor*, see Mary Elsbernd, "The Reinterpretation of *Gaudium et Spes* in *Veritatis Splendor*," *Horizons* 29, no. 2 (2002): 225–39. On the perception of the late pope by progressives as a "restorationist," see Charles Curran, *Catholic Moral Theology in the United States: A History* (Washington, DC: Georgetown University Press, 2008), 98.

10. See, e.g., Tracey Rowland, "Pope John Paul II: Authentic Interpreter of Vatican II," in *John Paul the Great: Maker of the Post Conciliar Church* (San Francisco: Ignatius, 2005), 27–48.

11. On the historical genesis of this debate and its immediate aftermath, see William H. Shannon, *The Lively Debate: Response to Humanae Vitae* (New York: Sheed and Ward, 1970); and John T. Noonan, *Contraception: A History of Its Treatment by the Catholic Theologians and Canonists* (Cambridge, MA: Harvard University Press, 1986), esp. 409–500. On the impact of this debate on the Church in the face of the sexual revolution, see John S. Grabowski, *Sex and Virtue: An Introduction to Sexual Ethics* (Washington, DC: Catholic University of America Press, 2003), 10–21.

tions of sexual ethics and to questions of fundamental moral theology.[12]

Moral theology in the United States emerged from the preconciliar stasis of a field still largely dominated by Neo-Thomism and the manuals of moral theology to the center of the post–*Humanae vitae* storm.[13] This shift into the limelight of public controversy paralleled the movement of Catholics in the United States from a somewhat enclosed subculture to positions of prominence in American culture and political life.[14] Organized public protests to its teaching,[15] an aggressive rethinking of received positions in the area of sexuality,[16] and the emergence of new revisionist approaches to the discipline characterized American Catholic moral theology after the encyclical.[17] Countering these developments was the work of a small but

12. The trajectory of this debate is catalogued in the volumes of the Paulist Press Readings in Moral Theology series, edited by Charles Curran and Richard McCormick, SJ, which capture many of the chief points of contention both regarding methodology and in regard to specific areas of teaching.

13. For a concise overview of the history of Catholic moral theology in the United States, see John A. Gallagher, *Time Past, Time Future: An Historical Study of Catholic Moral Theology* (New York: Paulist, 1990), 184–202. Charles Curran also notes the impact of papal condemnations of Americanism and modernism in the late nineteenth century on American Catholic moral theology. See *Catholic Moral Theology in the United States*, 35–38. For an insightful analysis of changes wrought in the US Church by the Second Vatican Council and their impact on the field of moral theology, see David Cloutier and William C. Mattison III, "Introduction," in *New Wine, New Wineskins: A Next Generation Reflects on Key Issues in Catholic Moral Theology* (Lanham, MD: Sheed & Ward, 2005), 1–23.

14. On the relation of this transition to debates in moral theology, see David McCarthy, "Shifting Settings from Subculture to Pluralism: Catholic Moral Theology in Evangelical Key," *Communio* 31, no. 1 (Spring 2004): 86

15. The most notable example was the "Washington Statement" released the day after the encyclical was promulgated. For the text, see "Statement by Catholic Theologians Washington D.C., July 30, 1968," in *Readings in Moral Theology*, vol. 8, *Dialogue about Catholic Sexual Teaching*, ed. Charles Curran and Richard McCormick (New York: Paulist, 1993), 135–37.

16. A rather notorious example is provided by the study commissioned by the Catholic Theological Society in America published in 1977. See Anthony Kosnick et al., *Human Sexuality: New Directions in American Catholic Thought* (New York: Paulist, 1977). In their effort to broaden the traditional criteria for evaluating sexual activity, the authors could find little in the way of moral critique to direct toward any form of sexual activity with the possible exception of bestiality. This was the basis for James Burtchaell's tongue-in-cheek description of the work's "liberating norms ... whereby the only discouraged form of sex is doing with a Doberman." See *The Giving and Taking of Life: Essays Ethical* (Notre Dame, IN: University of Notre Dame Press, 1989), 288.

17. Richard McCormick with his ground-breaking 1973 Pere Marquette Lecture and his years as the author of the "Notes on Moral Theology" section in the journal *Theological Studies*

influential group of philosopher-theologians who used a revised natural law theory to defend received positions in the area of sexuality and ethical theory.[18] This highly polarized climate was the place where John Paul II's teaching was heard and in varying degrees "received."[19]

Yet the effort to force John Paul II's teaching into the confines of existing disagreements or into newer debates sparked by them in American Catholic moral theology has been in many ways unsuccessful. In part this was because neither the revisionist nor traditionalist "camps" could account for the anthropological depth or coherence of this teaching. Efforts by proponents or critics to invoke the late pope's thought often failed to do justice to the many facets of his presentation of the human person: Scripture, action theory, Christology, gift theory, and experience. His multifaceted presentation generates a kind of excess that overflows shallow categorizations or reductions of his thought to preexisting positions. It is precisely in this anthropological excess—which has the form of the human person addressed by Christ in the drama of salvation and offered fulfillment through

---

helped to articulate the approach to moral reasoning known as proportionalism. See *Ambiguity in Moral Choice* (Milwaukee: Marquette University Press, 1973). Charles Curran's approach has been more eclectic, moving over the years from a self-described "relational responsibility" approach to moral judgment in his earlier works to an acceptance of the Wesleyan quadrilateral of authority that holds in tension Scripture, tradition, reason, and experience. For the meaning and evolution of Curran's "relational responsibility" model of personalism, see the overview provided by Timothy O'Connell, "The Moral Person: Moral Anthropology and the Virtues," in *A Call to Fidelity: On the Moral Theology of Charles E. Curran* (Washington, DC: Georgetown University Press, 2002), 19–35; see esp. 26–29. On the four Wesleyan sources as characteristic of contemporary Catholic moral theology, see Charles E. Curran, *The Catholic Moral Tradition Today: A Synthesis* (Washington, DC: Georgetown University Press, 1999), 48; *Catholic Moral Theology in the United States*, 208–9. For Curran's take on the impact of *Humanae vitae* on the development of revisionist thought and dissent, see *Catholic Moral Theology in the United States*, 102–27.

18. In the United States, the central figure in this group was Germain Grisez. His massive multivolume work *The Way of the Lord Jesus* offered both a critique of revisionist thought and extended defenses of traditional positions. See especially the first volume of *Christian Moral Principles* (Chicago: Franciscan Herald Press, 1983).

19. For an overview of the ongoing clash between "revisionism" and the new natural law theory as formative for fundamental Catholic moral theology, see Todd Salzman, *What Are They Saying about Catholic Ethical Method?* (Mahwah, NJ: Paulist, 2003). The book is a bit simplistic in that it tends to view all revisionist approaches through the lens of proportionalism and really does not treat other approaches that are sympathetic to traditional positions outside of the "basic human goods" approach of Grisez.

the grace-enabled gift of self—that much of the continuing appeal of the late pope's thought to students and scholars lies. This study argues that it is precisely this anthropological depth evidenced in differing areas of John Paul II's moral teaching that accounts for both the propensity of critics and proponents alike to mischaracterize it and for its ongoing appeal to those less invested in reading it within the confines of other controversies.

This essay proceeds by first acknowledging some of the methodological difficulties that attend any analysis of the late pope's work and its reception, and also by considering some of the limitations of scope and subject matter particular to this essay. It then examines two concrete examples in his moral teaching where John Paul II's thought has been mischaracterized to varying degrees in the effort to utilize it to address existing debates, with the result that something of its anthropological depth has been missed. These two areas are the Theology of the Body catecheses and the encyclical *Veritatis splendor*. The essay concludes by noting some of the further challenges and promise of this anthropological excess for the ongoing reception of the late pope's teaching.

Apples and Oranges? Some Limitations of Method and Scope

To consider John Paul II in the context of other significant figures who have influenced the field of US Catholic moral theology is to run headlong into dissimilarities and dissonance. One could even ask if his inclusion in such a group is justified given the qualitatively different nature of his influence. While others have shaped the field by virtue of the substance of their thought and the questions they have pursued, the late pope did so, at least in part, simply on the basis of his authority and office. And this is true in a number of distinct ways.

First, in a general sense, one can ask whether the late pontiff's work would have commanded all that much attention—at least outside of Polish-speaking circles—had he not been elevated to the Chair of Peter. Certainly, his philosophical work in *Love and Responsibility* captured the attention of Paul VI and won him a spot on the Papal Study Commission for the Study of Family, Population, and Birth Rate.[20] He played an import-

20. Though, as Weigel notes, he was prevented from attending the decisive June 1966 meeting of the commission, at which a majority of those present embraced the position that

ant part in the drafting of *Gaudium et spes*, which influenced subsequent Catholic moral theology, but was by no means its sole architect.[21] His visit to the United States as a cardinal in 1976 would probably have left little imprint in the United States without his election to the papacy two years later. It was only with the surprise move of the 1978 conclave that the bulk of his work as a philosopher was rushed into translation in English and other languages and that scholars turned their attention to this (in the West) relatively unknown Polish intellectual.[22] So, one might ask, have scholars paid attention to his thought because of its own intrinsic merit or because of its promulgation by the Church's universal pastor?

A second and related complicating feature of including John Paul II in such a list of influential figures is that, more than many of his predecessors, he used the authority of his office to directly influence and direct the field of moral theology in ways individual theologians could not. He wrote documents intended to both shape and critically evaluate the field in both its foundations and in regard to specific topics.[23] He also authored documents that reshaped received Catholic positions on moral issues.[24] He disciplined individual revisionist theologians.[25] And he sought to clarify the ec-

---

formed the basis of the "Majority Report" advocating change in the traditional teaching on contraception. See *Witness to Hope*, 207.

21. On Wojtyła's impact on drafting the text and its reception by the Council, see Rocco Buttiglione, *Karol Wojtyla: The Thought of the Man Who Became Pope John Paul II*, trans. Paolo Guietti and Francesca Murphy (Grand Rapids, MI: Eerdmans, 1997), 193–99. Cf. Weigel, *Witness to Hope*, 166–69.

22. It is true that *Love and Responsibility* had been translated into French and Italian in the early 1960s, which enabled it to be read by Paul VI. The English version did not appear until 1981 (trans. H. T. Willets [New York: Farrar Strauss and Giroux, 1981]). The English translation of his philosophical *magnum opus*—*The Acting Person*, Analecta Husserliana Series, trans. Andrej Potocki, ed. Anna-Teresa Tymieniecka (Boston: D. Reidel 1979)—is notoriously poor for a variety of reasons. For an overview of these problems, see Kenneth Schmitz, *At the Center of the Human Drama: The Philosophical Anthropology of Karol Wojtyla/Pope John Paul II* (Washington, DC: Catholic University of America Press, 1993), 58–60.

23. This is obviously the case with *Veritatis splendor*, which is considered below.

24. One significant example is *Evangelium vitae's* prudential opposition to the use of the death, which led to the revision of the *Catechism of the Catholic Church*. On the anthropological basis of this teaching and its significance, see Thomas R. Rourke, "The Death Penalty in Light of the Ontology of the Person: The Significance of *Evangelium Vitae*," *Communio* 25 (1998): 397–413.

25. On the case of Charles Curran, see *Vatican Authority and American Catholic Dissent*, ed. William W. May (New York: Crossroad, 1987).

clesial relationship between individual theologians, the universities where they taught, and the Church of which he was the spiritual head.[26] In other words, it is not just that others noticed his work because of the authority and position of its author, but he also used and traded on this very authority to affect the methodology used and positions taken within moral theology. In these ways, the Chair of Peter that John Paul II occupied served him as a bully pulpit from which to attempt to mold and reshape the field.

A third problematic feature of the inclusion of John Paul II in this consideration has to do with the genre and nature of papal teaching itself. While the work of individual theologians is just that, popes seldom write their own work in quite the same way. Many papal texts and addresses are written by other persons, vetted by still others, and finally approved by the pontiff. Even in the case of popes who write much of their own material, as was the case with John Paul II, there is still a level of involvement on the part of others that exceeds the normal feedback sought by scholars before publishing their work. So it is in some respects comparing the work of an individual to that produced by a committee—a committee composed of Vatican theologians and officials. And it is not always clear where the work of the individual pope ends and that of others begins.[27]

A fourth problem in analyzing the thought of John Paul II in particular stems from the prolific nature and wide-ranging scope of his teaching. Unlike other figures whose thought usually contains particular kinds of conceptual unity and lines of organic development, the very nature of the late pope's ministry to the universal Church required an equally universal scope in his teaching.[28] As a result, there is no question of offering anything like

26. These efforts would include the 1979 Apostolic Constitution *Sapientia christiana* on pontifical universities, the 1990 Apostolic Letter *Ex corde ecclesiae* on Catholic universities in general, the 1990 Congregation for the Doctrine of the Faith Instruction on the Ecclesial Vocation of the Theologian *Donum veritatis*, and the 1998 Apostolic Letter Moto Proprio *Ad tuendam fidem* updating the 1983 Code of Canon Law regarding the Profession of Faith and juridical penalties for certain kinds of dissent.

27. In some respects, the challenge for the commentator on papal texts is not unlike that facing the biblical scholar wrestling with issues of authorship—and at times it seems that sources consulted by exegetes are actually more forthcoming about these matters than are Vatican insiders.

28. The problem becomes more complex in the case of popes such as John Paul II or Benedict XVI, who had careers as private scholars prior to their elevation to the papacy. Commentators naturally tend to look for lines of continuity between the work of the individual thinker

a thorough or systematic analysis of this teaching in a study of this length. What follows is necessarily partial but intentionally suggestive. The effort in this study is to locate diverse areas of the late pope's thought in terms of content and method, which nevertheless highlight areas where this teaching has not been adequately understood because it often exceeds the categories in which it was received. It is precisely here—in the "excess" of ideas that elude efforts to categorize or pigeonhole his thought—that some of the reasons for the late pontiff's continuing appeal to scholars and students become apparent. While it may be the case that it was his office that initially drew many to consider his work, its authority alone does not explain the fruitfulness of his ideas.

Regardless of how one views John Paul II's relationship to the Council, it is apparent that he tried to respond to and exemplify in his own moral teaching many of the marks of renewal of which it spoke. Moral theology, the Council had taught, needed "livelier contact with the mystery of Christ" and to be "more thoroughly nourished by scriptural teaching."[29] Engagement of various kinds with Scripture (through meditation, exegesis, analysis, and even phenomenological reading) and preoccupation with the person and mystery of Christ permeate the late pope's writings. This biblical and Christological focus converged in his understanding of the human person. The ideas of *Gaudium et spes*, nos. 22 and 24—that Christ reveals us to ourselves and that human fulfillment is found in the sincere gift of self—form hermeneutical keys to the corpus of his thought. It is largely because of this Christological anthropology—the differences noted above in genre, authorship, and authority when compared to other influential figures notwithstanding—that John Paul II's teaching continues to generate interest and to

---

and universal teaching issues during his pontificate—in spite of the differences in genre and authorship. In the case of Karol Wojtyła / John Paul II, such a unifying theme or idea is supplied by his recurring focus on the person. Even at the beginning of his pontificate, commentators from around the globe pointed to the concept of person as the overarching focus of Wojtyła's philosophical project. See, e.g., Abelardo Lobato, "La Persona en el Pensamiento de Karol Wojtyla," *Angelicum* 56 (1979): 207. Cf. John Hellman, "John Paul II and the Personalist Movement," *Cross Currents* 30 (1980–81): 409–19; Elzbieta Wolicka, "Participation in Community: Wojtyla's Social Anthropology," *Communio* 8 (1981): 108–18; and P. Gilbert, "Personne et Acte: À Propos d'un Ouvrage Rècent," *Nouvelle Revue Théologique* 196 (1984): 731–37.

29. Second Vatican Council, Decree on Priestly Formation, *Optatum totius*, no. 16. The citation is from Walter M. Abbott, SJ, ed., *The Documents of Vatican II* (Piscataway, NJ: New Century, 1966), 452.

reward careful study.[30] The "excess" of John Paul II's thought that so often eludes both proponents and critics has the form of the human person as a dynamic embodied subject invited by Christ to give him or herself in love.

The Theology of the Body: More Than Sex Appeal

Certainly one area where interest in the late pope's teaching has continued unabated after his death has been the catecheses given over the first years of his pontificate, which have come to be known as the Theology of the Body (TOB). Popular presentations on this teaching have mushroomed and become a staple of many religious education programs and "theology on tap"–style lectures. At the same time, both the catecheses themselves and their popularizations have garnered a growing amount of scholarly attention as scholars have sought to understand and critically evaluate their appeal.[31] What sometimes goes unrecognized is the common ground that popular promoters and critics of TOB find in reducing the subject matter of the catecheses largely to a discussion and defense of traditional Catholic teaching on sex.

The "brand name" of popularizations of TOB in the United States be-

30. Even if John Paul II's office were a significant part of the reason why others originally studied his thought, this teaching had a depth that encouraged further consideration.

31. For a thoughtful examination of this popularity that locates the appeal of the catecheses in the cultural hunger for "authenticity," see David Cloutier, "Heaven Is a Place on Earth? Analyzing the Popularity of Pope John Paul II's Theology of the Body," in *Sexuality and the U.S. Catholic Church: Crisis and Renewal*, ed. Lisa Sowle Cahill, John Garvey, and T. Frank Kennedy, SJ (New York: Herder and Herder, 2006), 18–31.

Fortunately, this deeper scholarly interest has also led to the production of a better and more critical English translation of the catecheses. The staff of the English edition of the Vatican newspaper *L'Osservatore Romano* produced the original English translations. These were collected and published in four volumes in the United States by the Daughters of Saint Paul: *The Original Unity of Man and Woman:* (1981), *Blessed Are the Pure of Heart* (1983), *The Theology of Marriage and Celibacy* (1986), and *Reflections on Humanae Vitae* (1984). In 1997, these volumes were gathered into a single work by the same publisher (*The Theology of the Body: Human Love in the Divine Plan*) along with teaching that had served as its historical catalyst (*Humanae vitae*) or was its later fruit, such as John Paul II's Apostolic Letter on the Dignity and Vocation of Women *Mulieris dignitatem* (1988) and the encyclical *Evangelium vitae* (1995). But the catecheses in these texts still suffered from the inconsistent translation of having been produced by different members of a newspaper staff. In 2006, Michael Waldstein published a new critical translation of the text that not only consistently translated the official Italian text but also checked it against the original Polish and included new and previously unpublished material. See *Man and Woman He Created Them: A Theology of the Body*, trans. Michael Waldstein (Boston: Pauline, 2006).

longs to Christopher West. He has become a kind of one-man cottage industry of seminars, audio, video, and print products on the catecheses.[32] In addition to these, West has produced numerous books on the subject.[33] In these works, West sees the catecheses as offering a kind of "gospel of sex" to a contemporary culture sorely in need of such a message. He believes that the heart of this good news is John Paul II's view of the centrality of marriage and sex within the Christian message. He claims: "Of all the ways that God chooses to reveal his life and love in the created world, John Paul II is saying marriage—enacted and consummated by sexual union—is most fundamental."[34] Indeed, marriage and sex disclose the very structure of Christian revelation; they are the grammar through which God's plan is made known to us.[35] Within this gospel of the body, the sexual drive, for West, takes on roles traditionally ascribed to grace: "God gave us sexual desire to be the power to love as He loves, so that we can participate in divine life and fulfill the very meaning and being of our existence."[36]

Reviews of West's account of TOB have been mixed—and for good reason. It is undoubtedly true that he has been successful in increasing the level of interest in the late pope's catecheses and creating a more positive view of the Church's teaching on sexuality among many Catholics both young and old. Much of his message has positioned John Paul II's teaching as a positive and appealing presentation of the goodness and beauty of sex in a

32. For some sense of West's array of presentations and products, see his website http://www.christopherwest.com/.

33. These include: Christopher West, *Good News about Sex and Marriage* (Cincinnati: Servant, 2000); idem, *The Theology of the Body Explained: A Commentary on John Paul II's 'Gospel of the Body'* (Boston: Pauline, 2003); idem, *The Theology of the Body for Beginners* (West Chester, PA: Ascension Press, 2004); idem, *The Love That Satisfies* (West Chester, PA: Ascension Press, 2007); idem, *The Theology of the Body Explained: A Commentary on John Paul II's Man and Woman He Created Them*, rev. ed. (Boston: Pauline, 2007); idem, *Heaven's Song: Sexual Love as It Was Meant to Be* (West Chester, PA: Ascension Press, 2008).

34. West, *Good News*, 21.

35. This is an idea that runs throughout his works—a kind of nuptial hermeneutic. West writes: "we cannot understand the inner 'logic' of the Christian mystery without understanding its primordial revelation in the nuptial meaning of our bodies and that biblical vocation to become 'one flesh.'" *Theology of the Body Explained* (2003), 14. Cf. idem, *Good News*, 19; *The Love That Satisfies*, 13; and *Heaven's Song*, 28.

36. West, *Good News*, 21. In a later work that builds on Benedict XVI's teaching on love in his first encyclical, West compares *eros* to "the fuel of a rocket meant to launch us into the stars and beyond." See *The Love That Satisfies*, 34.

culture that has shown itself prone to fascination with the topic.[37] In particular, this work has helped many parish and diocesan religious education programs regain a voice in relating the faith to questions of sexuality after these programs had been debilitated first by internal Church disagreement in the polemics that followed *Humanae vitae* and then by the wave of sexual abuse scandals that subsequently rocked the Church.[38] But scholars who have examined West's account of TOB have raised significant questions about it. They argue that it gives marriage and sex an undue preeminence in the Christian life;[39] that it romanticizes marital sex, making it bear a weight of meaning and experiential fulfillment that it cannot carry;[40] and that in varying ways it seems to fail to come to grips with the reality of sin in present human existence.[41] There is disagreement as to what degree these problems are unique to West or whether they have their roots in John Paul II and are simply amplified or exacerbated by him.[42]

37. Cloutier points out that West's own relationship to the culture is a complex one. He sees the culture as misguided in its sexual fixation but at the same time blindly groping toward a deeper reality. See "Heaven Is a Place," 24–25.

38. Cf. Grabowski, *Sex and Virtue*, 20.

39. See William Mattison III, "'When They Rise from the Dead, They Neither Marry Nor Are Given to Marriage': Marriage and Sexuality, Eschatology, and the Nuptial Meaning of the Body," in Pope John Paul II's Theology of the Body," in *Sexuality and the U.S. Catholic Church*, 41–43. On this point, Mattison is generally careful to distinguish between West and John Paul II.

40. In some cases, this charge appears to be leveled against both West and John Paul II. Thus Mattison refers to a "myopic fixation on extraordinary" in this regard. See "When They Rise from the Dead," 43–46. Cloutier complains about TOB's "extraordinarily romanticized view of self-giving." "Heaven Is a Place," 19. In other cases, the primary target is John Paul II himself as representative of a particular kind of personalism. Thus David Matzko McCarthy criticizes the view of sex as total self-giving because he believes that it "says too much to be right … sex has no room to be ordinary." Individual sexual acts thus carry the weight of "representing a lifetime of friendship between husband and wife." See *Sex and Love in the Home: A Theology of the Household* (London: SCM, 2001), 43 and 47. Lisa Sowle Cahill too finds the language of "total self-giving used by the pope as dependent upon "a very romanticized view of sex and even marital love." See *Sex, Gender, and Christian Ethics*, New Studies in Christian Ethics (Cambridge: Cambridge University, 1996), 203.

41. The point is deftly argued against West by Cathleen Kaveny, "What Women Want: Buffy, the Pope, and the New Feminists," *Commonweal* 130, no. 19 (2003): 21–22. Her criticisms are echoed and elaborated by Mattison, "When They Rise from the Dead," 46–49.

42. Among the most careful not to conflate the two is Mattison, "When They Rise from the Dead." In a more recent piece coauthored with David Cloutier, however, he apparently throws in the towel on this effort. Noting recent critiques of West engendered by some of his statements, they write: "While we generally agree with such critiques, we cannot but help recognize the dominance and even major ecclesial support West's work, in person and in books,

A full evaluation of West's works or their treatment by critics is beyond the scope of this study. In particular, the charge that both he and the late pope grant sexual intercourse a romanticized preeminence in the marriage relationship deserves serious examination beyond that which can be given here. But the argument that John Paul II and West share a common starting point and purpose in regard to contemporary culture in regard to their examinations of the body deserves to be challenged. To argue that both are simply trying to harness contemporary culture's sexual fascination in their presentations is to read John Paul II through the lenses of West's popularized portrayal.[43] This conflation of West and the late pontiff has a number of significant problems. First, it assumes that both share a common stance in regard to the sexually saturated culture of the Western world, particularly the United States. This overlooks the fact that John Paul II had a far more nuanced and critical stance toward that culture than does West. It is true that there is an element of simple critique in West's engagement of popular culture.[44] But it does not approach the nuanced analysis of the struggle between "the civilization of love" versus its antithetical "anti-civilization" in the *Letter to Families* or that between "the culture of life" versus the "culture of death" in *Evangelium vitae*. This dialectical opposition between clashing cultures is integral to the late pope's understanding of marriage, sexuality, and family, and hence frames the TOB catecheses.[45] Second and related to the preceding point, this conflation ignores the degree to which West's

---

has achieved … Thus, our treatment of West and TOB here is not meant to claim that West necessarily 'gets John Paul II right,' but rather that West's reading of the Pope is (a) not an unreasonable interpretation of the Pope's work (including possible weaknesses) and (b) especially likely to be a common means of 'receiving' TOB in the church, since few laypeople are likely to slug through 600 pages of talks." "Bodies Poured Out: Marriage beyond the Theology of the Body," in *Leaving and Coming Home: New Wineskins for Catholic Sexual Ethics*, ed. David Cloutier (Eugene, OR: Cascade Books, 2010), 207. This appears to cede to West the role of the official interpreter of TOB at least for the Church in the United States. David Matzko McCarthy's essay in the same volume ("Cohabitation and Marriage," 119–41) also focuses primarily on the work of West (and Michael Lawler) rather than John Paul II.

43. Mattison suggests that both are engaged in a common project of attempting to "despoil the Egyptians" in this regard. See "When They Rise from the Dead," 50–51.

44. Cf. Cloutier, "Heaven Is a Place," 24–25.

45. See, e.g., Martin Tripole, SJ, "John Paul II the Countercultural Pope," in *Creed and Culture: Jesuit Studies of Pope John Paul II* (Philadelphia: Saint Joseph's University Press, 2004), 35–55; and in the same volume, John C. Haughey, SJ, "A Critical Reading of Pope John Paul II's Understanding of Culture," 75–92.

own reading of the pope is at times conditioned by the Freudian pansexual-ism of his own American culture.[46] Third and more basically, the claim of a common starting point between West and John Paul II tends to reduce the whole point and content of the catecheses to being "all about sex."

It is here, in this very reduction, that one finds common ground be-tween West's popularizations and some of TOB's sharpest revisionist crit-ics. Others too have tended to equate key concepts from TOB with shills for traditional positions on sex. "The nuptial meaning of the body," for Margaret Farley, is simply new language for excluding divorced and remar-ried Catholics from a sexual relationship in a second marriage.[47] Similarly, Lisa Sowle Cahill contends that the intersubjectivity of sex captured in the notion of "language of the body" is ultimately stripped of its real meaning and implications by a prior commitment to the norm of *Humanae vitae*.[48] For Luke Timothy Johnson, the whole point of TOB, in spite of the effort to use biblical texts and language and phenomenological analysis of expe-rience, is to offer a vain *apologia* for Pope Paul VI's failed 1968 encyclical:

John Paul II's conferences finally come down to a concentration on "the transmission of life." By the time he reaches his explicit discussion of *Humanae vitae*, it is difficult to avoid the conclusion that every earlier textual choice and phenomenological re-flection has been geared to a defense of Paul VI's encyclical. However, there is virtual-ly nothing in this defense that is strengthened by the conferences preceding it.[49]

Michael Lawler and Todd Salzman similarly read TOB as a defense of nat-ural (i.e., procreative) complementarity with a view to the exclusion of con-

---

46. This manifests itself in the propensity toward sexual reductionism in West's portrayal of the Christian message and particularly in his frequent identification of the power of *eros* and that of grace noted above. On the genesis of this Freudian pansexualism in American attitudes toward sex, see the fascinating historical treatment provided by Peter Gardella, *Innocent Ec-stasy: How Christianity Gave America an Ethic of Sexual Pleasure* (New York: Oxford, 1986).

47. See her work *Just Love: A Framework for Christian Sexual Ethics* (New York: Contin-uum, 2008), 309.

48. See Cahill, *Sex, Gender and Christian Ethics*, 202. Cahill contrasts the late pope's con-clusions with the challenge to traditional norms posed by the work of André Guindon, *The Sexual Language: An Essay in Moral Theology* (Ottawa: University of Ottawa, 1976).

49. See Luke Timothy Johnson, "A Disembodied 'Theology of the Body': John Paul II on Love, Sex, and Pleasure," *Commonweal* 128, no. 2 (2001): 11–17, here 14. In addition to this unsuccessful attempt to defend *Humanae vitae*, Johnson believes that TOB suffers from an uneven handling of Scripture; a focus on male agency; inattention to the actual experience of married people, particularly women; and a failure to treat sexual pleasure or pain.

traception, reproductive technologies, and sex between partners of the same sex.[50] As such, TOB is limited in that it is merely "a heterosexual theology of the body for reproduction" that does not take into account the experience of persons who do not fit this pattern.[51] What is needed are multiple theologies of the body that can account for the situation of others—"single people, widows and widowers, celibates, and homosexuals."[52]

Both West in his popularizing exposition of TOB and scholars who are critical of it seem to agree on a number of things. First, they concur that the catecheses—both in their key concepts and their overall sweep—have sex as their primary point. Second, they agree that, in spite of their novel language and tone, the catecheses of TOB are largely a defense of traditional sexual norms. For West, this is a good thing. The catecheses represent the Church's perennial wisdom offered in a positive and compelling form for contemporary culture. For revisionist critics, this reveals their problematic and potentially deceptive nature. It is "the old wine of biologism, physicalism, and classicism of the manuals of moral theology in the new wineskin of Thomistic personalism and a theology of the body."[53] What can be made of this rather surprising common ground on the part of those who are otherwise so at odds in their assessment of the TOB and its value?

This unexpected agreement has support from some obvious features of the catecheses. Clearly, issues of sexuality were a major concern of Karol Wojtyła's in writing the reflections that he later gave as general audiences during the first years of his reign as Pope John Paul II. His philosophical work and pastoral work had convinced him of the need for a new exposition of the bases of Catholic teaching in sexuality.[54] This conviction was reinforced by his experience on the "Birth Control Commission" of Paul VI,

50. See Michael Lawler and Todd Salzman, *The Sexual Person: Toward a Renewed Catholic Anthropology* (Washington DC: Georgetown University Press, 2008), 84–91. Against this view they argue that these traditionally prohibited forms of sexual expression can be justified sin some cases. In the case of homosexual expression, this requires "sexual orientation complementarity" between the two partners.

51. Salzman and Lawler, *Sexual Person*, 91. Cf. Ronald Modras, "Pope John Paul II's Theology of the Body," in *John Paul II and Moral Theology*, 149–56.

52. Salzman and Lawler, *Sexual Person*, 86. Cf. Charles Curran, *The Moral Theology of Pope John Paul II* (Washington, DC: Georgetown University Press, 2005), 168.

53. Salzman and Lawler, *Sexual Person*, 91.

54. For a good overview of this philosophical effort as reflected in *Love and Responsibility*, see Buttiglione, *Karol Wojtyla*, 83–116.

the firestorm of disagreement that followed the encyclical, and the impact of the sexual revolution that he could see in his contact with the Western world and to some degree in his own communist Poland.[55] The fact that TOB closes with a series of audiences that reflect on the moral norm proposed by *Humanae vitae* adds credibility to the charge that this issue was the catalyst and *telos* of TOB from its inception.[56]

But a closer examination suggests that there is more to this issue than meets the eye. Certainly, sex and ethical norms are concerns of TOB—but they are not the only such concerns. Both in its particular components and as a whole, TOB's focus is the whole person, of which sex is but one integral component.

In regard to particular features of the catecheses, the key concepts mentioned above are by no means univocal in describing features of sexual activity or expression. Scholars have argued, for example, that the "spousal meaning of the body" has to do with far more than its capacity for sexual self-gift.[57] It has to do rather with the human capacity for self-donation and communion regardless of one's state in life—whether single, married, or celibate.[58] In this regard, it can be understood as an integral component

55. On Wojtyła's pastoral work with married couples and families in Poland, see Weigel, *Witness to Hope*, 194–97.

56. But Waldstein's consultation of the official Italian text and the original Polish manuscript makes clear that the *L'Osservatore Romano* translation used headings for individual catecheses and groups or cycles of them that did not reflect those in Wojtyła's original text. Hence the material originally published in English under the title of *Reflections on Humanae Vitae* was actually the third part of a treatment of the sacrament of marriage dealing with conjugal ethics and spirituality ("He Gave Them the Law of Life as Their Inheritance"). This suggests a different "goal" for the TOB than Johnson's reading.

57. Earlier English translations of TOB usually rendered the Italian *significatio sponsale del corpo* as the "nuptial meaning of the body," though Waldstein points to seven other variations in the *L'Osservatore romano* translation. Waldstein consistently translates the phrase as "the spousal meaning of the body," which he regards as a superior rendering of the Italian. See his "Introduction," in *Male and Female*, 11–12.

58. Waldstein notes that the term is the key concept in the catecheses, being used some 117 times, and that it has a wide range of meaning, including the gift of character of human existence, the call to communion, and the virginal gift of self in the eschatological state. See *Male and Female*, 682–83. For a good synthetic overview of the concept and its range of meaning, especially in the early cycle of the catechesis, see Earl Muller, SJ, "The Nuptial Meaning of the Body," in *John Paul II on the Body: Human, Eucharistic, Ecclesial*, Festschrift for Avery Cardinal Dulles, SJ, ed. John McDermott, SJ, and John Gavin, SJ (Philadelphia: Saint Joseph's University Press, 2008), 87–120, and in the same volume the equally substantive response by John McDermott, SJ, "Response to 'The Nuptial Meaning of the Body,'" 121–53.

of the human capacity for friendship and love central to the moral teaching of St. Thomas.[59] Likewise, "the language of the body" has to do with the whole range of the body's capacity to communicate its sacramentality and gift character in nonverbal ways, particularly in the state of original innocence.[60] One can also use it to understand the body's inherent communicability in and through the experience of suffering.[61] Sexual union that communicates a promise of fidelity and unconditional self-gift is simply a unique and privileged instance of this communicability.

Furthermore, the treatment of sex in TOB is not merely focused on questions of sexual activity, it is also very much concerned with issues of sexual difference—the status of "masculinity and femininity."[62] Even some critics of TOB pick up on this concern, though they tend to read John Paul II as advocating a narrow understanding of sex complementarity in which men and women are incomplete without the other[63] and in which women are simultaneously romantically exalted but seen as subordinate to men.[64]

59. For a good study of the anticipation of this concept of Pope John Paul II, see Thomas Petri, OP, "Locating a Spousal Meaning of the Body in the *Summa Theologiae*: A Comparison of a Central Idea Articulated in the Theology of the Body by Pope John Paul II with the Mature Work of Saint Thomas Aquinas" (STD diss., Catholic University of America, 2010).

60. Cf. Mary Healy, *Men and Women Are from Eden: A Study Guide to John Paul II's Theology of Body* (Cincinnati: Servant Books, 2005), 24–28.

61. See the insightful treatment of the body's capacity to communicate in and through suffering by Peter Harman, "Towards a Theology of Suffering: The Contribution of Karol Wojtyla / Pope John Paul II" (STD diss., Catholic University of America, 2009), 303–415.

62. It is for this reason that Christopher C. Roberts includes an overview of TOB in a recent study of the phenomenon of sexual difference in the Christian tradition (undertaken in part because of debates over same-sex marriage). See *Creation and Covenant: The Significance of Sexual Difference in the Moral Theology of Marriage* (New York: T&T Clark, 2007), 171–83. His concern is primarily a defense of the Augustinian account of sexual difference as articulated by Karl Barth. Roberts sees John Paul II as an ally of Barth's account for the most part, but criticizes him for his neglect of Christology and turn to Mariology for his derivation of distinct roles and qualities of women.

63. This is the reading of Farley, *Just Love*, 141–42. Prudence Allen, RSM, describes this as "fractional sex complementarity" and does not see it as an accurate reading of John Paul II's thought. See her study "Integral Sex Complementarity and the Theology of Communion," *Communio* 17 (1990): 523–44.

64. See Susan Ross, "'Then Honor God in Your Body' (1 Cor. 6:20): Feminist and Sacramental Theology on the Body," *Horizons* 16, no. 1 (1989): 7–27. Cf. Cahill, *Sex, Gender and Christian Ethics*, 204–5. An examination of this charge of romanticization (and simultaneous denigration) of women in TOB is beyond the scope of this paper. But the fact of this controversy does support the basic claim that the catecheses are focused on more than questions of sexual activity.

While the late pope does use the language of "complementarity," he does so as a way to describe the way in which the "originality" of men and women as persons corresponds to one another.[65] If the body reveals the person, then the bodily differences of men and women reveal unique and original ways of existing as a person within their shared humanity.[66] The categories in which sexual difference is described here and in John Paul II's more weighty Apostolic Letter *Mulieris dignitatem* are Trinitarian—personal difference disclosed thorough mutual relation within an underlying unity of nature.[67]

Both this broader reading of the spousal meaning of the body and the concern with sexual difference help to bring into focus the basic anthropological thrust of TOB. While John Paul II used the language of "a theology of the body," he also characterized these audiences on numerous occasions as an effort to elaborate "an adequate anthropology."[68] In some ways, one sees in these audiences many of the concerns of his work as a professional philosopher carried forward—the self-awareness and self-determination of the acting person experienced through the bodily dimension of personal existence, of which sexual difference is typically a key component.[69] It is for

---

65. John Paul II states that "the knowledge of man passes through masculinity and femininity, which are, as it were, two 'incarnations' of the same metaphysical solitude before God and the world—*two reciprocally completing ways of 'being a body' and at the same time of being human*—as two complementary dimensions of self-knowledge and self-determination and, at the same time, *two complementary ways of being conscious of the meaning of the body.*" *Male and Female*, 10:1, 166 (emphasis original).

66. The late pope says of man and woman: "Their *unity denotes* above all *the identity of human nature; duality, on the other hand, shows what, on the basis of this identity, constitutes the masculinity and femininity* of created man." *Male and Female*, 9:1, 161 (emphasis original).

67. On the original reciprocity of male and female as existing persons, see *Male and Female* 15:3–5, 187–90, and *Mulieris dignitatem*, no. 10. For an analysis of the Trinitarian basis of this difference, see John S. Grabowski, "Mutual Submission and Trinitarian Self-Giving," *Angelicum* 74 (1997): 501–8.

68. See *Male and Female*, 13:2, 14:3, 15:1, 23:3, 25:2, 26:2. Waldstein notes that the Italian *adeguato* does not carry the connotation of "barely good enough" that "adequate" can denote in English. Instead, it should be understood as indicating something "commensurate with its object" (cf. ibid., 55:2, 678).

69. Though at times John Paul II seems to be so focused on the bodily nature of human existence that he loses sight of sexual difference as essential to actual persons and thus makes overtly self-contradictory statements, such as "Although in its normal constitution, the human body carries within itself the signs of sex and is by its nature male or female, *the fact that man is a 'body' belongs more deeply to the structure of the personal subject than the fact that in his somatic constitution he is also male or female.*" See *Man and Woman*, 8:1, 157 (emphasis original).

this reason that the pope's analysis of "original solitude" at the heart of human life and existence is a key to the whole of TOB.[70] Already in the command given by God not to eat of the tree in the middle of the Garden, the transcendence of the human person is evident in the freedom to eat or not eat.[71] This theological notion of transcendence has its roots in Wojtyła's early study of the thought of John of the Cross.[72] From the Doctor of Fontiveros, Wojtyła imbibed the idea that faith is not merely something that one has—it must be consciously lived through praxis, by which one grows and bears fruit.[73] Such praxis at the root of the transcendence of the human person is expressed vertically in his or her relationship with God and horizontally in the relationship between the sexes.

In TOB, this focus on the self-transcendence of the person is joined to phenomenological analysis of action and experience, and used as a method to mine dimensions of biblical texts often untouched by more standard exegesis—the solitude of the self-aware subject addressed by God, the longing for communion, the discovery of oneself in the encounter with an irreducible other, the freedom found in the gift of self in love.[74] This highly tex-

70. Commentators have pointed out the centrality of original solitude in the pope's anthropology: "Original solitude is an essential experience of the human being, both male and female; it remains at the root of every other human experience and so accompanies man throughout his whole life's journey." Carl Anderson and Jose Granados, *Called to Love: Approaching John Paul II's Theology of the Body* (New York: Doubleday, 2009), 27. For a more extensive consideration, see Mary Shivanandan, *Crossing the Threshold of Love: A New Vision of Marriage in Light of John Paul II's Anthropology* (Washington, DC: Catholic University of America Press, 1999), esp. 95–101.

71. Cf. *Male and Female*, 5:4, 7:3–4.

72. On Wojtyła's "Carmelite Personalism," see Waldstein, "Introduction," in *Male and Female*, 23–34.

73. On this, see Alvaro Huerga, "Karol Wojtyla, comentador de San Juan de la Cruz," *Angelicum* 56 (1979): 348–66. According to Huegera, John of the Cross took this distinction between "having faith" and "living faith" from his reading of a book by Luis de Granada.

74. While Johnson is critical of the pope's disengaged and overly academic analysis, he admits that John Paul II is generally careful in his handling of biblical texts. See "A Disembodied Theology of the Body,'" 13. For more thorough and generally positive assessment of the use of Scripture in TOB, see Michel Ségin, "The Biblical Foundations of the Thought of John Paul II on Human Sexuality," *Communio*, 20 (1993): 266–89; and William Kurz, SJ, "The Scriptural Foundations of *Theology of the Body*," in *John Paul II on the Body*, 27–46. Kurz points to the pope's awareness of historical critical exegeis as well as patristic and medieval readings, but highlights his pastoral engagement with Scripture as God's inspired word for Christians looking for its guidance. In his response to Kurz, Christopher Cullen, SJ, concurs in regard to the late pope's

tured biblical analysis is then stretched across a theological tableaux—the triptych of human existence as created, fallen, and imbued with the grace of redemption.[75] The template of the drama of redemption adds to the existential urgency of the analysis. The catecheses reverberate with the existential weight of human freedom confronted with the call of God, the struggle of the human heart torn between the poles of love and inordinate desire, and the longing for the freedom of love given and received. The reader is invited to "identify in" and find his or her own experience illuminated by the biblical texts considered. The experience that they capture well is that of the Christian who seeks to turn his or her faith into the daily praxis of "life in the Spirit" lived within the limits of fallen, historical existence.[76] TOB thus offers an experientially focused method of reading Scripture that envisions the human person as an icon illuminated by the mysteries of creation, the fall, redemption, and the eschaton.

That this iconic anthropology has application to issues beyond sexual activity and morality was noticed both by John Paul II and by scholars interested in his thought. In the concluding catechesis of the TOB he noted: "One must immediately observe, in fact, that the term 'theology of the body' goes far beyond the content of the reflections presented here. These reflections do not include many problems belonging, with regard to their object, to the theology of the body (e.g., the problem of suffering and death, so important in the biblical message)."[77] Though he himself did not develop this anthropology in that direction, scholars have found aspects of TOB to be relevant to his teaching in his 1984 Apostolic Letter *Salvifici doloris* in articulating "a theology of the suffering body."[78] Others have found these

---

sophistication as a biblical interpreter, but argues that his method of "exemplary actualization" of some biblical texts (such as Ephesians 5) exceeds what they actually say on current questions. See "A Response to William Kurz, S.J.," in ibid., *John Paul II on the Body*, 47–64.

75. Mary Healy suggests that this triptych can perhaps be understood as a "quadriptych" that splits redeemed existence between the experience of grace in the confines of present fallen history ("redeemed humanity") and the eschatological completion of the redemption ("glorified humanity"). See *Men and Women*, 9–12, 43–65. This fourfold division has the advantage of making clear that the full restoration of the paradise of humanity's original state is eschatological—a point sometimes lost in the rhetoric of West's popular portrayal.

76. This is part of what I take Cullen to mean by John Paul II's approach the scriptures as embodying "exemplary actualization."

77. *Male and Female*, 133:1, 660.

78. In addition to the study of Harman, "Towards a Theology of Suffering," see José Granados, "Toward a Theology of the Suffering Body," *Communio* 33 (2006): 540–63.

reflections to be relevant to articulating an account of the bodily presence and moral agency of the unborn, the comatose, the mentally handicapped, and other vulnerable persons.[79] Still others have explored the fruitfulness of TOB for a range of issues—not just sex or suffering but also vocation, revelation, technology, work, prayer, and eschatology.[80]

This diverse range of issues and applications to which TOB lends itself, as well as its theological depth in treating the human person in the panorama of salvation history, belies its reduction to a catchy new way to present old Catholic views of sex. Both enthusiastic popularizers like West and revisionist critics of the catecheses share this simplistic reading. TOB certainly does treat sex and in so doing attempts to defend traditional norms, but it does so in the context of developing a larger vision of the person called to make a gift of him or herself through the body—a gift lived in differing ways in the single, married, and celibate states.[81] This gift character of the human vocation integral to creation is debilitated by sin but progressively recovered through the healing work of grace made possible by union with Christ. As such, it is better read as a presentation of a gospel in which sex plays a part than "a gospel of sex."

Veritatis Splendor: The Drama of the Encounter with Christ

If the reception of TOB was skewed by its being commandeered by differing sides of the debate over the teaching of *Humanae vitae* and other traditional sexual norms as well as by the dearth of effective catechesis in its aftermath, then the encyclical *Veritatis splendor* was widely seen as the late pope taking sides in the methodological controversies that the very same debate had spawned. In this case, it was John Paul II weighing in on and authoritatively taking sides in debates over absolute moral norms, conscience, fundamental option theory, proportionalism, and action theory. Revision-

79. See the fine analysis provided by Jeffrey Tranzillo, "The Silent Language of a Profound Sharing of Affection: The Agency of the Vulnerable in Selected Writings of Pope John Paul II" (PhD diss., Catholic University of America, 2003).

80. These issues among others are treated by Mary Timothy Prokes, FSE, *Toward a Theology of the Body* (Grand Rapids, MI: Eerdmans, 1996). While not written as a commentary on John Paul II's catecheses, Prokes's work is clearly influenced and inspired by them.

81. *Humanae vitae* speaks of the need to develop a total vision of the person and his or her vocation (cf. no. 7). In this sense, one can see the catecheses as a response to the encyclical and the controversy it generated.

ists who believed themselves targeted by the teaching and their traditional-ist opponents who saw it as vindication for their own positions shared this reading. The problem with this reading is that it fixates on the second chapter of the document and largely dismisses its first and third chapters to the status of mere window dressing or parenesis. A casualty of this narrow reading is the mediation on the encounter with Jesus and the rich young man of Matthew 19 in chapter 1, which makes the biblical motif of the call to discipleship the foundation of the rest of the document.

Revisionist treatments of the document, while applauding John Paul II's stand against the relativism and individualism of the wider culture, found both its center of gravity and its Achilles heel in its treatment of technical questions of moral theology. Thus Richard McCormick, SJ, focused on the analysis of the moral object as the key to the document. But the fact that the encyclical makes "repeated appeals to actions wrong *ex objecto* does not aid analysis, rather it hides it."[82] Charles Curran objected to what he saw as the overwhelming focus on law within the document, especially laws that take the form of objectionless moral norms.[83] As was the case for McCormick, the key issue is how the act is described. John Paul II's moral absolutes are merely formal norms: "all would agree that murder is wrong because murder is by definition unjustified killing."[84]

A second common charge leveled against *Veritatis splendor* by revisionists was that it mischaracterized their positions. Curran makes this claim in regard to its presentations of autonomous ethics, its mention of accusations of physicalism in official Church teaching, its discussion of the relationship of conscience and truth, the evaluation of the theology of the fundamental option, and its action theory.[85] McCormick gives a wide survey of literature critical of the document that echoes the contention that the document mischaracterizes proportionalism in the positions that it opposes.[86] Others

---

82. See "Some Early Reactions to *Veritatis Splendor*," in *John Paul II and Moral Theology*, 5–34, here 28.

83. See Charles Curran, "*Veritatis Splendor*: A Revisionist Perspective," in *Veritatis Splendor: American Responses*, ed. Michael Allsopp and John O'Keefe (Kansas City, MO: Sheed and Ward, 1995),

84. Ibid., 232.

85. Ibid., 233–37.

86. McCormick, "Some Early Reactions," 12–25. McCormick's analysis also includes some studies favorable to the document, though his own sympathy for revisionist positions is evident

press the claim further. The document, they argue, without naming any specific authors describes positions that no one would accept and then rejects these positions—a classic case of erecting and toppling straw men.[87] In the words of James Gaffney, "'proportionalism,' as presented here by the pope is quite simply a bugaboo."[88]

Still other revisionist critics of the encyclical see John Paul II's primary point as the assertion of Church authority to quash dissent to traditional positions. In other words, the real issue is ecclesiological—the nature of the Church and the function of authority within it. For McCormick, this ecclesiology is clearly restorationist, envisioning a view of the Church "as a pyramid where truth and authority flow uniquely from the pinnacle" as opposed to Vatican II's "concentric model wherein the reflections of all must flow from the periphery to the center if the wisdom resident in the Church is to be reflected persuasively and prophetically to the world."[89] Curran faults the document for its assumption that the "hierarchical magisterium just has the truth" rather than attending to the role of reason and human experience in arriving at truth.[90] Further compounding this imbalanced ecclesiology are problems of the lack of consultation in its composition and questions about the authorship of its key second chapter.[91]

---

throughout. For his analysis of the encyclical as "the final solution" to the "problem of proportionalism," see his "Killing the Patient," in *Considering Veritatis Splendor*, ed. John Wilkins (Cleveland: Pilgrim, 1994), 14–20. For a somewhat less partisan overview of reactions to *Veritatis splendor*, see James Keenan, SJ, *A History of Catholic Moral Theology in the Twentieth Century: From Confessing Sins to Liberating Consciences* (London: Continuum, 2010), 128–34.

87. See, e.g., Joseph Selling, "The Context and Arguments of *Veritatis Splendor*," in *The Splendor of Accuracy: An Examination of the Assertions Made by Veritatis Splendor*, ed. Joseph Selling and Jan Jans (Grand Rapids, MI: Eerdmans, 1994), 22–70.

88. See "The Pope on Proportionalism," in *Veritatis Splendor: American Responses*, 60–71, here 70. A similar argument is made by Louis Janssens in "Teleology and Proportionality: Thoughts about the Encyclical *Veritatis Splendor*," in *Splendor of Accuracy*, 99–113.

89. McCormick, "Some Early Reactions," 29. Cf. Gabriel Daly, OSA, "Ecclesial Implications," *Doctrine and Life* 43 (1993): 532–37.

90. See Curran, "*Veritatis Splendor*: A Revisionist Perspective," 239.

91. McCormick complains that revisionist theologians were not consulted in the process of drafting the document and echoes the speculation of others (such as Ronald Modras and Joseph Selling) that the primary author of the document's second chapter was not the late pope. He mentions Andrez Szostek (whose dissertation at the University of Lublin included then Cardinal Wojtyła on his board) and John Finnis as possibilities. See "Some Early Reactions," 9–10, 29.

These analyses of the primary point of the document map rather neatly onto the contentious debates over method in moral theology, which emerged in the storm that followed *Humanae vitae*. This historical connection is cemented by the suggestion that John Paul II's real point in the document was in fact the debate over moral norms regarding sex in general and contraception in particular. Some scholars make this connection historically (i.e., that *Humanae vitae* was a catalyst for the growth of dissent at which *Veritatis splendor* was aimed),[92] others see it as a recurring "obsession" of Pope John Paul II that manifests itself in this document,[93] and still others simply saw it as a subtext for the document as a whole.[94]

Interestingly, some of the chief opponents of revisionist thought share a similar reading of the primary concerns of the document. Thus Germain Grisez locates the heart of the document in its depiction of the idea of moral absolutes as a truth taught by revelation. This for Grisez is a stake aimed at the heart of dissenting positions that cannot be evaded. Attempts to reduce such moral norms to the status of generalities regarding love, guidelines for judgments of conscience, discreet acts incapable of reversing a fundamental option, or the idea that such norms indicate only "premoral" or "ontic" evil are weighed against revelation (in the form of particular biblical texts) and found wanting.[95] In the end, such dissenting theologians have three choices: "to admit that they have been mistaken, to admit that they do not believe God's word, or to claim that the Pope is grossly misinterpreting the Bible."[96] While Grisez anchors his argument in appeals to specific biblical texts, the heart of the matter for him still centers on moral absolutes and Church teaching authority.

92. See, e.g., David Hollenbach, SJ, "Tradition, Historicity, and Truth in Theological Ethics," in *Christian Ethics: Problems and Prospects*, ed. Lisa Sowle Cahill and James Childress (Cleveland: Pilgrim, 1996), 62.

93. This is the term used by Ronald Burke, "*Veritatis* Splendor: Papal Authority and the Sovereignty of Reason," in *Veritatis Splendor: American Responses*, 119–36; see esp. 127–28.

94. Thus the angry lament of Bernard Häring, "A Distrust That Wounds," in *Considering Veritatis Splendor*, ed. John Wilkins (Cleveland: Pilgrim, 1994), 9–13. James Hannigan provides a more balanced analysis. Hannigan denies that sex is either the primary point or dominant subtext of the document, but notes that it does raise important questions for sexual ethics in its idea of moral perfection, engagement with revelation, treatment of intrinsically evil acts, and engagement with culture. See "*Veritatis Splendor* and Sexual Ethics," in *Veritatis Splendor: American Responses*, 208–23.

95. See Germain Grisez, "Revelation versus Dissent," in *Considering Veritatis Splendor*, 1–8.

96. Ibid., 7–8.

John Finnis claims to offer an alternative to the common but reduction-ist reading of the encyclical that it is really about sex—instead, he argues, its real point is faith.[97] But like Grisez, much of his argument is devoted to offering an indictment of proportionalist reasoning. The invocation of pro-portionate reason to create exceptions to moral absolutes allows the genie out of the bottle such that no reason for a moral action can ever be disqual-ified as disproportionate. The immediate result is that the basis of moral judgment is shifted to "whatever one *feels* appropriate, all things consid-ered."[98] The more long-term result is the broader cultural impact. The in-troduction of exceptions in regard to the teaching regarding contraception has resulted in widespread acceptance of abortion by Catholics in countries like the United States.[99] But these problems are merely symptomatic of a deeper crisis of morality and belief in post-Christian culture that appear in the Church as "reconceptions" of revelation and faith. Such reconceptions need to be banished by solemn judgments of the magisterium, which high-lights their incompatibility with Christian faith, as *Veritatis splendor* shows the incompatibility of the denial of moral absolutes with Catholic teach-ing.[100] Finnis therefore does regard the encyclical in a larger cultural and epistemological context, but those things on which he focuses in the doc-ument are familiar: absolute moral norms, the pitfalls of proportionalism, and the need for authoritative teaching by the Church.

Absent in these analyses of the key ideas of *Veritatis splendor* is attention to John Paul II's significant engagement with Scripture. This feature of the document did not go wholly unnoticed by scholars. Even when discussed, however, the encyclical's use of Scripture was frequently attached to one of the contested methodological foci identified above. In the case of Grisez, individual biblical texts are culled from the encyclical to refute revisionist attempts to defuse or evade the notion of moral absolutes.[101] For Curran, the invocation of Scripture, including the mediation on Jesus's encounter

97. See John Finnis, "Beyond the Encyclical," in *Considering Veritatis Splendor*, 69–76.

98. Ibid., 71. Emphasis original.

99. See ibid. It would therefore seem that Finnis sees sex as an important subtext of the document after all.

100. See ibid., 75–76.

101. Critics of Grisez complained that the piecemeal invocation of texts used in a "bitter and simplistic attack" on other theologians implied a simplistic notion of revelation akin to fundamentalism. See Seán Fagan, "The Encyclical in Focus," *Tablet* 247 (1993): 1519.

with the Rich Young Man of Matthew 19, serves to reinforce the legal model of morality that dominates the encyclical.[102] William Spohn largely concurs: "The encyclical promises a Christonomous ethics of discipleship but it cannot deliver because it reduces morality to a matter of rules and principles."[103] Gareth Moore sees the document's use of Scripture as largely unsuccessful—an attempt to support its condemnation of modern moral theories that the scriptures do not address.[104]

This study contends that these readings fail to do justice to the actual engagement with Scripture in the document, particularly in its presentation of discipleship in the first chapter. Many commentators found positive things to say about this section in spite of their views of the rest of the document or its overall purpose. Thus McCormick gushed, "All Catholic moral theologians should and will welcome this beautiful Christ-centered presentation unfolded in Chapter One."[105] Grisez called it "an inspiring articulation of the Gospel's teaching about following Jesus."[106] Summarizing the general good feeling generated by chapter 1, Oliver O'Donovan remarked: "Everyone has had a nice word to say about this first section." However, as he noted, "Not everyone has appreciated its innovative strength as a programme for moral theology . . . in these pages which shape the moral discourse of the Church as an evangelical proclamation."[107] The typical readings of the document by both critics and proponents surveyed above support the truth of O'Donovan's observation. The first chapter was nice or even beautiful, but

102. Curran writes that "the pope's purpose has shaped and limited the use of scripture. The moral life is understood primarily in terms of commandments (to the exclusion of and underplaying of other elements such as the change of heart, virtues, vision, attitudes, moral imagination, goals, etc.), and the role of Jesus and consequently of the Church is reduced to teaching commandments." See "*Veritatis Splendor*: A Revisionist Perspective," 225; cf. 230–32. Interestingly, Grisez too focuses on the specific moral norms identified in Jesus's exchange with the Rich Young Man, finding a certain amount of common ground with Curran in his reading of the text. See "Revelation versus Dissent," 2.

103. See "Morality on the Way to Discipleship: The Use of Scripture in *Veritatis Splendor*," in *Veritatis Splendor: American Responses*, 83–105, here 102.

104. See Gareth Moore, "Some Remarks on the Use of Scripture in *Veritatis Splendor*," in *Splendor of Accuracy*, 71–97.

105. See Richard McCormick, "*Veritatis Splendor* and Moral Theology," *America* 169, no. 13 (1993): 9.

106. Grisez, "Revelation versus Dissent," 3.

107. Oliver O'Donovan, "A Summons to Reality," in *Considering Veritatis Splendor*, 41–45, here 42.

it had little to do with the rest of the letter. A more careful reading of the text reveals that it does make strong claims about the nature of moral theology that are relevant to the rest of the document. It does this through the articulation of a dramatic biblical anthropology into which the reader is invited as a participant.

John Paul II identifies the unnamed Rich Young man of Matthew 19:16 as a type of "every person, who consciously or not, *approaches Christ the Redeemer of man and questions him about morality*."[108] He is thus identified with Adam—an association that recalls not just his point of departure in the catecheses on the body, but also Wojtyła's work as a playwright in works such as *The Jeweler's Shop* and *The Radiation of Fatherhood*. He is "John Q. Everyman," who wrestles with the moral good and questions concerning the meaning of life. Readers are thus encouraged to identify with the Young Man and to hear Jesus's words addressed to them in this dramatic encounter.[109] This reading of Scripture is not addressed solely to spectators at a theatrical performance, but also to participants in an existential drama. The Young Man's questions to Christ are those that well up from the depths of the readers' own hearts, pulled from their lips because of "the attractiveness of the person of Jesus."[110] His answers ring true because he is the Answer to the existential dilemmas that bedevil the human heart, as the "Alpha and the Omega of human history," particularly in his Incarnation and in the mystery of the Cross.[111]

In John Paul II's narration of this dramatic encounter on the stage of the Gospel, the reference to the commandments serve not to buttress a law-dominated morality, but to highlight the call to discipleship as a gift of grace. The commandments themselves are reflective of God's gracious initiative, but "not even the most rigorous observance of the commandments, succeeds in 'fulfilling' the Law."[112] Instead, human beings still find themselves in slavery to sin, which makes God's law appear alien and as a bur-

---

108. Pope John Paul II, Encyclical Letter, *Veritatis splendor*, no. 7. The citation is from the Daughters of Saint Paul edition, Vatican translation (Boston: St. Paul Books and Media, 1993), 17. Emphasis original. All subsequent references to this document are from this edition.

109. This chapter of Matthew's Gospel serves "as a useful guide *for listening once more* in a lively and direct way to [Jesus'] ... moral teaching." *Veritatis splendor*, no. 6, p. 16. Emphasis original.

110. *Veritatis splendor*, no. 8, p. 18.   111. *Veritatis splendor*, no. 8, p. 18.

112. *Veritatis splendor*, no. 11, p. 21.

den.[113] The Young Man, like fallen Adam, is unable to take the next step—the perfection to which he is called requires "maturity in self-giving," which itself is a gift of grace.[114] Discipleship requires an interior transformation effected through participation in the sacraments, which provide the "source and power" of the gift of self in love in union with Christ's own Eucharistic self-gift.[115] Following Jesus is therefore not exterior imitation based on norms, but interior transformation in conformity with Christ lived in the Holy Spirit who is himself the "new law" of Christian life.[116] This transformation contains the happiness that the Young Man seeks.[117]

This call to transformation in discipleship is not addressed to an elite few, but to all. The universal call to holiness reaffirmed at Vatican II is articulated through the dramatic call to the perfection of discipleship given to the Young Man: "*The invitation*, 'go sell your possessions and give money to the poor,' and the promise 'you will have treasure in heaven,' *are meant for everyone*, because they bring out the full meaning of the commandment of love of neighbor, just as the invitation which follows, 'Come follow me,' is the new, specific form of the commandment of love of God."[118] To make this identification is already a significant departure from the standard Catholic reading of the text, which saw in this interlocutor of Jesus a pious layman who kept the commandments now called to the perfection of the evangelical counsels.[119] The Young Man challenged with this general invitation shows once again the transcendence of the human person called to the gift of self in love—vertically in love of God and horizontally in love of neighbor. Sadly, the Young Man turns away from this call even offered as a gift, demonstrating human freedom in its negative form.

---

113. Cf. *Veritatis splendor*, nos. 17–18.   114. Cf. *Veritatis splendor*, no. 17.

115. *Veritatis splendor*, no. 21, p. 35.

116. See *Veritatis splendor*, no. 24, echoing the teaching of St. Thomas in the *Summa theologiae* I-II, q. 106, a. 1. On this theme of transformation in the document (issued on the Feast of the Transfiguration), see J. A. DiNoia, OP, "The Moral Life as Transfigured Life," in *Veritatis Splendor and the Renewal of Moral Theology* (Princeton, NJ: Scepter, 1999), 1–10.

117. On the eudaimonism of the document, see Livio Melina, "The Desire for Happiness and the Commandments in the First Chapter of *Veritatis splendor*," in *Veritatis Splendor and the Renewal of Moral Theology*, 143–60.

118. *Veritatis splendor*, no. 18, p. 31. Emphasis original.

119. This reading is at least as old as Athanasius's famous *Life of Anthony*. My reading differs from that of John O'Keefe, who sees asceticism at the root of the encyclical's notion of perfection. See "No Place for Failure? Augustinian Reflections on *Veritatis splendor*," in *Veritatis Splendor: American Responses*, 16–37.

This dramatic anthropology gleaned from the encounter between Jesus and the Rich Young Man as everyman is not limited to the first chapter of *Veritatis splendor*. It echoes through the rest of the document. The inviolability of the commandments safeguarded in the defense of absolute moral norms reinforces the need for grace to embrace the call of discipleship offered as a gift.[120] Moral norms thus protect but do not exhaust the corresponding gift of oneself in love in response to this gracious call, a truth eloquently proclaimed by the sacrificial self-gift of the martyrs.[121] This response is undertaken in less dramatic form by the choice of particular goods pursued in concrete moral choices. The choice of such goods that specify the moral object of particular acts is therefore necessarily a "first-person" endeavor on the part of the disciple.[122] The transcendence of the person to freely respond to God's invitation requires this. The authority of the Church to defend genuine moral goods and the norms that protect them is necessary to make it a place where this dramatic encounter between Christ and the human person can occur.[123] Thus understood, morality is not primarily obedience to rules but about a transformative encounter with Christ, who reveals us to ourselves.

The connections identified here between the dramatic biblical anthropology of chapter 1 and the rest of the document do not represent an exhaustive list. But they do help to challenge a reading of the document that minimizes the import of chapter 1 as mere biblical parenesis, while focusing on the "real issues" contained in chapter 2. O'Donovan is correct in

---

120. "*The gift does not lessen but reinforces the moral demands of love.*" *Veritatis splendor*, no. 24, p. 37. Emphasis original. In no. 83, a similar point is made about the gift of the Holy Spirit enabling us to interiorize the law and to live it in true freedom. On the social import of moral absolutes in the document, see Romanus Cessario, OP, "Moral Absolutes in the Civilization of Love," in *Veritatis Splendor and the Renewal of Moral Theology*, 195–208.

121. On the witness of the martyrs and moral norms, see *Veritatis splendor*, nos. 90–93. For a thoughtful, critical evaluation of the document's invocation of martyrdom and particularly the story of Susanna, see Katherine TePas, "'If You Wish to Be Perfect . . .': Images of Perfection in *Veritatis splendor*," in *Veritatis Splendor: American Responses*, 48–59.

122. "In order to grasp the object of an act which specifies the act morally, it is therefore necessary to place oneself *in the perspective of the acting person.*" *Veritatis splendor*, no. 78, p. 99. Emphasis original. For an incisive study of the importance of this contention, see Martin Rhonheimer, "Intrinsically Evil Acts and the Moral Viewpoint: Clarifying a Central Teaching of *Veritatis Splendor*," in *Veritatis Splendor and the Renewal of Moral Theology*, 161–93.

123. "*In order to make this 'encounter' with Christ possible, God willed his Church.*" *Veritatis splendor*, no. 8, p. 17. Emphasis original.

underscoring the potentially revolutionary character of chapter 1 for the Church's moral teaching. For John Paul II, moral theology both proceeds from and is ordered to an encounter between the human person and Christ. The Church and its teaching and sacramental life is the place where this transformative encounter takes place. These notes sounded most forcefully in the document's first chapter are reprised in different ways and in different style and subject matter in those that follow.[124]

As in the case of the TOB catecheses, the effort to fit John Paul II's teaching in *Veritatis splendor* into the lines of post–*Humanae vitae* debate leads to a reduction and loss of its anthropological depth. And as in the case of those catecheses on the body, that which is lost is precisely that which makes it engaging for the reader willing and able to put in the effort to engage the document. The appeal to experience in the context of the biblical drama of salvation enables the reader to "identify in" and find him- or herself as the one addressed and invited by Christ to transformation through the gift-call of discipleship. Deeper engagement with Scripture and "livelier contact with the mystery of Christ and the history of salvation" are keys to the renewal of moral theology called for by the Second Vatican Council.[125] These marks are prominently displayed in the dramatic biblical anthropology of the opening chapter of *Veritatis splendor*. An examination of the implications of taking the encounter with Christ as the starting point and goal of moral theology offers a rich vein for reconceptualizing the methodology of the discipline in conjunction with the field's deeper engagement with Scripture and virtue ethics.[126]

124. In addition to theories about different authors accounting for the differences in style and sources within the various chapters, it is worth considering whether some of these differences are the result of John Paul II's distinctive phenomenological style of analysis. The phenomenological method employed in the encyclical circles the reality of the moral life, allowing it to disclose itself through the media of Scripture, philosophical themes of fundamental moral theology, and social engagement.

125. See Second Vatican Council, Decree on Priestly Formation, *Optatum toius*, no. 16.

126. Some critics of the encyclical did indeed perceive this potentially transformative impact of the document on the field but warned of its dangers. Lisa Sowle Cahill, e.g., described its "confessional and even fideist mode which pulls the rug out from under the church's and moral theologians credibility as advocates of the human and the common goods." See "Veritatis Splendor," *Commonweal* 120, no. 14 (1993): 15–16. While disagreeing with the negative consequences of her assessment, Lorenzo Albacete notes that in some respects she grasped the implications of the document better than some of its proponents. See "The Relevance of Christ or the *Sequla Christi*," *Communio* 21 (1994): 255.

Conclusion

This study has argued that the "reception" of Pope John Paul II's teaching within Catholic moral theology in the United States to this point has been incomplete at best and in some ways inaccurate. A significant reason for this limited reception is that both proponents and critics of his teaching have sought to plug some of his ideas into the contours of existing debates within the field or the wider culture. This has clearly been the case with the popular promotion of and critical reaction to the TOB catecheses as well as with the typical readings of *Veritatis splendor* by major revisionist and traditionalist scholars. In both of these cases, there has been a corresponding reduction or loss of the anthropological depth within the discussion of these teachings. It is as if proponents and critics have plucked the fruit of individual insights or ideas that support their own positions while ignoring the tree that supports and unifies them. That "tree" is the human person, a dynamic acting subject, addressed by Christ in the existential drama of salvation, and called to fulfillment through the grace-powered action expressive of the gift of self. The individual insights or ideas gleaned from the late pope's thought are intelligible and fruitful because of the anthropology that nourishes them.

It is this anthropological foundation too that accounts for much of the continuing appeal of John Paul II's teaching some six years after his death. The appeal to experience in both TOB and *Veritatis splendor* encourages the reader to "identify in" and to discover him- or herself in the biblical text examined. Scripture becomes the place to encounter Christ and to allow him to engage the reader in a dialogue that leads to self-discovery. The process is simultaneously intellectually stimulating and ethically and spiritually challenging. Wojtyła's "Carmelite personalism" learned from John of the Cross pulls the reader to search for ways to go beyond merely "having faith" to the praxis of "living faith" and bearing fruit in the Christian life. His anthropology is thus both dynamic and holistic, engaging the reader as a whole person. It is also relevant to a consideration of much more than individual norms concerning sexual behavior.

The analysis of the particular examples afforded by the reception of TOB and *Veritatis splendor* does not constitute an exhaustive list of areas where the anthropological depth and consistency of John Paul II's moral teaching has been missed. Another example that could be considered is the widely echoed claim of methodological inconsistency between the late pope's teaching in regard to sexuality and that within his social teaching.[127] According to a common narrative, Vatican II represented a shift in Catholic teaching from a "classicist worldview" composed of absolute norms deduced from unchanging biological structures to an inductive, dynamic, and historically conscious method of moral reasoning in which norms are more flexibly and contextually understood. Revisionist thought has embraced this historically conscious worldview and applied it across the board. Pope John Paul II embraced a historically conscious approach in his social and political teaching but has maintained a classicist approach in his sexual teaching and life ethics.[128] This claim has already been indirectly challenged by studies that have shown a consistent view of the human person underlying John Paul II's teaching in these various areas, but more work needs to be done on this subject.[129] One can also more directly challenge the premise of the argument by questioning the coherence of appeals to "historical consciousness" that do not acknowledge their own historical conditioning or refuse to ground an appeal to experience within a particular tradition.[130]

127. This has been a consistent theme in the work of Charles Curran. For his reading of this methodological shift in the history of twentieth-century Catholic moral theology, see *Catholic Moral Theology*, 103–7. "Historical consciousness" understood in this way is also a methodological point of departure for Salzman and Lawler in *The Sexual Person*.

128. On this charge of inconsistency in John Paul II, see Curran, *Moral Theology of Pope John Paul II*. Some more recent studies question whether John Paul II's later social teaching shows something of a retreat from a "historically conscious" approach to more of a natural law methodology. See Ethna Regan, *Theology and the Boundary Discourse of Human Rights* (Washington, DC: Georgetown University Press, 2010), 42.

129. For an outstanding study that demonstrates the continuity of Wojtyła / John Paul II's anthropology from his philosophical work in *The Acting Person* to the biblical anthropology of TOB to his social encyclicals, see Gerard Beigel, *Faith and Social Justice in the Teaching of Pope John Paul II* (New York: Peter Lang, 1997). Thomas Williams, LC, in a recent study similarly demonstrates the continuity in Wojtyła's personalist analysis of human dignity in the sexual ethics of *Love and Responsibility* and John Paul II's papal defense of human rights. See *Who Is My Neighbor? Personalism and the Foundations of Human Rights* (Washington, DC: Catholic University Press, 2005), 105–216.

130. Brian Johnstone, CSsR, points out that the concepts such as "historical consciousness" developed by Vico and "historicity" developed by Hegel were imported into discussions of shifts in theological worldviews by Bernard Lonergan. But these appeals rest on an attribution of a kind of ontological subjectivity to the world that it does not possess. Furthermore, proponents of "historical consciousness" seldom apply the limitations imposed by this approach to

Another area of ongoing scholarly work that holds promise for fostering a deeper reception of the anthropological depth of John Paul II's teaching is a growing interest in the sources of this teaching. Certainly, his elevation to the papacy created a flurry of interest in phenomenology on the part of scholars who had never studied the method or who dismissed it as a strange species of "continental philosophy." Much of this interest centered on the classification of Wojtyła's "Lublin Thomism" or "Thomistic personalism" and whether it was more phenomenological or Thomistic. More recent scholarship has begun to attend to existential understanding of faith the Wojtyła gleaned from his study of John of the Cross and to the deeper dimensions of his appropriation of the thought of St. Thomas.[131] Such work serves to uncover the ontological depth in the late pope's account of the transcendence of the human person in moral choice and action in the face of more superficial appeals to human "experience."

Ultimately, only time will indicate the full measure of Pope John Paul II's impact on the field of Catholic moral theology in the United States and throughout the world. This study has indicated some of the reasons as to why the reception of that teaching to this point has been incomplete. There is an anthropological depth and coherence in John Paul II's thought that resists its reduction to either a simple answer to or a problem indicated by a preexisting debate. And it is this underlying vision of the person that continues to draw students and scholars to consider his thought as a method for engaging Scripture and experience in fashioning a compelling account of the moral life. This holistic anthropological vision points the way to the heart of the renewal of moral theology for which the Council called. It may well be this that proves to be Pope John Paul II's most lasting contribution to the field.

---

their own theories. Johnstone makes these observations in an unpublished paper on Salzman and Lawler's *The Sexual Person* presented at a faculty colloquium at the Catholic University of America on November 8, 2010.

131. In addition to Waldstein's consideration of Wojtyła's "Carmelite personalism" and Petri's study of the Thomistic foundations of the spousal meaning of the body noted above, see the collection of essays in *John Paul II and St. Thomas Aquinas*, ed. Michael Dauphinais and Matthew Levering (Washington, DC: Catholic University of America Press, 2006). On the history of personalism in general and Wojtyła's Thomistic appropriation of it, see Williams, *Who Is My Neighbor?*, 105–24.

CHAPTER 10

Catechesis and Moral Theology

Toward a Renewed Understanding of Christian Experience

Introduction

While different in many respects, the fields of moral theology and catechetics have significant shared concerns. Both of these theological disciplines have to do with the intersection of truth and life. Moral theology relates to the way in which we live in light of what we profess about God. Catechesis is the handing on of the truth of the Christian faith in a way that produces life in those who receive it. At the heart of this intersection between truth and life is "the mystery of Christ."[1]

But the effort to understand this intersection of truth and life raises for

---

This paper was first presented at the Intellectual Tasks of the New Evangelization Conference, US Conference on Catholic Bishops, September 14, 2013. I am grateful to many of those present for helpful feedback and suggestions on its content. I am particularly indebted to David Long, Cabrini Pak, Siobhan Benitez Riley, and Brett Smith for helpful comments on later drafts, one of which was subsequently published in *Nova et Vetera* 13, no. 2 (2015): 459–87.

1. The phrase is used to describe the catechetical task by Pope John Paul II in his Apostolic Exhortation *Catechesi tradendae*: "The primary and essential object of catechesis is, to use an expression dear to St. Paul, and also to contemporary theology, 'the mystery of Christ'" (no. 5). The citation is from The Holy See, accessed August 14, 2013, http://www.vatican.va/holy_father/john_paul_ii/apost_exhortations/documents/hf_jp-ii_exh_16101979_catechesi-tradendae_en.html. Another way to understand this is to see the four pillars of the *Catechism of the Catholic Church* as an interconnected whole with the Person of Christ as its dynamic center. One can make a further distinction between the ministry of catechesis and the study of effective means to engage in it or the discipline of catechetics.

us the question of experience, which seems to be a burning issue—perhaps *the* burning issue—in both of these areas of theology. What is the nature of Christian experience—or, perhaps more broadly, human experience—and what is its role in passing on the faith or in reflecting on its moral requirements? How do we discern the difference between distorted and authentic accounts of experience in these endeavors? The recent history of both moral theology and catechesis and the controversies within them raise such questions and indicate something of their gravity and pressing nature. In what follows I argue that a recovery of the centrality of the encounter with Christ for Christian moral teaching and catechesis is the key to understanding the place of authentic Christian experience within these disciplines.

My argument proceeds in a number of steps. First, I offer a rather compressed overview of the history of Catholic moral theology and catechesis in the modern period, focusing on some important parallels between them. Next, I examine the way in which both of these theological disciplines have come to focus on experience as a central category and some of the questions and problems that this has produced within them. I then argue for the need to refocus these theological endeavors on the encounter of the human person with Christ, utilizing documents such as *Gaudium et spes*, *Catechesi tradendae*, and *Veritatis splendor*. The final section considers something of the contribution of this Christological focus, drawing on the thought of St. Augustine as a particularly fruitful resource for understanding the role of experience within the theological endeavor.

A Parallel History

The Post-Reformation Context

Even a cursory examination of the history of what came to be called Catholic moral theology and catechesis in the modern period reveals some striking parallels, in no small part because of the common historical and intellectual context in which these disciplines functioned. The Council of Trent, confronting the challenge of the multiple Reformations dividing the Western Church, sought to respond through the adoption of a kind of battle posture and a new focus on uniformity of practice, teaching, and action.[2]

2. On the multiplicity of "Reformations" in the sixteenth century, see David Bentley Hart, *The Story of Christianity* (London: Quercus Press, 2012), 190–93. On the "battle posture" ad-

For the first time in its history, the Catholic Church established seminaries so that clergy would receive a minimum of theological and pastoral education. It was Trent's recommendation that in these seminary courses moral topics be treated separately from dogmatic ones (in order to better prepare future confessors) that gave impetus to the birth of moral theology as a separate discipline.[3]

The impact of the Council on the Church was a lasting one. Just three years after the close of the Council (1566), a universal catechism was produced that came to be known as "the Catechism of the Council of Trent."[4] This work would serve as the basis for catechetical instruction and as the model for local catechisms for centuries. In the emerging science of moral theology, the aftermath of Trent saw the birth of a new genre—the manuals of moral theology. Many of these works purported to be modeled on the *secunda pars* of St. Thomas Aquinas's *Summa theologiae*—yet in many cases they bore the imprint of the fourteenth-century revival of nominalist thought, which was foreign to the thought world of St. Thomas and produced a very different conception of the moral life.[5] According to Servais Pinckaers, OP, in his incisive account of the history of Catholic moral teaching, many of the manualists "read Thomas through nominalist lenses," leading them to construct a "morality of obligation" focused on the dialectic of law and freedom rather than a morality of happiness realized through virtue. This influence gave them a voluntarist cast that, when brought into contact with changing economic systems and the issues generated by the

---

opted by the Catholic Church at Trent, see Timothy O'Connell, *Principles for a Catholic Morality*, rev. ed. (San Francisco: HarperCollins, 1990), 18–19.

3. On the "separateness" of moral theology after Trent, see O'Connell, *Principles for a Catholic Morality*, 18; and John Mahoney, SJ, *The Making of Moral Theology: A Study of the Roman Catholic Tradition* (New York: Oxford, 1987), 24. Mahoney emphasizes the impact of auricular confession on the development of Catholic moral teaching from the early Church to the modern period (cf. 1–36). See also John Gallagher, *Time Past, Time Future: An Historical Study of Catholic Moral Theology* (Mahwah, NJ: Paulist, 1990), 33–34.

4. See Mahoney, *Making of Moral Theology*, 24.

5. For an overview of the emergence of the manuals and their history, see Gallagher, *Time Past, Time Future*, 29–47. For a summary of their content, see ibid., 48–97. On the impact of nominalism on the manuals and an incisive analysis of the differences between their moral teaching and that of St. Thomas, see Servais Pinckaers, OP, *The Sources of Christian Ethics*, trans. Mary Thomas Noble, OP (Washington, DC: Catholic University of America Press, 1995), 254–79, 327–99.

contact of Europe with the New World, helped spawn the competing systems of casuistry of the seventeenth and eighteenth centuries.[6]

Yet this insular world of the post-Tridentine Catholic Church was not
wholly immune from the encroachments of the modern world. The rationalism of the Enlightenment, the impact of scientific thinking and empir-
icist methodology, and the legacy of positivist thought all left an imprint
on the Neo-Scholastic Catholic thought of the modern period.[7] Revelation was often conceived as a deposit of truths, understood and elaborated
propositionally by the authority of the Church to be consigned to memory
through catechetical memorization. Catholic moral teaching bore the same
tendencies toward objectivism and authoritarianism with the added focus
on law and its application through a case-based casuistry.[8]

Impulses toward Renewal

In the twentieth century, it became increasingly clear to many Catholic
theologians that this insular thought world was in need of significant renewal. The tonic offered by these forms of catechetical instruction or moral
teaching had become insipid and stale. Alongside the impulses toward renewal seen in biblical studies and liturgical theology, the field of catechetics
also saw the stirrings of such renewal in the early twentieth century.[9] The

6. For a summary of this casuistry and its basic principles, see Gallagher, *Time Past, Time
Future*, 98–122. For a more contextual and sympathetic overview of modern casuistry, see the
essays collected in James F. Keenan, SJ, and Thomas Shannon, eds., *The Context of Casuistry*
(Washington, DC: Georgetown University Press, 1995). For a critique of the "morality of obligation" that the manuals embody and the competing moral systems that they spawned (even a
gentle critique of the equiprobabalism of St. Alfonsus Liguori), see Pinckaers, *Sources of Christian Ethics*, 266–77. Cf. Romanus Cessario, OP, *An Introduction to Moral Theology*, Catholic
Moral Thought Series (Washington, DC: Catholic University of America Press, 2001), 229–42.

7. See, e.g., the fine study of Gerald McCool, *Catholic Theology in the Nineteenth Century:
The Quest for a Unitary Method* (New York: Seabury Press, 1977); and Joseph Ratzinger, "The
Renewal of Moral Theology: Perspectives of Vatican II and *Veritatis splendor*," ed. Livio Melina,
Communio 32 (2005): 357–68, esp. 358.

8. David Bohr mentions objectivism, legalism, rationalism, and authoritarianism as tendencies of what he describes as the "classical worldview." See his *Catholic Moral Tradition: In
Christ a New Creation*, rev. ed. (Huntington, IN: OSV Press, 1999), 81–87. I would argue that
these are apt descriptions of Neo-Scholastic moral theology—the effort to apply it to Scholastic theologians such as St. Thomas can be effectively challenged (and has been by scholars such
as Pinckaers, on whom Bohr relies).

9. I am indebted in this brief overview of the history of the catechetical movement to the

approach to catechesis that focused on a rote memorization of doctrine (enshrined in the United States in the Baltimore Catechism) came to be seen by many as inadequate. Hence Johannes Hofinger, one of the key figures of the catechetical renewal in the middle to late twentieth century, would remark retrospectively:

Let us recall the lengthy, difficult and pictureless catechisms of those days, splendid models no doubt of precise formulation of the Church's doctrine, but equally splendid models of a completely unpsychological presentation of that doctrine. To make matters worse, children were generally required to learn these unchildlike catechisms by heart, word for word. We do not need to say that the result in many cases was mere mechanical memorizing of texts, the meaning of which was often grasped in part or perhaps not at all; and that these memorized texts offered the well-meaning, but helpless, child next to no nourishment for his religious life.[10]

This perceived inadequacy would give birth to a renewal movement that proceeded in three distinct stages. In the words of Bernard Marthaler,

Up to the present the modern catechetical movement has evolved though three more or less distinct stages. The first began with a quest to find a more effective method than the one then in use and then gradually evolved into a second phase, which was more concerned with content than method. And most recently, the third phase sees catechetics broadening its ken to include a variety of educational ministries and instructional strategies.[11]

The first phase, centered in Germany, has come to be called the "Munich method." Drawing on the insights of educational psychology, this approach used stories (frequently drawn from Scripture), highlighting particular doc-

---

outstanding analysis provided by Brian Pedraza, "Reform and Renewal in Catechesis: The Council, the Catechism, and the New Evangelization." *Josephinum Journal of Theology* 19, no. 1 (2012): 141–71.

10. Johannes Hofinger and Francis J. Buckley, *The Good News and Its Proclamation: Post Vatican II Edition of The Art of Teaching Christian Doctrine* (South Bend, IN: University of Notre Dame Press, 1968), 3–4. Other authors were more caustic, referring to the approach as a "catechetical straight-jacket." The phrase is that of Gerard Sloyan, *Speaking of Religious Education* (New York: Herder, 1968), 16. Still others would describe it as embodying a "minimalistic and legalistic view of the Catholic faith" that was "authoritarian and fear-centered." See Mary Perkins Ryan, "The Identity Crisis of Religious Education," *Living Light* 5, no. 4 (1968–69): 6–18, here 8.

11. Berard Marthaler, "The Modern Catechetical Movement in Roman Catholicism: Issues and Personalities," in *Sourcebook for Modern Catechetics*, vol. 1, ed. Michael Warren (Winona, MN: St. Mary's Press, 1983), 276.

trinal points contained in such stories, and then considered their application to the life of the hearer.[12] The second phase, drawing more directly on the renewal underway in biblical, liturgical, and patristic studies, focused on the proclamation of Jesus Christ as the heart of catechesis.[13] This kerygmatic approach saw the encounter with the Person of Christ mediated through Scripture and the liturgy as the unifying center of catechesis too often fragmented between doctrinal assent and Christian living. The high-water mark of this phase was reached in the first of the catechetical study weeks at Eichstätt in 1960.[14]

But this new focus on content over method also had its critics. It seemed to some that the old Neo-Scholastic doctrinal catechesis had been replaced by an equally narrow emphasis on Scripture.[15] This merely served to replace "old scholasticism with the new biblicism."[16] This sense, coinciding with the teaching of Second Vatican Council, led at subsequent study weeks (held at Bangkok in 1962, Manila in 1967, and Medellin in 1968) to the decisive shift to the third phase: a focus on human experience as the heart and locus of catechesis. Drawing on the developmental psychology of Jean Piag-

12. The approach was based on the psychological research of Johann Friedrich Herbart. See Marthaler, "Modern Catechetical Movement," 276. Something like this approach can be seen in the popular American Christian book and video series aimed at children known as *Veggie Tales*.

13. One of the key figures in this phase of the movement, Josef Andreas Jungmann was best known as a scholar of liturgy. His work *Die Frohbotshaft und unsere Glaubensverkündgung* (Regensburg: Freidrich Puster, 1936), edited and published in English as *The Good News Yesterday and Today*, trans. William A. Huesman (New York: Sadlier, 1962), and the reaction to it helped to launch this second phase. In this his work can be understood as part of the emphasis on *ressourcement* that preceded the Second Vatican Council. See Michael Warren, "Jungmann and the Kergymatic Theology Controversy," in *Sourcebook for Modern Catechetics*, 194; and Mary C. Boys, *Biblical Interpretation in Religious Education: A Study of the Kerygmatic Era* (Birmingham, AL: Religious Education Press, 1980).

14. On the significance of this meeting, see Marthaler, "Modern Catechetical Movement," 280. The papers collected and published by Jungmann's student Johannes Hofinger bear witness to the broad acceptance of the kerygmatic approach. See *Teaching All Nations: A Symposium on Modern Catechetics*, ed. Johannes Hofinger, trans. Clifford Howell (New York: Herder, 1961).

15. On this, see Alfonso Nebrada, *Kerygma in Crisis* (Chicago: Loyola University Press, 1965).

16. The phrase is that of José M. Calle, "Catechesis for the Seventies Part II," *Teaching All Nations* 7 (1970): 94. On this, see also Kenneth Barker, who argues that the kerygmatic worldview remained essentially "supernaturalist." See his *Religious Education, Catechesis, and Freedom* (Birmingham, AL: Religious Education Press, 1981), 62.

et, this approach saw experience as the key to learning and hence turned to the experience of the subjects of catechesis with its individual and cultural particularity.[17] Catechesis was now aimed at helping those who took part in it draw out the presence of God from within their own experience and concrete social situation. This emphasis on personal experience and inculturation would at Medellin be joined to a focus on liberating praxis from a then-emerging theology of liberation.[18] For many, this anthropological and experiential turn was simply following the trajectory of Vatican II's Pastoral Constitution *Gaudium et spes*.

By comparison, moral theology was something of a late bloomer in terms of the theological renewal of the twentieth century, but here too the impact of new biblical scholarship and the subsequent interpretation of the Council played important roles. The insights of biblical scholarship began to be utilized by influential moral theologians such as Germany's Redemptorist Bernard Häring.[19] When Häring and Jesuit Joseph Fuchs took teaching posts in Rome, they brought with them these new approaches to the discipline, ensuring the further dissemination of these ideas.[20] Such early work in the field and the awareness it created undoubtedly was behind the statement in the Council's Decree on Priestly Formation that moral theology needed "livelier contact with the mystery of Christ" and that it should be "more thoroughly nourished by scriptural teaching."[21] This sum-

17. See Marthaler, "Modern Catechetical Movement," 279; and Boys, *Biblical Interpretation in Religious Education*, 213–14.

18. On the importance of inculturation as emphasized at the Bangkok study week, see Nebrada, *Kerygma in Crisis*, 45; and "The Implications of Vatican II for the Mission in Asia," *Teaching All Nations* 4 (1967): 320–21. On Medellin's emphasis on liberating praxis, see Francis Houtart, "Reflections in the New Thinking in Latin America," in *Medellin Papers* (Manilla: East Asia Pastoral Institute, 1969), 72–73; and Berard Marthaler, *Catechetics in Context: Notes and Comments on the General Catechetical Directory Issued by the Sacred Congregation for the Clergy* (Huntington, IN: Our Sunday Visitor, 1973), 13.

19. Häring's three-volume work *Gesetz Christ* (1954) represents an effort to combine the insights of biblical scholarship with the standard pre–Vatican II genre of a moral manual. The work was translated into English as *The Law of Christ: Moral Theology for Priests and Laity*, 3 vols., trans. Edwin G. Kaiser (Westminster, MD: Edwin Newman Press, 1961).

20. See O'Connell, *Principles for a Catholic Morality*, 21; and Bohr, *Catholic Moral Tradition*, 73.

21. Second Vatican Council, Decree on Priestly Formation, *Optatum totius*, no. 16. The citation is from *The Documents of Vatican II*, ed. Walter M. Abbott, SJ (Piscataway, NJ: New Century, 1966), 452. All citations of the Council's documents are to this edition.

mons received further impetus by the robust affirmation of *Dei verbum* that the study of sacred Scripture is "the soul of sacred theology."[22] This coupled with the Council's employment of an inductive approach to engagement with the modern world in *Gaudium et spes* would seem to parallel the biblical and experiential turns in the catechetical movement, albeit in less developed form.

The New Primacy of Experience

The shift to experience in the third phase of the catechetical movement, which reached a high-water mark at Medellin and then was widely diffused in catechetical programs in the 1970s and 1980s, can be seen as part of a process of change that spanned much of the twentieth century.[23] This change was a kind of fermentation that produced a new mixture that then permeated the Church—a slow chemical reaction that changed the catechetical "solution" in significant ways. In spite of its broad influence and acceptance, this process of change was occasionally punctuated by rumbling reactions in the form of words of warning on the part of Church authority or by participants in the renewal themselves. Such rumblings came to a head in the controversy over the *Catechism of the Catholic Church*. By contrast, the field of moral theology after the Council produced far more volatile compounds and as a result was wracked by an ongoing series of explosive debates and sharp confrontations, at the heart of which was the effort to incorporate the turn to experience in new ways.

In the aftermath of the Council, there was some impetus for the promulgation of a new universal catechism; however, many bishops countered that in the face of growing theological and cultural diversity such a project was impracticable and undesirable—at least at that moment in time.[24] The

22. Dogmatic Constitution on Divine Revelation, *Dei verbum*, no. 24. The citation is from *Documents of Vatican II*, 127.

23. The phrase is that of Mary Charles Bryce, "Evolution of Catechesis from the Catholic Reformation to the Present," in *A Faithful Church: Issues in the History of Catechesis*, ed. John H. Westerhoff III and O. C. Edwards Jr. (Wilton, CT: Morehouse-Barlow, 1981), 228.

24. A new universal catechism was championed in particular by Bishop Pierre Marie Laconte of France, who saw it as part of the unfinished business of Vatican I. But others pushed for a directory that would be adapted to local and individual situations. See Marthaler, *Catechesis in Context*, xvi–xviii. Joseph Ratzinger, who would oversee the production of the *CCC*

publication of the *General Catechetical Directory* (*GCD*) can be understood as something of a compromise solution in this debate.[25] The *GCD* affirms many of the insights of the renewal and the various stages that preceded it, reconnecting the presentation of doctrine to the person of Jesus Christ consciously appropriated in the faith experience of adults.[26] But it also contains some significant words of warning. Describing a kind of catechetical "crisis" facing the Church, the *GCD* warns on the one hand against those who oppose the movement of renewal altogether, speaking of "those who are unable to understand the depth of the proposed renewal, as though the issue here were merely one of eliminating ignorance of the doctrine which must be taught." On the other hand, the document also warns against tendencies recognizable in the third stage, pointing to "those who are inclined to reduce the Gospel message to the consequences it has in men's temporal existence."[27] Pope Paul VI would reiterate a similar warning four years later in his apostolic exhortation *Evangelii nuntiandi*.[28]

---

some decades later, also opposed a universal catechism immediately after the Council. He writes: "in 1966 the full extent of the problem had simply not become visible; that a process of fermentation had just begun which could lead only gradually to the clarifications necessary for a new common word." See Joseph Ratzinger and Christoph Schönborn, *Introduction to the Catechism of the Catholic Church* (San Francisco: Ignatius, 1995), 12.

25. The directory was promulgated by the Sacred Congregation for Clergy on April 11, 1971. See The Holy See, accessed September 2, 2013, http://www.vatican.va/roman_curia/congregations/cclergy/documents/rc_con_cclergy_doc_11041971_gcat_en.html. Citations of the document will be to this version. For an overview of the *GCD* and its teaching, see Marthaler, *Catechesis in Context*.

26. Cf. *GCD*, nos. 20, 26, and 74. The shift as the primary objects of catechetical ministry from children to adults is itself a significant one, highlighting the gains of the renewal that preceded it. See Anne Marie Mongoven, "Directories as Symbols of Catechetical Renewal," in *The Echo Within: Emerging Issues in Religious Education*, ed. Kate Dooley, OP, and Mary Collins (Allen, TX: Thomas More Publishing, 1997), 135.

27. *GCD*, no. 9.

28. "We must not ignore the fact that many, even generous Christians who are sensitive to the dramatic questions involved in the problem of liberation, in their wish to commit the Church to the liberation effort are frequently tempted to reduce her mission to the dimensions of a simply temporal project. They would reduce her aims to a man-centered goal; the salvation of which she is the messenger would be reduced to material well-being. Her activity, forgetful of all spiritual and religious preoccupation, would become initiatives of the political or social order. But if this were so, the Church would lose her fundamental meaning. Her message of liberation would no longer have any originality and would easily be open to monopolization and manipulation by ideological systems and political parties. She would have no more authority to proclaim freedom as in the name of God. This is why we have wished to emphasize, in the same

The opposing assessments of both the needs of the Church and the trajectory of the third phase of the catechetical renewal came to a head in the controversy over Pope John Paul II's promulgation of the *Catechism of the Catholic Church* (*CCC*), which first appeared in 1993. Opponents of the project saw it as a retreat from the work of the catechetical movement and the renewal it engendered, especially the embrace of the particularity of human experience, pluralism, and liberating praxis.[29] Its defenders saw it as an effort to integrate the whole of the Church's tradition with the insights of the modern catechetical movement (particularly the reconnection with Scripture and the renewed focus on the Person of Christ) and as a corrective to some of the excesses of the third stage.[30] The slow chemical burn ignited in the third phase finally boiled over in full-blown divisive controversy.

Even before this controversy erupted, the great catechetical scholar Johannes Hofinger sought to point a way forward for the catechetical movement. In an essay published in 1984 (the year of his death), Hofinger gave his own assessment of the renewal to date, describing the third phase as a kind of "eulogy" to the movement that itself needed to be transcended in "a fourth phase still to come."[31] He likened the movement's work and their stages to the construction of a building. The pioneers of the first stage laid

---

address at the opening of the Synod, 'the need to restate clearly the specifically religious finality of evangelization. This latter would lose its reason for existence if it were to diverge from the religious axis that guides it: the kingdom of God, before anything else, in its fully theological meaning…'" Pope Paul VI, Apostolic Exhortation, *Evangelii nuntiandi*, no. 32. The citation is from the Vatican translation, available at The Holy See, accessed September 2, 2013, http://www.vatican.va/holy_father/paul_vi/apost_exhortations/documents/hf_p-vi_exh_19751208_evangelii-nuntiandi_en.html.

29. Interestingly, the universal catechism faced criticism from its inception. At the time of its announcement, the international journal *Concilium* devoted an entire issue to criticizing the very concept (see vol. 204 [1989]). The criticism continued after the appearance of the text. See, e.g., the generally critical essays contained in the volume *Introducing the Catechism of the Catholic Church: Traditional Themes and Contemporary Issues*, ed. Berard J. Marthaler (New York: Paulist, 1994).

30. See, e.g., Avery Dulles, SJ, "The Challenge of Catechism," *First Things* 49 (1995): 46–53; and Joseph Ratzinger, "Handing on the Faith and the Sources of Faith," in *Handing on Faith in an Age of Disbelief*, trans. Michael J. Miller, ed. Joseph Ratzinger, Dermott J. Ryan, Godfried Danneels, and Francis Marcharski (San Francisco: Ignatius, 2006), 15. Ratzinger's essay was originally delivered as a lecture in 1983.

31. Hofinger, "Looking Backward and Forward: Journey of Catechesis," *Living Light* 20, no. 4 (1984): 348–57, here 355. On the significance of these remarks, see Pedraza, "Reform and Renewal in Catechesis," 27–28.

the foundation on which the kerygmatic approach erected walls. The anthropological and experiential turn of the third phase produced a roof but left it lying on the ground next to the structure. The phase still to come must raise this roof and set it on the walls of the structure—experience must be reconnected with doctrine and the Person of Christ.[32]

The recent history of moral theology shows it to be even more combustible than catechetics, but once again it has been the notion of experience that has provided much of the fuel for the controversy. As is well known, it was only the intervention of Pope Paul VI and his expansion of the study commission created by his predecessor John XXIII that enabled the fathers of the Second Vatican Council to avoid being sidetracked by the emerging and contentious debate over oral contraception ("the pill").[33] On this commission it was both the failure of traditional Neo-Scholastic natural law arguments, often heavily colored by physicalism (itself a fruit of nominalism), as well as the voices of lay members drawing on their own experience that tipped a majority of members to advocate for a revision of the traditional teaching.[34] Revisionist thinkers often pointed to the experience of couples whom they had counseled as causing them to rethink the traditional teaching.[35]

32. Hofinger, "Looking Backward and Forward," 356. Elsewhere he would write: "By the time [the *GCD*] and the *National Catechetical Directory of Catholics in the United States* appeared, religious education had been unfavorably influenced by formidable waves of secularism and an unwillingness to accept the normative directions of the Church." Johannes Hofinger, "The Catechetical Sputnik," in *Modern Masters of Religious Education*, ed. Marlene Mayr (Birmingham, AL: Religious Education Press, 1983), 32.

33. See William H. Shannon, *The Lively Debate: Response to Humae Vitae* (New York: Sheed & Ward, 1970), 46–50, 52–54; and John T. Noonan, *Contraception: A History of Its Treatment by the Catholic Theologians and Canonists*, enlarged ed. (Cambridge, MA: Harvard University Press), 469–71.

34. Journalist Robert McClory emphasizes the experiential testimony of lay members of the commission in his *Turning Point: The Inside Story of the Papal Birth Control Commission, and How Humanae Vitae Changed the Life of Patty Crowley and the Future of the Church* (New York: Crossroad, 1995).

35. Charles Curran provides an example, though he makes the argument differently at different points in his career. In early work before the encyclical, he cites the difficulty experienced by couples struggling to live according to the Church's teaching. See, e.g., "Family Planning," in *Christian Morality Today: The Renewal of Moral Theology* (Notre Dame, IN: Fides, 1966), 47–64, esp. 47–48. In later work, he points to the example of John R. Cavanagh, a member of the papal birth control commission who was affected by survey results of couples who had negative experiences of "rhythm" as well as his own experience as a psychiatrist, which

After the unexpected reaffirmation of the teaching by Pope Paul VI in his encyclical *Humanae vitae*, the ensuing firestorm of debate spawned whole new moral methodologies that sought, among other things, to provide justification for the judgment of individuals and couples who on the basis of their consciences and experience rejected the norm proposed by the pope. Modern Catholic proportionalism with its elaborate weighing of the balance of premoral goods or evils in the human act considered in its totality was a sophisticated elaboration of a basis for just such an individual and experiential approach to moral reasoning. In many ways, it represents a reprise of the case-based moral reasoning of the manuals in the new context of the ongoing critique of the encyclical, but instead of privileging the opinions of authorities in the resolution of conflict cases, that weight was now given to individual conscience in the concreteness of the situation.[36] Other less widely imitated revisionist methodologies would also give new weight to the concept of experience, for example, the effort to understand human sexual activity in descriptive/experiential categories in the infamous 1977 CTSA (Catholic Theological Society of America) report.[37]

---

moved him to advocate for a change in the teaching. See "Theory and Practice; Faith and Reason: A Case Study of John R. Cavanagh," in *Critical Concerns in Moral Theology* (Notre Dame, IN: University of Notre Dame Press, 1984), 203–32, esp. 221–24. Curran also begins to utilize social scientific data to ground his advocacy for "pastoral solutions" to difficulties posed by Church teaching. See his "The Pastoral Minister: The Moral Demands of Discipleship and the Conscience of the Believer," in *Critical Concerns in Moral Theology*, 233–56.

36. For some of the historical parallels between modern casuistry and this approach, see Thomas Shannon, "Method in Ethics: A Scotist Contribution," in *The Context of Casuistry*, Moral Traditions Series, ed. James Keenan, SJ, and Thomas Shannon (Washington, DC: Georgetown University Press, 1995), 3–24, esp. 3–4. For a sympathetic historical account of the genesis of this method as a whole, see Bernard Hoose, *Proportionalism: The American Debate and Its European Roots* (Washington, DC: Georgetown University Press, 1987). For incisive critiques of the method as modern casuistry, see Servais Pinckaers, OP, "La question des actes intrinsèquement mauvais et le 'proportionalisme,'" *Revue Thomiste* 83 (1982): 181–212; and Christopher Kaczor, *Proportionalism and the Natural Law Tradition* (Washington, DC: Catholic University of America Press, 2011).

37. See Anthony Kosnick et al., *Human Sexuality: New Directions in American Catholic Thought* (Mahwah, NJ: Paulist, 1977). The work argued that the traditional criteria for evaluating sex should be broadened from "unitive and procreative" to "creative and integrative," with the understanding that these categories entailed that sexual expression must be self-liberating, other-enriching, honest, faithful, socially responsible, life-serving, and joyous (see esp. 86–95). Critics of the work pointed out that such fuzzy experiential criteria could not effectively rule out any form of sexual expression, with the possible exception of bestiality. Cf. James

But the herald and bellwether of the new role of experience in Catholic moral theology in the United States has been Charles Curran. First, in formulating his own methodology to ground a critical stance toward *Humanae vitae*, he outlined the "relational responsibility" approach to the moral life (his own blending of Neibuhrian ethics, American pragmatism, and an eclectic borrowing of proportionalist terminology from his close collaborator Richard McCormick, SJ, and others).[38] Second, Curran has long been at the forefront of the argument that Catholic social teaching around the time of the Council underwent a methodological shift from a deductive and classicist approach in its moral reasoning to a historically conscious, inductive, and experiential approach.[39] The shift is sometimes attributed to John XXIII in *Pacem in terris* but more frequently to the Council's Pastoral Constitution *Gaudium et spes*. The same shift has not occurred in Catholic sexual and biomedical ethics, leaving the Church's teaching in a "schizophrenic" state, vacillating between conflicting worldviews and methodologies.[40] Third, in his work as a historian and commentator on the field, Curran has called attention to the recent adoption by many Catholic moralists of the "Wesleyan Quadrilateral" of sources for ethical reasoning: experience, Scripture, tradition, and reason. This approach characterizes the work of prominent revisionist scholars such as Lisa Sowle Cahill, Margaret Farley, Todd Salzman, Michael Lawler, and, in his current work, Curran himself.[41]

Burtchaell, *The Giving and Taking of Life: Essays Ethical* (Notre Dame, IN: University of Notre Dame Press, 1989), 288.

38. For largely sympathetic overviews and analyses of Curran's thought and its development, see the essays collected in *A Call to Fidelity: On the Moral Theology of Charles E. Curran*, Moral Traditions Series, ed. James J. Walter, Timothy O'Connell, and Thomas Shannon (Washington, DC: Georgetown University Press, 2002).

39. For an overview and critique of Curran's position and its widespread impact, see John S. Grabowski and Michael Naughton, "Catholic Sexual or Social Teaching: Inconsistent or Organic?," *The Thomist* 57 (1993): 555–78. For a more recent version of Curran's argument, see his *Catholic Social Teaching 1891–Present: A Historical, Theological and Ethical Analysis* (Washington, DC: Georgetown University Press, 2002), esp. 23–37, 53–96.

40. For conflicting views on the "schizophrenia," see John S. Grabowski and Michael Naughton, "Doctrinal Development: Does It Apply to Family and Sex?," *Commonweal* 124, no. 13 (1997): 18–20, and the reply by Charles Curran in *Commonweal* 124, no. 13 (1997): 20.

41. See Charles Curran, *Catholic Moral Tradition Today: A Synthesis* (Washington, DC: Georgetown University Press, 1999), 48. Cf. Michael G. Lawler and Todd Salzman, "Human Experience and Catholic Moral Theology," *Irish Theological Quarterly* 76 (2011): 35–56.

The listing of experience in the first position among these sources is not an accident. It is, both implicitly and in some cases explicitly, the dominant source, being used at times as a "trump" to Scripture or the Church's tradition on particular points, such as the approval of sexual activity on the part of certain same-sex couples. There is some divergence among these moralists as to whether experience is best understood through social scientific study and data (Cahill),[42] or personal and even anecdotal experience (Farley),[43] or some mixture of them (Salzman and Lawler).[44] In this methodology, experience is given pride of place, and the conclusions it has generated have occasioned public negative evaluations of recent works in sexual ethics by Church authorities.[45] The category of experience thus continues to be the fuel that ignites explosive public controversy in Catholic moral theology.

42. See the somewhat complex argument in Lisa Sowle Cahill, *Sex, Gender, and Christian Ethics*, New Studies in Christian Ethics (Cambridge: Cambridge University Press, 1996). She draws primarily on social scientific research to ascertain "goods" integral to human flourishing (46–72), views sexual orientation (and the body more generally) as largely socially constructed (97–102), and, finding biblical condemnations of homosexual activity to be ambiguous and inconclusive (156–60), she opts to give more weight to the biblical themes of compassion and solidarity with the marginalized. All of this means that incorporating homosexual people within the Christian community "does not necessarily denigrate the ideals of virginity … of faithful, mutual heterosexual marriage" (158), especially when their experience can be understood as conducive to their human flourishing (as measured through social scientific criteria).

43. See Margaret Farley, RSM, *Just Love: A Framework for Christian Sexual Ethics* (New York: Continuum, 2008). Like Cahill, Farley sees Scripture and tradition as ambiguous and inconclusive sources for a contemporary evaluation of same-sex relationships (273–80). While she finds that the sciences contribute useful information to understanding the reality of sexual orientation and preference, however, she finds them inconclusive for formulating a moral evaluation (280–86). She therefore turns to experience to determine whether such activity can conduce to human flourishing. And by experience she specifies that she means "primarily the testimony of women and men whose sexual preference is for others of the same sex" (286–88, here 286).

44. See Todd Salzman and Michael Lawler, *The Sexual Person: Toward a Renewed Anthropology*, Moral Traditions Series (Washington, DC: Georgetown University Press, 2008), 228–29. Other scholars point to accounts of experience embedded in literature or art. For the former, see Anna Marie Vigen, "Conclusion," in *God, Science, Sex and Gender: An Interdisciplinary Approach to Christian Ethics*, ed. Patricia Beatiie Jung and Anna Marie Vigen (Champaign: University of Illinois Press, 2010), 240. For the latter, see John Corvino, *What's Wrong with Homosexuality?* (New York: Oxford, 2013), 16.

45. The works in question are Farley's *Just Love* and Salzman and Lawler's *Sexual Person*. On September 15, 2010, the US Conference of Catholic Bishops Committee on Doctrine issued a public statement calling attention to problems of both method and conclusions in Salzman

My contention is that the fundamental flaw in such works is not that they engage experience, but that they misrepresent its place in the theological endeavor. By exaggerating its importance and using it to "trump" Scripture, tradition, or moral norms grounded in reason's apprehension of human nature, experience has an exaggerated and even distorted importance. Experience becomes the primary *locus theologicus* overriding and reshaping the other sources. Furthermore, there does not seem to be adequate recognition of the fact that human experience is itself distorted and wounded by the presence and effects of sin in the human person and in the world around him or her. Authentic Christian experience is not an independent source standing outside of the tradition—it is the fruit of the encounter with the person of Christ. Hence, to address the questions and controversies that experience has generated in the histories of both catechetics and moral theology, we need to refocus the theological endeavor on this transforming encounter. This is the path to renewal marked out in the teaching of the Council itself and in subsequent documents that continue its trajectory.

The Encounter with Christ as the Heart of the Church and Theology

In differing ways, both Pope John Paul II and Joseph Ratzinger / Benedict XVI have sought to focus the attention of the Church and its intellectual endeavors on the encounter with the Person of Christ, which is at the heart of Christian life. In so doing, they saw themselves as carrying forward and implementing the renewal begun at the Second Vatican Council. This focus has become programmatic in the pontificate of Pope Francis.[46]

---

and Lawler's text (including but not limited to those on same-sex relationships). Two years later, on June 4, 2012, the Vatican's Congregation for the Doctrine of the Faith published a notification on Farley's book, citing both general and specific problems in the work. For the text of the notification, see The Holy See, accessed October 24, 2016, http://www.vatican.va/roman_curia/congregations/cfaith/documents/rc_con_cfaith_doc_20120330_nota-farley_en.html.

46. Thus in the first major document of his pontificate that was largely his own, he wrote: "I invite all Christians, everywhere, at this very moment, to a renewed personal encounter with Jesus Christ, or at least an openness to letting him encounter them; I ask all of you to do this unfailingly each day. No one should think that this invitation is not meant for him or her, since 'no one is excluded from the joy brought by the Lord.'" Pope Francis, Apostolic Exhortation, *Evangelii gaudium*, no. 3, citing Pope Paul VI, Apostolic Ex-

In his apostolic exhortation *Catechesi tradendae* given at the beginning of his pontificate (1979), Pope John Paul II pointed to Christ as the heart of the ministry of catechesis, writing,

at the heart of catechesis we find, in essence, a Person, the Person of Jesus of Nazareth, "the only Son from the Father … full of grace and truth," who suffered and died for us and who now, after rising, is living with us forever. It is Jesus who is "the way, and the truth, and the life," and Christian living consists in following Christ, the *sequela Christi* … Accordingly, the definitive aim of catechesis is to put people not only in touch but in communion, in intimacy, with Jesus Christ: only He can lead us to the love of the Father in the Spirit and make us share in the life of the Holy Trinity.[47]

The ministry of catechesis exists to put the Church and its members in conscious contact—"in communion"—with the Person of Jesus Christ. We can debate how well the *CCC* and its various parts accomplish this goal, but this is undoubtedly its aim, as John Paul II would indicate in the constitution that promulgated it.[48]

Some fourteen years later, addressing the even more tumultuous field of moral theology in the first chapter of his encyclical letter *Veritatis splendor,* John Paul II would restate the import of this personal encounter in even more sweeping and (literally) dramatic terms. The problem is that most commentators on the document, fixating on the technical analysis of controversial issues in its second chapter (particularly the negative evaluation

hortation, *Gaudete in Domino*, no. 22. The citation is from The Holy See, accessed December 2, 2013, http://www.vatican.va/holy_father/francesco/apost_exhortations/documents/papa-francesco_esortazione-ap_20131124_evangelii-gaudium_en.html.

47. *Catechesi tradendae*, no. 5.

48. See John Paul II, Apostolic Constitution, *Fidei depositum*, no. 2: "In reading the *Catechism of the Catholic Church* we can perceive the wondrous unity of the mystery of God, his saving will, as well as the central place of Jesus Christ, the only-begotten Son of God, sent by the Father, made man in the womb of the Blessed Virgin Mary by the power of the Holy Spirit, to be our Saviour. Having died and risen, Christ is always present in his Church, especially in the sacraments; he is the source of our faith, the model of Christian conduct and the Teacher of our prayer." The citation is from The Holy See, accessed September 12, 2013, http://www.vatican.va/holy_father/john_paul_ii/apost_constitutions/documents/hf_jp-ii_apc_19921011_fidei-depositum_en.html. Reflecting on the *CCC*, Joseph Ratzinger observes that writing the third part "was no doubt the most difficult" and that "it does not claim to offer the only possible or even the best systematic formulation of moral theology." See his "Is the *Catechism of the Catholic Church* Up to Date?" in *On the Way to Jesus Christ* (San Francisco: Ignatius, 2005), 140–63, here 159.

of proportionalism's appeal to individual conscience and the experience of action in its concreteness to override absolute moral norms), have virtually ignored the genuinely revolutionary character of this teaching. This neglect is equally evident by both revisionist critics of the document as well as many of its traditionalist defenders.[49]

Commenting on the encounter between Christ and the Rich Young Man of Matthew 19, John Paul sees him as a type of "every person, who consciously or not, *approaches Christ the Redeemer of man and questions him about morality.*"[50] He is thus identified as a type of "Adam"—a John Q. Everyman who wrestles with the nature of the moral good and questions about the ultimate purpose of life. Readers are thus encouraged to identify themselves with the figure of the Young Man and to hear Jesus's words as addressed to the questions arising within their own hearts.[51] The pope draws upon his own early work as playwright to invite readers of the encyclical to hear themselves addressed by Christ as participants in an existential drama.

In John Paul II's presentation of this drama, which unfolds on the stage of the Gospel account, the reference to the commandments serves not to articulate a law-centered morality, as some critics alleged, but to highlight the invitation to discipleship as a gift of grace. The commandments themselves are reflective of God's covenantal invitation to humanity, but "not even the most rigorous observance of the commandments, succeeds in 'fulfilling' the Law."[52] Instead, human beings still find themselves enslaved to the power of sin, which makes God's law appear as an alien intrusion upon their autonomy.[53] The Young Man, like Adam after his fall, is unable to respond on his own volition—he finds himself impotent in the face of a call to perfection, which requires "mature human freedom," itself a gift of grace.[54] Disciple-

49. See the overview of the debate and the literature in John S. Grabowski, "The Luminous Excess of the Acting Person: Assessing the Impact of Pope John Paul II on American Catholic Moral Theology," *Journal of Moral Theology* 1, no. 1 (2012): 116–47, esp. 136–44. Parts of the following two paragraphs are adapted from that essay (141–42).

50. Pope John Paul II, Encyclical Letter, *Veritatis splendor*, no. 7. The citation is from the Daughters of Saint Paul edition, Vatican translation (Boston: St. Paul, 1993), p.17 Emphasis original. All subsequent references to this document are from this edition.

51. This chapter of Matthew's Gospel serves "as a useful guide *for listening once more* in a lively and direct way to [Jesus's] … moral teaching." *Veritatis splendor*, no. 6, p. 16. Emphasis original.

52. *Veritatis splendor*, no. 11, p. 21.   53. Cf. *Veritatis splendor*, nos. 17–18.

54. Cf. *Veritatis splendor*, no. 17, p. 29.

ship requires not merely outward conformity of behavior but an interior transformation of the person mediated through the Church's sacramental worship, which provides the "source and power" of the gift of self in love in union with Christ's own Eucharistic self-gift.[55] Following Jesus is therefore not exterior imitation based on moral rules, but the communication of a new interior life in Christ lived through the Holy Spirit, who is himself the "new law" of Christian life.[56] It is this transforming encounter that bestows the happiness that the Young Man seeks.[57]

Oliver O'Donovan was one of the few commentators on the document who recognized the genuinely transformative character of its first chapter: "Not everyone has appreciated its innovative strength as a programme for moral theology ... in these pages which shape the moral discourse of the Church as an evangelical proclamation."[58] *Veritatis splendor* is indeed revolutionary for the discipline of moral theology—and for theology generally—in at least three distinct ways. First, this invitation to discipleship is not addressed to an elite few (the traditional Catholic understanding), but to all. The universal call to holiness reaffirmed at Vatican II is here rearticulated through the dramatic call to the perfection of discipleship given to the Young Man.[59] Second, the purpose of the Church's life and mission is refocused on this encounter: "*In order to make this 'encounter' with Christ possible, God willed his Church.*"[60] Some of the implications of this sweeping statement have begun to take shape in the current ministry and teaching

55. *Veritatis splendor*, no. 21, p. 35.

56. See *Veritatis splendor*, no. 24, echoing the teaching of St. Thomas in the *Summa theologiae* I-II, q. 106, a. 1. On this theme of transformation in the document (issued on the Feast of the Transfiguration), see J. A. DiNoia, OP, "The Moral Life as Transfigured Life," in *Veritatis Splendor and the Renewal of Moral Theology* (Princeton, NJ: Scepter, 1999), 1–10.

57. On the eudaimonism of the document, see Livio Melina, "The Desire for Happiness and the Commandments in the First Chapter of *Veritatis Splendor*," in *Veritatis Splendor and the Renewal of Moral Theology*, 143–60.

58. "A Summons to Reality," in *Considering Veritatis Splendor*, ed. John Wilkens (Cleveland: Pilgrim, 1994), 41–45, here 42. Cf. the assessment of Lorenzo Albacete, "The Relevance of Christ or the *Sequela Christi*," *Communio* 21 (1994): 255.

59. "*The invitation*, 'go sell your possessions and give money to the poor,' and the promise 'you will have treasure in heaven,' *are meant for everyone*, because they bring out the full meaning of the commandment of love of neighbor, just as the invitation which follows, 'Come follow me,' is the new, specific form of the commandment of love of God." *Veritatis splendor*, no. 18. Emphasis original.

60. *Veritatis splendor*, no. 7. Emphasis original.

of Pope Francis.[61] Third, and most directly pertinent to the concern of this study, is that the encounter with the Person of Christ is made the hermeneutical key to understand experience—both human and Christian. Christ reveals the contents of the human heart to those who encounter him—the experience of impotence in the face of the struggle with sin, himself as the concrete fulfillment of the hunger for happiness and love, and the liberating freedom of the grace-empowered "yes" of discipleship.

I would argue that this evangelical and Christological turn of *Veritatis splendor* is an effort to reconnect with and extend the trajectory for renewal mapped out in the Pastoral Constitution *Gaudium et spes*. In an essay written shortly before his election as pope, Joseph Ratzinger describes *Veritatis splendor* as an effort to reconnect with the Council's great themes of Scripture, Christology, and human reason. The efforts to implement the biblical dimension of this renewal were stymied by a variety of factors: the complexity of contemporary problems that seem to go beyond the resources of scriptural wisdom, the diversity and difficulty of biblical materials themselves, and the ecumenical context in the Bible was read and applied to ethical matters.[62]

On his elevation to the Chair of Peter, Pope Benedict XVI continued to focus the Church on the Person of Christ and on the Council's program of renewal. In the beginning of his first encyclical, Pope Benedict wrote: "*We have come to believe in God's love*: in these words the Christian can express the fundamental decision of his life. Being Christian is not the result of an ethical choice or a lofty idea, but the encounter with an event, a person, which gives life a new horizon and a decisive direction."[63]

For Benedict, however, a proper hermeneutic of tradition was an integral part of this program of renewal. In his first Christmas address to the Roman curia, he contrasted a "hermeneutic of discontinuity and rupture" with one of "reform and renewal." Of the former, he said:

---

61. It is certainly apparent in his Apostolic Exhortation *Evangelii gaudium*.

62. See Ratzinger, "Renewal of Moral Theology," 359–62. To this list might be added the bitterly divisive controversy of the birth control debate in the Church.

63. *Deus caritas est*, no. 1 (emphasis original). The citation is from The Holy See, accessed September 10, 2013, http://www.vatican.va/holy_father/benedict_xvi/encyclicals/documents/hf_ben-xvi_enc_20051225_deus-caritas-est_en.html.

The hermeneutic of discontinuity risks ending in a split between the pre-conciliar Church and the post-conciliar Church. It asserts that the texts of the Council as such do not yet express the true spirit of the Council. It claims that they are the result of compromises in which, to reach unanimity, it was found necessary to keep and reconfirm many old things that are now pointless. However, the true spirit of the Council is not to be found in these compromises but instead in the impulses toward the new that are contained in the texts.[64]

By contrast, Pope Benedict described the hermeneutic of reform and renewal as follows:

Here I shall cite only John XXIII's well-known words, which unequivocally express this hermeneutic when he says that the Council wishes "to transmit the doctrine, pure and integral, without any attenuation or distortion." And he continues: "Our duty is not only to guard this precious treasure, as if we were concerned only with antiquity, but to dedicate ourselves with an earnest will and without fear to that work which our era demands of us"… It is necessary that "adherence to all the teaching of the Church in its entirety and preciseness"… be presented in "faithful and perfect conformity to the authentic doctrine, which, however, should be studied and expounded through the methods of research and through the literary forms of modern thought. The substance of the ancient doctrine of the deposit of faith is one thing, and the way in which it is presented is another"… retaining the same meaning and message.[65]

In other words, the updating in light of contemporary questions and experience for which the Council called (*aggiornamento*) cannot be separated from its program of returning to the sources of faith (*ressourcement*).[66]

It is true that the Pastoral Constitution offers for the first time in a conciliar document an extended treatment of human person and his or her experience in the modern world.[67] The very complexity of modern life, the

64. Pope Benedict XVI, "Address of His Holiness Benedict XVI to the Roman Curia Offering Them His Christmas Greetings," December 22, 2005. The citation is from The Holy See, accessed September 12, 2013, http://www.vatican.va/holy_father/benedict_xvi/speeches/2005/december/documents/hf_ben_xvi_spe_20051222_roman-curia_en.html.

65. Ibid.

66. Marcellino D'Ambrosio observes that *ressourcement* and *aggiornamento* were "inextricably intertwined" in *la nouvelle théologie*, which preceded the Council. See his essay "*Ressourcement* Theology, *Aggiornamento*, and the Hermeneutics of Tradition," *Communio* 18 (1991): 530–55.

67. On the novelty of *Gaudium et spes* in this regard, see Walter Kasper, "The Theological Anthropology of *Gaudium et Spes*," *Communio* 23 (1996): 129–40, esp. 129.

advancements of human science and technology, render the human person increasingly opaque to him- or herself. In analyzing and addressing this problem, anthropology becomes "the Archimedean point" and unifying center of the document.[68] Yet if anthropology is the starting point and hinge of the Pastoral Constitution, Christology is the key to its understanding of the human person. In a famous text the Council fathers write:

The truth is that only in the mystery of the incarnate Word does the mystery of man take on light. For Adam, the first man, was a figure of Him Who was to come, namely Christ the Lord. Christ, the final Adam, by the revelation of the mystery of the Father and His love, fully reveals man to man himself and makes his supreme calling clear. It is not surprising, then, that in Him all the aforementioned truths find their root and attain their crown.[69]

Even the widely hailed inductive approach to "reading the signs of the times" is put in the eschatological and Christological framework of the Gospel's use of the phrase.[70] While the final text of *Gaudium et spes* does not invoke Matthew 16:1–4, it retains its meaning: "To carry out such a task the Church has always had *the duty of scrutinizing the signs of the times* and of interpreting them in the light of the gospel."[71]

It is thus possible to read the first chapter of *Veritatis splendor* as a commentary and elaboration of the teaching of *Gaudium et spes*, no. 22, as to how "Christ reveals us to ourselves."[72] Included in this revelation is an illumination of both the person's interior life ("the heart")—its hungers, aspirations, and darkness—and the world in which the person lives—a world

68. The term is that of ibid., 133–34.

69. *Gaudium et spes*, no. 22. The citation is from *Documents of Vatican II*, 220. Walter Kasper calls this statement "the standard and short form of the Pastoral Constitution." Kasper, "Theological Anthropology of *Gaudium et Spes*," 137.

70. The phrase "signs of the times" was first used by John XXIII in *Humanae salutis* referencing Mt 16:1–4. Early drafts of *Gaudium et spes* equated the phrase with the Roman phrase *vox temporis, vox dei*—an understanding at odds with the Christological and eschatological overtones of Mt 16:1–4.

71. *Gaudium et spes*, no. 4 (emphasis added). The original Latin text reads: "Ad tale munus exsequendum, per omne tempus Ecclesiae officium incumbit signa temporum perscrutandi et sub Evangelii luce interpretandi." The citation is from The Holy See, accessed September 12, 2013, http://www.vatican.va/archive/hist_councils/ii_vatican_council/documents/vat-ii_const_19651207_gaudium-et-spes_lt.html.

72. It bears remembering that this text was a hermeneutical key to the teaching of Pope John Paul II as a whole and that Karol Wojtyła was one of the authors of *Gaudium et spes*.

also composed of both lights and shadows. Experience—both human and Christian—is neither wholly good or bad, but it is fundamentally opaque without the light of Christ.

Authentic Christian experience is born from the life-changing encounter of the human person with Jesus Christ. It is first and foremost a fruit of this encounter—not an autonomous higher vantage from which to critique the sources through which this encounter is mediated (Scripture and the liturgical worship of the Church).[73] Neither should it be conceived as independent and coequal source alongside Scripture, tradition, and reason.[74] And such experience does not simply emerge spontaneously from within persons and communities—even those engaged in the noble struggle for justice and human dignity. Instead, as the fruit of the encounter with the Redeemer of the human race, experience can be likened to the "matter" of the theological enterprise to which revelation corresponds as its form.

Confession, Conversion, and Healing: Insights from the Doctor of Grace

Understanding Christian experience as the fruit of the encounter with the Person of Christ is neither a return to some form of ancient Gnosticism nor a species of modern fideism.[75] In many ways it marks a recovery of ear-

73. Aidan Nichols forcefully makes the point: "I can never appeal to Christian experience against that Church to deny its common faith or disparage its way of life. To appeal away from the Church would be to cut off the branch on which I am sitting, to cut myself off from the source of experience I am claiming, to commit epistemological suicide. Experience is only an aid to discernment; it is not itself the living source of enlightenment in Christian theology." *The Shape of Catholic Theology: An Introduction to Its Sources, Principles, and History* (Collegeville, MN: Liturgical Press, 1991), 246.

74. Both Wesley himself and subsequent generations of Methodist teachers were clear that Scripture was the ruling source in this quadrilateral—it is in Scripture that Christian faith is revealed, and then it is subsequently illumined by tradition brought to life in the experience of the believer and finally confirmed by reason. On this, see the essays in W. Stephen Gunter, Scott Jones, Ted Campbell, Rebekah Miles, and Randy Maddox, eds., *Wesley and the Quadrilateral: Renewing the Conversation* (Nashville: Abingdon, 1997).

75. In this I disagree with the assessment of Lisa Sowle Cahill, who raised the specter of fideism in her reaction to *Veritatis splendor*, warning of "its confessional and even fideist mode which pulls the rug out from under the Church's moral theologian's credibility as advocates of the human and common goods." See "*Veritatis Splendor*," *Commonweal* 120, no. 14 (1993): 15–16.

ly Christianity's understanding of the relationship of Christ to the world and to humanity. It is not accidental that the Christological anthropology of *Gaudium et spes* has deep biblical and patristic roots, as it reflects the renewal of patristic studies that flowered in the *ressourcement* prior to the Council.[76]

A brief consideration of the thought of one particularly important Western patristic author can serve to illustrate the point—St. Augustine of Hippo. Augustine's *Confessions,* written a few years after his ordination as a bishop, offers a uniquely Christian autobiographical reflection on this encounter in a style accessible to the classical tastes of late Roman culture.[77] His (to his contemporaries) shocking discussion of his vices and the sway that they exercised over his mind and will as he wandered far from God, the source of truth and happiness; the breakthroughs of truth in his restless search, culminating in the dramatic *tolle lege* moment in the garden of Milan; and the liberating illumination of his conversion and baptism offer a kind of phenomenology of the hermeneutic function of the encounter with Christ described above.

In this phenomenology, "confession" becomes a key to healing and renewal. Reviewing the sins of his past life, Augustine says that "the recalling of my wicked ways is bitter in my memory but I do it so that you may be sweet to me."[78] His vicious actions had forged for him "a chain to hold me prisoner." He continues, "By servitude to passion, habit is formed, and habit to which there is no resistance becomes necessity. By these links, as it were, connected one to another ... a harsh bondage held me under restraint."[79]

---

76. In terms of such roots, one could point to the Pauline notion of Christ as the Second Adam, or the New Testament's understanding of Christ as the image of God. Such notions are developed in the thought of Fathers such as Irenaeus, Athanasius, and Gregory Nazianzus, among others. In the case of Gregory, scholars have argued that his experience of Christ is a key to the whole of his Christology. See Andrew Hofer, OP, *Christ in the Life and Teaching of Gregory of Nazianzus*, Oxford Early Christian Studies (New York: Oxford University Press, 2013).

77. For an overview of the *Confessions* in their historical and literary context, see Peter Brown, *Augustine of Hippo: A Biography*, new ed. (Berkley: University of California Press, 2001), esp. 151–75. Brown vacillates between characterizing the work as conventional and iconoclastic in terms of Roman and Christian literary antecedents.

78. *Confessions* II, i, 1. The citation is from the translation by Henry Chadwick for Oxford's World's Classics series (1992; rev. ed., New York: Oxford University Press, 2008), 24. All citations are to this version.

79. *Confessions* VIII, v, 10 (p. 140).

Like the Prodigal Son of the Gospel, he wandered far from God and in so doing lost himself.[80] Conversely, in finding God, Augustine finds himself because God is "more inward than my most inward part."[81] Yet this interior has depths that are ultimately impenetrable to human introspection. In his long prayer, he confesses the inscrutability of his own heart and motives: "How does it come about that the various kinds of love are felt in a single soul with different degrees of weight … Man is a vast deep, whose hairs you, Lord, have numbered … Yet it is easier to count his hairs than the passions and emotions of his heart."[82]

His encounter with Christ liberated him, like Lazarus from the tomb, from the "mass of habit" under which he lay dead, but he would still have to "come forth" and "lay bare his inmost self in confession."[83] But even then the human heart remains frail and inscrutable, so Augustine begs the source of this healing and transforming grace: "grant what you command, and command what you will."[84] Even as a bishop, Augustine regards himself as a convalescent receiving therapy.[85] It is this knowledge of himself gained from his own experience of struggle, failure, and progressive healing that leads the bishop of Hippo to frequently describe Christ as the divine physician: "The Lord, though, like an experienced doctor, knew better what was going on in the sick man, than the sick man himself. Doctors do for the indispositions of bodies what the Lord can also do for the indisposition of souls."[86] The hospital used by this Divine Doctor is the Church: "Let us, the wound-

80. The biblical story prodigal son is a recurring allusion in the narrative of the *Confessions*. See II, x, 18; III, vi, 11; IV xvi, 30; V, xii, 22.

81. *Confessions* III, vi, 11 (p. 43). The original is: *intimior intimo meo*. Brown describes the *Confessions* as a "manifesto of the inner world." See *Augustine of Hippo*, 161.

82. *Confessions* IV, xiv, 22 (p. 66)

83. *Serm.*, 67, 2.

84. *Confessions* X, xxix, 40 (p. 202). Brown notes that this prayerful refrain was one of the things that shocked Pelagius in his reading of the *Confessions* (see *Augustine of Hippo*, 173).

85. Brown points us to Book X in this regard: "For the insistence on treatment by 'confession' has followed Augustine into his present life. The amazing book ten of the *Confessions* is not the affirmation of a cured man; it is the self-portrait of a convalescent." See *Augustine of Hippo*, 170–71.

86. *Serm.*, 229O. The citation is from *The Works of St. Augustine: A Translation for the 21st Century. Sermons* III/6 (184–229Z), trans. Edmund Hill, OP, ed. John Rotelle, OSA (New York: New City, 1993), 323. For other instances in which Augustine describes salvation in medical terms, see *Serm.*, 229E (ibid., 283); *Confessions* VII, xx, 26; X, xxx, 42; *De doctrina christiana*, 1, 27; 4, 95; *Enchiridion*, 3.11; 22.81; 23.92; 32.121; *De nuptiis*, Book 2, 9.III; 38.XXIII.

ed, entreat the physician, let us be carried to the inn to be healed ... therefore Brothers, in this time the Church too, in which the wounded man is healed, is the inn of the traveler."[87] The scriptures provide the convalescing Christian with the grammar to describe his or her experience of captivity, release, and transformation by grace. They are also the means by which the Divine Physician imparts healing through the medium of human words.[88] The Psalms do this in a particular way as they describe the full range of human experience and emotion and because they are the prayer of Christ himself in the members of his Body.[89] The ministry of catechesis aims to penetrate both the hearts and minds of those it forms with the grammar and reality of this graced experience.[90]

To use a contemporary example of a similar understanding of this kind of engagement with experience, one can consult the recovery literature of present-day twelve-step programs. The experience of addiction to a particular behavior or substance brings the person to an awareness of his or her own powerlessness, often described as "hitting bottom." Having accepted the reality of this hopeless situation, the person then makes a decision to turn his or her life over to the care and power of a loving God—what the Christian might describe as a "conversion." The new reality imparted by this psychic change is not an end in itself; instead, it must be reinforced by a series of practices that develop new habits of living and interaction, and deepen the person's ongoing dependence on God. The literature of the pro-

87. *Tractates on the Gospel of John*, 41.13.2. The citation is from *Saint Augustine Tractates on the Gospel of John 28–54*, trans. John W. Rettig (Washington, DC: Catholic University of America Press, 1993), 148–49.

88. "With Augustine we find the roots of a genuinely scriptural form of pragmatism aimed at healing the world through the Word." C. C. Pecknold, *Transforming Postliberal Theology: George Lindbeck, Pragmatism and Scripture* (New York: T&T Clark, 2005), 60. For an overview of Augustine's view of Scripture, see Tarmo Toom, "Augustine on Scripture," in *The T&T Clark Companion to Augustine and Modern Theology*, ed. C. C. Pecknold and Tarmo Too (London: T&T Clark, 2013), 75–90.

89. See *Confessions* IX, xi, 8–11. On this, see Brown, *Augustine of Hippo*, 171–72, esp. 254: "the Psalms were the record of the emotions of Christ and His members. Just as he had taken on human flesh, so Christ had, opened himself to human feeling." Others have pointed to the Gospel's portrayal of Christ as making the prayer of the Psalms his own. See the outstanding study by Mary Healy, "The Hermeneutic of Jesus," *Communio* 37 (2010): 477–95.

90. For an excellent and in-depth overview of Augustine's understanding of the ministry of catechesis, see William Harmless, *Augustine and the Catechumenate* (Collegeville, MN: Liturgical Press, 1995).

gram in which the person is engaged provides a grammar to describe an experience that is at once individual and shared—both the experience of the hopelessness of addiction and the grace of recovery.

The theology of the Doctor of Grace, particularly his formulation of the doctrine of original sin, makes clear that this is the human condition generally. Human beings are all fallen in Adam, infected by the restless burning of the disordered forms of *concupiscentia* that drive us to seek our happiness in created things when our hearts are only satisfied by their Creator.[91] The experience of such fallen creatures is a perilous foundation for the search for truth, subject as it is to the vicissitudes of darkened minds, warring hearts, and interior depths that exceed the person's own ability to plumb. Even the convalescent Christian—"the recovering sinner"—following the transforming encounter with Christ must continue to habituate him- or herself to the healing effects of grace made available in the Church and its sacraments, and use the literature and language of the community (i.e., the scriptures) to learn to rightly evaluate and characterize personal experience both past and present.[92] Appeals to the category of experience in theology—whether in catechetics or moral theology—must be subject to this sober form of Christian realism that Augustine exemplifies. Thus the recovery of Christian experience depends in many respects upon understanding it as an experience of recovery.[93]

91. Cf. *Confessions* I, i, 1. Augustine follows 1 Jn 2:15–16 in describing a threefold disorder within the fallen human being: "Do not love the world or the things of the world. If anyone loves the world, the love of the Father is not in him. For all that is in the world, sensual lust, enticement for the eyes, and a pretentious life, is not from the Father but is from the world" (New American Bible). For the bishop of Hippo, baptism removes the guilt of original sin but not the disorder created by it (cf. *De nuptiis*, Book 1, 25.XXIII; 28.XXV). The "concupiscence of the flesh" *concupiscentia carnis* may be utilized "without fault" in marriage when directed to the good of the procreation of children (cf. *De Bono conjugali*, 6). In the prelapsarian state, sexual desire would have been ordered because it would have been governed by the will (see *De nuptiis*, Book 2, 59.XXXV; *De civitate dei*, Book 14, 10, 15–19). For an excellent overview of Augustine's complex views of sexual desire, see John Cavidini, "Feeling Right: Augustine on the Passions and Sexual Desire," *Augustinian Studies* 36, no. 1 (2005): 195–217.

92. This is an example of what it means to hold that experience provides the "matter" of theological reflection to which revelation gives form. Nichols argues that experience and the magisterium are the "aids" to understanding the sources of theology, such as Scripture and tradition. The first of these he characterizes as "situated at the subjective pole of ecclesial life" and the second at its "objective pole," but both are thoroughly ecclesial. See *Shape of Catholic Theology*, 235–47, here 235.

93. Others have drawn upon Augustine's powerful account of the enslaving power of hab-

Conclusion

This essay has argued that an adequate response to the questions of experience generated by developments and controversies within the fields of moral theology and catechetics depends upon the recovery of the encounter with the Person of Christ as the source for these disciplines and for understanding the place of authentic Christian experience within them. Negatively, this encounter serves to reveal the distorted and sinful elements within human experience, both individual and social. Without the light of Christ, manifestations of evil often lay unrecognized in the morass of unreflective personal motivation, the impulse of habit, the blur of ordinary social interchange, or the shadows cast by structures of sin within a fallen world. Positively, this encounter serves to transform and enlarge the horizon in which this experience is understood and to provide a shared grammar in which the experience of healing and transformation can be expressed in the life of the Christian community.

These theological disciplines take part in the critical and constructive tasks that flow from this encounter at the heart of the Church's life. Moral theology serves both to identify actions, attitudes, and structures that are antithetical to the life of the Christian community and to help to discern individual and communal practices that foster and reinforce its participation in the life of grace. Additionally, it also critically engages new questions that arise as a result of social, economic, or technological developments. Catechetics too has a critical function in reflecting on and discerning effective from ineffective catechetical methods. The ministry of catechesis itself helps mediate the encounter with Christ, which is at the source of the Church's life through the handing on of the Gospel.[94] Through reflection

---

it and the impotence of the human will to consider addiction and recovery from a Christian theological perspective. See, e.g., the study of Christopher C. H. Cook, *Alcohol, Addiction and Christian Ethics* (Cambridge: Cambridge University Press, 2006). As to whether Augustine's own account of his struggle with his sexual habits in Book VIII of the *Confessions* should be considered as a depiction of a sexual addiction, I hesitate to make such a characterization at the distance of some sixteen centuries of a remarkably vivid writer whose cultural and scientific understanding of these realities is different than our own.

94. "Catechesis is nothing other than the process of transmitting the Gospel, as the Christian community has received it, understands it, celebrates it, lives it and communicates it in many ways." *General Directory for Catechesis*, no. 105.

on Scripture, it also helps to provide the language and categories in which this transformative encounter can be understood, expressed, and refined.

The experience engaged in these fields of theological study and ministry is neither independent of the transforming encounter with Christ at the heart of the Church nor of the sources that mediate it—Scripture, tradition, and the liturgy. This experience, rather, is the fruit of this encounter and is given shape and expression by the shared grammar of revealed truth and through the praxis of the community. Reason certainly plays a vital role in the theological endeavor, but reason itself is in need of the healing work of grace in order to function rightly, and the light of faith to grasp the full measure of truth. It may be the case that something like the four sources of Wesley's quadrilateral of authority can be understood to function within Catholic theology, but only if it is clear that they are not of equal weight.[95] In particular, to give experience pride of place is to risk distorting the nature of condition of fallen humanity and the healing work of Christ's redemption.

As St. Augustine reminds us, the Church can thus be likened to a hospital where its convalescents are treated by the Great Physician himself with the medicine of the Gospel and the sacraments.[96] It is precisely this healing encounter with Christ that the Church seeks to offer in the great effort of our time—the New Evangelization.[97]

95. The weight given to these sources by Wesley himself as identified by contemporary scholars of Methodism (see note 74 above) seems congruent with the understanding argued here.

96. One thinks here not only of Augustine's frequent use of this medicinal image noted above, but also of the remarks of Pope Francis in his September 2013 interview comparing the Church to a "field hospital" in which the wounded are treated. See the text of the interview by Antonio Spadaro, SJ, "A Big Heart Open to God," *America*, September 30, 2013, http://www. americamagazine.org/pope-interview.

97. Cf. Pope Francis: "The joy of the gospel fills the hearts and lives of all who encounter Jesus. Those who accept his offer of salvation are set free from sin, sorrow, inner emptiness and loneliness. With Christ joy is constantly born anew. In this Exhortation I wish to encourage the Christian faithful to embark upon a new chapter of evangelization marked by this joy, while pointing out new paths for the Church's journey in years to come." *Evangelii gaudium*, no. 1.

CHAPTER 11

Not Just Love

The Anthropological Assumptions of Catholic Teaching on Same-Sex Attraction and Activity

Introduction

Our popular culture proclaims with increasing energy and confidence the ascendancy and momentum of what has come to be identified as the LGBT— for lesbian, gay, bisexual, and transsexual (or "LGBTQLMNOP")—cause. Hit songs preach the message of accepting and celebrating diverse sexual orientations, telling individuals that they were "born this way."[1] Others capture the increasingly popular portrayal of acceptance of gay relationships and marriage as an issue of justice, intoning that it's the "same love" that draws same-sex couples together as their opposite-sex counterparts.[2] Such views are

Originally published as *Justice through Diversity? A Philosophical and Theological Debate* (Lanham, MD: Rowman & Littlefield, 2016), pp. 615–37. I am indebted to Dan Grabowski, Rebekah Grabowski, Christopher Klofft, and Thomas Petri, OP, for helpful comments and suggestions on earlier versions of this essay.

1. This was the name of a chart-topping album and single released by the performer known as Lady Gaga in May 2011. A section of the song lyrics conveys the relevant message: "Whether life's disabilities / Left you outcast, bullied or teased / Rejoice and love yourself today / 'Cause baby, you were born this way / No matter gay, straight or bi / Lesbian, transgendered life / I'm on the right track, baby / I was born to survive." See "Born This Way Lyrics," Metrolyrics, accessed June 4, 2014, http://www.metrolyrics.com/born-this-way-lyrics-lady-gaga.html. Lady Gaga has subsequently started a charitable foundation by the same name. See "Born This Way Foundation," Huffington Post, accessed June 4, 2014, http://www.huffingtonpost.com/news/born-this-way-foundation/.

2. "Same Love" was the name of a popular song released by Macklemore and Ryan Lewis in

not limited to entertainers and the media who cover them; journalists, bloggers, and public intellectuals add their voices to the growing chorus of tolerance, which can be surprisingly intolerant of those with opposing views. We are told that "marriage equality" and other LGBT issues are the civil rights issues of our time, with the implication that those who oppose them are bigots who will ultimately be found on the wrong side of history.[3] The advancing tide of state and judicial approval of same-sex marriage and repudiation of "defense of marriage" statutes can be understood as civil law catching up to where the culture went some fifty years ago with the widespread acceptance and use of contraception and the adoption of "no-fault" divorce by many states.[4] With the abandonment of both the link between marriage and procreation and a real notion of marital permanence, marriage has been increasingly conceived as a private arrangement ordered only to the happiness of individuals who enter it.

What is perhaps more surprising is the way in which revisionist Catholic moral theologians have increasingly echoed and advanced the ideas of the wider culture, albeit in more nuanced ways. Catholic teaching on sexuality has been subject to new and critical scrutiny across the board since the forceful backlash against *Humanae vitae*'s reassertion of the tradition's opposition to contraception in 1968,[5] but most early Catholic revisionist thought in the period following the encyclical focused on arguing for exceptions to what had been regarded as exceptionless moral norms prohibiting contraception, masturbation, sex outside of marriage, and homogenital activity. So, the typical argument ran, sexual activity by homosexual persons in a stable, committed relationship was nonideal, but it was better than imposing mandatory celibacy on persons acting in accord with a sta-

2012. The entire song is an apologia for the immutable nature of same-sex attraction, the need for equal treatment of same-sex-attracted persons in society, and a polemic against conservative and especially religious opposition to such views. See "Same Love Lyrics," Metrolyrics, accessed June 4, 2014, http://www.metrolyrics.com/same-love-lyrics-macklemore-ryan-lewis.html.

3. There is even an online journal of news and opinion titled *The New Civil Rights Movement*. See their website, accessed June 4, 2014, http://thenewcivilrightsmovement.com/.

4. This is the opinion of Catholic journalist and pundit Phil Lawler. See his piece "Three Important Perspectives on Same Sex Marriage," Catholic Culture, accessed June 8, 2014, http://www.catholicculture.org/commentary/otn.cfm?id=978.

5. For an overview of this reaction, see my analysis in *Sex and Virtue: An Introduction to Sexual Ethics*, Catholic Moral Thought Series (Washington, DC: Catholic University of America Press, 2003), 10–22.

ble orientation they did not choose.[6] Now, however, one increasingly finds revisionist moral theologians who assert the "naturalness" of homogenital activity for those persons who have a homosexual orientation, cast doubt on the link between sex and procreation even within the natural world, and argue that justice requires evaluating same-sex relationships on exactly the same basis as those between opposite-sex partners.[7] The Church's teaching is discounted as culturally and scientifically outdated and hurtful in its exclusion of same-sex-attracted people from the fulfillment offered by caring and committed sexual relationships.

This essay offers a critical evaluation of these arguments and their assumptions with a view to uncovering the sharply differing conceptions of the human person and of the concept of justice at work in them as opposed to those found in official Catholic teaching on homosexuality. It is the contention of this chapter that, while revisionist analyses tend to view persons as individuals whose identities are largely shaped by sexual desire and whose activity must be evaluated according to standards of justice understood as fairness, Catholic teaching resists these reductions, advancing an anthropology that sees human dignity as grounded in a shared human nature instantiated in sexually diverse persons called to lives of justice shaped by Trinitarian love.

This essay proceeds by first providing an overview of some important and influential recent Catholic revisionist approaches to same-sex attraction and activity: Todd Salzman and Michael Lawler's idea of "sexual orien-

6. In regard to the justification of sexual activity by same-sex-attracted individuals, some used the language of ontic or premoral evil of Catholic proportionalism to justify these exceptions, while others used the language of a "relational responsibility" approach to justify such compromises. For an example of the first approach, see Philip Keane, SS, *Sexual Morality: A Catholic Perspective* (Mahwah, NJ: Paulist, 1977), 71–91. An example of the second approach is provided by the work of Charles Curran in the 1970s and 1980s. See, e.g., his "Moral Theology, Psychiatry and Homosexuality," in *Transition and Tradition in Moral Theology* (Notre Dame, IN: University of Notre Dame Press, 1979), 59–80; and idem, "Moral Theology and Homosexuality," in *Critical Concerns in Moral Theology* (Notre Dame, IN: University of Notre Dame Press, 1984), 73–98. For an overview of these and other positions in Catholic theology in the post–*Humanae vitae* debate on this issue, see James P. Hannigan, *Homosexuality: The Test Case of Christian Ethics* (New York: Paulist, 1988).

7. An early example of some of these views can be found in the thought of Gregory Baum, who argued that having homosexual orientation could be considered akin to being left-handed—it is neither good nor bad, just different. See his essay "Catholic Homosexuals," *Commonweal* 99 (1974): 479–81. More current examples of these positions are provided below.

tation complementarity," recent challenges to the idea of sexual dimorphism in the natural world and hence in human relationships, and Margaret Farley's justice-centered evaluation of same-sex and opposite-sex relationships on equal terms. It then critically evaluates these arguments, with a view to surfacing some of their anthropological and ethical assumptions as well as how these differ from those found in the Catholic theological tradition and recent Church teaching. The concluding section aims to show that Catholic teaching points to the need for a clear articulation of a common human nature, the reality of sexual differential as an essential feature of human personhood, and an understanding of justice that can account for both unity and difference among persons.

Some Recent Revisionist Arguments on Same-Sex Attraction and Activity

Salzman and Lawler's "Sexual Orientation Complementarity"

In 2008, Todd Salzman and Michael Lawler of Creighton University published a volume titled *The Sexual Person: Toward a Renewed Catholic Anthropology*. In it they sought to promote a critical dialogue on Catholic teaching on sexuality, teaching that they argued was still rooted in a classicist view of the world dominated by a deductive understanding of human reason and a static understanding of nature.[8] The work endeavored to give a comprehensive treatment of the history of Catholic teaching on sexual issues, the current divisions within Catholic moral theology, and an array of contemporary issues that bear upon sexuality—issues of sexual equality, contraception, cohabitation, reproductive technologies, and homosexuality. While many of the positions that the work advanced and even the methodology it used proved to be controversial,[9] it is the novel treatment of sexual orientation and same-sex activity that is of interest here.

8. Todd Salzman and Michael Lawler, *The Sexual Person*, Moral Traditions Series (Washington, DC: Georgetown University Press, 2008), 1–3. The arguments of the book were reprised in textbook form in their *Sexual Ethics: A Theological Introduction* (Washington, DC: Georgetown University Press, 2012).

9. On September 15, 2010, the US Conference of Catholic Bishops (USCCB) Committee on Doctrine issued a public statement calling attention to problems of both methodology and conclusions in Salzman and Lawler's text (including but not limited to those on same-sex relationships). See "Inadequacies in the Theological Methodology and Conclusions of the

Appropriating the notion of sexual complementarity found in magisterial teaching on sexuality, these authors seek to invest it with new meaning. Catholic teaching, they claim, rests on an understanding of this reality that prioritizes "heterogenital and reproductive complementarity"—the physical differences of men and women that capacitate them for procreation.[10] In opposition to this, they advance what they call "personal complementarity," which can account for the multiple dimensions of sexuality—interpersonal, affective, and even parental. This "personal" focus can accommodate sexual orientation as a part of a "holistic" understanding of complementarity as a basis for discerning the truly human character of sexual acts. The "heterogenital complementarity" valorized in Church teaching is "necessary" but "not sufficient" in order "to realize a truly human act" because: "Heterosexual rape and incest take place in a heterogenitally complementarity way, but no one would claim that they are personally complementary."[11] Traditional arguments against same-sex activity are dismissed as irrelevant or even discriminatory.[12] Instead, for persons with a homosexual orientation, if the actions are otherwise just and loving,[13] Salzman and Lawler argue: "For those who are by 'nature' homosexual ... Homosexual acts are natural, reasonable, and moral, and heterosexual acts are unnatural, unreasonable, and immoral."[14]

Two observations are worth making at this point. First, the term "natural" here is being used to describe that which is experienced by individuals

---

Sexual Person: Toward a Renewed Anthropology by Todd A. Salzman and Michael G. Lawler," US Conference of Catholic Bishops, accessed June 8, 2014, http://www.usccb.org/about/doctrine/publications/upload/Sexual_Person_2010-09-15.pdf. Especially problematic in this work's method is the weight given to experience, understood both social scientifically and anecdotally. For a critique of this trend in this work and revisionist moral theology generally, see my "Catechesis and Moral Theology: Toward a Renewed Understanding of Christian Experience," *Nova et Vetera* 13, no. 2 (2015): 459–87.

10. Salzman and Lawler, *Sexual Person*, 140–43. They point out that the term "complementarity" is a relatively recent addition to the vocabulary of Catholic teaching, appearing in Pope John Paul II's (1981) Apostolic Exhortation, *Familiaris consortio*, no. 19.

11. Salzman and Lawler, *Sexual Person*, 149.

12. Salzman and Lawler write: "Relying on the historical critical method espoused by the Magisterium, we have demonstrated that traditional interpretations of scripture condemning homosexual acts lack legitimacy." They go on to describe the "rhetoric" of this teaching as "entrenched, and sometimes discriminatory and hurtful." *Sexual Person*, 232.

13. They rely heavily on the work of Margaret Farley for their arguments concerning justice. Her work is considered below.

14. Salzman and Lawler, *Sexual Person*, 233.

as in accord with their own individual desires and sense of self. As shown below, this is a very different understanding than that found within the Catholic tradition. Second, there is a significant disjunction between "the personal" and the physical in Salzman and Lawler's anthropology.[15]

Nature as Rainbow: The Challenge to Sexual Dimorphism

If Salzman and Lawler's work tends toward a privatized account of nature shaped by individual experience, other recent revisionist works have argued against the priority of sexual dimorphism on which Catholic sexual teaching rests. This is the thrust of many of the essays in the ecumenical and interdisciplinary 2010 volume *God, Science, Sex, Gender: An Interdisciplinary Approach to Christian Ethics*, which was based on a series of symposia held at Loyola University Chicago in 2007.[16]

At the heart of the argument is the iconoclastic work of evolutionary biologist Joan Roughgarden, who argues against the accuracy of the "sexual selection" paradigm, which has driven biological theory on sexual behavior since Darwin.[17] Surveying evidence from the world of nature, she argues against the existence of universal roles for male and female members of species, for the existence of multiple genders within the sex of various animals, for the presence of both sexes in plants and fish, and for frequent homosexual activity in many animal species. She proposes instead a theory of "social selection" in which gender flexibility and homosexual behavior is understood as a common and integral part of the natural world.

The point of this research, however, is not just to revise biological theorizing, but also to draw out implications for human life and behavior. Thus

15. The USCCB analysis frames this dualistic tendency well: "In their view, personal complementarity is independent of bodily complementarity, and exists even when contradicted by bodily non-complementarity. The implication here is that the personal and the bodily are separable. Rather than an integral part of the human person, the human body becomes merely an instrument of the human spirit, an instrument that can be manipulated according to one's desire" (15).

16. Patricia Beattie Jung and Aana Marie Vigen, eds., *God, Science, Sex, Gender: An Interdisciplinary Approach to Christian Ethics* (Chicago: University of Illinois Press, 2010). The essays represent a variety of disciplines: science—particularly evolutionary biology—philosophy, theology, ethics, and literature.

17. See Joan Roughgarden, "Evolutionary Biology and Sexual Diversity," in *God, Science, Sex, Gender*, 89–104. This essay revisits her book *Evolution's Rainbow: Diversity, Gender, and Sexuality in Nature and People* (Oakland: University of California Press, 2009).

Roughgarden argues: "Both science and religious doctrine are complicit in the persecution of gay, lesbian, and transgender people. Indeed, to some, being unnatural is sinful in itself."[18] To the contrary, she asserts: "Homosexuality is not against nature, it is an adaptive part of nature."[19] Building on this line of argument, the editors of the volume, Patricia Beattie Jung and Aana Marie Vigen, argue that discoveries in the sciences, the relativization of procreation as a purpose for human sexual activity, and fact that there are some 5.5 million intersexed persons in the world today all serve to call into question the sexual dimorphism upon which traditional Christian teaching rests.[20] Like the work of Salzman and Lawler, the thrust of this volume undercuts the idea of a shared human nature that could be the basis of moral judgment,[21] but it broadens this into a critique of a sexually dimorphous order within the natural world as a whole. Diversity and difference are the order that the natural world displays. Human sexual diversity is a part of this larger complex whole.

Farley's "Just Love"

Perhaps the most influential recent revisionist argument on the subject is that put forward by Margaret Farley, RSM, in her 2008 work *Just Love: A Framework for Christian Sexual Ethics*.[22] Like Salzman and Lawler's work, this text received praise in some academic circles but drew a negative evaluation from Church authorities.[23] Like Salzman and Lawler, she privileg-

18. Roughgarden, "Evolutionary Biology and Sexual Diversity," 101. Her focus in these comments was on the controversy over same-sex marriage and the ordination of openly gay clergy in the Episcopal and Anglican churches.

19. Ibid., 103.

20. See Jung and Vigen, "Introduction," *God, Science, Sex, Gender*, 1–19, esp. 6–8.

21. Vigen in her conclusion to the volume notes: "after reading and reflecting on the array of analyses offered in this volume, I am not sure how much can be said definitely of an 'essential human nature' whether in biological, theological, philosophical, or ethical terms." See "Conclusion," *God, Science, Sex, Gender*, 256.

22. Margaret Farley, RSM, *Just Love: A Framework for Christian Sexual Ethics* (New York: Continuum, 2008).

23. In addition to receiving critical acclaim by some scholars and reviewers, the work received the Louisville Grawemeyer Award in Religion in 2008. On June 4, 2012, the Congregation for the Doctrine of the Faith (CDF) published a notification on Farley's book, citing both general and specific problems in the work. For the text of the notification, see The Holy See, accessed October 24, 2016, http://www.vatican.va/roman_curia/congregations/cfaith/documents/rc_con_cfaith_doc_20120330_nota-farley_en.html.

es the role of experience in her invocation of "the Wesleyian quadrilateral" of authority;[24] however, more than them she sees this experience as largely provided by the testimony of gay men and women themselves.

As she has argued for some time, Farley sees Scripture and tradition as ambiguous and inconclusive sources for a moral evaluation of present-day same-sex relationships.[25] But while she finds that the sciences contribute useful information to understanding the reality of sexual orientation and preference, she also finds them to be inconclusive for formulating criteria for a moral evaluation.[26] She therefore turns to experience to determine whether such activity can conduce to human flourishing. And by experience she specifies that she means "primarily the testimony of women and men whose sexual preference is for others of the same sex."[27] This determination of human flourishing is not completely subjective, however, because for Farley, sexual activity in same-sex relationships must conform to more general standards of justice that bear upon the evaluation of sexual activity in any relationship. Such standards flow from the reality of the individual person in his or her autonomy and relationality as well as the individual's social location. The specific norms by which any sexual activity should be evaluated include the following: the prohibition of unjust harm; the free consent of sexual partners; respect for the mutuality and equality of these partners; and some form of commitment, fruitfulness, and social justice.[28]

24. This approach purports to offer four complementary sources of authority for approaching and evaluating moral questions: experience, Scripture, tradition, and reason. In addition to Salzman, Lawler, and Farley, this approach can be found in the work of Lisa Sowle Cahill and the more recent work of Charles Curran. See Charles Curran, *Catholic Moral Tradition Today: A Synthesis* (Washington, DC: Georgetown University Press, 1999), 48. Cf. Michael G. Lawler and Todd Salzman, "Human Experience and Catholic Moral Theology," *Irish Theological Quarterly* 76 (2011): 35–56.

25. See Farley, *Just Love*, 273–80. She offered similar arguments in her earlier essay "An Ethic for Same-Sex Relations," in *A Challenge to Love: Gay and Lesbian Catholics in the Church*, ed. Robert Nugent (New York: Crossroad, 1984), 93–106.

26. See Farley, *Just Love*, 280–86.

27. Ibid., 286–88, here 286.

28. Ibid., *Just Love*, 208–32. By "fruitfulness," Farley does not necessarily mean procreation as an end of sexual activity. All persons—including gays, lesbians, and the ambiguously gendered—can "participate in the rearing of new generations" and the fruitfulness "of all interpersonal love" (227). For an extended reflection on what she means by "commitment," see her earlier work *Personal Commitments: Beginning, Keeping, Changing* (San Francisco: Harper & Row, 1986).

Like many other feminist theorists, Farley has adopted the common post-Kantian understanding of justice as fairness.[29] In other words, justice demands that all sexual relationships be evaluated by exactly the same criteria—whether between gay or straight people, married or unmarried. When sexual activity between same-sex partners fulfills these criteria, it can be considered "just"; as to whether it contributes to their personal fulfillment, we should listen to the testimony of their experience and take their word for it. Like Salzman and Lawler, she does not see the body as playing a significant role in her understanding of personal flourishing, and she prioritizes experience in moral evaluation. Even more than them she dispenses with the concept of a shared nature as a basis for ethical consideration, and to this she adds the focus on justice understood as fairness to equal and autonomous individuals.

Analysis and Critique

A full analysis of the preceding arguments is beyond the scope of this essay. Given the highly polarized nature of the debate, virtually any statement on this topic is likely to be contested and controversial rather than "a last word." Instead, these reflections aim to further uncover some of the presuppositions of the above arguments, with a view to contrasting them with those underlying official Catholic teaching on same-sex attraction and activity. Of particular concern for this treatment are the notions of person and nature, the status of sexual difference and attraction within them, and how these bear upon an understanding of justice.

"Shades of Gay"? The Mutability of Sexual Orientation

Much like the ideas found in popular advocacy for LGBT causes, in differing ways the various revisionist arguments considered above presuppose the a priori nature and fixity of sexual orientation. Sexual orientation is conceived as a given, prior to any choice, volition, or activity for both same-sex attracted and opposite-sex attracted people.[30] Sexual activity for

---

29. For a more extensive utilization of this understanding of justice in a feminist context (which Farley cites in her work), see Susan Moller Okin, *Justice, Gender, and the Family* (New York: Basic Books, 1989).

30. Salzman and Lawler offer this definition of sexual orientation: "'a psychosexual attrac-

same-sex-attracted people is simply action in accord with who they are, and as such it can be deemed "just" or wholly "natural."

But this assumption is open to question on a variety of grounds. First, not only are the causes of sexual orientation themselves disputed,[31] but also there is simply no one agreed-upon definition of the concept. In fact, some have argued that the very concept of sexual orientation is a modern invention dating from the nineteenth century designed to serve as a placeholder for a conventional morality in a culture that had largely abandoned a Christian framework for thinking about sex.[32] Second, even scientific accounts of sexual orientation have recognized varying degrees of malleability within it, often viewing it as a continuum and acknowledging that individuals can and do act sexually in ways that differ from their primary orientation for extended periods of time.[33] Third, there is also evidence that sexual attraction

tion (erotic, emotional, affective) toward particular individual *persons*' of either the same or the opposite sex, depending on whether the orientation is homosexual or heterosexual." *Sexual Person*, 65 (emphasis original; citing Robert Nugent).

31. After reviewing evidence for a variety of theories explaining the bases of sexual orientation both biological (such as genetic and neurohormonal) and developmental (such as the psychoanalytic explanation of a disruption in a child's relationship with a parent that interferes with the development of gender identity, which is a component of sexual attraction and identification), Gerald Coleman wisely concludes that "no one theory of homosexuality can explain such a diverse phenomenon." See the overview he provides in *Homosexuality: Church Teaching and Pastoral Practice* (New York: Paulist, 1995), 48–55, here 54. Though Coleman's treatment is a bit dated, Salzman and Lawler make a similar point: "Concerning the genesis of homosexual and heterosexual orientations, the scientific community generally agrees that there is no single isolated cause. The experts point to a variety of genetic, hormonal, psychological, and social '*loading*' factors, from which the orientation may derive." *Sexual Person*, 65 (emphasis original).

32. Michael Hannon writes in a provocative recent essay: "Contrary to our cultural preconceptions and the lies of what has come to be called 'orientation essentialism,' 'straight' and 'gay' are not ageless absolutes. Sexual orientation is a conceptual scheme with a history and a dark one at that … Over the course of several centuries, the West had progressively abandoned Christianity's marital architecture for human sexuality. Then, about one hundred and fifty years ago, it began to replace that longstanding teleological tradition with a brand new creation: the absolutist but absurd taxonomy of sexual orientations. Heterosexuality was made to serve as this fanciful framework's regulating ideal, preserving the social prohibitions against sodomy and other sexual debaucheries without requiring recourse to the procreative nature of human sexuality." See "Against Heterosexuality," *First Things* 241 (March 2014): 27–34, here 27–28. Similar critiques of the concept of sexual orientation have been put forward by gay academics.

33. Thus the widely used scale developed by Kinsey and his associates in 1948 envisions sexual orientation as a seven-point scale, with 0 being an exclusively heterosexual person and 6 be-

and inclination can be shaped and altered over time by behavior.[34] Fourth and even more controversially, there are groups that argue for the possibility of long-term change of same-sex attraction in individuals through therapeutic intervention.[35] Others dispute this claim and argue that these efforts actually cause harm to those who undergo them.[36] But in spite of the highly contested nature of the data and the categories in which to interpret them, these factors indicate that sexual orientation is neither univocal in its meaning nor immutable in its impact on human behavior.

It is true that in its recent teaching the Church has acknowledged the reality of same-sex attraction as an unchosen reality for many people.[37] Yet

---

ing exclusively homosexual, with many gradations (representing most of the adult population) in between. The Klein Sexual Orientation Grid takes this further, factoring in sexual desire and arguing that orientation can and does change over time. See Fritz Kline, *The Bisexual Option* (New York: Arbor House, 1978). Many recent studies document the fluidity of sexual orientation and attraction among persons belonging to these various groups. See, e.g., J. D. Weinrich and Fritz Klein, "Bi-Gay, Bi-Straight, and Bi-Bi: Three Bisexual Subgroups Identified Using Cluster Analysis of the Klein Sexual Orientation Grid," *Journal of Bisexuality* 2 (2002): 109–39; O. F. Kernberg, "Unresolved Issues in the Psychoanalytic Theory of Homosexuality and Bisexuality," *Journal of Gay and Lesbian Psychotherapy* 6, no. 1 (2002): 9–27; and Neil Whitehead and Briar Whitehead, *My Genes Made Me Do it: A Scientific Look at Sexual* Orientation, 3rd ed. (published by the authors, 2013), accessed June 13, 2014, http://www.mygenes.co.nz/download.htm.

34. Nicanor Austriaco, OP, argues that sexual orientation can be understood in Thomistic terms as a *habitus* formed from the matrix of disposition, choice, and action. See his essay "Understanding Sexual Orientation as a *Habitus*: Reasoning from the Natural Law, Appeals to Human Experience, and the Data of Science," in *Leaving and Coming Home: New Wineskins for Catholic Sexual Ethics*, ed. David Cloutier (Eugene, OR: Wipf & Stock, 2010), 101–18.

35. For an overview of such "reparative" or "gender-affirming" therapies, see Joseph Nicolosi, *Shame and Attachment Loss: The Practical Work of Reparative Therapy* (Downers Grove, IL: IVP Academic, 2009). See also the report by the National Association for the Research and Therapy of Homosexuality (NARTH), "What Research Shows: NARTH's Response to the APA Claims on Homosexuality," *Journal of Human Sexuality* 1 (2009): 1–121. For an overview of clinical issues in treating same-sex-attracted persons that is open but not limited to this reparative approach, see the thoughtful analysis provided by Philip Sutton, "Who Am I: Psychological Issues in Gender Identity and Same Sex Attraction," in *Fertility and Gender: Issues in Reproductive and Sexual Ethics*, ed. Helen Watt (Oxford: Anscombe Bioethics Centre, 2011), 70–98.

36. See Salzman and Lawler, *Sexual Person*, 65. For a clinical perspective opposed to that of NARTH, see the American Psychological Association (APA) report *Appropriate Therapeutic Responses to Sexual Orientation* (Washington, DC: APA, 2009), 1–130.

37. See, e.g., the CDF's 1975 Declaration on Sexual Ethics, *Persona humana*, no. 8; idem, *Letter to the Bishops of the Catholic Church on the Pastoral Care of Homosexual Persons* (1986),

the way in which it has done so is instructive in a number of ways. First, the Church in its official teaching has resisted the reduction of the person to their sexual inclinations, speaking of "homosexual persons" or "persons with homosexual tendencies" (as opposed to "homosexuals"), and it has acknowledged that the number of such persons "is not negligible."[38] In insisting that "it is deplorable that homosexual persons have been and are the object of violent malice in speech or action … [and that] the intrinsic dignity of each person must always be respected in word, action, and law," the Church has highlighted the importance of using language in ways that fosters just social relations.[39] Second, while acknowledging deep-seated homosexual tendencies in some people, magisterial teaching has also resisted the deterministic assumption that this inclination must be expressed in sexual activity that reflects it. All persons have disordered inclinations, including sexual ones, but these do not compel action based on them.[40] Third, the Church's official teaching has not univocally used the language of "homosexual orientation," though this can be found within it. As seen in the preceding analysis, it also speaks of "inclinations" or "deep-seated tendencies" to describe the reality of same-sex attraction.

What these observations make clear is that in the Church's view a person is more than his or her desires or inclinations. Having disordered inclinations is a shared human condition for those living within a fallen world.[41]

---

no. 3. For an overview of Church teaching on same-sex attraction and activity and its pastoral implications, see the balanced overview provided by Coleman, *Homosexuality*. See also John F. Harvey, *Homosexuality and the Catholic Church: Clear Answers to Difficult Questions* (Westchester, PA: Ascension Press, 2007). For more concise treatments, see Grabowski, *Sex and Virtue*, 335–40; and William E. May, Ronald Lawler, and Joseph Boyle, *Catholic Sexual Ethics: A Summary Explanation and Defense*, 3rd ed. (Huntington, IN: Our Sunday Visitor, 2011), 286–96.

38. See the *Catechism of the Catholic Church (CCC)*, 2358–59. The citation is from the second edition, Libreira Editrice Vaticana; English translation by the US Catholic Church (Washington, DC: USCC, 1997), 566.

39. CDF, *Letter* (1986), no. 10. See also the excellent discussion of the power of language and the need to avoid reductive or denigrating epithets for same-sex-attracted people (even when these come from within the gay community) provided by Coleman, *Homosexuality*, 30–32.

40. As Coleman observes, "a person can be homosexual in orientation without having acted on this psychosexual attraction." Ibid., 16. The same could be said for heterogenital activity outside the context of the marriage covenant.

41. Official Church teaching has described this inclination as an "objective disorder" (see CDF, *Letter*, no. 3; *CCC*, 2358) insofar as it inclines persons toward activity that the Church

Same-sex-attracted persons are not morally culpable for inclinations that they did not choose. Like their opposite-sex-attracted brethren, they are morally responsible for what they do with their disordered inclinations. Further, they have the same dignity and the same capacity for growth in virtue and holiness that all human beings possess.

In light of these considerations, Salzman and Lawler's novel language of "sexual orientation complementarity" can be understood to be problematic in a number of respects. It ignores the malleability of "sexual orientation" observable in both human behavior and scientific data. Furthermore, it reifies sexual attraction or inclination, making it an intrinsic and defining feature of personhood, more basic than physical sexual difference. This in turn seems to obscure the insight that the identity of the person and his or her corresponding dignity is greater than his or her dominant sexual attraction. Finally, it reduces the category of nature and "the natural" into an individually constituted reality.

While the Church's teaching on sexual orientation has undergone development in recent decades, its opposition to same-sex activity has been a constant feature of its teaching from the beginning. This is because it has understood in light of the witness of both Scripture and human reason that such activity "closes[s] the sexual act to the gift of life" and "do[es] not proceed from a genuine and affective sexual complementarity."[42] That is to say, such activity is violation of both the procreative nature of sex and union of equally human but sexually differentiated persons.

"Birds Do It": Sexual Dimorphism in Nature and Human Nature

The appeal to the procreative purpose of sexuality recalls the traditional category of "sins against nature" as a way of characterizing sexual acts that in themselves are not apt for procreation.[43] But it is precisely the concept of the "natural" that arguments such as those of Salzman and Lawler seek to

---

understands to be disordered. As Coleman notes, however, the Church does not teach that homosexual persons are themselves disordered. See his thoughtful analysis of this language in *Homosexuality*, 94–96.

42. *CCC*, 2357. Salzman and Lawler complain that this "affective complementarity" is really just a way of referring to heterogenital complementarity for reproduction (*Sexual Person*, 146–49), but their own "holistic complementarity" prescinds from bodily sexual difference altogether.

43. See, e.g., Thomas Aquinas, *Summa theologiae* (*ST*) II-II, q. 154, a. 12.

reclaim by arguing that same-sex activity can be natural for same-sex couples who have "sexual orientation complementarity." This dissolution of the category of nature seems to be intensified by the argument that the order of the natural world is shot through with diverse sexualities and same-sex activity. But this argument too is in need of closer examination.

Even in the volume that emerged from the Loyola colloquia there were those who questioned Roughgarden's extrapolations from outliers of diverse sexual manifestation in nature and animal behavior to an alleged rainbow of sexual diversity shining through the whole of the natural world.[44] The reaction of most of her fellow evolutionary biologists to her work has been even more critical.[45] In point of fact, the overwhelming majority of literature in evolutionary biology turns on the basic and widespread nature of sexual dimorphism as the driver for mating and sexual behavior. Proponents of this growing discipline tell us that mating strategies of modern men and women (including same-sex-attracted ones, albeit in different ways) are largely a genetic imprint left by the evolutionary history of our early human ancestors.[46] Furthermore, even if one accepts some diversity of sexual behavior in the animal world, it remains a stark biological fact that sexual dimorphism is the basis of the continuation of almost all animal species—at least mammalian ones. Offspring can naturally come into the world only through the union of male and female. Whether explicated in biblical or Aristotelian terms, this teleology apparent in both animal and human sexuality is an inescapable one.

It also remains true philosophically that observable biological phenomena are not the same as nature in a metaphysical sense. For St. Thomas and the Catholic moral tradition, "nature" refers to a set of properties or inclinations that a thing characteristically pursues for its fulfillment and that

44. Terry Grande, Joel Brown, and Robin Colburn, in their essay "The Evolution of Sex," in *God, Science, Sex, Gender*, 105–22, argue against Roughgarden that, a few exceptions notwithstanding, "the existence of sexual dimorphism is a fact" (116). They also disagree with her contention that sex selection is defunct, arguing that it is obvious throughout the natural world though it can be extended by "social selection" in higher animals and humans (117–18).

45. Roughgarden attributes the reaction to *Nature's Rainbow* by her peers to homophobia. See "Evolutionary Biology and Sexual Diversity," 102.

46. See, e.g., David Buss, *The Evolution of Desire*, rev. ed. (New York: Basic Books, 2003); and Helen Fisher, *Why We Love: The Nature and Chemistry of Romantic Love*, reprint ed. (New York: Holt, 2004). Cf. David Blankenhorn, *The Future of Marriage*, reprint ed. (New York: Encounter, 2009), 11–68.

identify it as a member of a species.[47] To discern this nature, one must abstract from individual instances of action to the inclinations at which they aim. In the case of human nature, these inclinations are spiritual realities apprehended by reason—not merely biological or psychological impulses. Furthermore, these inclinations belong to humanity as a species, not simply to individuals. While individual persons possess human nature, this nature is a shared set of goods toward which they are inclined.

Salzman and Lawler's "sexual orientation complementarity" represents an effort to overwrite and reconstitute this common human nature with the same-sex attraction experienced by individuals. Roughgarden's coloring of the natural world with the hues of the LGBT rainbow is an attempt to write sexual diversity into the whole of nature, further dissolving the duality of sex, which the Church sees as basic to humanity and to creation as a whole. Ultimately, these efforts fail to understand the concept of nature and a natural order, which is at the basis of Catholic moral reasoning. And it is not just the Church's moral doctrine that turns on the concept of nature—this is true of its teaching in its doctrines of human solidarity, original sin, the Incarnation, and the redemption.[48]

Justice beyond Sameness

Recent Catholic teaching has insisted on the goodness and profound significance of the sexual differentiation of male and female created in the image of God as "two equally valuable but different expressions of the one nature of humanity."[49] Responding to the growing modern confusion about sex dif-

47. On the inclinations of human nature in the teaching of St. Thomas, see *ST* I-II, q. 94, a. 2. John Paul II acknowledged that "the Church has often made reference to the Thomistic doctrine of natural law, including it in her own teaching on morality." *Veritatis splendor*, 44. The citation is from the Daughters of Saint Paul edition, Vatican translation (Boston: St. Paul, 1993), 59. For an excellent overview of Aquinas's conception of the inclinations and their function in his ethic of virtue, see Servais Pinckaers, OP, *The Sources of Christian Ethics*, trans. Mary Thomas Noble (Washington, DC: Catholic University of America Press, 1995), 400–456.

48. John Finnis forcefully argues this point against attempts by revisionist thinkers to argue for a concept of human nature as mutable. See his "The Natural Law, Objective Morality, and Vatican II," in *Principles of Catholic Moral Life* (Chicago: Franciscan Herald, 1980), 113–49, esp. 141–42.

49. This is the expression of Walter Kasper in his "The Position of Women as a Problem of Theological Anthropology," trans. John Saward, in *The Church and Women: A Compendium*, ed. Helmut Moll (San Francisco: Ignatius Press, 1988), 58–59.

ferences caused in varying ways by second-wave feminism, the sexual revolution, the current dissociation of sex and gender, and its own internal controversy following *Humanae vitae*, the Church has repeatedly affirmed the goodness and profound significance of sexual difference.[50] Created together in the image of God (Gn 1:27), men and women are both fundamentally equal as human yet irreducibly different as persons. As noted above, this difference is sometimes described in the language of "complementarity." Thus the *Catechism of the Catholic Church* teaches that "Man and woman were made 'for each other'—not that God made them half-made and incomplete: he created them to be a communion of persons, in which each can be 'helpmate' to the other, for they are equal as persons ('bone of my bones...') and complementary as masculine and feminine."[51] Hence male and female together are in the image of God who, as Revelation discloses to us, is also a communion of persons in the mystery of his Trinitarian life.[52]

Throughout his pontificate, Pope John Paul II sought to deepen the Church's awareness of the goodness and the profound anthropological significance of sexual difference. In his weekly general audiences, which have come to be known as the Theology of the Body, he spoke often of the "originality" of men and women in their existence as persons:

50. The contentious debate, which started with the issue of birth control, quickly spread to other issues of sexual ethics. In this same period the Church has been further polarized by ongoing arguments in favor of the ordination of women that have not been entirely resolved by authoritative statements by the magisterium in *Inter insignores* (1976) and *Ordinatio sacerdotalis* (1994).

At the same time, there are persons with physically ambiguous sexual characteristics (the "intersexed" persons mentioned above) and those who experience a disconnect between their physical sex and their psychological experience of themselves as persons—sometimes called transgender persons. A treatment of these complex phenomena would require a separate essay. Here I would simply note that the focus in Catholic teaching is on the typical manifestation of sexual difference within humanity, not on these exceptional cases that account for a tiny fraction of the current human population.

51. *CCC*, 372, p. 95.

52. Of course, this does not mean that God is male or female. As a divine and spiritual being, God transcends the distinctions of biological sex. But both Scripture and the Church's tradition have analogously applied qualities of human masculinity and femininity to God *simpliciter* or to the Persons of the Trinity. See *CCC*, 370, and John Paul II, Apostolic Letter, *Mulieris dignitatem*, no. 8.

the knowledge of man passes through masculinity and femininity, which are, as it were, two incarnations of the same metaphysical solitude before God and the world—*two reciprocally completing ways of "being a body" and at the same time of being human*—as two complementary dimensions of self-knowledge and self-determination and, at the same time, *two complementary ways of being conscious of the meaning of the body.*[53]

The bodily differences of men and women reveal unique ways of existing as a person within a shared human nature. As the late pope says, "their unity *denotes* above all *the identity of human nature; duality on the other hand, shows what, on the basis of this identity, constitutes the masculinity and femininity* of created man."[54] Yet these differences are themselves a summon to communion with others through the sincere gift of self in love—a reality that John Paul II described as "the spousal meaning of the body."[55]

Persons are not autonomous individuals whose identities are conferred by their desires or self-creating subjects who create themselves *ex nihilo* by their choices. Pope Benedict XVI in his final Christmas address to the Roman curia made the point forcefully in remarks that deserve to be cited at length because of their profundity. Commenting on the famous phrase of feminist thinker Simone de Beauvoir: "one is not born a woman, one becomes so," he observes:

53. The citation is from John Paul II, *Man and Woman He Created Them: A Theology of the Body*, trans. Michael Waldstein (Boston: Pauline, 2006), 10:1, p. 166. Emphasis original.

54. John Paul II, *Man and Woman* 9:1, p. 161. Emphasis original. The same focus on the mutual relation and irreducible difference of men and women as persons within a shared human nature can be found in his more weighty teaching in the Apostolic Letter, *Mulieris dignitatem*, no. 10. This distinction between person and nature as a key to understanding sexual difference has been highlighted in recent Catholic theological reflection on sexual difference. In addition to Kasper's essay cited above, Michele Schumacher speaks of "one nature in two modes"; see "'The Nature of Nature in Feminism,' Old and New: From Dualism to Complementary Unity," in *Women in Christ: Toward a New Feminism*, ed. Michele Schumacher (Grand Rapids, MI: Eerdmans, 2004), 38–41. Put more sharply, one might speak of sexual difference as accidental on the level of nature but essential to existing human persons. Cf. Grabowski, *Sex and Virtue*, 110–11.

55. Waldstein in the index to *Man and Woman*, 682–83, notes that this term is an important and wide-ranging one in the TOB catecheses, appearing some 117 times. For an overview of the range of meaning of the term as employed in these catecheses, see Earl Muller, SJ, "The Nuptial Meaning of the Body," in *John Paul II on the Body: Human, Eucharistic, Ecclesial*, Festschrift for Avery Cardinal Dulles, SJ, ed. John McDermott, SJ, and John Galvin, SJ (Philadelphia: St. Joseph's University Press, 2008), 87–120.

These words lay the foundation for what is put forward today under the term "gender" as a new philosophy of sexuality. According to this philosophy, sex is no longer a given element of nature, that man has to accept and personally make sense of: it is a social role that we choose for ourselves, while in the past it was chosen for us by society. The profound falsehood of this theory and of the anthropological revolution contained within it is obvious. People dispute the idea that they have a nature, given by their bodily identity that serves as a defining element of the human being. They deny their nature and decide that it is not something previously given to them, but that they make it for themselves … The words of the creation account: "male and female he created them" (Gn 1:27) no longer apply. No, what applies now is this: it was not God who created them male and female—hitherto society did this, now we decide for ourselves. Man and woman as created realities, as the nature of the human being, no longer exist. Man calls his nature into question. From now on he is merely spirit and will. The manipulation of nature, which we deplore today where our environment is concerned, now becomes man's fundamental choice where he himself is concerned. From now on there is only the abstract human being, who chooses for himself what his nature is to be. Man and woman in their created state as complementary versions of what it means to be human are disputed. But if there is no pre-ordained duality of man and woman in creation, then neither is the family any longer a reality established by creation.[56]

The separation of "gender" from sex begun in second-wave feminism thus acts as a solvent to the very concept of human nature and of sexually differentiated and irreducible persons created in the image of God. This "profound falsehood" reduces human beings to self-created spirits whose bodily and sexual reality is shaped by either uncontrollable desire or an act of the will. The end result is a seemingly endless array of "genders" constituted by an individual's sexual preferences.[57]

56. The French is "on ne naît pas femme, on le deviant." See Pope Benedict XVI, "Address of His Holiness Benedict XVI on the Occasion of Christmas Greetings to the Roman Curia," The Holy See, accessed June 4, 2014, http://www.vatican.va/holy_father/benedict_xvi/speeches/2012/december/documents/hf_ben-xvi_spe_20121221_auguri-curia_en.html. Thus Catholic new feminists reacting to de Beauvoir and her impact on modern thought argue for the need to reunite these realities. See Beatriz Vollmer Coles, "New Feminism: A Sex-Gender Reunion," in *Women in Christ,* 52–66.

57. A sign of such confusion can be witnessed in the recent decision by Facebook to gives its users some fifty different options for their gender self-identification. On this, see Aimee Lee Ball, "Who Are You on Facebook Now? Facebook Customizes Gender with 50 Different Choices," *New York Times*, April 4, 2014, http://www.nytimes.com/2014/04/06/fashion/facebook-customizes-gender-with-50-different-choices.html?_r=0.

A concept of justice invoked as a source for the moral evaluation of human sexual activity must be able to account for the basic equality of dignity and rights of all persons grounded by a shared human nature *and* the irreducible differences between men and women as persons, which are the basis of marriage itself both naturally and sacramentally.[58] To abstract from the concrete realities of human nature and personhood is to invoke a concept of justice that is itself an abstraction. The concept of justice invoked by Farley, and by Salzman and Lawler who rely on her, presupposes a view of persons as autonomous and largely self-creating subjects who must be treated as basically interchangeable. Justice understood as mere fairness must abstract itself from the contingencies of difference and the body and view all individuals, relationships, and sexual activity on equal and interchangeable terms. Conversely, the concept of justice defended by the Church is specified by reference to the body, by sexual difference and its life-giving potential, even while defending the dignity and rights of persons grounded in a shared human nature. But more than this it is specified by the demands of justice toward the Creator, who made male and female in his own image and endowed them with the capacity to become co-creators with him in the generation of new human life.[59]

Conclusion: Toward a Trinitarian Account of Justice and Love

Alasdair MacIntyre famously argued that the concepts of justice and rationality require a tradition to render them intelligible.[60] The analysis above supports this contention in regard to the application of justice to an evalua-

58. This is why the Church can simultaneously defend the basic human and civil rights of same-sex-attracted persons while resisting the claim that their inclination bestows on them a right to redefine marriage, which has God as its author. See the CDF's *Non-Discrimination against Homosexual Persons: Some Considerations Concerning the Response to Legislative Proposals,* nos. 12, 15. Surely all persons—including same-sex-attracted persons—need friendship, love, and communion with God and with other human beings. Yet contrary to the messages preached by our popular culture, neither friendship nor personal fulfillment requires sexual expression.

59. For an analysis of the demands of "justice toward the Creator" in the context of a personalist analysis of sexuality, see Karol Wojtyła, *Love and Responsibility*, trans. H. T. Willets (San Francisco: Ignatius, 1981), 211–61.

60. Alasdair MacIntyre, *Whose Justice? Which Rationality?* (Notre Dame, IN: University of Notre Dame Press, 1989).

tion of same-sex attraction and activity. But it would specify this further by noting that the concept of justice requires an anthropology to concretize it, and that this anthropology is itself embedded within a larger understanding of the world and its relationship to its Creator.[61]

Revisionist arguments to justify same-sex activity end up making autonomy, desire, and choice the hallmarks of personhood. Ironically, in the promotion and celebration of sexual diversity, certain differentiating features of personhood—most notably bodily sexual difference—are suppressed by a cookie-cutter approach to justice as fairness between autonomous individuals. Sexual acts by same-sex-attracted persons must be evaluated by the same criteria as those by opposite-sex-attracted persons. The problem, created by the fact that only those in the latter group can actually marry, can be solved by either reducing marriage to just another form of commitment or redefining marriage to accommodate same-sex couples. The problem that only sexual acts by men and women are capable of generating new human life can be addressed by seeing procreation as just one form of a larger "fruitfulness" inherent to any interpersonal love. These arguments seem to oscillate between a monist reduction of persons to a basic interchangeable identity and an atomist fixation on difference.[62]

Ultimately, the anthropology proposed by Catholic teaching on same-sex attraction and activity reflects its integrative approach to the person and the universe. Male and female, procreation and interpersonal union, person and nature, equality and difference are all held in a fruitful tension. From the vantage point of the Church's theological tradition, this fruitful tension finds its source in the mystery at the heart of all reality—the revelation of God as a Trinity of Persons. Human sexual dimorphism and the I-Thou communion of love of which it is the basis find their completion in the I-Thou-We community of the family. This is but a created reflection of the eternal communion of Persons of Father, Son, and Holy Spirit, who are

61. One problem with Salzman and Lawler's dismissal of the Catholic natural law tradition as being embedded in a "classicist" worldview as opposed to their own "historically conscious" one is that they ignore the historicist presuppositions imbedded in this schema, which Bernard Lonergan imported into theology from Vico and Hegel. That is, they fail to acknowledge themselves as part of a historically situated (and hence limited) tradition.

62. The problem of whether sameness or difference was more basic to reality—known as the problem of the One and the Many—was one of the oldest philosophical conundrums to bedevil the ancient world.

irreducibly distinct in their mutual relations while each possesses the full-ness of the one divine nature. Both unity and difference are equally basic.[63] Justice in relations between persons must account for these realities, as must the love that is justice's completion. Sexual expression by same-sex-attract-ed individuals or unmarried opposite-sex-attracted individuals falls short of the full measure of love.

63. This can be understood as Christian revelation's response to the ancient problem of the One and Many and its replication in modern debates about the status of sexual difference. See John S. Grabowski, "Mutual Submission and Trinitarian Self-Giving," *Angelicum* 74 (1997): 499–500.

Index